BLOODLINE OF THE HOLY GRAIL

Also by the same Author

GENESIS OF THE GRAIL KINGS

REALM OF THE RING LORDS

Laurence Gardner, a Fellow of the Society of Antiquaries of Scotland, is an internationally known sovereign genealogist and historical lecturer. Distinguished as the Chevalier Labhràn de St. Germain, he is Presidential Attaché to the European Council of Princes, a constitutional advisory body established in 1946. He is also Prior of the Sacred Kindred of St. Columba, a Knight Templar of St. Anthony and Attaché to the Grand Protectorate of the Imperial Dragon Court of Hungary, 1408. Formally attached to the Noble Order of the Guard of St. Germain, founded by King James VII of Scots in 1692 and ratified by King Louis XIV of France, he is the appointed Jacobite Historiographer Royal.

BLOODLINE OF THE HOLY GRAIL

The Hidden Lineage of Jesus Revealed

Revised and Expanded Edition

Laurence Gardner

le Chevalier Labhràn de St. Germain

FAIR WINDS
PRESS
GLOUCESTER, MASSACHUSETTS

Dedicated to the Memory
of
Dr. Whitman Pearson,
a questing pilgrim of the Holy Grail

Here is the Book of thy Descent;
Here begins the Book of the Sangréal.

The Perlesvaus

Bible references are from
AUTHORIZED KING JAMES VERSION
Oxford Edition

CONTENTS

GENEALOGICAL CHARTS

1)   The House of Herod
        Gospel Kings and Governors of Judaea (37 BC - AD 99)

2)   Early Emperors and Bishops of Rome
        To the time of Constantine the Great (44 BC - AD 337)

3)   Sicambrian Franks and the First Merovingians
        Progenitors of the Sorcerer Kings (4th - 6th century)

4)   Merovingian Kings
        The House of Meroveus (5th - 8th century)

5)   The Carolingians
        House of Charlemagne (8th - 10th century)

6)   Houses of Wales and Brittany
        Arimatheac dynasties (1st - 10th century)

7)   The Holy Families of Britain
        Saints and Sovereign Houses (1st - 6th century)

8)   Family of Saint Helena
        Supplement to the chart *The Holy Families of Britain*

9)   Arthurian Descent
        Houses of Siluria, Camulod, Dalriada and Gwynedd

10)   Arthur and the House of Avallon del Acqs
        Including Merlin, Vortigern and Aurelius (4th - 6th century)

11)   Bloodline of the Holy Grail
        Messianic descent in Britain and Europe (1st - 7th century)

12)   Strathclyde and the Gwyr-y-Gogledd
        Supplement to the chart *Arthur and the House of
        Avallon del Acqs*

13)   Kings of Scots Dalriada
        The Western Highlands and Isles (AD 500 - 841)

14)   Early Kings of Scots
        Carolingian contemporaries (8th - 10th century)

15)   Scots Imperial Descent
        Supplement to the chart *The Holy Families of Britain*

PLATES

MAPS AND ILLUSTRATIONS

ACKNOWLEDGEMENTS and INTRODUCTION

For their valued assistance in the preparation of this work, I am indebted to the good offices of the Royal House of Stewart, the European Council of Princes, the Sacred Kindred of Saint Columba and the Order of Knights Templars of Jerusalem. I would similarly like to thank all the archivists and librarians who have aided my endeavour, especially those at the British Library, Bibliothèque Nationale de France, Bibliothèque de Bordeaux, Somerset County Library, Birmingham Central Library, Glasgow Mitchell Library, the Royal Irish Academy and the National Library of Scotland.

My utmost gratitude is due to the directors and staff of Multi MediaQuest International for working with me on this special edition, along with HRH Prince Michael of Albany for affording me privileged access to Household and Chivalric papers. I am also most thankful to my wife Angela, whose tireless effort has brought this work to fruition, and to my son James for his encouragement during my quest.

My recognition is due to the composer, Sir Adrian Wagner who, in the family tradition of such masterworks as *Lohengrin* and *Parsifal*, has endorsed this book with his companion music album, *Holy Spirit and the Holy Grail* <http://www.mediaquest.co.uk/awhshg.html>. Likewise to Sir Peter Robson for his artistic liaison by way of the specially conceived *Bloodline of the Holy Grail* paintings series <http://www.entropic-art.com>.

To those many friends who have smoothed the path of this venture in one way or another I offer my appreciation. In particular, I am grateful to Helen Wagner, Tracy Knight, Stephen Knight, John Baldock, Scarlett Nunn, Chev. David Roy Stewart, Chev. Jack Robertson, Rev. David Cuthbert Stalker, Karen Lyster, Gretchen Schroeder, Laura Wagner, Tony Skiens, Jaz Coleman, Jack Miller, Chris Rosling, Leo van de Pas, Dr. A. R. Kittermaster and Ian F. Brown. Also to David and Virginia Kingston of Crop Phenomena Investigations, to Diane Morland and Felicity Jordan of Fountain International, to Sam and Jean Wright of Probe International, and to Robert and Veronica Cowley of the Research for Lost Knowledge Organization.

For their generous support in aiding my work internationally, my special thanks to Eleanor Robson and Steve Robson of Peter Robson Studio; to Duncan Roads, Ruth Parnell, Marcus Allen and Tom Bosco of *Nexus*; to Adriano Forgione of *Hera*; to JZ Knight and all at Ramtha's School of Enlightenment; to Christina Zohs of *The Golden Thread*; to Jeanette Limondjian of Barnes & Noble, to Nancy and Mike Simms of Entropic Fine Art, to Ananda Tara Shan and all at The Theosophical Fellowship, to Laura Lee, Whitley and Ann Strieber, and to Robert Sessions of Penguin Books.

Additionally, my thanks to Michael Mann and the directors and staff of Element Books for their enthusiastic initial launch of this title. And, after some five years of involvement, my appreciation to Biddles Printers for their consistently high quality of production through the various editions. Neither must I forget the inceptive serialization by the *Daily Mail*, which set the course for the book's success, along with the continued and much appreciated backing which has been received from bookstores far and wide.

Since this book is very much a synthesis of interrelated subject matter, I am greatly beholden to those specialist authors whose individual mastery in their respective fields has facilitated the coverage of specific aspects. Their personal research, expertise and pre-eminent published works have been invaluable. Apart from a comprehensive Bibliography, selected reading material is identified within the Notes and References, while attention is drawn to some individual writers in the general text.

Finally, I must convey my gratitude to all those readers who have supported and encouraged my work since the publication of the first edition of *Bloodline of the Holy Grail*. Especially to those many thousands who have written to me with a variety of useful comments and contributions — all of which have helped to pave the way towards this newly designed volume. In revising and reshaping the book, I have expanded certain elements of the content to elaborate on some past themes, while also introducing various new items in an endeavour to answer some of the most asked questions. In maintaining a closer publishing liaison than was hitherto possible, I have also been enabled to influence the general layout and presentation, enhancing the work with colour plates and introducing a rather more personal flavour for this Author's Special Edition.

Laurence Gardner
May 2001

PICTURE CREDITS

Thanks must go to those below in respect of the following photographic illustrations and copyright images:

Bridgeman Art Library, London: 20; British Library, London: 14; Entropic Fine Art, Ontario <http://www.entropic-art.com/>: 10, 19, 22; E. T. Archive, London: 3, 8, 21; Galleria Uffizi, Scala Museum, Florence: 6, 13; Kunstistorisches Museum, Vienna: 4; Mary Evans Picture Library, London: 2, 15, 23; Mary Evans Picture Library, London / Edwin Wallace: 16; National Gallery, London: 7; National Gallery of Art, Washington: 11; Tate Gallery, London: 9, 12, 24; Walker Art Gallery, Liverpool: 17.

While every effort has been made to ensure that permissions are granted, if there are any errors or oversights regarding copyright material, we apologise and will make suitable acknowledgement in any future edition.

FOREWORD

Bloodline of the Holy Grail is a remarkable achievement in the field of genealogical research. Rare is the historian acquainted with such compelling facts as are gathered in this work. The revelations are entirely fascinating, and will surely be appreciated by many as real treasures of enlightenment. Herein, is the vital story of those fundamental issues which helped to shape the Christian Church in Europe and the Crusader States.

To some, perhaps, aspects of this book will appear heretical in nature. It is the right of any individual to take this view since the inherent disclosures are somewhat removed from the orthodox tradition. However, the fact remains that Chevalier Labhràn has penetrated the very depths of available manuscripts and archival data concerning the subject, moving far beyond the bounds of any conventional domain. The resultant unveiled knowledge is presented in a very articulate, interesting and tantalising manner.

This work offers an incredible insight into centuries of strategic governmental alignments, together with their associated deceits and intrigues. For around two-thousand years, the destinies of millions of people have been manipulated by unique, though often whimsical, personalities, who have perverted the spiritual aspirations of our civilization. With marvellous detail, the author has removed the constraints of vested interest to relate numerous suppressed accounts of our heritage. In so doing, he resurrects the politically silenced history of a resolute royal dynasty which the Church has long sought to vanquish in order to further its own ends. Now, in this new age of understanding, may the truth prevail, and may the Phoenix rise once again.

HRH Prince Michael of Albany
Head of the Royal House of Stewart

Origins of the Bloodline

Whom Does the Grail Serve?

Following the Jewish Revolt in Jerusalem during the 1st century AD, the Roman overlords were reputed to have destroyed all records concerning the Davidic legacy of Jesus the Messiah's family. The destruction was far from complete, however, and relevant documents were retained by Jesus's heirs, who brought the Messianic heritage from the Near East to the West. As confirmed by the Ecclesiastical History of Eusebius, the 4th-century Bishop of Caesarea,[1] these heirs were called the *Desposyni* (ancient Greek for 'of the Master'),[2] a hallowed style reserved exclusively for those in the same family descent as Jesus.[3] Theirs was the sacred legacy of the Royal House of Judah — a dynastic bloodline that lives on today.

During the course of this book, we shall study the compelling story of this sovereign lineage by unfolding a detailed genealogical account of the Messianic Blood Royal (the *Sangréal*) in direct descent from Jesus and his brother James. However, in order to cover this ground, it will first be necessary to consider the Old and New Testament Bible stories from a different perspective to that normally conveyed. This will not be a rewriting of history, but a reshaping of familiar accounts — bringing history back to its original base, rather than perpetuating the myths of strategic restyling by those with otherwise vested interests.

Throughout the centuries, an ongoing Church and governmental conspiracy has prevailed against the Messianic inheritance. This heightened when Imperial Rome diverted the course of Christianity to suit an alternative ideal and has continued to the present day.

Many apparently unconnected events of history have in fact been chapters of that same continuing suppression of the line. From the Jewish Wars of the 1st century through to the 18th-century American

Revolution and beyond, the machinations have been perpetuated by English and European governments in collaboration with the Anglican and Roman Catholic Churches. In their attempts to constrain the royal birthright of Judah, the High Christian movements have installed various figurehead regimes, including Britain's own House of Hanover—Saxe-Coburg—Gotha. Such administrations have been compelled to uphold specific religious doctrines, while others have been deposed for preaching religious forbearance.

Now, at the turn of a new Millennium, this is a time for reflection and reform in the civilized world—and to accomplish such reform it is appropriate to consider the errors and successes of the past. For this purpose there is no better record than that which exists within the chronicles of the *Sangréal*.

The definition Holy Grail first appeared in the Middle Ages as a literary concept, based (as will be later discussed) on a series of scribal misinterpretations. It derived immediately as a translation from *Saint Grail* and from the earlier forms *San Graal* and *Sangréal*. The Ancient Order of the Sangréal, a dynastic Order of the Scots Royal House of Stewart, was directly allied to the continental European Order of the Realm of Sion.[4] and the knights of both Orders were adherents of the *Sangréal*, which defines the true Blood Royal (the *Sang Réal*) of Judah: the Bloodline of the Holy Grail.

Quite apart from its dynastic physical aspect, the Holy Grail also has a spiritual dimension. It has been symbolized by many things, but as a material item it is most commonly perceived as a chalice, especially a chalice that contains, or once contained, the life-blood of Jesus. The Grail has additionally been portrayed as a vine, weaving its way through the annals of time. The fruit of the vine is the grape—and from the grape comes wine. In this respect, the symbolic elements of the chalice and the vine coincide, for wine has long been equated with the blood of Jesus. Indeed, this tradition sits at the very heart of the Eucharist (Holy Communion) sacrament, and the perpetual blood of the Grail chalice represents no less than the enduring Messianic bloodline.

In esoteric Grail lore, the chalice and vine support the ideal of 'service', whereas the blood and wine correspond to the eternal spirit of 'fulfilment'. The spiritual Quest of the Grail is, therefore, a desire for fulfilment through giving and receiving service. That which is called the Grail Code is itself a parable for the human condition, in that it is the quest of us all to achieve through service. The problem is that the precept of the code has been overwhelmed by an avaricious society complex, based on the notion of the 'survival of the fittest'. Today, it is plain that wealth, rather than health, is a major stepping-stone towards being socially fit, whilst another criterion is obedience to the law.

Above such considerations, however, there is a further requirement: the requirement to toe the party line while paying homage to the demigods of power. This prerequisite has nothing to do with obeying the law or with behaving properly — it relies totally on not rocking the boat and on withholding opinions that do not conform. Those who break ranks are declared heretics, meddlers and troublemakers, and as such are deemed socially unfit by thier governing establishment. Perceived social fitness is consequently attained by submitting to indoctrination and forsaking personal individuality in order to preserve the administrative *status quo*. By any standard of reckoning, this can hardly be described as a democratic way of life.

The democratic ideal is expressed as 'Government *by* the people *for* the people'. To facilitate the process, democracies are organized on an electoral basis whereby the few represent the many. The representatives are chosen *by* the people to govern *for* the people — but the paradoxical result is generally their government *of* the people. This is contrary to all the principles of democratic community and has nothing whatever to do with service. It is, therefore, in direct opposition to the Grail Code.

At a national and local level, elected representatives have long managed to reverse the harmonious ideal by setting themselves upon pedestals above their electorate. By virtue of this, individual rights, liberties and welfare are controlled by political dictate, and such dictates determine who is socially fit and who is socially unfit at any given time. In many cases this even corresponds to decisions on who will survive and who will not. To this end, there are many who seek positions of influence for the sheer sake of gaining power over others. Serving their own interests, they become manipulators of society, causing the disempowerment of the majority. The result is that, instead of being rightly served, that same majority is reduced to a state of servitude.

It is not by chance that, from the Middle Ages, the motto of Britain's Princes of Wales has been *Ich dien* (I serve). The motto was born directly from the Grail Code during the Age of Chivalry. By gaining kingly succession through hereditary lineage rather than being elected, it was important for those next in line to promote the ideal of service. But have the monarchs actually served? More to the point, whom have they served? In general — and certainly through the feudal and Imperial eras — they have 'ruled', in collusion with their ministers and the Church. Rule is not service, and it has no part in the justice, equality and tolerance of the democratic ideal. It is therefore quite inconsistent with the maxim of the Holy Grail.

Accordingly, *Bloodline of the Holy Grail* is not restricted in content to genealogies and tales of political intrigue, but its pages hold the key to the essential Grail Code—the key not only to an historical mystery but to a way of life. It is a book about good government and bad government. It tells how the patriarchal kingship of people was supplanted by dogmatic tyranny and the dictatorial overlordship of land. It is a journey of discovery through past ages, with its eye set firmly on the future.

In this present age of computer technology, satellite tele-communications and an international space industry, scientific advancement takes place at an alarming rate. With each stage of development arriving ever more quickly, the functionally competent will emerge as the 'survivors', while the rest will be considered 'unfit' by an impetuous establishment that serves its own ambitions but not its subjects.

So, what has all this to do with the Grail? Everything. The Grail has many guises and many attributes—as will be revealed. Yet, in whatever form it is portrayed, the Grail quest is governed by an overriding desire for honest achievement. It is the route by which all can survive among the fit, for it is the key to harmony and unity at every social and natural station. The Grail Code recognizes advancement by merit, and acknowledges community structure—but above all things it is entirely democratic. Whether apprehended in its physical or its spiritual dimension, the Grail belongs to leaders and followers alike, enjoining that all should be as one in a common, unified service.

In order to be numbered among the fit, it is necessary to be fully informed. Only through awareness can preparation be made for the future. Dictatorial rule is not a route to information; it is a positive constraint designed to prevent free access to the truth. Whom, therefore, does the Grail serve? It serves those who quest despite the odds—for they are the champions of enlightenment.

Pagan Idols of Christendom

In the course of our journey we shall confront a number of assertions which may at first seem startling, but this is often the case when bringing history back to its base, for most of us have been conditioned to accept certain interpretations of history as matters of fact. To a large extent we have all learned history by way of strategic propaganda,

4

whether Church or politically motivated. It is all part of the control process; it separates the masters from the servants and the fit from the unfit. Political history has, of course, long been written by its masters—the few who decide the fate and fortunes of the many. Religious history is no different, for it is designed to implement control through fear of the unknown. In this way the religious masters have retained their supremacy at the expense of devotees who genuinely seek enlightenment and salvation. In relation to political or religious history it is apparent that establishment teachings often border on the fantastic, but they are nonetheless rarely questioned. When less than fantastic, however, they are often so vague that they actually make little sense when examined with any depth of scrutiny.

In biblical terms our Grail quest begins with the Creation, as defined in the book of Genesis. Some 222 years ago, in 1779, a consortium of London booksellers issued the mammoth 42-volume *Universal History*—a work that came to be much revered and which stated with considered assurance that God's work of Creation began on 21 August 4004 BC.[5] A debate ensued over the precise month, for some theologians reckoned that 21 March was the more likely date. All agreed, however, that the year was accurate and everyone accepted that there were only six days between cosmic nothingness and the emergence of Adam.

At the time of publication, Britain was in the grip of her Industrial Revolution. It was an unsettled period of extraordinary change and development but, as with today's rapid rate of advancement, there were social prices to pay. The prized skills and crafts of yesteryear became obsolete in the face of mass production and society was regrouped to accommodate an economically-based community structure. A new breed of winners emerged, while the majority floundered in an unfamiliar environment that bore no relation to the customs and standards of their upbringing. Rightly or wrongly, this phenomenon is called Progress, and the relentless criterion of progress is that very precept propounded by the English naturalist Charles Darwin: the 'survival of the fittest'.[6] The problem is that people's chances of survival are often diminished because they are ignored or exploited by their masters—those same pioneers who forge the route to progress, aiding (if not guaranteeing) their own survival.

It is easy now to appreciate that the 1779 *Universal History* was wrong. We know that the world was not created in 4004 BC. We also know that Adam was not the first man on Earth.[7] Such archaic notions have been outgrown—but to the people of the late 18th century this impressive history was the product of men more learned than most and it was, naturally, presumed correct. It is therefore worth posing ourselves a question at this stage: How many of today's accepted facts of science and history will also be outgrown in the light of future discoveries?

Dogma is not necessarily truth; it is simply a fervently promoted interpretation of truth based on available facts. When new influential facts are presented, scientific dogma changes as a matter of course — but this is rarely the case with religious dogma. In this book we are particularly concerned with the attitudes and teachings of a Christian Church which pays no heed to discoveries and revelations, and which still upholds much of the incongruous dogma that dates from medieval times. As H. G. Wells so astutely observed during the early 1900s, the religious life of Western nations is "going on in a house of history built upon sand".

Charles Darwin's theory of evolution in *The Descent of Man* in 1871[8] caused no personal harm to Adam, but any thought of his being the first living human was naturally discredited. Like all the organic life-forms on the planet, humans had evolved by genetic mutation and natural selection through hundreds of thousands of years. The announcement of this fact struck religious-minded society with horror. Some simply refused to accept the new doctrine, but many fell into despair. If Adam and Eve were not the primal parents, there was no Original Sin and the very reason for atonement was, therefore, without foundation!

The majority completely misunderstood the concept of Natural Selection. They deduced that, if survival was restricted to the fittest, then success must be dependent on outdoing one's neighbour! Thus, a new sceptical and ruthless generation was born. Egotistical nationalism flourished as never before and domestic deities were venerated as were the pagan gods of old. Symbols of national identity — such as Britannia and Hibernia — became the new idols of Christendom.

From this unhealthy base was generated an Imperialist disease and the stronger, advanced countries claimed the right to exploit less developed nations. The new age of empire-building began with an undignified scramble for territorial domain. The German Reich was founded in 1871 through the amalgamation of hitherto separate states. Other states combined to form the Austro-Hungarian Empire. The Russian Empire expanded considerably and, by the 1890s, the British Empire occupied no less than one-fifth of the entire global land mass. This was the impassioned era of resolute Christian missionaries, many of them dispatched from Queen Victoria's Britain. With the religious fabric sorely rent at home, the Church sought a revised justification abroad. The missionaries were especially busy in such places as India and Africa, where the people already had their own beliefs and had never heard of Adam. More importantly, though, they had never heard of Charles Darwin!

In Britain, a new intermediate stratum in society had emerged from the employers of the Industrial Revolution. This burgeoning middle class set the true aristocracy and the governing establishment far beyond the reach of people at large, effectively creating a positive class structure—a system of divisions in which everyone had a designated place. The chieftains wallowed in Arcadian pursuits, while the merchant opportunists competed for station through conspicuous consumption. The working man accepted his serfdom with songs of allegiance, a dream of Hope and Glory, and a portrait of the tribal priestess Britannia above his mantelshelf.

Students of history knew it would not be long before empires set their sights against each other, and they forecast a day when competing powers would meet in mighty opposition. The conflict began when France endeavoured to recover Alsace-Lorraine from German occupation, while the pair battled over the territory's iron and coal reserves. Russia and Austria-Hungary locked horns in a struggle for dominion of the Balkans and there were disputes resulting from colonial ambitions in Africa and elsewhere. The fuse was lit in June 1914 when a Serbian nationalist murdered Archduke Francis Ferdinand, the heir to the Austrian throne. At this, Europe exploded into a great war, largely instigated by Germany. Hostilities were commenced against Serbia, Russia, France and Belgium, and the counter-offensive was led by Britain. The struggle lasted for more than four years, coming to an end when a revolt erupted in Germany and Emperor (Kaiser) William II fled the country.

Following all the technological advancements of a manufacturing age, history had made little progress in social terms. Engineering achievements had led to unprecedented martial ability, while Christianity had become so fragmented as to be barely recognizable. Britain's pride emerged intact, but the German Reich was not of a mind to take its losses lightly. With the old regime overthrown, a fervent new party rose to dominance. Its despotic Fuehrer (leader), Adolf Hitler, annexed Austria in 1937 and swept into Poland two years later. The second great war—truly a World War—had begun: the fiercest territorial struggle to date. It was waged through six years and was centred upon the very core beliefs of religion itself: the rights of everyone in a civilized environment.

Quite suddenly, the Church and the people realized that religion was not, and never had been, about patriarchs and miracles. It was about belief in a neighbourly way of life, an application of moral standards and ethical values, of faith and charity, along with the constant quest for freedom and deliverance. At last any continuing general dispute about the evolutionary nature of human descent was put aside; that was the province of scientists and the majority relaxed in acceptance of the fact.

The Church emerged as a far less fearful opponent of scholars, and the new environment was more agreeable to all concerned. For many, the text of the Bible had no longer to be regarded as inviolable dogma and venerated for its own sake. Religion was embodied in its precepts and principles, not in the paper on which it was printed.

This new perspective gave rise to endless speculative possibilities. If Eve had truly been the only woman in existence and her only offspring were three sons, then with whom did her son Seth unite to father the tribes of Israel? If Adam was not the first man on Earth, what actually was his significance? Who or what were the angels? The New Testament also had its share of mysteries. Who were the apostles? Did the miracles really happen? And most importantly, did the Virgin Birth and the Resurrection genuinely take place as described?

We shall consider all of these questions before we embark on the trail of the Grail Bloodline itself. In fact, it is imperative to understand Jesus's historical and environmental background, in order to comprehend the facts of his marriage and parental fatherhood. As we progress, many readers will find themselves treading wholly new ground – but it is simply the ground that existed before it was carpeted and concealed by those whose motives were to suppress the truth for the sake of retaining control. Only by rolling back the carpet of strategic concealment can we succeed in our Quest for the Holy Grail.

Bloodline of the Kings

It is now generally acknowledged that the opening chapters of the Old Testament do not represent the early history of the world as they appear to suggest.[9] More precisely, they tell the story of a family: a family that became a race comprising various tribes – a race that in turn became the Hebrew nation. If Adam was the first of a type, then he was seemingly a progenitor of the Hebrews and the tribes of Israel.[10] Indeed, as described in this book's companion volume, *Genesis of the Grail Kings*, he was actually the first of a predestined line of priestly governors.

Two of the most intriguing Old Testament characters are Joseph and Moses. Each played an important role in the formation of the Hebrew nation and both have historical identities that can be examined quite independently of the Bible. Genesis 41:39-43 tells how Joseph was made Governor of Egypt:

> And Pharaoh said unto Joseph ... Thou shalt be over my house and according unto thy word shall all my people be ruled: only in the throne will I be greater than thou ... and he made him ruler over all the land of Egypt.

Referring to Moses, Exodus 11:3 informs us similarly that:

> Moses was very great in the land of Egypt, in the sight of the Pharaoh's servants, and in the sight of the people.

Yet for all this status and prominence, neither Joseph nor Moses appear in any Egyptian record under their given biblical names.

The annals of Ramesses II (c.1304-1237 BC) specify that Semitic people were settled in the land of Goshen and it is further explained that they went there from Canaan for want of food. But why should Ramesses' scribes mention this Nile delta settlement at Goshen? According to standard Bible chronology, the Hebrews went to Egypt some three centuries before the time of Ramesses and made their exodus in about 1491 BC, long before he came to the throne. So, by virtue of this first-hand scribal record, the standard Bible chronology as generally promoted is seen to be incorrect.

It is traditionally presumed that Joseph was sold into slavery in Egypt in the 1720s BC and was made Governor by the Pharaoh a decade or so later. Afterwards, his father Jacob (whose name was changed to Israel)[11] and seventy family members followed him into Goshen to escape the famine in Canaan. Notwithstanding this, Genesis 47:11, Exodus 1:11 and Numbers 33:30 all refer to 'the land of Ramesses' (Egyptian: 'the house of Ramesses')[12] — but this was a complex of grain storehouses built by the Israelites for Ramesses II in Goshen some 300 years after they were supposedly there!

It transpires, therefore, that the alternative Jewish Reckoning is more accurate than the Standard Chronology: Joseph was in Egypt not in the early 18th century BC, but in the early 15th century BC. There he was appointed Chief Minister to Tuthmosis IV (c.1413-1405 BC). To the

Egyptians, however, Joseph (Yusuf the Vizier) was known as Yuya and his story is particularly revealing — not just in relation to the biblical account of Joseph, but also in respect of Moses. The Cairo-born historian and linguist Ahmed Osman has made an in-depth study of these personalities in their contemporary Egyptian environment and his findings are of great significance.[13]

When Pharaoh Tuthmosis died, his son married his sibling sister Sitamun (as was the pharaonic tradition) so that he could inherit the throne as Pharaoh Amenhotep III. Shortly afterwards he also married Tiye, daughter of the Chief Minister (Joseph/Yuya). It was decreed, however, that no son born to Tiye could inherit the throne and, because of the overall length of her father Joseph's governorship, there was a general fear that the Israelites were gaining too much power in Egypt. So when Tiye became pregnant, the edict was given that her child should be killed at birth if a son. Tiye's Israelite relatives lived at Goshen and she owned a summer palace a little upstream at Zarw, where she went to have her baby. She did indeed bear a son, but the royal midwives conspired with Tiye to float the child downstream in a reed basket to the house of her father's half-brother Levi.

The boy, Aminadab (born c.1394 BC), was duly educated in the eastern delta country by the Egyptian priests of Ra. Then, in his teenage years he went to live at Thebes. By that time, his mother had acquired more influence than the senior queen, Sitamun, who had never borne a son and heir to the Pharaoh, only a daughter who was called Nefertiti. In Thebes, Aminadab could not accept the Egyptian deities with their myriad idols and so he introduced the notion of Aten, an omnipotent god who had no image. Aten was thus akin to the Hebrews' Adon — a title borrowed from the Phoenician and meaning 'Lord' — in line with Israelite teachings. At that time Aminadab (the Hebrew equivalent of Amenhotep: 'Amun is pleased') changed his name to Akhenaten (Servant of Aten).

Pharaoh Amenhotep then suffered a period of ill health and, since there was no direct male heir to the royal house, Akhenaten married his half-sister Nefertiti in order to rule as co-regent during this difficult time. In due course, however, when Amenhotep III died, Akhenaten was able to succeed as Pharaoh, gaining the official style of Amenhotep IV. He and Nefertiti had six daughters and a son called Tutankhaten.

Pharaoh Akhenaten closed all the temples of the Egyptian gods and built new temples to Aten. He also ran a household that was distinctly domestic — quite different from the kingly norm in ancient Egypt. On many fronts he became unpopular, particularly with the priests of the former national deity Amun (or Amen) and of the sun god Ra (or Re), as a result of which plots against his life proliferated. Loud were the threats of armed insurrection if he did not allow the traditional gods to be worshipped alongside the faceless Aten. But Akhenaten refused and was eventually forced to abdicate in short-term favour of his cousin Smenkhkare, who was succeeded by Akhenaten's son Tutankhaten. On taking the throne at the age of about eleven, however, Tutankhaten was obliged to change his name to Tutankhamen, but he only lived for a further nine or ten years, meeting his death while still comparatively young.

Akhenaten, meanwhile, was banished from Egypt. He fled with some retainers to the remote safety of Sinai, taking with him his royal sceptre topped with a brass serpent. To his supporters he remained very much the rightful monarch — the heir to the throne from which he had been ousted — and he was still regarded by them as the *Mose*, *Meses* or *Mosis*, meaning 'heir' or 'born of' — as in Tuthmosis (born of Tuth) and Ramesses (fashioned of Ra).

Evidence from Egypt indicates that Moses (Akhenaten) led his people from Pi-Ramesses (near modern Kantra) southward, through Sinai, towards Lake Timash.[14] This was extremely marshy territory and, although it was manageable on foot with some difficulty, any pursuing horses and chariots would have foundered disastrously.

Among the retainers who fled with Moses were the families of Jacob-Israel: the Israelites. Then, at the instigation of their leader, they constructed the Tabernacle[15] and the Ark of the Covenant at the foot of Mount Sinai. Once Moses had died, they began their invasion of the country left by their forefathers so long before, but Canaan (Palestine) had changed considerably in the meantime, having been infiltrated by waves of Philistines and Phoenicians. The records tell of great sea battles and of massive armies marching to war. At length, the Israelites (under their new leader, Joshua) were successful and, once across the Jordan, they took Jericho from the Canaanites, gaining a real foothold in their traditional Promised Land.

Following Joshua's death, the ensuing period of rule by appointed Judges was a catalogue of disaster until the disparate Hebrew and Israelite tribes united under their first king, Saul, in about 1048 BC. Eventually, however, with the conquest of Canaan as complete as possible, David of Bethlehem married Saul's daughter to become King of Judah (corresponding to half the Palestinian territory) in around 1008 BC. Subsequently, he also acquired Israel (the balance of the territory) to become overall King of the Jews.

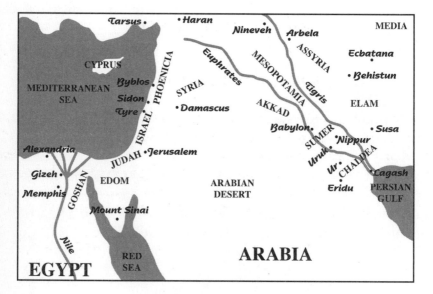

Old Testament Bible Lands

In the Beginning

Jehovah and the Goddess

Together with the military exploits of the Israelites, the Old Testament compilers described the evolution of the Jewish faith from the time of Abraham. The story is not that of a unified nation devoted to the God Jehovah, but tells of a tenacious sect who fought against all odds to contrive the dominant religion of Israel. In their opinion, Jehovah was male, but this was a sectarian concept that gave rise to severe and manifold problems.

On the wider contemporary stage, it was generally understood that the creation of life must emanate from both male and female sources. Other religions—whether in Egypt, Mesopotamia, or elsewhere—accordingly had deities of both sexes. The primary male god was generally associated with the sun or the sky, while the primary goddess had her roots in the earth, the sea and fertility. The sun gave its force to the earth and waters, from which sprang life: a very natural and logical interpretation.

In relation to such theistic ideas, one of the more flexible characters mentioned in biblical texts is King David's son, Solomon, celebrated not just for the magnificence and splendour of his reign, but for the wisdom of the man himself. Much later, Solomon's legacy was crucial to emergent Grail lore because he was the true advocate of religious toleration. Solomon was king centuries before the period of the Israelites' captivity in Babylon and he was very much a part of the old environment.

During Solomon's era, Jehovah was afforded considerable importance, but other gods were acknowledged as well. It was a spiritually uncertain age in which it was not uncommon for individuals to hedge their bets in respect of alternative deities. After all, with such a plethora of different gods and goddesses receiving

13

homage in the region, it might have been shortsighted to decry all but one—for who was to say that the devout Hebrews had got it right.

In this regard, Solomon's renowned wisdom was based on considered judgement. Even though he worshipped Jehovah, the God of a minority sect, he had no reason to deny his subjects their own gods (1-Kings 11:4-10). He even retained his own beliefs in the divine forces of nature, no matter who or what was at the head of them.

Veneration of the primary female deity was of long standing in Canaan, where she took the form of the goddess Ashtoreth. She was equivalent to Ishtar, the major goddess of the Babylonians. As Inanna, her Sumerian temple was at Uruk (the biblical Erech, modern Warka) in southern Mesopotamia, while in nearby Syria and Phoenicia she was reported by the ancient Greeks to have been called Astarte.

The Holy of Holies (Inner Sanctum) of Solomon's Temple, was deemed to represent the womb of Ashtoreth (alternatively called Asherah, as mentioned several times in the Old Testament). Ashtoreth was openly worshipped by the Israelites until the 6th century BC. As the Lady Asherah, she was the supernal wife of El, the supreme male deity, and they were together the Divine Couple. Their daughter was Anath, Queen of the Heavens, and their son, the King of the Heavens, was called He. As time progressed, the separate characters of El and He were merged to become Jehovah. Asherah and Anath were then similarly conjoined to become Jehovah's female consort, known as the Shekinah or Matronit.

The name Jehovah is a late and somewhat Anglicized trans-literation of Yahweh, which is itself a form of the four-consonantal Hebrew stem *YHWH* into which two vowels have been rightly or wrongly interpolated.[1] Originally, these four consonants (which later became a sort of acronym for the One God) represented the four members of the heavenly family: Y represented El the *Father*; H was Asherah the *Mother*; W corresponded to He the *Son*, and H was the *Daughter*, Anath. In accordance with the royal traditions of the time and region, God's mysterious bride, the Shekinah, was also reckoned to be his sister. In the Jewish cult of the Kabbalah (an esoteric discipline that reached its height in medieval times) God's dual male-female image was perpetuated. Meanwhile other sects perceived the Shekinah (or Matronit) as the female presence of God on Earth. The divine marital chamber was the Sanctuary of the Jerusalem Temple but, from the moment the Temple was destroyed, the Shekinah was destined to roam the Earth while the male aspect of Jehovah was left to rule the heavens alone.

In practical terms, the cementing of the Hebrew ideal of the one male God did not actually occur until after their fifty years of captivity in Babylon (*c.*586-536 BC). When the Israelites were first deported there by Nebuchadnezzar, they were effectively disparate tribes belonging to at least two major ethnic streams (Israel and Judah), but they returned to the Holy Land with a common national purpose as Jehovah's 'chosen people'.

Much of what we now know as the Old Testament (the Hebrew Bible) was first written down in Babylon.[2] It is hardly surprising, therefore, that Sumerian and Mesopotamian stories were grafted onto the early Jewish cultural tradition - including accounts of the Garden of Eden (the Paradise of Eridu[3]), the Flood[4] and the Tower of Babel.[5] The patriarch Abraham had migrated to Canaan from Ur of the Chaldees (in Mesopotamia), so the cultural grafting was justifiable, but the fact remains that stories such as that of Adam and Eve were by no means restricted to Hebrew tradition. In this regard, their lives and historical relevance are discussed at length in *Genesis of the Grail Kings*.

Alternatives to the Bible's version of the Adam and Eve story may be found in the writings of Greeks, Syrians, Egyptians, Sumerians and Abyssinians (ancient Ethiopians). Some accounts tell of Adam's first consort, Lilith, before he was enchanted by Eve. Lilith was handmaiden to the Shekinah and she left Adam because he tried to dominate her. Escaping to the Red Sea, she cried "Why should I lie beneath you? I am your equal!" A Sumerian terracotta relief depicting Lilith (dating from around 2000 BC), shows her naked and winged, standing on the backs of two lions and holding the rods and rings of divine rulership and wisdom. Although not a goddess in the traditional sense, her incarnate spirit was said to flourish in Solomon's most renowned lover, the Queen of Sheba. Lilith is described in the sacred book of the esoteric Mandaeans of Iraq as the Daughter of the Underworld[6] and, throughout history to the present day, she has represented the fundamental ethic of female opportunity.

When the Israelites returned from Babylon to Jerusalem, the first five Books of Moses[7] were collated into the Jewish Torah (the Law). The rest of the Old Testament was, however, kept separate. For a number of centuries, it was regarded with varying degrees of veneration and suspicion but, in time, the Books of the Prophets[8] became especially significant in stabilizing the Jewish heritage.[9] The main reason for hesitation was that, although the Jews were understood to be God's chosen people, Jehovah had not actually treated them very kindly. He was their all-powerful tribal Lord and had promised the patriarch, Abraham, to exalt their race above all others. And yet, for all that, they had faced only wars, famines, deportation and captivity! To counter the nation's growing disenchantment, the Books of the Prophets reinforced Jehovah's promise by announcing the Coming of a Messiah, an anointed King or Priest who would serve the people by leading them to salvation.[10]

This prophecy was sufficient to ensure the rebuilding of Solomon's Temple and the Wall of Jerusalem, but no Messianic saviour appeared. The Old Testament ends at this point in the 4th century BC. Meanwhile, the bloodline of David continued, although not actively reigning. Then, more than 300 years later, a whole new chapter of sovereign history began when the revolutionary heir of Judah stepped boldly into the public domain. He was Jesus the Nazarene, the King *de jure* of Jerusalem.

Heritage of the Messiah

The New Testament picks up the story again in the final years BC. But the untold intervening period was immensely significant, for it set the political scene into which the awaited Messiah was to make his entrance.

The era began with the rise to power of Alexander the Great of Macedonia, who defeated the Persian Emperor Darius in 333 BC. Destroying the city of Tyre in Phoenicia, he then moved into Egypt and built his citadel of Alexandria. With full control of the enormous Persian Empire, Alexander then pressed on through Babylonia, moving ever eastward, until he finally conquered the Punjab. At his early death in 323 BC his generals took control. Ptolemy Soter became Governor of Egypt, Seleucus ruled Babylonia, while Antigonus governed Macedonia and Greece. By the turn of the century, Palestine was also enveloped within the Alexandrian Empire.

At that stage a new force gathered momentum in Europe: the Republic of Rome. In 264 BC the Romans ousted the Carthaginian rulers of Sicily—also capturing Corsica and Sardinia. The great Carthaginian general, Hannibal, then retaliated by seizing Saguntum (in modern Spain) and advanced with his troops across the Alps, but he was checked by the Romans at Zama. Meanwhile Antiochus III (a descendant of the Macedonian general Seleucus) became King of Syria. By 198 BC he had rid himself of Egyptian influences to become master of Palestine. His son, Antiochus IV Epiphanes, then occupied Jerusalem—an action that promptly gave rise to a Jewish revolt under the Hasmonaean[11] priest Judas Maccabaeus. He was killed in battle, but the Maccabees achieved Israelite independence in 142 BC.

In a continuing struggle, the Roman armies destroyed Carthage and formed the new province of Roman North Africa. Further campaigns brought Macedon, Greece and Asia Minor under Roman control. But disputes raged in Rome because the Carthaginian (or Punic) wars had ruined the Italian farmers while simultaneously enriching the aristocracy, who built large estates utilizing slave labour. The Democrat leader Tiberius Graccus put forward proposals for agrarian reform in 133 BC, but he was murdered by the Senatorial Party. His brother took up the farmers' cause and he too was murdered, with the Democrat leadership passing to the military commander Gaius Marius.

By 107 BC Gaius Marius was Consul of Rome. But the Senate found its own champion in Lucius Cornelius Sulla, who eventually deposed Marius and became Dictator in 82 BC. A horrifying reign of terror ensued until the Democrat statesman and general Gaius Julius Caesar gained popularity and was duly elected to primary office in 63 BC.

In that same year, Roman legions marched into the Holy Land, which was already in a state of sectarian turmoil. The Pharisees, who observed the rather strict ancient Jewish laws, had risen in protest against the more liberal Greek culture. In so doing, they also opposed the priestly caste of Sadducees, and the unsettled environment rendered the region ripe for invasion. Seeing their opportunity, the Romans, under Gnaeus Pompeius Magnus (Pompey the Great), subjugated Judaea and seized Jerusalem, having annexed Syria and the rest of Palestine.

Meanwhile, the Roman hierarchy was undergoing its own upheavals. Julius Caesar, Pompey and Crassus formed the first ruling Triumvirate in Rome, but their joint administration suffered when Caesar was sent to Gaul and Crassus went to supervise matters in Jerusalem. In their absence, Pompey changed political camps, deserting the Democrats for the Republican aristocrats — whereupon Caesar returned and civil war ensued. Caesar was victorious at Pharsalus, in Greece, and eventually gained full control of the Imperial provinces when Pompey fled to Egypt.

Until that time, Queen Cleopatra VII had been ruling Egypt jointly with her brother, Ptolemy XIII. But then Caesar visited Alexandria and conspired with Cleopatra, who had her brother assassinated and began to rule in her own right. Caesar went on to campaign in Asia Minor and North Africa, but on his return to Rome in 44 BC he was murdered by Republicans on the Ides of March. His nephew Gaius Octavius (Octavian) formed a second Triumvirate with General Mark Antony and the statesman Marcus Lepidus. Octavian and Mark

Antony defeated the foremost of Caesar's assassins, Brutus and Cassius, at Philippi in Macedonia, but Antony then deserted his wife Octavia (Octavian's sister) to join Cleopatra. At this, Octavian declared war on Egypt, and was victorious at the Battle of Actium, following which Antony and Cleopatra committed suicide.

Palestine, at that juncture, was composed of three distinct provinces: Galilee in the north, Judaea in the south, and Samaria between. Julius Caesar had installed the Idumaean Antipater as Procurator of Judaea, with his son Herod as the Governor of Galilee — but Antipater was killed shortly afterwards, whereupon Herod was summoned to Rome and there appointed King of Judaea.

To the majority of his subjects, Herod was an Arab usurper. He had converted to a form of Judaism, but he was not of the Davidic succession. In practice, Herod's authority was confined to Galilee since Judaea was actually governed by the Roman Procurator at Caesarea. Between the two of them, the regime was harsh in the extreme, and more than 3,000 summary crucifixions were carried out to coerce the population into submission.[12] Prohibitive taxes were levied, torture was commonplace, and the Jewish suicide rate leapt alarmingly.

This was the brutal environment into which Jesus was born: a climate of oppression controlled by a puppet monarchy backed by a highly organized military occupational force. The Jews were desperate for their long-awaited Messiah ('Anointed One' — from the Hebrew verb *maisach*, 'to anoint'), but there was no thought of this Messiah being divine. What the people wanted was a forceful liberator to secure their freedom from the Roman overlords. Among the famous Dead Sea Scrolls, the text known as the *War Rule* sets out a strategy for the ultimate battle, naming the Messiah as the supreme military commander of Israel.[13]

Scrolls and Tractates

The Dead Sea Scrolls are now the most useful aids to understanding the Judaean culture of the pre-Gospel era,[14] but they were discovered by pure chance as recently as 1947. A Bedouin shepherd boy, Mohammed ed-Di'b, was searching for a lost goat in the cliff-hill caves of Qumrân, near Jericho, when he found a number of tall earthenware jars. Professional archaeologists were called in and excavations were subsequently undertaken — not only at Qumrân but at nearby Murabba'at and Mird in the Wilderness of Judaea.[15] Many more jars were discovered in 11 different caves. Altogether the jars contained around 500 Hebrew and Aramaic manuscripts—among them Old Testament writings and numerous documents of community record, with some of their traditions dating back to about 250 BC. The Scrolls had been hidden during the Jewish Revolt against the Romans (between AD 66 and 70) and were never retrieved. The Old Testament book of Jeremiah (32:14) states prophetically, 'Thus saith the Lord of Hosts .... Take these evidences ... and put them in an earthen vessel, that they may continue many days'.[16]

Among the more important manuscript texts, the *Copper Scroll* lists an inventory and gives the locations for the treasures of Jerusalem and the Kedron Valley cemetery. The *War Scroll* contains a full account of military tactics and strategy. The *Manual of Discipline* details law and legal practice along with customary ritual and describes the importance of a designated Council of Twelve to preserve the faith of the land. The fascinating *Habakkuk Pesher* gives a commentary on the contemporary personalities and important developments of the era. Also in the collection is a complete draft of Isaiah which, at more than 30 feet (around 9 metres) in length, is the longest scroll and is centuries older than any other known copy of that Old Testament book.

To complement these discoveries, another significant find from the post-Gospel era had been made in Egypt two years earlier. In December 1945 two peasant brothers, Mohammed and Khalifah Ali, were digging for fertilizer in a cemetery near the town of Nag Hammadi when they came upon a large sealed jar containing thirteen leather-bound books. The books' papyrus leaves contained an assortment of scriptures, written in the tradition that was later to be called Gnostic (esoteric insight). Inherently Christian works, but with Jewish overtones, they became known as the Nag Hammadi Library.[17]

The books were written in the ancient Coptic language of Egypt during early Christian times. The Coptic Museum in Cairo ascertained that they were, in fact, copies of much older works originally composed in Greek. Indeed, some of the texts were discovered to have very early origins, incorporating traditions from before AD 50. Included in the fifty-two separate tractates are various religious texts and certain hitherto unknown Gospels. They tend to portray an environment very different from that described in the Bible. The cities of Sodom and Gomorrah, for example, are not presented as centres of wickedness and debauchery, but as cities of great wisdom and learning. More to our purpose, they describe a world in which Jesus gives his own account of the Crucifixion, and in which his relationship with Mary Magdalene reaches enlightening new proportions.

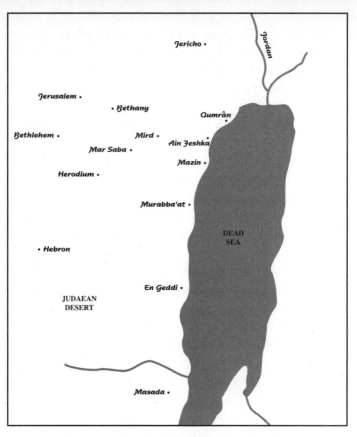

Qumrân — Land of the Dead Sea Scrolls

Secrets of the Scribal Codes

The excavations at Qumrân have produced relics dating from about 3500 BC, at which time (during the Bronze Age) the settlement was a Bedouin[18] camp. The period of formal occupation seems to have commenced in about 130 BC. Jewish chronicles describe a violent Judaean earthquake in 31 BC[19] and this is confirmed at Qumrân by a break between two distinct times of habitation.[20] According to the Copper Scroll, old Qumrân was called Sekhakha.

The second residential period began during the reign of Herod the Great (c.37-4 BC). Herod was an Idumaean Arab, installed as King of Judaea by the Roman authorities who had first taken control of the region under Julius Caesar. Apart from the evidence of the Scrolls, a collection of coins has also been amassed from the Qumrân settlement,[21] relating to a time-span from the Hasmonaean ruler John Hyrcanus (135-104 BC) to the Jewish Revolt of AD 66-70.

The uprising in 168 BC, in which the priestly caste of Hasmonaean Maccabees came to prominence, was prompted largely by the action of King Antiochus IV Epiphanes of Syria, who had foisted a system of Greek worship upon the Jewish community. The Maccabees later reconsecrated the Temple but, successful as the Jews were against Antiochus, internal social damage had been done because the campaign had necessitated fighting on the Sabbath. A core of ultra-strict Jewish devotees known as the Hasidim (Pious Ones) strongly objected to this and, when the triumphant House of Maccabaeus took control and set up their own King and High Priest in Jerusalem, the Hasidim not only voiced their opposition but marched *en masse* out of the city in order to establish their own 'pure' community in the nearby Wilderness of Qumrân. Building work started in around 130 BC.

Many relics of the time have since been discovered and, during the 1950s, more than a thousand graves were unearthed at Qumrân. A vast monastery complex from the second habitation was also revealed, with meeting rooms, plaster benches, a huge water cistern and a maze of water conduits. In the Scribes' room were ink-wells and the remains of the tables on which the Scrolls had been laid out — some more than 17 feet (*c*.5 metres) in length.[22] It was confirmed, by archaeologists and scholars, that the original settlement had been damaged in the earthquake and rebuilt by the incoming Essenes in the later Herodian era. The Essenes were one of three main philosophical Jewish sects (the other two being the Pharisees and the Sadducees).

Many biblical manuscripts have been found at Qumrân, relating to such books as Genesis, Exodus, Deuteronomy, Isaiah, Job and others. There are, in addition, commentaries on selected texts and various documents of law and record. Among these ancient books are some of the oldest writings ever found — predating anything from which the traditional Bible was translated. Of particular interest are certain biblical commentaries compiled by the Scribes in such a way as to relate the Old Testament texts to the historical events of their own time.[23] Such a correlation is especially manifest in the Scribes' commentary on the Psalms and on such prophetical books as Nahum, Habakkuk and Hosea. The technique applied to link Old Testament writings like these with the New Testament era was based on the use of 'eschatological knowledge' — a form of coded representation that used traditional words and passages to which were attributed special meanings relevant to contemporary understanding.[24] These meanings were designed to be understood only by those who knew the code.

The Essenes were trained in the use of this allegorical code, which occurs in the Gospel texts in particular relation to those parables heralded by the words 'for those with ears to hear'. When the Scribes referred to the Romans, for example, they wrote of the *Kittim* — ostensibly a name for Mediterranean coastal people, which was also used to denote the ancient Chaldeans, whom the Old Testament describes as 'that bitter and hasty nation which shall march through the breadth of the land to possess dwelling places that are not theirs' (Habakkuk 1:6). The Essenes resurrected the old word for use in their own time and enlightened readers knew that *Kittim* always stood for Romans.[25]

In order that the Gospels should be beyond Roman understanding, they were largely constructed with dual layers of meaning — evangelical scripture on the surface and political information beneath — and the carefully directed messages were generally based on the substitution codes laid down by the Scribes. However, a working knowledge of the code was not available until some of the Dead Sea Scrolls were recently published. Only since then has an appreciation of the cryptic technique facilitated a much greater awareness of the political intelligence that was veiled within the Gospel texts. The most extensive work in this field has been conducted by the noted theologian Dr. Barbara Thiering, a lecturer at Sydney University from 1967.

Dr. Thiering explains the code in very straightforward terms. Jesus, for example, was referred to as 'the word of God'. Thus, a superficially routine passage such as that in 2-Timothy 2:9, 'The word of God is not bound', would be apprehended at once to concern Jesus — in this case meaning that Jesus was not confined. Similarly, the Roman Emperor was called the Lion. Being 'rescued from the lion's mouth', therefore, meant escaping the clutches of the Emperor or his officers.

Study of the Scrolls — particularly the *Pesharim*,[26] the *Manual of Discipline*, the *Community Rule* and the *Angelic Liturgy* — reveals a number of such coded definitions and pseudonyms[27] that were previously misunderstood or considered of no particular importance. For instance, the 'poor' were not poverty-stricken, under-privileged citizens; they were those who had been initiated into the higher echelons of the community and who, on that account, had been obliged to give up their property and worldly possessions. The 'many' was a title used for the head of the celibate community, whereas the 'crowd' was a designation of the regional Tetrarch (Governor) and a 'multitude' was a governing council. Novices within the religious establishment were called 'children'. The doctrinal theme of the community was known as the Way and those who followed the principles of the Way were known as the Children of Light.

The term 'lepers' was often used to denote those who had not been initiated into the higher community, or who had been denounced by it. The 'blind' were those who were not party to the Way and could therefore not see the Light. In these respects, texts mentioning 'healing the blind' or 'healing a leper' refer more specifically to the process of conversion to the Way. Release from excommunication was described as being 'raised from the dead' (a term that is of particular importance and will be returned to later). The definition 'unclean' related mostly to uncircumcised Gentiles, while the description 'sick' denoted those in public or clerical disgrace.

Such information, hidden in the New Testament, was of considerable relevance when written and it remains very important today. Methods of disguising the true meanings included allegory, symbolism, metaphor, simile, sectarian definition and pseudonyms. The meanings were fully apparent nevertheless to 'those with ears to hear'.

There are, in fact, very similar forms of jargon in modern English. Those of other countries would have difficulty understanding such common English expressions as 'the Speaker addressed the Cabinet', 'the silk prepared his brief', or 'the chair opposed the board'. So too was there an esoteric language of New Testament times — a language that included clouds, sheep, fishes, loaves, ravens, doves and camels. All of these classifications were pertinent, for they were all people — just as are today's screws, fences, sharks, bulls and bears. Currently, we call our top entertainers 'stars', while entertainment investors are called 'angels'. What, then, might an unenlightened reader 2000 years from now make of the statement, 'The angels talked to the stars'?

Additionally, some of the esoteric terms in the New Testament were not merely descriptive of people's social status, but were titles which had special relevance to Old Testament tradition. The doctrine which the community regarded as its guiding message was the Light, and this was represented by a high-ranking triarchy (corresponding, respectively, to Priest, King and Prophet) who held the symbolic titles of Power, Kingdom and Glory. In the clerical patriarchy the *Father* was supreme and his two immediate deputies were designated his *Son* and his *Spirit*.[28]

Armageddon

Some of the most important non-biblical records of the New Testament era have been preserved in the writings of Flavius Josephus, whose *Antiquities of the Jews* and *Wars of the Jews* were written from a personal standpoint, for he was the military commander in the defence of Galilee during the Jewish Revolt in the 1st century AD.

Josephus explains that the Essenes were very practised in the art of healing and received their therapeutic knowledge of roots and stones from the ancients.[29] Indeed, the term Essene might well refer to this expertise, for the Aramaic word *asayya* meant physician and corresponded to the Greek word *essenoi*.

A fundamental belief of the Essenes was that the universe contained the two cardinal spirits of Light and Darkness. Light represented truth and righteousness, whereas Darkness depicted perversion and evil. The balance of one against the other in the cosmos was settled by celestial movement and people were individually apportioned with degrees of each spirit, as defined by their planetary circumstances of birth. The cosmic battle between Light and Darkness was thus perpetuated within humankind and between one person and another: some contained proportionately more Light, others proportionately more Dark.

God was held to be the supreme ruler over the two cardinal spirits, but to find the Way to the Light required following a long and arduous path of conflict. Such a path culminated in a final weighing of one force against the other at a Time of Justification, later called the Day of Judgement. It was thought that, as the time drew near, the forces of Darkness would gather in strength during a Period of Temptation.Those who followed the Way of Light sought to avoid the impending evaluation with the plea, 'Lead us not into Temptation, but deliver us from evil'.

By tradition, the Spirit of Darkness was identified with Belial (Worthless), whose children (Deuteronomy 13:13) worshipped gods other than Jehovah. The Spirit of Light was upheld by the hierarchy and was symbolized by a seven-branched candlestick, the Menorah. In the time of the Davidic kings, the Zadokite priest was considered the foremost proponent of the Light.

But just as the Spirit of Light had its representative on Earth, so too did the Spirit of Darkness. It was an appointment held by the Chief of the Scribes, whose purpose was to provide a formal opposition within the hierarchical structure.[30] A primary responsibility of the designated Prince of Darkness, was to test female initiates within the celibacy, in which capacity he held the Hebrew title of Satan (Accuser). The equivalent title in Greek was *Diabolos* (Aggressor), being the origin of the English word 'devil'. (The Satan's office was not unlike that of the Devil's Advocate, who probes the background of potential candidates for canonization in the Roman Catholic Church.)

In the book of Revelation (16:16), the great final war between Light and Darkness—between good and evil—is forecast to take place at Armageddon (*Har Megiddo*: the Heights of Megiddo), an historically important Palestinian battlefield where a military fortress guarded the plains of Jezreel, south of the Galilean hills. The *War Scroll* describes in detail the forthcoming struggle between the Children of Light and the Sons of Darkness.[31] The tribes of Israel were to be on one side, with the *Kittim* (Romans) and various factions on the other. In the context of this climactic war, however, there is no mention of an omnipotent Satan—such mythical imagery played no part in the community's perception of the Final Judgement. The conflict was to be a purely mortal affair between the Light that was Israel and the Darkness of Imperial Rome.

Much later, the fundamental notion behind this ancient concept was purloined and adapted by the emergent Church of Rome. The symbolic battle of Har Megiddo was removed from its specific location and reapplied on a world scale, with Rome (the hitherto Darkness) usurping the Light in its own favour. In order that the rule of the Catholic bishops should prevail, it was strategically decreed that the Day of Judgement had not yet come. Those who obeyed the revised principles of the Roman Catholic Church were promised the right of entry to the Kingdom of Heaven, as sanctified by the bishops. The one-time hill-fort of Har Megiddo was thereby invested with supernatural overtones, so that the very word Armageddon took on the hideous ring of apocalyptic terror. It implied the fearsome ending of all things, from which the only sure route to salvation was absolute compliance with the rule of Rome. In this regard, it has proved to be one of the most ingenious political manoeuvres of all time.

Jesus, Son of Man

The Virgin Birth

The Gospels of the New Testament are written in a manner not common to other forms of literature. However, their method of construction was no accident, for they had a common purpose and were not intended to relate history. The aim of the Gospels was to convey an evangelical message (Greek: eu-aggelos—'bringing good news'). The English word Gospel is an Anglo-Saxon translation from the Greek, meaning precisely the same thing.

The original Gospel of Mark was written in Rome in around AD 66. Clement of Alexandria, the 2nd-century churchman, confirmed that it was issued at a time when the Jews of Judaea were in revolt against the Roman occupiers and were being crucified in their thousands. The Gospel writer, therefore, had his own safety to consider and could hardly present a document that was overtly anti-Roman; his mission was to spread the Good News, not to give cause for its condemnation. Mark's Gospel was a message of brotherly support, a promise of independent salvation for those subject to the overwhelming domination of Rome. Such a forecast of deliverance eased the people's minds and took some pressure off the governors whose subjugation was felt throughout the growing Empire.

The Gospel of Mark subsequently became a reference source for those of Matthew and Luke, whose authors severally expanded upon the theme. For this reason, the three are known together as the Synoptic Gospels (Greek: syn-optikos—'[seeing] with the same eye'), even though they do not concur in many respects.

The Gospel of John differs from the others in content, style and concept, being influenced by the traditions of a particular community sect. It is, nevertheless, far from naive in its account of Jesus's story and, consequently, has its own adherents who preserve its distinction from the Synoptic Gospels. John also includes countless small details which do not appear elsewhere—a factor that has led many scholars to conclude that it is a more accurate testimony in general terms.

The first published Gospel, that of Mark, makes no mention of the Virgin Birth. The Gospels of Matthew and Luke bring it into play with varying degrees of emphasis, but it is totally ignored in John. In the past, as now, clerics, scholars and teachers have thus been faced with the difficulty of analysing the variant material, as a result of which they have made choices of belief from a set of documents that are very sketchy in places. In consequence, bits and pieces have been extracted from each Gospel, to the extent that a whole new pseudo Gospel has been concocted. Students are simply told that 'the Bible says this', or 'the Bible says that'. When being taught about the Virgin Birth they are directed to Matthew and Luke. When being taught about other aspects they are directed to the Gospel or Gospels concerned, as if they were all intended to be constituent chapters of the same overall work which, of course, they were not.

Over many centuries, various speculations about biblical content have become interpretations and these have been established by the Church as dogma. The emergent doctrines have been integrated into society as if they were positive facts. Pupils in schools and churches are rarely told that Matthew says Mary was a virgin but that Mark does not; or that Luke mentions the manger in which Jesus was placed whereas the other Gospels do not; or that not one Gospel makes even the vaguest reference to the stable which has become such an integral part of popular tradition. Selective teaching of this kind applies not only to the Bethlehem Nativity, but to any number of incidents in Jesus's recorded life. Instead, Christian children are taught a tale that has been altogether smoothed over; a tale that extracts the most entertaining features from each Gospel and merges them into a single embellished story that was never written by anyone.

The concept of the Virgin Birth of Jesus sits at the very heart of the orthodox Christian tradition. Even so, it is mentioned in only two of the four Gospels and nowhere else in the New Testament. Matthew 1:18-25 reads:

> Now the birth of Jesus Christ was on this wise:
> When as his mother Mary was espoused to
> Joseph, before they came together, she was
> found with child of the Holy Ghost. Then
> Joseph her husband, being a just man, and not
> willing to make her a public example, was
> minded to put her away privily.

But while he thought on these things, behold, the angel of the Lord appeared unto him in a dream, saying, Joseph, thou son of David, fear not to take unto thee Mary thy wife: for that which is conceived in her is of the Holy Ghost. And she shall bring forth a son, and thou shalt call his name Jesus: for he shall save his people from their sins.

Now all this was done, that it might be fulfilled, which was spoken of the Lord by the prophet, saying, Behold, a virgin shall be with child, and shall bring forth a son, and they shall call his name Emmanuel, which being interpreted is, God with us.

The prophet referred to is Isaiah who, in 735 BC, when Jerusalem was under threat from Syria, proclaimed to the troubled King Ahaz, 'Hear ye now, O house of David .... Behold, a virgin shall conceive, and bear a son, and shall call his name Immanuel' (Isaiah 7:13-14).[1] But there is nothing in this to suggest that Isaiah was predicting the birth of Jesus more than 700 years later. Such an anachronistic revelation would actually have been of little use to Ahaz in his hour of need. Like so many instances in the New Testament, this illustrates how events of the Gospels were often interpreted to conform with ambiguous prophecies.

That apart, popular understanding of the Gospel text is based on numerous other misconceptions. The Semitic word translated as 'virgin' was *almah*, which actually meant no more than a 'young woman'.[2] The comparative word denoting a physical virgin was *bethulah*. In Latin, the word *virgo* meant, quite simply, 'unmarried' and, to imply the modern English connotation of 'virgin', the Latin noun would have to be qualified by the adjective *intacta* (i.e. *virgo intacta*), denoting sexual inexperience.[3]

The physical virginity attributed to Mary becomes even less credible in relation to the dogmatic Catholic assertion that she was a 'virgin forever'.[4] It is no secret that Mary had other offspring, as confirmed in each of the Gospels: 'Is this not the carpenter's son? Is not his mother called Mary and his brethren, James, and Joses, and Simon, and Judas?' (Matthew 13:55). In both Luke 2:7 and Matthew 1:25, Jesus is cited as Mary's 'firstborn son'. The above quotation from Matthew, furthermore, describes Jesus as 'the carpenter's son' (that is, the son of Joseph) and Luke 2:27 clearly refers to Joseph and Mary as

Jesus's 'parents'. Matthew 13:56 and Mark 6:3 both indicate that Jesus also had sisters.

The portrayal of Jesus as the son of a carpenter is yet another example of how a later language misinterpreted an original meaning. It is not necessarily a deliberate mistranslation, but it does show how some old Hebrew and Aramaic root words, enveloped within the Greek texts, have no direct counterparts in other tongues. The term translated into English as 'carpenter' represents the much wider sense of the ancient Greek, *ho tekton*, which is a rendition of the Semitic word *naggar*.[5] As pointed out by the Semitic scholar Dr. Geza Vermes, this descriptive word could perhaps be applied to a trade craftsman, but would more likely define a scholar or teacher. It certainly did not identify Joseph as a woodworker. More precisely it defined him as a man with skills—a learned man and a master of his occupation. Indeed, better translations of *ho tekton*, relate to a Master Craftsman or a Master of the Craft—a term still used in modern Freemasonry.

In much the same way, the mention in Luke of the baby Jesus's being placed in a manger has given rise to the whole concept of the Nativity being set in a stable, complete with its familiar cast of attentive animals. But, there is no basis whatever for this image; no stable is mentioned in any original or authorized Gospel. In fact, Matthew 2:11 states quite clearly that the baby Jesus lay within a house: 'And when they were come into the house, they saw the young child with Mary his mother, and fell down, and worshipped him'.[6]

It is also worth noting that the precise words used in Luke 2:7 relate that Jesus was laid in a manger because there was no room '*in* the inn', not '*at* the inn',[7] as is so frequently misquoted (notwithstanding the fact that there were no inns in the region). The author and biographer A. N. Wilson specifies, however, that the original Greek (from which the New Testament was translated into English) actually states that there was 'no *topos* in the *kataluma*'—denoting that there was 'no *place* in the *room*'.[8] In reality, it was quite common for mangers (animal feeding boxes, or troughs) to be used as substitute cradles.

Dynastic Wedlock

According to Hebrews 7:14, Jesus was of the tribe of Judah. It is evident, therefore, that he was of the family line of King David. The scriptures also say that Jesus was a Nazarene, but this does not mean that he came from the town of Nazareth. Although Luke 2:39 suggests that Joseph's family came from Nazareth, the term Nazarene (or Nazarite) was strictly sectarian and had nothing whatever to do with the settlement.

In Acts 24:5, St. Paul is brought on a charge of religious sedition before the Governor of Caesarea: 'For we have found this man a pestilent fellow, and a mover of sedition among all the Jews throughout the world, and a ringleader of the sect of the Nazarenes'. The Arabic term for Christians is *Nasrani* and the Islamic Koran refers to Christians as *Nasara* or *Nazara*. These variants ultimately derive from the Hebrew, *Nozrim*, a plural noun stemming from the description *Nazrie ha-Brit* (Keepers of the Covenant), a designation of the Essene community at Qumrân on the Dead Sea.[9]

It is actually a point of contention whether the settlement of Nazareth existed at all during Jesus's lifetime, for it does not appear on contemporary maps, neither in any books, documents, chronicles or military records of the period, whether of Roman or local compilation.[10] Even St. Paul, who relates many of Jesus's activities in his letters, makes no allusion to Nazareth. This being the case, every reference to Nazareth in English translations of the Gospels must be regarded as incorrect—stemming from a misunderstanding of the word Nazarene. As far as has been ascertained, Nazareth (which does not feature in the Hebrew Talmud) was of no significance before the Roman destruction of Jerusalem in AD 70, long after the crucifixion of Jesus.

John the Baptist and Jesus's brother James were both Nazarenes, but the older, equivalent sectarian term, Nazarite, can be traced back to the Old Testament figures of Samson and Samuel. Nazarites were ascetic individuals bound by strict vows through predetermined periods, as related in Numbers 6:2-21. In the Gospel era, Nazarites were associated with the Essene community of Qumrân—the environment of Joseph and Mary. The community observed some highly regulated disciplines in relation to dynastic betrothal and matrimony, so we should refer the question of Mary's said virginity to this specific context.

Both Matthew 1:18 and Luke 2:5 state that Mary was 'espoused' to Joseph and she is thereafter referred to as his 'wife'. As determined in this regard, the word 'espoused' does not mean betrothed or engaged—it refers to contractual wedlock. But, in what circumstance would a married woman also be virginal? To answer this question we must refer to the original Semitic word *almah*—the word that has been translated as 'virgin' (from *virgo*) and incorrectly thought to mean *virgo intacta*.

As we have seen, the real meaning of *almah* was 'young woman' (and it had no sexual connotation). It was quite feasible, therefore, for Mary to be both an *almah* and Joseph's wife. Let us look again at how

Matthew describes that, when Joseph learned of Mary's pregnancy, he had to decide whether or not to hide her away. It is of course perfectly normal for a wife to become pregnant, but this was not the case for Mary.

As the wife of a dynastic husband, Mary would have been governed by the regulations applicable to Messianic (anointed) lines such as those of King David and Zadok the Priest. In fact, Mary was serving a statutory probationary period as a married woman of the dynastic hierarchy—a period of espousal during which sexual relations were forbidden—and Joseph would have had just cause for personal embarrassment when Mary was discovered to have conceived. The situation was resolved only when the high-ranking Abiathar priest (the designated Gabriel)[11] granted approval for the confinement.

From the time of King David, the dynasty of Abiathar (2-Samuel 20:25) was established in the hierarchy of senior priests. The line of Zadok was the primary priestly heritage and the line of Abiathar was second in seniority. In addition to the traditional priestly styles, the Essenes also preserved the names of the Old Testament archangels within their governing structure.[12] Hence, the Zadok priest was also the archangel Michael, while the Abiathar priest (whatever his personal name) was also the angel Gabriel.[13] Being subordinate to the Zadok/Michael (the Lord—'like unto God'), the Abiathar/Gabriel was the designated Angel of the Lord (the ambassador of the Michael-Zadok). This angelic system is detailed in the Book of 1-Enoch 4:9, whilst the War Scroll 9:15-17 identifies the angels' order of priestly ranking during the Gospel era.

In the Luke account, it was through the mediation of the angel Gabriel that Mary's pregnancy was granted approval, being of holy consequence. This is known as the Annunciation, but it was not so much a matter of announcing as one of sanctioning.

Prior to Jesus's birth, the High Zadok (the Michael) was Zacharias. His wife was Mary's cousin Elizabeth,[14] and his deputy, the Abiathar (the Gabriel), was Simeon the Essene.[15] It was he who gave the formal consent for Mary's confinement, even though she and Joseph had disobeyed the rules of dynastic wedlock.

It is evident that these dynastic rules were no ordinary matter and were quite unlike the Jewish marital norm.[16] Parameters of operation were explicitly defined, dictating a celibate lifestyle except for the procreation of children and, only then, at set intervals. Three months after a betrothal ceremony, a First Marriage was formalized to begin the espousal in the month of September. Physical relations were allowed after that, but only in the first half of December. This was to ensure that any resultant Messianic birth occurred in the Atonement month of September. If the bride did not conceive, intimate relations were suspended until the next December, and so on.[17]

Once a probationary wife had conceived, a Second Marriage was performed to legalize the wedlock. However, the bride was still regarded as an *almah* until completion of the Second Marriage which, as qualified by Flavius Josephus, was never celebrated until she was three months pregnant.[18] The purpose of this delay was to allow for the possibility of a miscarriage. Second Marriages thus took place in the month of March. The reason that full wedlock was not achieved until pregnancy had been firmly established was to accommodate the dynastic husband's legal change of wife if the first should prove barren.

In the case of Joseph and Mary, it is apparent that the rules of dynastic wedlock were infringed, since Mary gave birth to Jesus at the wrong time of year (Sunday 1 March, 7 BC).[19] Sexual union must therefore have taken place six months before the designated December, in June, 8 BC — at about the time of their initial betrothal — some three months before their First Marriage in the September. And so it was that Mary not only conceived as an *almah*, but also gave birth as an *almah* before her Second Marriage.

Once Mary's unauthorized pregnancy had been confirmed, Joseph would have been granted the choice of not going through with the Second Marriage ceremony. To save embarrassment he could have placed Mary in monastic custody ('put her away privily', as in Matthew 1:19), where the eventual child would be raised by the priests.

But if the child were a boy, he would be Joseph's firstborn descendant in the Davidic succession. It would have made little sense to bring him up as an unidentified orphan, leaving a possible younger brother to become his substitute in the kingly line. Joseph and Mary's unborn child was plainly a significant prospect and demanded special treatment as an exception to the general rule. The angel Gabriel would, therefore, have advised that, since a sacred legacy was at stake, Joseph should go ahead with the Second Marriage ceremony: 'for that which is conceived in her is of the Holy Ghost' (Matthew 1:20).

Following this dispensation, the normal rules would have been applied once more — the first being that no physical contact was allowed between man and wife until some while after the child had been born: 'Then Joseph being raised from his sleep did as the angel of the Lord had bidden him, and took unto him his wife: And knew her not till she had brought forth her firstborn son: and he called his name Jesus' (Matthew 1:24-25). All that remained was for the Gospel writers to wrap the whole sequence in a blanket of enigma, and this was made possible by the Old Testament prophecy of Isaiah.

Descent from King David

Strange as it may seem, the Gospel of Mark—from which both Matthew and Luke took their leads—makes no mention of the Nativity. John 7:42 does allude to the birth at Bethlehem, but not as a mysterious event. Neither does John suggest that Mary's conception was virginal. In fact, the Gospel refers only to Jesus's Davidic descent: 'Hath not the scripture said, that Christ cometh of the seed of David, and out of the town of Bethlehem, where David was?' Even the Gospel of Matthew, which implies the notion of Virgin Birth, opens with the statement, 'The book of the generation of Jesus Christ, the son of David, the son of Abraham'.

Paul's Epistle to the Romans 1:3-4 refers to 'Jesus Christ our Lord, which was made of the seed of David according to the flesh; And declared to be the Son of God'. Again, in Mark 10:47 and Matthew 22:42 Jesus is called the 'son of David'. In Acts 2:30, Peter, referring to King David, calls Jesus the 'fruit of his loins, according to the flesh'.

All things considered, the divinity of Jesus is figuratively portrayed, whereas his human descent from David ('in accordance with the flesh') is consistently stated as a matter of fact.[20] Indeed, Jesus generally referred to himself as the Son of Man (as for instance in Matthew 16:13). When asked by the High Priest whether he was in truth the Son of God, Jesus replied, 'Thou hast said'—implying that the priest had said it, not he (Matthew 26:63-64). In Luke 22:70, Jesus answered in virtually identical terms: 'Then said they all, Art thou then the son of God? And he said unto them, Ye say that I am'.

The Messianic Dispute

One of Jesus's foremost problems was that he had been born into an environment of controversy over whether or not he was legitimate. It was for that very reason that Mary and Joseph took him to Simeon the Gabriel for legitimizing under the Law (Luke 2:25-35). Despite this endeavour by his parents, Jesus evoked a mixed response and the Jews were polarised in two opposing camps on the subject of his lawful status in the kingly line. He had been conceived at the wrong time of year and had been born before Joseph and Mary's wedlock was formalized by their Second Marriage. Six years later his brother James was born within all the rules of dynastic wedlock and there was no disputing his legitimacy. Hence, the opposing factions each had a prospective Messiah to support.

The Hellenists (westernized Jews) claimed that Jesus was the rightful Christ (Greek: *Christos* — King), whereas the orthodox Hebrews contended that the kingly entitlement lay with James. The argument persisted for many years but, in AD 23, Joseph — the father of both candidates — died and it became imperative to resolve the dispute one way or the other.

Through long prevailing custom, the Davidic kings were allied to the dynastic Zadokite priests and the prevailing Zadok was Jesus's own kinsman, John the Baptist.[21] He had risen to prominence in AD 26 upon the arrival of the Roman governor, Pontius Pilate. John the Baptist was very much of the Hebrew persuasion, but Jesus was a Hellenist. John therefore supported James, even though he acknowledged Jesus as legitimate and baptised him in the Jordan. It was because of the Baptist's attitude that Jesus realized he must make a stand for, if the prospect of a revived Jewish kingdom were to gain momentum, he would undoubtedly lose out to his brother James. In view of this, he decided to create his own organized party of supporters: a party that would not follow any conventional social policy. His vision was straightforward, based upon the logic that a split Jewish nation could never defeat the might of Rome. But he perceived too that the Jews could not accomplish their mission if they continued to hold themselves separate from the Gentiles (native non-Jews). Jesus's ambition for the Kingdom of Israel was one of harmonious, integrated society, but he was more than frustrated by the unbending Jews of rigid Hebrew principle.

Jesus knew full well that tradition had prophesied a Messiah who would lead the people to salvation, and he knew how desperately that Messiah was craved. John the Baptist was too much of a recluse to fulfil that role. James, meanwhile, was doing little to aid his own prospects, apart from relaxing in the comfort of High Priest Caiaphas' and the Baptist's support. And so, from a once reserved position, Jesus stepped into the public domain, resolving to give the people their long-awaited Messiah. After all, he was the firstborn son of his father, no matter what the wrangling priests and politicians had to say on the subject. In a short while he gathered his disciples, appointed his twelve Apostles (delegates) and began his ministry. In this, he sought acceptance in a world where he perceived no selection by class, conviction or fortune — promoting an ideal of princely service that was to carve its mark in time.

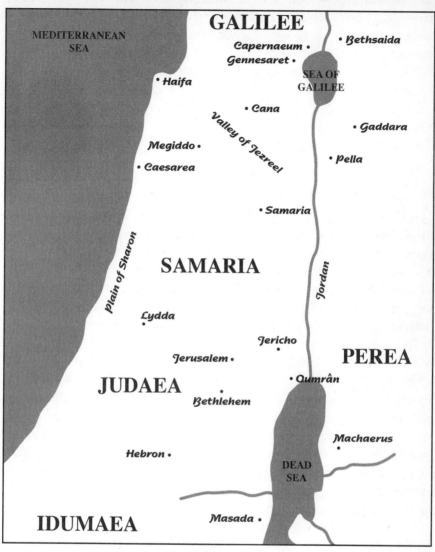

Gospel Locations

The Early Mission

Who Were the Apostles?

For all his apparent humility, there is very little to portray anything faint-hearted or pacifist about Jesus. He knew full well that his task would make him unpopular with the authorities. Not only would the Romans be at his heels, but so too would the Jews' own governing body of legal elders, the powerful Sanhedrin Council. Regardless, Jesus made his entry in due accord, stating at the outset, 'Think not that I am come to send peace on earth: I came not to send peace, but a sword' (Matthew 10:34).

Under those circumstances, it seems rather odd that a group of everyday working men would give up their livelihoods for a leader who announced, 'Ye shall be hated of all men for my name's sake' (Matthew 10:22). There was no formal Christianity to preach in those early times and Jesus promised neither earnings nor public status. However, the Gospels appear to indicate that his envoys forsook their various employments and followed blindly into the unknown to become 'fishers of men'. Who then were these mysterious Apostles? Can anything of the Qumrân scribal codes be applied to the texts, in order to make their identities and purpose more understandable?

Luke (6:13 and 10:1) tells that Jesus appointed eighty-two followers in all; seventy he sent out to preach and twelve were designated his immediate circle, his Apostles. It is no secret to Bible readers that the Apostles were armed, even though Sunday school tradition would have it otherwise. Indeed, Jesus made sure of their martial ability at the very start of his campaign, saying, 'He that hath no sword, let him sell his garment, and buy one' (Luke 22:36).

All four Gospels agree that Simon was the first recruit; three Gospels also mention his brother Andrew. But there is some disagreement between John and the Synoptic Gospels as to precisely where this recruitment took place. It was either at the Sea of Galilee (the Lake of Gennesaret), where the pair were mending their nets, or at a baptism ritual at Bethabara, beyond Jordan. Moreover, the accounts differ again as to who was present at the time. John 1:28-43 states that John the Baptist was there, whereas Mark 1:14-18 claims that it all happened while the Baptist was in prison.

The account in John's Gospel is undoubtedly the more correct, for the first disciples were recruited in March AD 29. In *The Antiquities of the Jews*, Flavius Josephus of Galilee (born AD 37) indicates that Jesus began his ministry in the fifteenth year of the rule of Tiberius Caesar — that is AD 29. John the Baptist was not discredited until a year later, in March AD 30 (as confirmed in John 3:24). He was executed by Herod the Great's successor, Herod-Antipas of Galilee, in September AD 31.

Luke 5:11 relates the story of Simon's enlistment as told in the Mark account, but makes no mention of Andrew. Next on the scene are James and John, the sons of Zebedee. Mark and Luke then declare that Jesus enrolled Levi. In Matthew, however, the next disciple is not called Levi, but Matthew. In John, an early recruit is Philip, who is said to come from Bethsaida, the home-town of Simon and Andrew. Philip, in turn, brought Nathanael of Cana into the fold and, from that point, no more is told of individual appointments.

Instead, it is next explained that Jesus gathered all his disciples together and from them chose his twelve personal delegates. Certain anomalies then become apparent. Levi disappears, as does Nathanael, but Matthew then appears in all listings. The Gospels of Matthew and Mark both name Lebbaeus Thaddaeus as one of the twelve, whereas the other Gospels do not, but Luke and Acts list Judas, the brother of James, in the twelve, whereas he does not appear in this context elsewhere. In Matthew and Mark we are also introduced to Simon the Canaanite, described in Luke and Acts as Simon Zelotes.

Mark narrates how Jesus gave Andrew's brother Simon the name of Peter sometime after their meeting, but Matthew and Luke indicate that he had this other name already. From John we learn that Simon and Andrew were the sons of Jona and that Jesus referred to James and John (the sons of Zebedee) as *Boanerges* or Sons of Thunder. In Mark and Luke, Levi the publican is described as a 'son of Alphaeus', while listed among the final recruits is James, another son of Alphaeus. Thomas, a constant Apostle throughout the Gospels, is referred to in John and Acts as Didymus (the Twin). This leaves only Philip, Bartholomew and Judas Iscariot, each of whom is listed by all the Gospel writers.

It is plain that the Apostles were not a group of sheep-like altruists, who abandoned all to join a charismatic faith healer (even though he was of kingly descent). Jesus's prospects were unknown and, at that stage, he had not gained any divine reputation. It is, therefore, evident that something vital is missing from the Gospels. However, since they were compiled so as not to arouse the suspicions of the Roman overlords, much of their content was phrased in esoteric language for an audience who would understand what was written between the lines.

On many occasions our attention is drawn to specific textual passages by the words, 'He that hath ears to hear, let him hear' (as for instance in Mark 4:9). In this regard, we now enter the enlightening world of the New Testament scribal codes and, on opening the door to the Apostles, we shall also gain insight into the politically formidable role of Jesus as the Messianic descendant of King David.

James and John

Jesus referred to James and John (the sons of Zebedee) by the descriptive Greek name of Boanerges: the Sons of Thunder (Mark 3:17). This is a positive example of cryptic information aimed at initiates. Thunder and Lightning were the titles of two high-ranking ministers of the Sanctuary. The symbolic titles derived from references to the phenomena at Mount Sinai,[1] described in Exodus 19:16, when thunder and lightning enveloped the mountain and Moses went up from the camp to meet with Jehovah. The Sanctuary was emblematic of the Tabernacle (Exodus 25:8) and the Essene Sanctuary was at the Monastery of Mird, nine miles south-east of Jerusalem—once the site of a Hasmonaean fortress.

The man known to Jesus as Thunder was Jonathan Annas, the son of Ananus, the Sadducee High Priest from AD 6 to 15. Jonathan (meaning Jehovah gave) was alternatively called Nathanael (Gift of God), being essentially the same name. His counterpart and political rival, known as Lightning, was Simon Magus (also called Zebedee or Zebadiah, meaning Jehovah hath given), the influential head of the Samaritan Magi. He is better known in the Gospels as Simon the Canaanite or Simon Zelotes.

So, were James and John the sons of Thunder (Jonathan Annas) or the sons of Lightning/Zebedee (Simon Magus)? The answer is that they were both—not by birth, but by distinction. As *Boanerges*, James and John were spiritual sons (deputies) of the Ananus priests; they were also under instruction from Simon, who was destined to hold the highest patriarchal office—that of the community Father.

At once we are presented with a very different picture of the Apostles' social prestige. Even James and John, who are identified as 'fishers', turn out to be prominent in Hellenist society. But why were they depicted (along with Simon-Peter and Andrew) in an environment of fishing boats? This is where the alternative account of John comes into its own, for symbolic fishing was a traditional part of the ritual of baptism.[2]

Gentiles who sought affiliation with the Jewish tribes could take part in the baptism, but could not be baptised in the water. Although they joined the Jewish baptismal candidates in the sea, they were permitted only to receive priestly blessings after they had been hauled aboard ships in large nets. The priests who performed the baptism were called 'fishers'. James and John were both ordained fishers, but Simon-Peter and Andrew were among the lay net-haulers (fishermen). It was in allusion to his own more liberal ministry that Jesus promised them canonical promotion, saying, 'I will make you to become fishers of men' (Mark 1:17).

The Apostles were clearly no ragtag band of righteous devotees, but an influential Council of Twelve under their supreme leader Jesus the Christ. Only much later did his royal style, Jesus Christ (King Jesus), become misconstrued as if it were a proper name in its own right.[3] It is worth reminding ourselves here that the Qumrân *Manual of Discipline* details the importance of a Council of Twelve to preserve the faith of the land.

Simon Zelotes

Simon Magus (or Zebedee) was head of the West Manasseh Magi,[4] a priestly caste of Samaritan philosophers who supported the legitimacy of Jesus. It was their ambassadors (the Magi, or wise men) who honoured the baby Jesus at Bethlehem. Simon was a master showman and manuscripts of his life deal with matters of cosmology, natural magnetism, levitation and psychokinesis.[5] He was a confirmed advocate of war with Rome and was accordingly known as Simon Kananites (Greek: the 'fanatic'). This was later mistranslated as Simon the Canaanite.

As an Apostle of Jesus, Simon was undoubtedly the most prominent in terms of social status, but he was also a keen Zealot commander and was often called Simon *Zelotes* (the Zealot). The Zealots were militant freedom fighters set on vengeance against the Romans who had usurped their heritage and their territory. To the Roman authorities, however, the Zealots were simply *lestai* (bandits).

Already, the Apostles have assumed a more daunting identity than their familiar image, but their purpose remains the same: to support and defend the oppressed of their homeland, being themselves of the elite class. The majority were trained priests, therapeutics and teachers; they would have displayed merciful skills in healing and been able to expound as orators of great wisdom and goodwill.

Judas Iscariot

Another well-born nationalist leader of renown was Judas, Chief of the Scribes.[6] The Dead Sea Scrolls were produced under his tutelage and that of his predecessor, the fierce Judas of Galilee, founder of the Zealot movement.[7] Apart from his academic scholarship, Judas the Apostle was the tribal head of East Manasseh and a warlord of Qumrân. The Romans had a nickname for him: to them he was Judas Sicarius (a sica was a deadly, curved dagger). The Greek form of the nickname was Sikariotes (dagger man), and its corruption to Sicariote was, in due course, further corrupted to become 'Iscariot'.[8] Although always placed at the end of the Apostolic lists, Judas Sicariote would have been second in seniority only to Simon Zelotes.

Thaddaeus, James and Matthew

Lebbaeus Thaddaeus is described as a 'son of Alphaeus' and is also called Judas (Theudas) in two of the Gospels. He was an influential leader of the community and yet another Zealot commander. For more than fifty years, from 9 BC, Thaddaeus was head of the Therapeutate, an ascetic order that had evolved during the Egyptian occupation of Qumrân. Thaddaeus was a confederate of Jesus's father, Joseph, and took part in the people's rising against Pontius Pilate in AD 32.

James, said to be another 'son of Alphaeus', was actually Jonathan Annas, leader of the Thunder Party. The name James is an English variant of the name Jacob,[9] and the nominal style of Jacob was Jonathan's patriarchal entitlement. Just as the names of the angels and archangels were preserved within the higher priesthood, so too were the Jewish patriarchal names preserved by the community elders. They were led by a triumvirate of appointed officials to whom were applied the titular names Abraham, Isaac and Jacob. In this regard, Jonathan Annas was the Jacob patriarch for a time (the English equivalent being James).

As for Matthew (also called Levi), he too is described as a 'son of Alphaeus'. He was, in fact, Matthew Annas (the brother of Jonathan) — later to succeed as High Priest from AD 42 until deposed by Herod-Agrippa I. Matthew was intimately concerned with the promotion of Jesus's work and actively sponsored the Gospel issued under his name. As Jonathan's successor, he was the chief Levite priest and held the nominal title of Levi. He was also an appointed publican (a Jerusalem tax official), responsible for the collection of public revenues from the Diaspora Jews who had settled outside their homeland, but were still liable to taxation.[10] Income from Asia Minor was collected by the Levites and deposited at the Treasury in Jerusalem: 'And as Jesus passed forth from thence, he saw a man, named Matthew, sitting at the receipt of custom' (Matthew 9:9). Similarly, in reference to the same event, 'He went forth, and saw a publican, named Levi, sitting at the receipt of custom' (Luke 5:27).

Thaddaeus, James and Matthew (Levi) are all described as 'sons of Alphaeus', but they were not all brothers. As elsewhere, the word 'son' is used to denote a deputy position. The style 'of Alphaeus' did not imply relation to a person or a place, for it meant, quite simply, 'of the Succession'.

Philip, Bartholomew and Thomas

As John 1:45-49 indicates, Philip was an associate of Jonathan Annas (alternatively known as Nathanael). An uncircumcised Gentile Proselyte,[11] Philip was head of the Order of Shem.[12] The Coptic Gospel of Philip was written in his name. Bartholomew (also known as John Mark) was Philip's evangelical and political companion. He was chief of the Proselytes and an official of the influential Egyptian Therapeutate (the healing community) at Qumrân.[13]

The Gospels say little about Thomas, but he was among the most influential of Christian evangelists, known to have preached in Syria, Persia and India. He was eventually lanced to death at Mylapore, near Madras. Thomas — originally Crown Prince Philip — was born into the Herod family,[14] but lost his inheritance when his mother, Mariamne II, was divorced by King Herod after she tried to assassinate him. Philip's half-brother, Herod-Antipas, later became Tetrarch of Galilee. In ridicule, the local people likened Prince Philip to Esau — the son of Isaac who lost both his birthright and his father's blessing to his twin brother Jacob (Genesis 25-27) — and they called him *Teoma* (Aramaic for 'twin'): in Greek this name became Thomas and was sometimes translated as Didymus (similarly meaning 'twin').

Simon-Peter and Andrew

We are dealing here with the two Apostles who are often thought to have been the most prominent — yet in this sequence they are placed last. Indeed, the order in which the Apostles have been listed in this section pretty much represents the reverse of that followed in the Gospel lists. This is because such characters as Simon Zelotes, Judas Sicariote and Thaddaeus were far more powerful than their traditional end-of-list positions indicate. But, it was by no accident that the Gospel writers arranged the names as they did for, by this means, they diverted Roman attention from those Apostles in the very forefront of public life.

Hence, the Apostolic tables usually begin with the least influential members, Simon-Peter and Andrew, who were ordinary village Essenes and held no public office. In the context of their being 'fishermen' and not 'fishers', their role at the baptism ritual was strictly as laymen: they were in charge of the nets, but performed no priestly function (such as the bestowing of blessings) as did the ordained 'fishers' James and John.

For all that, Simon-Peter and Andrew's lack of public station was of great value to Jesus. It made the two brothers more readily available to him than others who had ministerial or legislative work to accomplish. The result was that Simon-Peter became Jesus's right-hand man and he was evidently a fellow of some solidity, being nicknamed *Cephas* (the Stone). In the Nag Hammadi Gospel of Thomas, Jesus refers to Simon-Peter as his 'guardian' and he was, presumably, Jesus's chief bodyguard. After losing his wife, Simon-Peter became a prominent evangelist and, despite the occasional disagreement with Jesus, was largely responsible for perpetuating the Gospel in Rome. He was eventually martyred by crucifixion during Emperor Nero's persecution of the Christians.

Priests and Angels

We have already encountered the fact that the angelic structure was maintained within the priestly hierarchy of the Qumrân community — so that the highest ranking priest was not only the Zadok dynast but was also the archangel Michael. Thus, he was the Michael-Zadok (the Melchizedek). Second in ranking was the Abiathar, who was also the angel Gabriel. It is now worth taking a closer look at the angelic order, for it will shed even more light on the Apostles' social status. In this context, various customary practices—both priestly and patriarchal—will become apparent, leading the way, quite naturally, to a whole new understanding of Jesus's miracles.

The first thing to note is that there is nothing spiritual or ethereal about the word 'angel'. In the original Greek, *aggelos* (more usually transliterated as *angelos*—Latin: *angelus*) meant no more than 'messenger'. Modern English derives the word 'angel' from this via Church Latin, but the Anglo-Saxon word *engel* came originally from the old French *angele*. An angel of the Lord was, thus, a messenger of the Lord or, more correctly, an ambassador of the Lord. An Archangel was a priestly ambassador of the highest rank (the prefix 'arch' meaning 'chief', as in archduke and archbishop).

The Old Testament describes two types of angel, the great majority of whom acted like normal human beings—as for example in Genesis 19:1-3, when two angels visited Lot's house, 'and [he] did bake unleavened bread, and they did eat'. Most Old Testament angels belong to this uncomplicated category, such as the angel who met Abraham's wife Hagar by the water fountain,[15] the angel who stopped Balaam's ass in its tracks,[16] the angel who spoke with Manoah and his wife[17] and the angel who sat under the oak with Gideon.[18]

Another class of angel seems to have been rather more than a messenger, possessing fearsome powers of destruction. This type of avenging angel features in 1-Chronicles 21:14-16: 'And God sent an angel unto Jerusalem to destroy it ... having a sword drawn in his hand stretched out over Jerusalem'. Quite a few angels are described as wielding swords, but they are never described as divine and there is no hint in the text of the graceful wings that are so often portrayed. The now familiar wings were devised by artists and sculptors to symbolize the angels' spiritual transcendence above the mundane environment.

This brings us to another category of daunting Old Testament phenomena which were said to rise above the earth by mechanical means. They were never called angels, and generally these blazing spectacles had wheels, as in Daniel 7:9: 'His throne was like the fiery flame, and his wheels as burning fire'. In Isaiah 6:1-2 there is a similar account of an airborne throne, and 'above it stood the seraphims: each one had six wings'. Yet another reference to such an apparatus occurs in Ezekiel 1, where the whole scenario—recounted at some length—is entirely in keeping with the others, including fire, wheels, and noisy, rotating rings.

Unrelated to the Bible, an ancient tractate from 3rd-century Alexandria, entitled *The Origin*, tells of the immortal Sophia, and of the ruler Saboath who 'created a great throne on a four-faced chariot called Cherubim .... And on that throne he created some other dragon-shaped seraphims'. Interestingly, it is narrated in Genesis 3:24 that the Lord stationed cherubims (chariots or mobile thrones) and a revolving sword of fire to protect the Garden of Eden.

The Cherubim appears again in an ancient Greek work called *The Hypostasis of the Archons*, which deals with the Rulers of Entirety and the Creation of Adam. Once more it concerns Saboath and his heavenly chariot — the Cherubim. There is mention of a similar vehicle in 2-Kings 2:11, when Elijah is taken up in a chariot of fire, and there are further descriptions of a like conveyance in the Sumerian *Epic of Gilgamesh*[19] from the Mesopotamian Bible land of old Iraq.

It is not the purpose of this book to examine the whys and wherefores of such phenomena — simply to present them as they are depicted in the ancient texts.[20] What is certain, however, is that these flying chariots (*cherubims*) with their accompanying *seraphims* (fiery dragon-shaped auxiliaries) were never at any time described as having human form, as angels always were. It was the fearful Christian dogma of the later Roman establishment which transformed the cherubims and seraphims into adoring celestial putti.

Notwithstanding these spectacular Old Testament portrayals, the angels of the New Testament were, without exception, all men and their appointments to angelic office were strictly dynastic. The Book of Enoch (representing the patriarch sixth in line from Adam) was written in the 2nd century BC. It forecast a restoration of the Messianic dynasties and laid down ground-rules for the structure of the priestly hierarchy.[21] Included was the premise that successive dynastic heads should carry the names of the traditional angels and archangels to denote their rank and position.

In the Old Testament days of King David, the senior priests were Zadok, Abiathar and Levi (in that order of precedence). The Essenes of Qumrân duly preserved their priestly heritage using those names as titles: Zadok, Abiathar and Levi, as we have seen. Also, in accordance with the Book of Enoch, the archangelic names were retained, under vow, as badges of priestly rank,[22] with the Zadok dynast also being the Michael; the Abiathar being the Gabriel and the Levi being the Sariel.[23]

We should, therefore, understand that the archangel Michael's battle with the dragon, in Revelation 12:7, corresponds to the conflict between the Zadokite succession and 'the beast of blasphemy' — Imperial Rome. The 'second beast' was that of the rigidly strict regime of the Pharisees, who thwarted the ambitions of the Hellenist Jews by segregating Jews from Gentiles. This was the beast to which was attributed the number 666 (Revelation 13:8) — the numerically evaluated polar opposite to the spiritual energy of water in the solar force.[24]

Outside the dynastic families (the heads of kingly and priestly successions who were expressly required to marry in order to perpetuate their lines), those of the high orders were generally required to remain celibate, as detailed in the *Temple Scroll*. Trainee priests were, therefore, in limited supply and were often raised within a monastic system from the community's illegitimate sons. Jesus might well have become one of those trainee priests, whose mother had been 'put away privily', were it not for the considered intervention of the angel Gabriel.

When procreation was embarked upon, a priestly dynast (such as the Zadok) had, temporarily, to suspend himself from his ordained role and pass his religious duties to another. When physical relations with his wife were completed, he would once more live apart from her and resume his celibate existence.

The Zadok/Michael of the early Gospel era was Zacharias (the husband of Mary's cousin, Elizabeth). His priestly deputy, the Abiathar/Gabriel, was Simeon. The story of Zacharias' procreational leave is very veiled in Luke 1:15-23, but his being rendered 'speechless in the Temple' actually means that he was prevented from speaking in his usual ordained capacity. Being concerned about his advancing age, Zacharias the Zadok transferred his priestly authority to Simeon the Abiathar so that Elizabeth could bear a son. That son was John the Baptist who, in time, succeeded as the Zadokite head.

At the time of Jesus's early ministry, the head of the Levi priests was Jonathan Annas. As chief of the Levite dynasty he held the third archangelic rank of Sariel, in which capacity he was the nominated King's Priest. Along with these three supreme archangels (chief ambassadors), Michael (the Zadok), Gabriel (the Abiathar) and Sariel (the Levi), there were also others with pre-eminent titles. These positions, however, were not dynastic and were denoted by the representative styles, *Father*, *Son* and *Spirit*. The Father was the equivalent of the Roman Pope of later times (Pope = Papa = Father) — the Roman style having been purloined directly from the original Jewish source. In essence, the Son and Spirit were his physical and spiritual deputies. The position of Father was elective and precluded its holder from certain other duties. For example, when Jonathan Annas became the Father, his brother Matthew (the Apostle) became his successor as the head of the Levi priests of the Succession. Hence, Matthew then became the Levi of Alphaeus.

The Levi priests (Levites) operated as subordinates of the archangels. At their head, but junior to the Levi dynast, was a Chief Priest (as distinct from a High Priest). He was angelically designated Raphael. His senior priests were styled in accordance with the original sons of Levi (as given in Genesis 29:34) and they were called Kohath, Gershon and Merari. The next priest in seniority was Amram (the Old Testament son of Kohath), followed by Aaron, Moses and the priestess, Miriam. They, in turn, were senior to Nadab, Abihu, Eleazar and Ithmar—the representative sons of Aaron.

It is at this stage that the primary aspect of the Grail Code begins to emerge, for the heir to the Davidic kingly succession held no angelic title and was not in priestly service. The King was obliged to serve the people and it was his express duty to champion them against establishment injustice. The very name David means 'beloved' and, as an upholder of this distinction, Jesus would have made a very fine king. It was this royal concept of humble service that the lay disciples found so hard to comprehend in their Messianic leader. This is well demonstrated in John 13:4-11, when Jesus washed the Apostles' feet. Peter queried the action, saying, 'Thou shalt never wash my feet', but Jesus was insistent, replying with finality, 'I have given you an example, that ye should do as I have done to you'. Such a charitable action is not the mark of a power-seeking dynast, but is emblematic of common fatherhood in the nature of true Grail kingship.

The Messiah

Water and Wine

Although not considered to be history in the traditional sense, the Gospels relate the story of Jesus by way of a continuous narrative. Sometimes they are in agreement; sometimes they are not but, at all times, their purpose was to convey an imperative social message with Jesus as the focal catalyst. Not all of that message was delivered in an overt fashion, however. Jesus is often said to have spoken in the form of parables, thereby simplifying his message with allegorical discourse. To some, these moralistic tales would appear superficial, but their undertones were frequently political, being based upon actual people and real situations.

The Gospels were constructed in a similar manner and it is important to recognize that many of the stories about Jesus are themselves the equivalent of parables for the benefit of 'those with ears to hear'. This has often led to some perfectly straightforward events being dubbed with supernatural overtones. A good example occurs in John 2:1-10: the story of Jesus substituting the water for wine at the Cana wedding feast. This well-known event was the first of many presumptuous actions by which Jesus made known his intention to circumvent tradition.

Although raised within a strict regime that was influenced by tradition and ancient laws, Jesus recognized that Rome could never be defeated while extremes of competitive doctrine existed within the Jewish community itself. There was no such thing as Christianity in those days—the religion of Jesus was Judaism and the Jews all worshipped one God, but even they were split into various factions, each with a different set of community rules. It was generally perceived, however, that Jehovah belonged to the Jews, but Jesus aspired to share Jehovah with the Gentiles in a way that did not require them to take on all the trappings of orthodox Judaism.

Jesus had little patience with the rigorous creeds of Jewish groups like the Pharisees, and he knew the people could not be freed from oppression until they had forsaken their own uncompromising sectarianism. He was also aware that a Messiah had long been anticipated — a saviour who was expected to introduce a new era of deliverance. He would, therefore, be revolutionary in outlook and would set himself apart from customary practice. As the heir to the Davidic royal house, Jesus knew that he was qualified to be that Messiah and that, if he should emerge as such, few would be unduly surprised.

What Jesus did not have was any designated social authority — he was neither a reigning King nor a High Priest. However, he paid little heed to such technicalities and proceeded to implement ritualistic changes regardless of his titular deficiency. On his first opportunity at the Cana wedding, he hesitated, claiming, 'Mine hour is not yet come'. But his mother waved aside his lack of entitlement and directed the servants, saying, 'Whatsoever he saith unto you, do it'.

The only account of this appears in John's Gospel, where the incident of the water and wine is described as the first of Jesus's miracles. But, it is not stated that they 'ran out of wine', as is so often misquoted. The text actually says, 'And when they wanted wine, the mother of Jesus saith unto him, They have no wine'. According to the ritual described in the Dead Sea Scrolls, the relevance of this is plain. At the equivalent of Communion, only fully initiated celibates were allowed to partake of wine.[1] All others present were regarded as unsanctified and were restricted to a purifying ritual with water; these included married men, novices, Gentiles and all lay Jews.

The Gospel text continues: 'There were set there six water-pots of stone, after the manner of the purifying of the Jews'. The significance of Jesus's action is that he took it upon himself to break with tradition when he abandoned the water and allowed the 'unclean' guests to take the sacred wine. The Ruler of the Feast (Greek: *Architriclinos*) 'knew not whence it was (but the servants which drew the water knew)'. He did not comment on any marvellous transformation, but simply remarked that he was surprised the good wine had made its appearance at that stage. As Mary declared, when instructing the servants to obey Jesus, the episode 'manifested forth his glory and his disciples believed on him'.

Communion with consecrated bread and wine was an age-old Essene tradition, not a product of later Christianity. In time, the Christian Church appropriated the original custom as its own Eucharistic sacrament, symbolizing the body and blood of Jesus in accordance with the Gospel references to its supposed institution at the Last Supper (as for instance in Matthew 26:26-28).

Represented with similar allegory in the Gospels is the episode known as the Feeding of the Five Thousand. Judaic law was strict, but Jesus's new ministry was intended to be quite open-hearted. Normally, Gentiles were afforded access to Jewish ritual only if they were committed converts, who had undertaken to observe the Jewish customs (including circumcision, if they were male). Jesus's thoughts, however, were of the uncircumcised Gentiles: Why should they not also gain access to Jehovah? After all, he had already allowed unclean Gentiles to take the consecrated wine at Cana.

The concept of a God shared by Jews and Gentiles alike became the very life-force of Jesus's mission. But it was an ideal that was more than revolutionary; to the die-hard orthodox Jews it was outrageous, for Jesus was assuming personal power over their own historical prerogative. He was making Jehovah (the God of the Chosen People) available to all and sundry, with few strings attached.

As we have already seen, Gentiles wishing to be baptised into Judaism underwent a ritual in which they, as 'fishes', were hauled into boats by 'fishermen' to be blessed by priestly 'fishers'. In a similar transference of imagery, the Levite officials of the Sanctuary were called 'loaves'.[2] In the rite of ordination (the ceremony of admission to the priestly ministry), the officiating Levite priests would serve seven loaves of bread to the priests, while to the celibate candidates they would administer five loaves and two fishes. There was some important legal symbolism in this, for whereas Gentiles might receive baptism as 'fishes', the Law was very firm in that only Jews could become 'loaves'.

Once again, Jesus resolved to flout convention and allow unclean Gentiles to partake of what was normally reserved for Jews who were candidates of the priesthood. In this regard, Jesus made his concession to the representatives of the uncircumcised non-Jews of the Ham fraternity (known figuratively as the Five Thousand).[3] Thus, he granted their Multitude (governing body) symbolic access to the ministry by serving them the five loaves and two fishes of the Jewish priestly candidates (Mark 6:34-44).

In the separate episode known as the Feeding of the Four Thousand,[4] the seven loaves of the senior priests were proffered by Jesus to the uncircumcised Multitude of Shem (Mark 8:1-10).

At the baptism ceremonies, the *fishermen* who caught the Gentile *fishes* would first take their boats out some little distance from the shore. The baptismal postulants would then wade into the water towards the boats. When everything was set, the priestly *fishers* would leave the shore and make their own way to the moored boats along a jetty—thereby 'walking on the water' to the boats.[5] Born into the tribe of Judah, not that of Levi, Jesus had no authority as a baptismal priest, but he nonetheless presumed to disregard the establishment and to usurp a priestly entitlement by walking on the sea to the disciples' boat (Matthew 14:25-26). He even tempted Peter to arrogate to himself the same right, but Peter was unable to comply for fear of sinking beneath legal reprisals (Matthew 14:28-31).

Such new insight on our part, both into the veiled meaning of the Gospel wording, and into Jesus's own political motivations, does not detract from his probable skills as a healer. Being attached to the Qumrân Therapeutate, he would not, however, have been unique in this regard. But then, a charismatic physician was not the anticipated image of a liberating Messiah expected to free the people from Roman oppression. What was particularly remarkable about this radical protagonist was that he applied his medical expertise to the said unworthy and unclean Gentiles; he did not restrict his aid to the Jewish society as the Pharisees and others would have preferred. This form of social ministry—a ministry of princely service, as promoted by the emergent Grail Code, was wholly indicative of Jesus's Messianic ideal for a unified people.

The King and his Donkey

Shortly after Jesus began his mission, John the Baptist was arrested because he had angered Herod-Antipas, the Governor of Galilee. Antipas had married Herodias, the divorced wife of his half-brother, Philip, and the Baptist repeatedly condemned the marriage, declaring that it was sinful. As a result, he was imprisoned for a year and then beheaded. On his ignoble demise, many of his followers turned their allegiance toward Jesus. Some had thought that John was the expected Messiah, but a number of his prophecies had not been fulfilled[6] and so he was discounted in this regard. One of the reasons why John's prophecies proved inaccurate was because of the differences between the commonly used solar and lunar calendars, further complicated by the Julian calendar introduced from Rome.

The Essenes were advocates of the Greek philosopher Pythagoras (c.570-500 BC), who in his great study of arithmetical ratios searched for meaning both in the physical and metaphysical worlds through mathematical proportions. Over the centuries, using his methodology, world events were foretold with surprising accuracy. One particular event so forecast was the beginning of a new World Order, an occurrence that was in many quarters determined to be the advent of the Saviour Messiah.

The years (which we now designate BC) were thus already on a predetermined countdown long before Jesus was born. As things turned out, the Messianic forecast was actually seven years astray when applied to Jesus — which explains why he was (as far as we may be concerned) born in the year 7 BC and not in the notional year 0 (754 AUC).[7] But, his brother James was actually born in the right year, as a result of which many considered James to be the legitimate heir. Much later, by way of a new Roman dating system, the notional year 0 was designated AD 1.

In the movement away from the Baptist's rigid Hebrew doctrine, even King Herod-Agrippa began to regard Jesus as the lawful heir to David, leaving James with few to champion his cause. Encouraged by this, Jesus decided to step up his campaign, but he acted too rashly and committed an offence that was to upset the governors and elders.

It had long been the Jewish custom to hold a Day of Atonement (*Yom Kippur*), on which day the people might be absolved of their misdeeds. The solemn ritual took place in the equivalent of September, and the Essene rite was performed by the Father in the seclusion of the Holy of Holies (inner sanctuary) of the monastery temple at Mird. To witness the atonement, the Father was allowed the company of one co-celebrant: a symbolic Son. In AD 32 the Father was Simon Zelotes, and his appointed Son was his immediate lieutenant Judas Sicariote. (John 13:2 gives Judas's status as Simon's son, but their exact relationship and its priestly significance are not made clear.)

When the act of Atonement was complete, three deputies were authorized to proclaim the fact from a high location west of the temple, symbolically spreading the word to Jews resident in other lands (those of the Diaspora). On this occasion, the deputies appointed were Jesus (representing King David), Jonathan Annas (representing the great mystic Elijah/Elias) and Thaddaeus (representing Moses), corresponding respectively to the symbolic roles of King, Priest and Prophet. But when the time came for Jesus to make his proclamation, he appeared not in the apparel of a king, but in the robes of a high priest: 'And he was transfigured before them. And his raiment became shining, exceeding white as snow; so as no fuller[8] on earth can white them .... And there appeared unto them Elias with Moses: and they were talking with Jesus' (Mark 9:2-4).

In AD 32, Simon Zelotes fell foul of the authorities, having led an unsuccessful revolt against the Governor of Judaea, Pontius Pilate. The reason for the revolt was that Pilate had been using public funds to have his personal water supply improved. A formal complaint was lodged against him in court,[9] whereupon Pilate's soldiers murdered the known complainants. Armed insurrection immediately ensued, led by the prominent Zealots, Simon Zelotes, Judas Sicariote and Thaddaeus. Perhaps inevitably, the revolt failed and Simon was excommunicated by edict of King Herod-Agrippa. Simon's political opponent, Jonathan Annas, was thus enabled to accede to the supreme office of the Father.

Under the Law, excommunication (to be regarded as spiritual execution, or death by decree) took four days for complete implementation. In the meantime, the excommunicatee was dressed in a shroud, shut away and held to be 'sick unto death'. In view of his patriarchal rank up to that point, Simon was incarcerated in the patrimonial burial chamber at Qumrân known as the Bosom of Abraham.[10] His devotional 'sisters', Martha and Mary, knew that his soul would be forever condemned if he was not reprieved (raised) by the third day, and so they sent word to Jesus that Simon was 'sick' (John 11:3).

At first Jesus was powerless to act, for only the Father or the High Priest could perform such a raising (resurrection) and Jesus held no priestly office. It happened, however, that Herod-Agrippa fell into an argument with the Roman governors, losing his jurisdiction to the short-term benefit of his uncle, Herod-Antipas, who had supported the Zealot action against Pilate. Seizing his opportunity, Antipas countermanded the order of excommunication and instructed that Simon should be 'raised from the dead'. Jesus was, therefore, in something of a quandary. He was heir to the kingly line, yet with no formal entitlement, but he wished to come to the aid of his friend and loyal supporter—and so he did. Although the time of spiritual death (the fourth day following excommunication) for Simon had arrived, Jesus decided to presume a priestly function and perform the release. In so doing, he confirmed the spiritually dead Simon's rank as that of Abraham's Steward, Eliezer (corrupted in the Gospels to Lazarus) and summoned him, under that distinguished name, to come forth from Abraham's Bosom.

And so it was that Lazarus was raised from the dead without official sanction from the new Father, neither from the High Priest, nor from the Sanhedrin Council. Jesus had blatantly flouted the rules, but Herod-Antipas then obliged Jonathan Annas to acquiesce in the *fait accompli* and, to the people at large, the unprecedented event was indeed a miracle.

Jesus had effected exactly what he wanted and, with this impressive action behind him, it remained only for him to be formally anointed and to appear before the people as their rightful Messiah in a way that would leave little room for dispute. How the Saviour Messiah was to achieve such recognition was long established for it had been prophesied in the Old Testament book of Zechariah (9:9): 'Rejoice greatly, O daughter of Zion; shout O daughter of Jerusalem: behold, thy King cometh unto thee: he is just, and having salvation; lowly, and riding upon an ass'.

The arrangements were made when Jesus and his disciples were in Bethany during the week before Passover, March AD 33. Firstly (as related in Matthew 26:6-7 and Mark 14:3), Jesus was anointed by Mary of Bethany, who poured a precious box of spikenard[11] over his head. A suitable beast of burden was found and, in accordance with Zechariah's prophecy, Jesus rode into Jerusalem on a donkey.[12] It has long been popularly supposed that this was a gesture of abject humility—and so it was—but it was also much more than that. From the time of King Solomon, to the Jewish deportation to Babylon following the fall of Jerusalem in 586 BC, the Davidic kings had all ridden to their installations on mules. The custom was representative of the monarch's accessibility to the lowliest of his subjects—an example, yet again, of the Messianic code of service.

The Messianic Queen

It has often been said that the New Testament does not state in any forthright manner that Jesus was married. By the same token, and more importantly, however, nowhere does it state that he was unmarried. In fact, the Gospels actually contain a number of specific pointers to his married status and it would have been very surprising if he had remained single, for the dynastic regulations were quite clear in this regard.

As we have seen, the rules of dynastic wedlock were no ordinary affair. Explicitly defined parameters dictated a celibate lifestyle except for the procreation of children at regulated intervals. A lengthy period of betrothal was followed by a First Marriage in September, after which physical relationship was allowed in December. If conception took place, a Second Marriage ceremony was then celebrated in March to legalize the wedlock. During that trial period, and until the Second Marriage, whether pregnant or not, the bride was regarded in law as an *almah* ('young woman' or, as erroneously cited, 'virgin').

Among the more colourful books of the Old Testament is *The Song of Solomon* — a series of love canticles between a sovereign bride and her bridegroom. The *Song* identifies the potion symbolic of espousal as the aromatic ointment called spikenard.[13] It was the same very expensive spikenard that was used by Mary of Bethany to anoint Jesus's head at the house of Lazarus (Simon Zelotes) and a similar incident (narrated in Luke 7:37-38) had occurred some time earlier, when a woman anointed Jesus's feet with ointment, wiping them afterwards with her hair.

John 11:1-2 also mentions this earlier event, then explains how the ritual of anointing Jesus's feet was performed yet again by the same woman at Bethany. When Jesus was seated at the table, Mary took 'a pound of ointment of spikenard, very costly, and anointed the feet of Jesus, and wiped his feet with her hair: and the house was filled with the odour of the ointment' (John 12:3).

In *The Song of Solomon* (1:12) is the bridal refrain, 'While the king sitteth at his table, my spikenard sendeth forth the smell thereof'. Not only did Mary anoint Jesus's head at Simon's house (Matthew 26:6-7 and Mark 14:3), but she also anointed his feet and wiped them afterwards with her hair in March AD 33. Two and a half years earlier, in September AD 30, she had performed this same ritual three months after the Cana wedding feast.

On both occasions the anointing was carried out while Jesus was seated at the table (as defined in *The Song of Solomon*). This was an allusion to the ancient rite by which a royal bride prepared her bridegroom's table. To perform the rite with spikenard was the express privilege of a Messianic bride and was performed solely at the First and Second Marriage ceremonies. Only as the wife of Jesus and as a priestess in her own right could Mary have anointed both his head and his feet with the sacred ointment.

Psalm 23 depicts God, in the male-female imagery of the era, as both the shepherd and the bride. Of the bride, the words say 'Thou preparest a table before me ... thou anointest my head with oil'.[14] According to the sacred marriage rite of ancient Mesopotamia (the land of Noah and Abraham), the Great Goddess, Inanna, took as her bridegroom the shepherd Dumuzi (or Tammuz)[15] and it was from this union that the concept of the Shekinah-and-Jehovah evolved in Canaan through the intermediate deities Asherah and El Elohim.

In Egypt, the anointing of the king was the privileged duty of the pharaohs' semi-divine sister-brides. Crocodile fat was the substance used in the anointing because it was associated with sexual prowess — and the sacred crocodile of the Egyptians was the *Messeh*, which corresponds to the Hebrew *Messiah*: 'Anointed One'.[16] In old Mesopotamia the intrepid royal beast — a four-legged monitor dragon — was called the *Mûs-hûs*.

It was preferred that the Pharaohs married their sisters — especially their maternal half-sisters by other fathers — because true dynastic inheritance was held in the female line. Alternatively, maternal first cousins were suitably regarded. The Kings of Judah did not adopt this as a general practice, but they did regard the female line as a means of

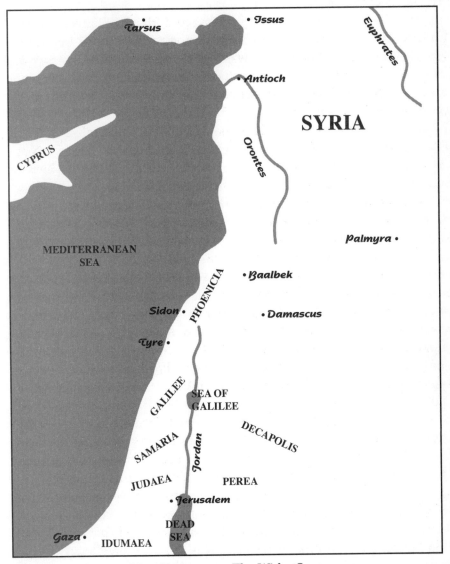

New Testament — The Wider Scene

transferring kingship and other hereditary positions of influence (even today, one is said to be truly a Jew if born of a Jewish mother). David attained his kingship, for example, by marrying Michal, the daughter of King Saul. Much later, Herod the Great gained his kingly status by marrying Mariamne of the Hasmonaean royal house.

Just as the men who were appointed to various patriarchal positions took on names that represented their ancestors — such as Isaac, Jacob and Joseph — so too were the women styled according to their genealogy and rank. Their nominal styles included Rachel, Rebecca and Sarah.[17] Wives of the Zadok and David male lines held the ranks of Elisheba (Elizabeth) and Miriam (Mary) respectively. That is why John the Baptists's mother is called Elizabeth in the Gospels and why Jesus's mother was Mary. It is also why Jesus's own wife would have been a Mary. These women underwent the ceremony of their Second Marriage only once they were three months pregnant, at which time the bride ceased being an *almah* and became a designated *mother*.

As we have seen, sexual relations were permitted only in December; husbands and wives lived apart for the rest of the year. At the outset of a period of separation, the wife was classified as a *widow* and was required to weep for her husband. This is described in Luke 7:38, when Mary of Bethany, on the first occasion, is said to have 'stood at his feet behind him weeping, and began to wash his feet with tears'. Once the period of symbolic widowhood had been established, and during these lengthy periods of separation, the wife was given the conventual designation *sister*, just as a modern nun might be. So who exactly was Mary of Bethany — the woman who twice anointed Jesus with spikenard in accordance with Messianic tradition?

To be precise, she is never called Mary of Bethany in the Bible. She and Martha are only ever referred to as 'sisters' at the house of Lazarus of Bethany. Mary's full title was Sister Miriam Magdala or, as she is better known, Mary Magdalene. Gregory I, Bishop of Rome 590-604, and St. Bernard, the Cistercian Abbot of Clairvaux 1090-1153, both confirmed that Mary of Bethany was synonymous with Mary Magdalene.

On the second occasion that Jesus was anointed with spikenard, Judas Sicariote declared his dissatisfaction at the way things were going. He stated his opposition (John 12:4-5) and thus paved the way for his betrayal of Jesus. Following the failed revolt by the Zealots against Pilate, Judas had become a fugitive. Jesus was of little political use to him, for he carried no influence with the Sanhedrin Council,[18] so Judas threw in his lot with Jesus's uncontroversial brother James, who was actually a member of that Council. Consequently, Judas not only had no interest in seeing Jesus anointed as a Messiah, but his new allegiance to James caused him to resent it once it had happened. Jesus, nevertheless, was adamant about the significance of his anointing by Mary (Mark 14:9): 'Verily I say unto you, Wheresoever this gospel shall be preached throughout the whole world, this also that she hath done shall be spoken of for a memorial of her'.

Apart from the fact that Jesus was said to love Mary Magdalene, there is not much in the Gospels to indicate their intimate closeness until Mary appears with Jesus's mother and Salome (the consort of Simon Zelotes[19]) at the Crucifixion. Not so, however, in the Nag Hammadi Gospel of Philip, where the relationship between Jesus and Mary is openly discussed:

> And the companion of the Saviour is Mary Magdalene. But Christ loved her more than all the disciples, and used to kiss her often on the mouth. The rest of the disciples were offended by it and expressed disapproval. They said unto him, Why do you love her more than all of us? The Saviour answered and said to them, Why do I not love you like her? ... Great is the mystery of marriage, for without it the world would not have existed. Now the existence of the world depends on man, and the existence of man on marriage.

Notwithstanding the particular references to the importance of marriage in this passage, the reference to kissing on the mouth is especially relevant; it relates once more to the offices of the sacred bride and bridegroom, and was not the mark of extra-marital love or friendship. As a part of the royal bridal refrain, such kissing is the subject of the first entry in *The Song of Solomon*, which opens, 'Let him kiss me with the kisses of his mouth: for thy love is better than wine'.

There is no talk in John's Gospel of any marriage service at Cana, only of a wedding feast and of the water and wine. The disciples were there, as were various guests including Gentiles and others who were technically unclean. This, then, was not the ceremony of the marriage itself but the sacred meal that preceded the betrothal. The custom was for there to be a formal host (as appears in the account); he would be in full charge as the Ruler of the Feast. Secondary authority rested only in the bridegroom and his mother — and this is entirely relevant for, when the matter of the communion wine arose, Jesus's mother said to the servants (John 2:5), 'Whatsoever he saith unto you, do it'. No invited guest would have had any such right of command and it is plain, therefore, that Jesus and the bridegroom were one and the same.

This betrothal communion (6 June AD 30) took place three months before Mary first anointed Jesus's feet at Simon's house (3 September AD 30). The rules were strictly defined: only as Jesus's bride would Mary have been permitted to perform this act. With her First Marriage duly completed in the September, she would also have wept for her husband (as in Luke 7:38) before they were parted for their statutory separation. Prior to this, as a betrothed *almah*, she would have been classified as a *sinner* and ranked as a *crippled woman*.[20] The couple would then not have come together for any physical union until the following December.

Suppression of the Marriage Evidence

One of the reasons why there is no obvious mention of Jesus's marital status in the New Testament is that the evidence was deliberately removed by Church decree. This was revealed as recently as 1958, when a manuscript of the Ecumenical Patriarch of Constantinople was discovered in a monastery at Mar Saba, east of Jerusalem, by Morton Smith, Professor of Ancient History at Columbia University, USA. The extracts quoted below are from his subsequent writings.[21]

Within a book of the works of St. Ignatius of Antioch was a transcription of a letter by Bishop Clement of Alexandria (*c*.AD 150-215). It was addressed to his colleague, Theodore, and included a generally unknown section from the Gospel of Mark. Clement's letter decreed that some of the original content of Mark was to be suppressed because it did not conform with Church requirement. The letter reads:

> For even if they should say something true, one who loves the Truth should not, even so, agree with them. For not all true things are the Truth; nor should that truth which seems true according to human opinions be preferred to the true Truth — that according to the faith.

> To them one must never give way; nor, when they
> put forward their falsifications, should one concede
> that the secret Gospel is by Mark—but should deny it
> on oath. For not all true things are to be said to all men.

In the removed section of the Gospel is an account of the raising of Lazarus—but an account that has Lazarus (Simon Zelotes) calling to Jesus from within the tomb even before the stone was rolled back.[22] This makes it quite clear that the man was not dead in the physical sense—which, of course, defeated the Church's insistence that the raising should be accepted as a supernatural miracle. Moreover, the original Gospel of Mark did not include any details of the events of the Resurrection and its aftermath; it ended simply with the women fleeing from an empty sepulchre. The concluding twelve verses of Mark 16, as generally published today, were spuriously attached at a later date.[23]

The relevance of this is that the Lazarus incident was part of that same sequence of events which climaxed when Mary Magdalene anointed Jesus at Bethany. The Synoptic Gospels do not say what happened on Jesus's arrival at Simon's house, for the raising of Lazarus is not included in them, but in John 11:20-29, it is described:

> Then Martha, as soon as she heard that Jesus
> was coming, went and met him: but Mary sat
> still in the house ... [Martha] called Mary her
> sister secretly, saying, The Master is come, and
> calleth for thee. As soon as she heard that, she
> arose quickly and came unto him.

No reason is ventured for Mary's hesitant behaviour although, apart from that, the passage seems straightforward enough. But the incident is described in much greater detail in the portion of Mark that was officially suppressed. It explains that Mary did come out of the house with Martha on the first occasion, but was then chastised by the disciples and sent back indoors to await her Master's instruction. The fact is that, as Jesus's wife, Mary was bound by a strict code of bridal practice. She was not permitted to leave the house and greet her husband until she had received his express consent to do so.[24] John's account leaves Mary in her rightful place without explanation, but the more detailed Mark text was strategically withheld from publication.

The suppression of the Lazarus story is why the accounts of anointing in the Gospels of Mark and Matthew are located at the house of Simon the leper, instead of at the house of Lazarus as in John. But the description, Simon the leper, is simply another more guarded way of referring to Simon Zelotes (Lazarus); he was classified as a 'leper' because he was rendered hideously unclean by his excommunication. This, in turn, explains the anomalous account of a leper entertaining prestigious friends at his fine house. However, the resultant fact was that, with his wife three months into her pregnancy, Jesus was not only a formally anointed Messianic Christ when he rode into Jerusalem on the donkey; he was also a father-to-be.

Betrayal

Politics and the Passover

Jesus rode into Jerusalem in style; coats and palm branches were scattered in his path and there was an amount of cheering, 'Hosanna to the son of David' (Matthew 21:9). But it has to be said that this frenetic activity was mainly that of the disciples (as described in Luke 19:36-39). The strewing of the palm fronds was intended to remind the people of the triumphant entry into Jerusalem of Simon Maccabaeus, the deliverer of Palestine from the yoke of Syrian oppression in 142 BC. But Jesus's face was not well known in the city; his familiar territory was Galilee and the land around. Indeed, Matthew 21:10 states: 'And when he was come into Jerusalem, all the city was moved, saying, Who is this?'

A prophecy of John the Baptist[1] had determined that March AD 33 would see the proclamation of the Saviour Messiah and the restoration of the true King. Many things had been carefully prepared for this time—the anointing, the donkey, the palm leaves and so forth—but nothing of consequence happened! According to Mark 11:11, Jesus entered the Temple, 'and when he had looked round and about upon all things, and now eventide was come, he went out unto Bethany'. Luke 19:40 tells that the Pharisees ordered the disciples to be rebuked for creating a disturbance. Matthew 21:12 adds, 'Jesus went into the temple of God, and cast out all them that sold and bought in the temple, and overthrew the tables of the money changers, and the seats of them that sold doves'. He then returned to Bethany. John (12:37) further explains that Jesus spoke to some people in the street, following which, 'though he had done so many miracles before them, yet they believed not on him'.

All things considered, the visit to Jerusalem was an unfortunate non-event. Jesus did not receive the acclaim he expected and he realized that his days were numbered, especially since he was a known associate of the Zealot commanders, Simon Zelotes, Judas Sicariote and Thaddaeus, who had led the revolt against Pilate. The Scribes and priests 'sought how they might take him by craft, and put him to death' (Mark 14:1). His plan to create an idyllic Judaea, free from the Roman oppression, had failed because his dream of unifying the people was not shared by his sectarian countrymen — in particular the stalwart Pharisees and Sadducees.

Also at that time, a serious rift occurred within the Apostolic group. Simon Zelotes had long been at odds with Jonathan Annas (James of Alphaeus) and their political rivalry came to a head. In their respective party roles as Lightning and Thunder, they were both contenders for the supreme position of Father. Simon was the Father from March AD 31, but lost his supremacy to Jonathan by default through his excommunication. Jonathan had been obliged to endorse the raising of Lazarus (by which Simon was restored to political and social life), but he was in no mood to relinquish the power he had only just gained, especially when Simon had been resurrected against the established rules.

There was also disagreement between Jonathan and Jesus over whether baptised male Gentile converts should have to submit to circumcision. Jesus was in favour of allowing the converts a choice in the matter, but Jonathan wanted circumcision made mandatory. Finally, Jonathan rejected the Zealot plan for open warfare against Rome, whilst Simon (always fiery in word and deed) promoted the martial view. In this, Jesus was inclined to side with Simon — not that he particularly sought a military solution, but he did not like Jonathan's complacent attitude.

Trapped in the middle of all this was Judas Sicariote, who determined to side with whoever looked to be the most politically valuable. Judas had been denounced as a Zealot leader, and in the light of that his only hope was Jonathan who, as the new Father, could authorize his spiritual reinstatement and negotiate on his behalf with the Roman Governor, Pontius Pilate. As for whether Jewish converts should be circumcised, Judas was strongly opposed to Jesus and supported Jonathan. At the same time, Judas could appreciate that Simon was in a weak position: Simon stood to face criminal charges (along with Judas and Thaddaeus) for leading the Zealot revolt. It was even possible that Jesus would be charged with them if it could be proved that he was an active supporter of the war faction. This provided a likely way out for Judas, for he could betray Jesus's sympathies and make known the whereabouts of Thaddaeus.

Soon afterwards, it was time for the Jewish celebration of the Passover, when hordes of pilgrims joined the Jerusalem residents for the ritual of the Paschal Lamb in accordance with Exodus 12:3-11. In the course of this, we are told that Jesus and his Apostles made their way to that legendary upper room where they were to eat the sacred Last Supper. But there are some questionable features about this. How was it that, at such a time when all the temporary accommodation in the city was full to bursting, the Apostles were so easily able to obtain a room of some considerable size for themselves? How also could the fugitive Zealots, Simon, Judas and Thaddaeus, possibly afford to move openly in Jerusalem, while being sought for leading the recent revolt?

The answer to these questions may be found in the Dead Sea Scrolls, wherein it is evident that the Last Supper did not take place in Jerusalem at all, but at Qumrân. Indeed, Josephus explains in *The Antiquities of the Jews* that the Essenes did not observe the traditional Jewish festivals in Jerusalem[2] and did not, therefore, uphold the ritual of the Paschal Lamb at the Passover.

More than 160 years earlier, when the pious Hasidim vacated Jerusalem for Qumrân in around 130 BC, their new environment became a substitute Holy City. The custom was continued by the later Essenes and, in this context, they often referred to Qumrân as 'Jerusalem' (*Yuru-salem*: City of peace). As evidenced by one of the Dead Sea Scrolls known as the *Community Rule*, the famous Last Supper corresponds, in fact, to the Messianic Banquet (the Lord's Supper). That it occurred at the same time as the Passover celebration in Jerusalem was entirely coincidental, for the Messianic Banquet had a quite different significance. The primary hosts of the banquet were the High Priest and the Messiah of Israel.[3] The people of the community were represented by appointed officers who together formed the Council of Delegate Apostles. The *Rule* lays down the correct order of precedence for the seating and details the ritual to be observed at the meal. It concludes:

> And when they gather for the community table ...
> and mix the wine for drinking, let no man stretch
> forth his hand on the first of the bread or the wine
> before the Priest, for it is he who will bless the first
> fruits of the bread and wine .... And afterwards,
> the Messiah of Israel shall stretch out his hands
> upon the bread, and afterwards all the congre-
> gation of the community will give blessings, each
> according to his rank.[4]

When the time came for communion, Judas left the room, ostensibly to offer alms to the poor (John 13:28-30). Actually, he went to make the final arrangements for Jesus's betrayal, while Jesus—who perceived his intention—said, 'That thou doest, do quickly' (John 13:27). There was, however, still time for the Baptist's prophecy concerning the restoration of the true Christ to be fulfilled—but the final deadline was that very night, the vernal equinox of 20 March AD 33.[5] Jesus knew that if this passed with no proclamation being made in his favour, then his ambition was over. From that night there would be no hope of satisfying the Messianic prediction and he would be denounced as a fraud. When Judas left the room, the time was already fast approaching midnight.

Following the banquet, Jesus and the remaining Apostles went to the old monastery at Qumrân, customarily known as the Mount of Olives. There is some disagreement at this point between John's Gospel and the Synoptic Gospels on the precise course of events but, one way or another, Jesus foretold his fate and outlined to his companions what their reactions would be. He declared that even Peter would deny him in the face of the unfulfilled prophecy. While some of Jesus's disciples slept in the monastery garden, Jesus walked among them (Matthew 26:36-45), agonizing that his bid to be recognized as the Saviour Messiah might have failed. Midnight passed—then Judas Sicariote arrived with the soldiers. The garden of the Mount of Olives was known as the 'Valley of oil'—Gethsemane.

The ultimate success of Judas's plan relied on retaining favour with the Father, Jonathan Annas. Whether Judas took a calculated gamble or whether he and Jonathan had come to some agreement beforehand is uncertain. But when the moment of seizure came, Jonathan certainly ranged himself alongside Judas. This is not really surprising, for Jonathan's daughter was married to the Pharisee High Priest, Joseph Caiaphas, while both Jonathan and Judas were politically opposed to Jesus's close friend Simon Zelotes. With the Gethsemane arrest duly made, 'the captain and officers of the Jews took Jesus, and bound him, and led him away to Annas first; for he was father-in-law to Caiaphas, which was the high priest that same year' (John 18:12-13).

It seems rather strange that Simon Zelotes, who must surely have been present at these events, is not mentioned in any of the Gospel accounts. Yet in Mark 14:51-52 there is a peculiar veiled reference to a person who might very well have been Simon: 'And there followed him a certain young man, having a linen cloth cast about his naked body ... and he left the linen cloth and fled from them naked'. Fleeing naked could well have been symbolic of Simon's having been unfrocked from his previous high ecclesiastical rank, while for him to be described as a 'young man' relegates him to his newly demoted status as a Community novice following his excommunication.

Crucify Him!

Jesus's trial was hardly a trial at all and the scenario, as presented in the Gospels, is full of ambiguities. Matthew 26:57-59 describes matters thus: 'They that had laid hold on Jesus led him away to Caiaphas the high priest, where the scribes and the elders were assembled .... Now the chief priests, and elders, and all the council, sought false witness against Jesus'.

Even if all these priests, scribes and elders were somehow conveniently gathered together in the early hours at a moment's notice, the fact remains that it was quite outside the law for the Jewish Council to sit at night. Luke 22:66 indicates that although Jesus was taken firstly to Caiaphas, the Sanhedrin did not meet until it was day. But the meeting would still have been illegal because the Sanhedrin Council was not allowed to sit during the Passover.[6]

The Gospels all state that Peter followed Jesus to the house in which Caiaphas was located, where he denied his master three times as predicted. The house was not in the city of Jerusalem, though; it was the Vestry House at Qumrân.[7] In his capacity as the prevailing High Priest, Caiaphas would necessarily have been at the Messianic Banquet (as laid down in the *Community Rule*) and would, therefore, have been resident in the community along with other officials of the Sanhedrin, on the night before the Passover Friday.

All accounts agree that Caiaphas passed Jesus over to the Roman Governor, Pontius Pilate, whose presence facilitated the immediate interrogation. This is confirmed in John 18:28-31, only for a further anomaly to emerge:

> Then led they Jesus from Caiaphas unto the hall of judgement: and it was early; and they themselves went not into the judgement hall, lest they should be defiled; but that they might eat the Passover.
> Pilate then went out unto them, and said, What accusation bring ye against this man? They answered and said unto him, If he were not a malefactor, we would not have delivered him up unto thee.

> Then said Pilate unto them, Take ye him, and
> judge him according to your law. The Jews therefore
> said unto him, It is not lawful for us to put any man
> to death.

In this regard, the truth is that the Sanhedrin was fully empowered not only to condemn criminals but to pass and implement the death sentence if necessary. The Gospels also claim that Pilate offered to reprieve Jesus because 'it was customary for the Governor to release a prisoner at the feast of the Passover'. Again this is simply not true — there never was such a custom.[8]

Although the Zealots, Simon (Lazarus) and Judas, feature in the events leading to Jesus's arrest, it would appear that Thaddaeus — the third of the key revolutionaries — is not mentioned after the Last Supper. But he does actually come into the story at the trial. Thaddaeus was a deputy of the Succession (of Alphaeus), a deputy to the Father and thus a devotional Son of the Father. In Hebrew, the expression Son of the Father would incorporate the elements *Bar* (Son) and *Abba* (Father) — so Thaddaeus might be described as 'Bar-Abba' and a man called Barabbas is intimately concerned with the possibility of Jesus's reprieve by Pontius Pilate.

Barabbas is described in Matthew 27:16 as 'a notable prisoner'; in Mark 15:7 as one who had 'committed murder in the insurrection'; in Luke 23:19 as a man who 'for murder had been cast into prison' and in John 18:40 as 'a robber'. The John description is rather too vague, for everyday robbers were not customarily sentenced to crucifixion. However, the English translated word does not truly reflect the original Greek implication, for *léstés* does not mean 'robber' so much as 'outlaw'. Mark's words point far more specifically to the insurgent role of Barabbas in the recent revolt.

What seems to have happened is that when the three prisoners Simon, Thaddaeus and Jesus were brought before Pilate, the cases against Simon and Thaddaeus were clear cut; they were known Zealot leaders and had been condemned men since the uprising. On the other hand, Pilate found it extremely difficult to prove a case against Jesus. Indeed, he was only there because the Jewish contingent had passed him over to Pilate for sentencing with the others. Pilate asked the Jewish hierarchy to provide him, at least, with a pretext — 'What accusation bring ye against this man?' — but he received no satisfactory answer. In desperation Pilate suggested they should take him and 'judge him according to your law', at which the Jews are said to have given the untrue excuse that 'It is not lawful for us to put any man to death'.

So Pilate then turned to Jesus himself. 'Art thou the King of the Jews?' he asked, to which Jesus replied, 'Sayest thou this thing of thyself, or did others tell it thee of me?' Confused by this, Pilate continued, 'Thine own nation and the chief priests have delivered thee unto me: what hast thou done?' The questioning progressed until, eventually, Pilate 'went out again unto the Jews, and saith unto them, I find in him no fault at all' (John 18:38).

At this point, Herod-Antipas of Galilee arrived on the scene (Luke 23:7-12). He was no friend of the Annas priests and it suited his purpose for Jesus to be released in order to provoke his nephew King Herod-Agrippa. Antipas therefore struck a deal with Pilate to secure the release of Jesus. The pact between Judas Sicariote and Jonathan Annas was thus superseded, without involving either of them, by way of an agreement between the Herodian Tetrarch and the Roman Governor. From that moment, Judas lost any chance of a pardon for his Zealot activities and his days were numbered. In accordance with the new arrangement, Pilate said to the Jewish elders (Luke 23:14-16):

> Ye have brought this man unto me, as one that perverteth the people: and, behold, I, having examined him before you, have found no fault in this man touching those things whereof ye accuse him: No, nor yet Herod: for I sent you to him; and lo, nothing worthy of death is done unto him. I will therefore chastise him, and release him.

Had the members of the Sanhedrin waited until after the Passover, they could have conducted their own trial of Jesus in perfect legality. But they had strategically passed the responsibility over to Pilate because they knew there was no true charge to substantiate. They had certainly not bargained for Pilate's sense of justice, nor for the intervention of Herod-Antipas. But Pilate managed to defeat his own objective. He tried to reconcile his decision to free Jesus with the notion that it might be regarded as a Passover dispensation and, in so doing, he opened the door to a Jewish choice: Jesus or Barabbas? At this, 'they cried out all at once, saying, Away with this man, and release unto us Barabbas' (Luke 23:18).

Pilate pursued his course in favour of Jesus, but the Jews cried 'Crucify him!' Yet again Pilate asked, 'Why, what evil hath he done? I have found no cause of death in him'. But the odds were stacked against him and, giving way to his misguided commitment, Pilate released Barabbas (Thaddaeus). The Roman soldiers placed a crown of thorns on Jesus's head and wrapped a purple robe around him. Pilate then handed him back to the priests, saying, 'Behold, I bring him forth to you, that ye may know that I find no fault in him' (John 19:4).

To Golgotha

At that stage, things were going well for the Jerusalem elders; their plan had all but succeeded. The ageing Thaddaeus may have been released, but both Simon and Jesus were in custody along with Judas Sicariote. Undoubtedly, the greatest betrayer of all was the prevailing Father, Jonathan Annas, the one-time Apostle known as James of Alphaeus (or Nathanael). The three crosses were duly erected in the Place of a Skull (Golgotha) and were set to bear Jesus and the two Zealot guerrilla leaders, Simon Zelotes and Judas Sicariote.

On the way to the Crucifixion at Golgotha a significant event occurred when a mysterious character named Simon the Cyrene offered to carry Jesus's cross (Matthew 27:32). Many theories have been put forward about who the Cyrene might have been, but his real identity does not matter too much. What matters is that he was there at all. There is an interesting reference to him in an early Coptic tractate called *The Second Treatise of the Great Seth*, discovered among the books of Nag Hammadi. Explaining that there was a substitution made for at least one of the three victims of the Crucifixion, it mentions the Cyrene in this connection. The substitution apparently succeeded, for the tractate declares that Jesus did not die on the Cross as presumed. Jesus is himself quoted as saying after the event, 'As for my death—which was real enough to them—it was real to them because of their own incomprehension and blindness'.

The Islamic Koran (chapter 4, entitled Women) specifies that Jesus did not die on the cross, stating: 'Yet they slew him not, neither crucified him, but he was represented by one in his likeness .... They did not really kill him'. Also, the 2nd-century historian, Basilides of Alexandria, wrote that the crucifixion was stage-managed (with Simon the Cyrene used as a substitute), while the gnostic leader, Mani (born near Baghdad in AD 214), made precisely the same assertion.

In the event, however, it would seem that Simon the Cyrene was a substitute for Simon Zelotes, not for Jesus. Clearly, the execution of two such men as Jesus and Simon could not go unchallenged and so a strategy was implemented to outwit the Jewish authorities (even though Pilate's men may well have been party to the subterfuge). It hinged upon the use of a comatosing poison and the performance of a physical deception.

If any man could mastermind such an illusion, that man was Simon Zelotes, Head of the Samaritan Magi and renowned as the greatest magician of his day. Both the *Acts of Peter* and the Church's *Apostolic Constitutions*[9] recount the story of how, some years later, Simon levitated himself above the Roman Forum. At Golgotha, however, things were very different: Simon was under guard and on his way to be crucified.

In the first instance it was necessary to extricate Simon from his predicament—and so a substitution was organized in the person of the Cyrene, who would have been in league with the released Thaddaeus (Barabbas). The deception began on the way to Golgotha when, by accepting Jesus's burden, the Cyrene was able to incorporate himself in the midst of the assembly. The switch itself was made at the Crucifixion site, under cover of the general preparatory confusion. Amid this bustle of erecting the crosses, the Cyrene seemingly disappeared—but actually took Simon's place.[10] In the Gospels, the following sequence of events is carefully veiled by giving very few details about the men crucified alongside Jesus, other than describing them as 'thieves'.

And so the scene was set—Simon (Zelotes) Magus had achieved his freedom and could successfully handle the proceedings from then on.

Crucifixion

Place of a Skull

Although the Crucifixion is generally portrayed as a relatively public affair, the Gospels affirm (for instance in Luke 23:49) that onlookers were obliged to watch the proceedings 'from afar off'. In Matthew, Mark and John, the site is named as Golgotha, whereas in Luke it is Calvary. However, both names (Hebrew: Gulgoleth, Aramaic: Gulgolta, Latin: Calvaria) derive from words that mean 'skull' and the meaning of Golgotha, as given in the Gospels, is straightforward: a 'place of a skull'.

Three centuries later, as the Christian faith spread its influence, various sites in and around Jerusalem were dubbed with supposed New Testament significance. On many occasions it was simply a case of finding a suitable place to hang a name — such were the demands of pilgrims and the tourist market. A suitable Calvary site was identified; a route along which Jesus carried his cross was mapped out and a convenient sepulchre was earmarked to represent the legendary tomb.

In the context of all this creativity, Golgotha (Calvary) was said to have been located outside Herod's wall, north-west of Jerusalem. It was a barren hill and was selected because it was roughly skull-shaped. Later Western tradition romanticised the place as 'a green hill far away' — a theme on which many artists have produced variations. Yet for all of this fanciful idealism, not one of the Gospels makes any mention at all of a hill. According to John 19:41, the location was a 'garden' in which there was a private sepulchre owned by Joseph of Arimathea (Matthew 27:59-60). Heeding the evidence of the Gospels instead of pandering to popular folklore, it is apparent that the Crucifixion was no hill-top spectacle with enormous crosses against the skyline and an epic cast of spectators. On the contrary, it was a small-scale affair on controlled land — an exclusive garden that was, in one way or another, the 'place of a skull' (John 19:17).

The Gospels have little more to say on the subject, but Hebrews 13:11-13 provides some very important clues to the location:

> For the bodies of those beasts, whose blood is brought into the sanctuary by the high priest for sin, are burned without the camp. Wherefore Jesus also, that he might sanctify the people with his own blood, suffered without the gate. Let us go forth therefore unto him without the camp, bearing his reproach.

From this we gather that Jesus suffered 'outside the gate' and 'outside the camp'. Also there is some association with a place where the bodies of sacrificed animals were burned. This reference is particularly important because the sites at which animal remains were burned were regarded as unclean. According to Deuteronomy 23:10-14, 'without the camp' described areas set aside as cesspits, middens and public latrines which were both physically and ritually unclean. By the same token, 'without the gate' defined various other unclean places, including ordinary cemeteries.[1] Furthermore, the Dead Sea Scrolls make it clear that, because it constituted an act of defilement to walk over the dead, human graveyards were identified with the sign of a skull. It follows, quite naturally, that the 'place of a skull' (Golgotha/Calvary) was a cemetery—a restricted cemetery garden that contained an empty sepulchre in the charge of Joseph of Arimathea.

A further clue comes from Revelation 11:8, which states that Jesus was crucified in 'the great city which spiritually is called Sodom and Egypt'. This positively identifies the cemetery location as Qumrân, which was designated Egypt by the Therapeutate[2] and was geographically associated with the Old Testament centre of Sodom.

Who, then, was Joseph of Arimathea? In the Gospels, he is described as an 'honourable counsellor [a member of the Sanhedrin], which also waited for the kingdom of God' (Mark 15:43). He was also 'a disciple of Jesus, but secretly, for fear of the Jews' (John 19:38). But although Joseph's allegiance to Jesus was a secret from the Jewish elders, it came as no surprise to Pontius Pilate, who accepted the man's involvement in Jesus's affairs without question. That same involvement was no surprise either to Jesus's mother Mary, or to Mary Magdalene, Mary Cleophas, or Salome. They all went along quite happily with Joseph's arrangements, accepting his authority without comment or demur.

Sometimes presumed to relate to the village of Arimeh on the plain of Gennesareth, Arimathea was, in fact, a descriptive title like so many others in the New Testament. It represented a particularly high status. Just as Matthew Annas held the priestly distinction 'Levi of Alphaeus' (Levi of the Succession), so Joseph was 'of Arimathea'. However (as with Matthew's style of Levi), Joseph was not his true baptismal name. Arimathea derived (like Alphaeus) from a combination of Hebrew and Greek elements — in this case, the Hebrew: *ha ram* or *ha rama* (of the height or top) and the Greek: *Theo* (relating to God), together meaning 'of the Highest of God' — *ha Rama Theo* — and, as a personal distinction, Divine Highness.

Meanwhile, we know that Jesus was the heir to the throne of David. The patriarchal title of Joseph was applied to the next in succession[3] and, in this respect, with Jesus regarded as the David, then his eldest brother, James, was the designated Joseph. Hence, Joseph of Arimathea emerges as Jesus's own brother James. It, therefore, comes as no surprise that Jesus was entombed in a sepulchre that belonged to his own royal family. Neither is it surprising that Pilate should allow Jesus's brother to take charge; nor that the women of Jesus's family should accept the arrangements made by Joseph (James) without question. The reason that Joseph kept his personal support for Jesus a secret from the Sanhedrin is self-evident, for he had his own separate following amid all ranks of the Hebrew community.

From the time the Dead Sea Scrolls were first discovered at Qumrân in 1947, digs and excavations went on well into the 1950s. During this period important finds were made in a number of different caves. The archaeologists discovered that one cave in particular had two chambers and two separate entrances quite a way apart. The access to the main chamber was through a hole in the roof path, whereas the adjoining hollow was approached from the side.[4] From the roof entrance, steps had been constructed down into the chamber and, to seal the entrance against rainfall, a large stone had to be rolled across the opening. According to the *Copper Scroll*, this sepulchre was used as a Treasury deposit and as such it has been dubbed the Rich Man's Cave. This, the sepulchre of the Joseph Crown Prince, was sited directly opposite the Bosom of Abraham.

The prophecy that the Messiah would ride into Jerusalem on an ass was not the only prediction made concerning the Messiah in the Old Testament book of Zechariah. Two other prophecies — Zechariah 12:10 and 13:6 — stated that he would be pierced and mourned in death by all Jerusalem and that he would be wounded in the hands as a result of his friends. Jesus realized that by being crucified he would qualify in all of these respects. He might have missed the deadline as far as John the Baptist's prophecy was concerned, but crucifixion offered him another chance. So, as John 19:36 states in relation to Zechariah, 'These things were done, that the scripture should be fulfilled'.

Crucifixion was both punishment and execution: death by torturous ordeal extended over a number of days. First the victim's outstretched arms were strapped by the wrists to a beam which was then hoisted into place horizontally across an upright post. Sometimes the hands were transfixed by nails as well, but nails alone would have been useless. Suspended with all his weight on his arms, a man's lungs would be compressed and he would die fairly quickly through suffocation. To prolong the agony, chest pressure was relieved by fixing the victim's feet to the upright post. Supported in this manner a man could live for many days, possibly even a week or more. After a while, in order to free up the crosses, the executioners would sometimes break the legs of the victims so as to increase the hanging weight and accelerate death.

On that Friday, the equivalent of 20 March AD 33, there was no reason for any of the three men crucified to have died within the day. Nevertheless, Jesus was given some vinegar and, having taken it, he 'gave up the ghost' (John 19:30). Soon afterwards, a centurion pierced Jesus's side with a spear and the fact that he bled (identified as blood and water) has been held to indicate that he was dead (John 19:34). In reality, vascular bleeding indicates that a body is alive, not dead. Dr. A. R. Kittermaster, in his 1979 report entitled *A Medical View of Calvary*, confirmed that "Dead or alive, the flow of water is difficult to explain, but blood does not flow from a stab wound which is inflicted after death. It would take a large, gaping laceration to cause any blood to flow from a dead body". At that stage, Judas and the Cyrene were still very much alive, so their legs were broken.

The Gospels do not say who gave the vinegar to Jesus on the cross, but John 19:29 specifies that the vessel was ready and waiting. A little earlier in the same sequence (Matthew 27:34), the potion was said to be 'vinegar mingled with gall' — that is soured wine mixed with snake venom. Dependent on the proportions, such a mixture could induce unconsciousness or even cause death. In this case, the poison was fed to Jesus not from a cup, but from a sponge and by measured application from a reed. The person who administered it was undoubtedly Simon Zelotes, who was meant to be upon one of the crosses himself.

Meanwhile, Joseph of Arimathea was negotiating with Pilate to remove Jesus's body before the Sabbath and place it in his sepulchre. Pilate was amazed that Jesus had died in so short a time (Mark 15:44): 'And Pilate marvelled if he were already dead: and calling unto him the centurion, he asked him whether he had been any while dead'. To speed matters up further, Joseph quoted to Pilate a Jewish rule based on Deuteronomy 21:22-23 and confirmed in the Qumrân *Temple Scroll*: 'And if a man have committed a sin worthy of death, and he be put to death, and thou hang him on a tree: His body shall not remain all night upon the tree, but thou shalt in any wise bury him that day'. Pilate therefore sanctioned the change of procedure from hanging (as manifest in crucifixion) to the old custom of burial alive. He then returned to Jerusalem leaving Joseph in control. (It is perhaps significant that in Acts 5:30, 10:39 and 13:29, the references to Jesus's torture all relate to his being 'hanged on a tree'.)

With Jesus in a seemingly lifeless coma and with the legs of Judas and the Cyrene newly broken, the three were brought down, having been on their respective crosses for less than half a day. The account does not state that the men were dead; it simply refers to the removal of their bodies—that is live bodies as against corpses.

Three Hours of Darkness

The next day was the Sabbath, about which the Gospels have little to tell. Only Matthew 27:62-66 makes any mention of this Saturday, but refers simply to a conversation between Pilate and the Jewish elders in Jerusalem, following which Pilate arranged for two guards to watch Jesus's tomb. Apart from that, all four Gospels continue their story from the Sunday morning thereafter.

Yet, if any day was important to the ongoing course of events, that day was the Saturday—the Sabbath day we are told so little about. This respected day of rest and worship was the key to everything that happened. It was what occurred on the Saturday that caused the women such amazement when they found the stone rolled from its position at daybreak on the Sunday. In practical terms, there was nothing startling about the displacement of the stone—anyone could have moved it. Indeed, the women would have rolled it away themselves, for they had no reason to anticipate a prevention of access. What was so unthinkable was that the stone had been moved on the Sabbath, a sacred day on which it was utterly forbidden to shift a burden. The mystery was not in the 'act' of removal, but in the 'day' of removal. For the stone to have been moved on the Sabbath was quite impossible!

There is some variation between the Gospels over what actually happened on the third day — the Sunday. Matthew 28:1 tells that Mary and Mary Magdalene made their way to the tomb, while Mark 16:1 includes Salome as well. Luke 24:10 introduces Joanna, but omits Salome, whereas John 20:1 has Mary Magdalene arriving entirely alone. Mark, Luke and John claim that when the woman/women arrived, the stone had already been displaced. In Matthew, however, the two sentries were on guard and the stone was still in position. Then, to the astonishment of the women and the sentries, 'the angel of the Lord descended ... and rolled back the stone'.

It subsequently became apparent that Jesus was not in the tomb where he had been laid. According to Matthew 28:5-6, the angel led the women into the cave. In Mark 16:4-5, they went in by themselves and were confronted by a young man in a white robe. Luke 24:3-4, however, describes two men standing inside. And John 20:2-12 tells how Mary Magdalene went to fetch Peter and another disciple before entering the cave with them. Then, after her companions had departed, Mary found two angels sitting within the sepulchre.

In the final analysis, it is not clear whether the guards existed or not. The number of women was either one, two, or three. Perhaps Peter was around; perhaps he was not. There was either an angel outside or a young man inside; conversely, there were two angels inside, who might have been sitting, or might have been standing. As for the stone, it was possibly still in position at daybreak, or maybe it had already been moved.

There is only one potential common denominator in all of this: Jesus was no longer there — but even that is not certain. According to John 20:14-15, Mary Magdalene turned away from the angels to find Jesus standing there, whereupon she took him to be the gardener. She moved towards him, but Jesus prevented her approach, saying, 'Touch me not' (John 20:17).

These are the four accounts on which the entire tradition of the Resurrection is based — and yet they conflict in almost every detail. Because of this, centuries of argument have ensued over whether it was Mary Magdalene or Peter who first saw the reappeared Jesus. But can we trace what actually happened after Joseph (James) left Jesus in the tomb on the previous Friday?

Initially, the Cyrene and Judas Sicariote — with their legs broken, but still very much alive — had been placed in the second chamber of the tomb. Jesus's body occupied the main chamber. Within the confines of the double-hollow, Simon Zelotes had already taken up his station, along with lamps and everything else required for the operation. (Interestingly, a lamp was among the items found within the cave during the 1950s.)

Then, according to John 19:39, Nicodemus arrived, bringing with him 'a mixture of myrrh and aloes, about an hundred pound weight'.[5] Extract of myrrh was a form of sedative commonly used in contemporary medical practice—but why such a vast quantity of aloes? The juice of aloes, as modern pharmacopoeias explain, is a strong and fast-acting purgative—precisely what would have been needed by Simon to expel the poisonous gall (venom) from Jesus's body.

It was of great significance that the day after the Crucifixion was the Sabbath day. Indeed, the timing of the whole operation to 'raise Jesus from the dead' (release him from excommunication) relied on the critical timing of the precise hour at which the Sabbath might be considered to begin. In those days, there was no concept of any fixed duration for hours and minutes. The recording and measurement of time was one of the official functions of the Levites who programmed the course of hours by ground-shadows on measured areas. Also, since about 6 BC, they had been able to make use of sundials. However, neither ground markings nor sundials were of any use when there were no shadows. Hence, there were twelve designated 'hours of day' (daylight) and, similarly, twelve 'hours of night' (darkness). The latter were measured by Levitical prayer sessions (like the canonical hours of the Catholic Church today. Indeed, the prevailing *Angelus* devotion—held at morning, noon and sunset—derives from the practice of the early Levite angels). The problem was however that, as the days and nights became longer or shorter, adjustments were necessary where hours overlapped.

On that particular Friday of the Crucifixion, a forward adjustment of a full three hours was required and, because of this, there is a noticeable discrepancy between the accounts of Mark and John over the timing of events on that day. Mark 15:24 states that Jesus was crucified at the third hour, whereas John 19:14-16 claims that Jesus was delivered for crucifixion at about the sixth hour. This anomaly occurs because Mark's Gospel relies on time as measured by Hellenist reckoning, whereas John's Gospel uses Hebrew time. The result of the time-change was (as Mark 15:33 describes) that 'When the sixth hour was come, there was a darkness over the whole land until the ninth hour'. These three hours of darkness were symbolic only; they occurred within a split second (as do changes in time today when we cross between different time-zones, or when we put clocks forward or backward for daylight saving). So, on this occasion, the end of the fifth hour was followed immediately by the ninth hour.

The key to the Resurrection story lies in those three missing hours (the daytime hours that became night-time hours), for the newly defined start of the Sabbath began three hours before the old twelfth hour—that is at the old ninth hour, which was then renamed the twelfth hour. But the Samaritan Magi of Simon Zelotes worked on an astronomical time-frame and did not formally implement the three-hour change until the original twelfth hour. This meant that, without breaking any of the rules against labouring on the Sabbath, Simon had a full three hours in which he could do what he had to do, even while others had begun their sacred period of rest. This was time enough to administer the medications to Jesus and to attend to the bone fractures of the Cyrene. Judas Sicariote was dealt with none too mercifully and was thrown over a cliff to his death (as obliquely related in Acts 1:16-18). The earlier reference in Matthew 27:5, which indicates that Judas hanged himself, refers more precisely to the fact that, at that stage, he set the scene for his own downfall.

The Empty Tomb

When the Sabbath began by Magian time (three hours after the standard Jewish Sabbath), there were still a full three night hours before Mary Magdalene arrived on the first dawn of the new week. Whether or not there were sentries on guard that night is quite irrelevant; any coming and going by Simon and his colleagues would have been effected by way of the second entrance which was some distance away. Whether or not the stone was moved is equally irrelevant. The important thing is that when Jesus appeared, he was alive and well.

Concerning the angel who moved the stone for the women, Matthew 28:3 reads, 'His countenance was like lightning, and his raiment white as snow'. As we have seen, Simon (Magus) Zelotes was politically styled 'Lightning'; his vestment was white and in rank he was indeed an angel. The sentence might thus be interpreted more literally as 'His countenance was like that of Simon Zelotes in his priestly vestment'. But why should this have been such a surprise to the women? Because as far as they knew, Simon had been crucified and entombed with his legs broken.

Not only was Simon present, but so too was Thaddaeus: 'There was a great earthquake, and an angel appeared' (Matthew 28:2). Just as Simon Zelotes was styled Lightning (with Jonathan Annas being Thunder), Thaddaeus was, in turn, designated Earthquake (in similar imagery concerning Mount Sinai, as in Judges 5:5). Simon and

Thaddaeus were, therefore, the two angels encountered by Mary (John 20:11-12). Simon was also the 'young man' in the white robe (Mark 16:5), the youthful description indicating his newly demoted status as a novice subsequent to the Lazarus excommunication.

The garden in which Jesus was crucified was under the jurisdiction of Joseph of Arimathea (Jesus's brother James). It was a consecrated area symbolizing the Garden of Eden, in relation to which James was identified with Adam, the man of the Garden. Thus, when Mary first saw Jesus and thought he was the gardener, the inference is that she believed she was looking at James. The reason that Jesus stopped Mary from touching him was that Mary was pregnant and, according to the rules for dynastic brides, she was allowed no physical contact with her husband at that time.

It is evident that Mary and most of the disciples were not party to the subterfuge of that Friday and Saturday. Indeed, it was in Simon's own interest to remain mysterious; escaping from the burial cave alive and with his legs unbroken could only add to his already great reputation. It was also in Jesus's own favour that his reappearance should be astounding to all. In the event, their joint effort — with the support of Thaddaeus, the Cyrene and brother James (Joseph) — held the mission together after its near collapse, enabling the Apostles to continue their work. If Jesus had truly died, his disciples would have scattered in fear and dismay, whereupon his cause would have died with him.[6] As it was, the mission received a whole new lease of life — the result of which was the birth of Christianity.

Raised From the Dead

> But if there be no resurrection of the dead, then is Christ not risen: And if Christ be not risen, then is our preaching vain, and your faith is also vain .... For if the dead rise not, then is not Christ raised ....

This is the case for the Resurrection as presented as an item of faith by St. Paul in 1-Corinthians 15:13-16. It has to be said that it does not constitute much of an argument for something that is apparently so fundamental to the Christian belief. In fact, if anything it is fully self-defeating. Had Paul been speaking in spiritual terms, his contemporaries might have accepted his claim more readily, but he was not. He was talking literally, referring to the notion of corpses returning to life in accordance with the prophecy in the book of Isaiah

(26:19): 'Thy dead men shall live, together with my dead body shall they arise'.

Immortality of the soul (rather than of the body) was around as a concept long before Jesus's time. In the ancient Greek world it was promoted by the followers of the Athenian philosopher Socrates (*c*.469-399 BC). Plato maintained in the 4th century BC that mind, not matter, was the root of reality. Even earlier, Pythagoras (*c*.570-500 BC) expounded the doctrine of reincarnation: the idea that, upon death in one life, the soul enters another body and begins life anew. Indeed, belief in reincarnation is common to many religions deriving from around the same time, including Hinduism and Buddhism.

However, Paul was not referring to the transmigration of souls; he was expressing a belief in which Christianity stands alone as a major religion — the notion that a dead person came back to life 'in the flesh'. The Apostles' Creed states that Jesus was 'crucified, dead and buried ... The third day he rose again from the dead'. Scholars have long challenged the literal interpretation of this statement and, in recent years, many churchmen have queried it too. But, old doctrines die hard and many feel that to dispense with the concept would be to dispense with the intrinsic ethic of Christianity itself. Yet, if Christianity has a worthwhile base — which it surely has — then that base must rest upon the moral codes and teachings of Jesus himself. Indeed, these social standards and their associated teachings are what the Gospels are all about. They are the very essence of the Good News.

It has often been pointed out that, after nearly 2,000 years, some three-quarters of the world's population does not subscribe to the idea of bodily resurrection. Many actually find the idea more disturbing than uplifting, as a result of which the Christian message is severely repressed. Few (of any religion or none) would dispute the inspiring neighbourly motive of Jesus's own ideal — an ideal of harmony, unity and service in a fraternal society. In fact, there is no better basis for a religion; yet the wrap of a constraining dogma prevails — along with a constant wrangling about matters of interpretation and ritual. While such disputes continue, there can be no true harmony and a divided Church society can provide no more than a limited service to itself and to others.

One of the main problems associated with the acceptance of Jesus's bodily resurrection from physical death is that its premise is supported by little, if anything, in the Gospels. We have already seen that verses 9 to 20 of Mark 16 were spuriously attached long after the Gospel was completed and published. And if Mark's was the first of the Synoptic Gospels, forming a base for the others, then legitimate doubt is cast on the authenticity of the final verses of Matthew and Luke. But, if we ignore all of this, to accept the four Gospels as they are presented, we are faced with a very vague picture in which many details are not only confusing but conflicting. At first Mary Magdalene thought Jesus was someone else. Then Peter and Cleophas talked with him for several hours thinking he was a complete stranger. Not until Jesus sat down to eat with his Apostles did they recognize him—at which point he vanished from their sight.

What emerges is that the concept of the Resurrection as we know it today was completely unknown to those of the time. Apart from those directly concerned with the overall Crucifixion scenario, the disciples were kept in the dark. They truly believed their master had died and would have been totally bewildered at his reappearance. These were not the high-ranking priests like Simon, Levi and Thaddaeus, but the less sophisticated Apostles like Peter and Andrew. Nonetheless, they would certainly have appreciated that Jesus's own forecast of how his temple would be raised in three days (John 2:19) had nothing to do with a later European interpretation that completely missed the point of the death symbolism.

As apparent in the story of Lazarus,[7] a man was regarded as dead when excommunicated—a form of spiritual death by decree. The process took four days for implementation, during which period the excommunicatee was held to be sick unto death. In this regard, Jesus had been formally denounced by the Sanhedrin Council of legal elders, by the High Priest, Joseph Caiaphas, and by the new Father, Jonathan Annas. His excommunication was absolute and, from the early hours of the Crucifixion Friday, he was officially 'sick'. The only way to escape 'death' on the fourth day was to be previously released (raised) from the denouncement by the Father or the High Priest, which is why Jesus made such a point of being raised on the third day. In any other context, the period of three days had no significance whatever. But with the establishment set so firmly against him, who was there to perform the raising?

The only man who might presume to undertake the rite was the deposed Father, the loyal Simon Zelotes. Irrespective of the machinations in Jerusalem, Simon's rank as the Father was still upheld by many, but Simon had been crucified along with Jesus, or so most of the disciples believed. As it transpired, though, Simon emerged fit and well along with Jesus, whom he had 'raised from the dead' in the early hours of the Sunday morning. To those who were not party to the scheme, the raising of Jesus was indeed a miracle and, as the Gospel states, 'When therefore he was risen from the dead, his disciples ... believed the scripture, and the word which Jesus had said' (John 2:22).

It was Paul (a later Hebrew convert to Hellenist ways) who established the blood and bones Resurrection doctrine, but even his enthusiasm was short-lived. However, since he had expressed himself so excitedly on the subject and had backed his fervour with such clinching non-arguments as we saw earlier ('if there be no resurrection from the dead, then is Christ not risen' — and so forth), Paul was regarded as a fanatic[8] by Jesus's brother James, whose Nazarenes never preached the Resurrection. Indeed, from those times of initial Pauline exaltation, the Resurrection diminished as a factor of fundamental concern. This is fully apparent in the later Epistles (letters) of Paul and in other New Testament books, where it hardly features at all.

More important was the fact that Jesus had seen fit to suffer for the sake of his ideals and Paul eventually sought to find a more explanatory basis for his earlier doctrine, declaring,

> There is a natural body, and there is a spiritual body. Flesh and blood cannot inherit the kingdom of God; neither doth corruption inherit incorruption. Behold, I shew you a mystery (1-Corinthians 15:44, 50-51).

It is essential to remember that Jesus was neither a Gentile nor a Christian. He was a Hellenist Jew whose religion was radical Judaism. In time, however, his original mission was usurped and taken over by a religious movement that was named after him in order to obscure his true heirs. That movement centred upon Rome and based its self-proclaimed authority on the statement of Matthew 16:18-19, in which Jesus supposedly said 'Thou art Peter, and upon this rock I will build my church'. Unfortunately, the Greek word petra (rock), relating to the Rock of Israel, was mistranslated as if it had been petros (stone), referring to Peter[9] (who was indeed dubbed Cephas — a stone, as in John 1:42). Jesus was actually affirming that his and Peter's mission was to be founded upon the Rock of Israel, not upon Peter himself. Irrespective of this, the new movement then decreed that only those who had received authority handed down directly from Peter could be leaders of the Christian Church. It was an ingenious concept which, as was intended, restricted overall control to a select, self-promoting fraternity. The Gnostic[10] disciples of Simon (Magus) Zelotes called it 'the faith of fools'.

The Gospel of Mary Magdalene confirms that, for a short time after Jesus had been raised from the dead, some of the Apostles knew nothing about it and went on believing that their Christ had been crucified. The Apostles 'wept copiously, saying, How can we possibly go to the Gentiles and preach the gospel of the kingdom of the Son of Man? If they were ruthless to him, won't they be ruthless to us?' Having already spoken with Jesus at the tomb, Mary Magdalene was able to reply: 'Stop weeping. There is no need for grief. Take courage instead, for his grace will be with you and around you, and will protect you'.

Peter then said to Mary, 'Sister, we know that the Saviour loved you more than other women. Tell us all that you can remember of what the Saviour said to you alone — everything that you know of him but we do not'.[11]

Mary recounted that Jesus had said to her: 'Blessed are you for not faltering at the sight of me: for where the mind is, there is the treasure'. Then 'Andrew responded, and said to the brethren, Say whatever you like about what has been said. I for one do not believe the Saviour said that'. Peter, agreeing with Andrew, added, 'Would he really have spoken privately to a woman, and not freely to us?' At this,

> Mary wept and said to Peter .... Do you think that I thought this all up myself, or that I am not telling the truth about the Saviour?
>
> Levi answered, and said unto Peter .... You have always been hot-tempered. Now I see you arguing with the woman as if you were enemies. But if the Saviour found her worthy, who are you, indeed, to reject her? The Saviour surely knows her well enough.

Levi, as we know,[12] was Matthew Annas, a priest and deputy of Alphaeus. His sensible opinion was the product of intellect and education. Peter and Andrew, on the other hand, were lesser educated villagers who, despite their length of time with Jesus and the more learned Apostles, still retained old establishment views of womanhood. Eventually, as we shall discover, Peter's sexist attitude was to achieve a position of prominence in the Romanized doctrine that was founded partially upon his teaching.

The early bishops of the Christian Church claimed their own Apostolic succession from Peter — the handing down of episcopal authority through the personal laying-on of hands. But those same bishops were described in the Gnostic *Apocalypse of Peter* as 'dry canals'.[13] It continues:

> They name themselves bishops and deacons as
> if they had received their authority directly
> from God .... Although they do not understand
> the mystery, they nonetheless boast that the
> secret of Truth is theirs alone.

As for the Resurrection, the matter remains a paradox. It is regarded as being of huge importance when it need not be; yet it has an express significance of which most people are quite unaware. The Gospel of Thomas quotes Jesus as saying, 'If spirit came into being because of the body, it is a wonder of wonders'.[14]

The Bloodline Continues

Times of Restitution

As we have seen, Mary Magdalene was three months pregnant at the time of the Crucifixion. She and Jesus had cemented their Second Marriage at the Bethany anointing in March AD 33. Apart from being able to derive this information directly from the Gospel sources, it is also a matter of straightforward calculation. A male heir to a dynastic succession was required ideally to have his first son at or close to his own fortieth birthday. (Four decades—40 years—was the recognized period of royal generation.[1]) The birth of a dynastic son and heir should always have been planned to occur in the then equivalent of September—the holiest month of the Jewish calendar—and it was for this reason that sexual relations were permitted only in December.

First Marriages also took place in the holy month of September—the month that included the Day of Atonement. A dynastic marriage would, therefore, theoretically be scheduled for the September of the bridegroom's thirty-ninth birthday, with sexual activity commenced in the December immediately following. In practice, however, there was always the chance that the first child might be a daughter and provision for this contingency was made by bringing the First Marriage ceremony forward to the bridegroom's thirty-sixth September. The first chance of a child then fell in his thirty-seventh September. If there was no conception in the first December, the couple would try again a year later—and so on. For a son to be born in or around the husband's fortieth year was fully acceptable within the generation standard.

Once a son was born, no further sexual contact between the parents was permitted for six years.[2] On the other hand, if the child was a daughter the ensuing period of celibacy was limited to three years until the 'times of restitution' (the return to the married state). As we have seen, the Second Marriage was solemnized in the March following conception, at which time the bride would be three months pregnant.

In accordance with these customs and rules, Jesus's First Marriage took place in September AD 30 (his thirty-sixth September), the very occasion on which Mary Magdalene first anointed his feet (Luke 7:37-38). There was, however, no conception that December, nor in the December of the next year. But, in December AD 32, Mary did conceive and duly anointed Jesus's head and feet at Bethany (Matthew 26:6-7, Mark 14:3 and John 12:1-3), formally sanctifying their Second Marriage in March AD 33.

Jesus had himself been born, against the rules, on 1 March 7 BC but, in order to regularize his status, he had been allocated the official birthday of 15 September in line with Messianic requirement. (It has long been customary for some monarchs to celebrate their actual birthdays and their separate official birthdays — as the Queen of Britain does today.) It was not until AD 314 that the Roman Emperor, Constantine the Great, arbitrarily changed the date of Jesus's official birthday to 25 December, on which date it is still celebrated, with many presuming it to be his real physical birthday.

Constantine's reason for making this change was two-fold. Firstly, it separated the Christian celebration from any Jewish association, thereby suggesting that Jesus was himself a Christian and not a Jew. Secondly, the adjustment of Jesus's official birthday was designed to coincide with the customary pagan Sun Festival of *Sol Invictus*. However, in the contemporary setting of Jesus's own time, 15 September AD 33 (six months after the Crucifixion) was his thirty-ninth official birthday and in that month a daughter was born to Mary Magdalene. She was named Tamar (Palm tree — assimilated in Greek to the name Damaris), a traditional Davidic family name. Jesus was then required to enter a fully celibate state for three years until the 'times of restitution', as detailed in Acts 3:20-21.[3]

> And he shall send Jesus Christ, which before was preached unto you: Whom the heaven must receive until the times of restitution of all things, which God hath spoken by the mouth of all his holy prophets since the world began.

This month of September AD 33 coincided with Simon Zelotes being formally re-established as the Father of the Community, at which juncture Jesus was finally admitted to the priesthood — a ritual in which he 'ascended into Heaven'.

Although recognized by many as the Davidic king, Jesus had long sought entry into the priesthood and particularly to the inner sanctum of the senior priests—the high monastery: the Kingdom of Heaven. Once Simon Zelotes had been reinstated, Jesus's wish was fulfilled: he was ordained and conveyed to Heaven by the Leader of the Pilgrims—his own brother James. In this fraternal context, James, by way of Old Testament imagery, was the designated Cloud.[4] It was a cloud that had led the ancient Israelites into the Promised Land (Exodus 13:21-22) and the appearance of God to Moses on Mount Sinai had been accompanied not just by thunder and lightning, but also by a cloud (Exodus 19:16). Thus, (like Thunder, Lightning and Earthquake) Cloud was also retained as a symbolic designation within the Essene community.

Jesus's elevation to the priesthood is recorded in the New Testament by the event generally known as the Ascension. Not only did Jesus speak himself in parables, the Gospel writers did the same, applying allegories and parallels that were meaningful to 'those with ears to hear'. Thus, passages of the Gospel texts which seem to be straightforward narrative (no matter how apparently supernatural their contexts) are also parables. As Jesus said to the disciples (Mark 4:11-12):

> Unto you it is given to know the mystery of the kingdom of God: but unto them that are without, all these things are done in parables: That seeing they may see, and not perceive; and hearing they may hear, and not understand.

The Ascension, then, is another parable, as described in Acts 1:9: 'And when he had spoken these things, while they beheld, he was taken up, and a cloud received him out of their sight'. As Jesus departed into the priestly realm of Heaven, two angelic priests announced that he would eventually return in the same manner:

> Behold, two men stood by them, in white apparel, which also said, Ye men of Galilee, why stand ye gazing up into heaven? This same Jesus which is taken up ... shall so come in like manner as ye have seen him go (Acts 1:10-11).

And so Jesus left the everyday world for three years, during which time Mary Magdalene, the mother of his child, would have no physical contact with him. From her sixth month of pregnancy, Mary had the right to call herself Mother, but once her daughter was born and the three years of celibacy commenced, she would have been ranked as a widow. Dynastic children were brought up and educated at a monastic community centre, in which their mothers (those designated widows or crippled women: wives in celibacy) also lived. It was because Jesus had himself been brought up in such enclosed conventual surroundings that so little is said about his childhood in the Gospels.

To Jesus a Son

Jesus's three-year period of monastic separation expired in September AD 36, following which physical relations with his wife were permitted once more in the December.

One very clear property of the language used in the New Testament is that words, names and titles which have a cryptic meaning are used with that same meaning throughout. Not only do they have the same meaning every time they are used, but they are used every time that same meaning is required. Undoubtedly the most thorough studies to date in this field of research have been conducted by Dr. Barbara Thiering, based on information contained in the Dead Sea Scrolls commentaries on Old Testament books. These commentaries hold the secrets of the *pesharim* (the routes to vital clues) and they were produced by the learned Scribes at Qumrân.

In some cases, individual derivations of coded names or titles may be complex or obscure, but more often they are straightforward, though rarely obvious. Frequently, cryptic information in the Gospels is heralded by the statement that it is intended 'for those with ears to hear'—this phrase is an inevitable precursor to a passage with a hidden meaning for those who know the code. The governing rules of the code are fixed and the symbolism remains constant—as in the case of Jesus himself.

By way of the inherent biblical *pesher* (singular of *pesharim* and meaning 'explanation' or 'solution'), Jesus is defined as the Word of God—as established from the very outset in the Gospel of John:

> In the beginning was the Word, and the Word was with God .... And the Word was made flesh, and dwelt among us, and we beheld his glory (John 1:1, 14).

There are no variables in the Gospel texts: whenever the phrase 'the Word of God' is used (with or without a capital W, according to translation), it means that Jesus either was present or is the subject of the narrative—as in Luke 5:1, when the word of God stood by the lake.

The phrase was also used in Acts to identify Jesus's whereabouts after the Ascension. So when we read that 'the apostles which were at Jerusalem heard that Samaria had received the word of God' (Acts 8:14), we may immediately understand that Jesus was in Samaria.

It follows, therefore, that when we read 'the word of God increased' (Acts 6:7) we should apprehend at once that Jesus 'increased',[5] as symbolized through the *pesher* in the parable of the Sower and the Seed (Mark 4:8): 'And other [seed] fell on good ground, and did yield fruit that sprang up and increased'. In short, the Acts reference means that 'Jesus [yielded fruit and] increased'—that is to say, he had a son. Perhaps not surprisingly, this first son was also named Jesus and we shall return to him in due course.

As required by the Messianic rules, the birth took place in AD 37— the year after Jesus returned to his marriage at the 'time of restitution'. Following the birth of a son, however, Jesus was now destined for no less than six more years of monastic celibacy.

In the Russian Church of St. Mary Magdalene, Jerusalem, there is a wonderful portrayal of Mary, which depicts her holding up a red egg to the viewer. This is the ultimate symbol of fertility and new birth. In a similar vein, *The Sacred Allegory* by Jan Provost—a 15th-century esoteric painting—shows Jesus with a sword, together with his wife Mary, who is crowned and wears the black garb of a Nazarite priestess, while releasing the dove of the Holy Spirit.

Paul's Mythological Jesus

During the years of Jesus's monastic separation (the heavenly state), his Apostles continued to preach—but they had no concept of founding a new religion. Albeit their message was radical, they were still Jewish and sought only to be reformers within Judaism, with Peter at the evangelical forefront of operations.

In direct opposition to the evolving movement was Saul of Tarsus, a staunchly orthodox Hebrew who was tutor to King Herod-Agrippa's son. Saul had no time for the liberal Hellenist views of Jesus; he believed that Jews were superior to all Gentiles, and considered James to be the rightful Messiah.

The year AD 37 was one of administrative change throughout the Roman Empire, and especially in Palestine. Emperor Tiberius had died and the new Emperor, Gaius Caligula, sacked Pontius Pilate to install his own man, Felix, as Governor in Judaea. Also ousted from their positions were Joseph Caiaphas the High Priest, and Simon Zelotes the Father. Theophilus, the brother of Jonathan Annas, took over as High Priest, and a whole new administration was in place — more answerable to Rome than any before.

In AD 40 Jesus was in Damascus, where the leading Jews attended a conference to discuss their position in relation to Rome. Just as Jesus knew that the Jews could never defeat Rome while divided from the Gentiles, Saul of Tarsus was equally sure that association with Gentiles represented a weakness that left the Jews vulnerable and exposed. Saul was particularly incensed when a statue of Caligula was set up within the Temple of Jerusalem — an outrage for which he put the blame squarely on Jesus and the Hellenists, whom he regarded as having split the Jewish nation. He too made his way to Damascus to state his case.

The account in Acts suggests that Saul went to Damascus, Syria, with a mandate from the High Priest in Jerusalem, but that cannot have been the case. The Jewish Sanhedrin had no jurisdiction whatever in Syria.[6] It is much more likely that Saul, who was attached to the House of Herod, was in fact operating for the Roman administration in an attempt to suppress the Nazarenes.[7] However, before Saul had a chance to make his presence felt at the conference, Jesus confronted him in the monastery buildings. When Saul entered at noon, the sun was at its height immediately above the vestry skylight,[8] and Jesus was there, ready to face his accuser. Then, having listened to Jesus's persuasive sermon, Saul realized that he had hitherto been blinded by sectarian dogma (Acts 9:8).

> Suddenly there shined round about him a light from heaven: And he fell to the earth, and heard a voice saying unto him, Saul, why persecutest thou me? (Acts 9:3-4).

Jesus subsequently instructed the disciple Ananias to further enlighten Saul, but Ananias hesitated, believing Saul to be an enemy agent: 'Lord, I have heard by many of this man, how much evil he hath done to thy saints at Jerusalem' (Acts 9:13). Nonetheless, the disciple obeyed, saying, 'Brother Saul, the Lord, even Jesus, that appeared unto thee in the way as thou camest, hath sent me, that thou mightest receive thy sight' (Acts 9:17).

The use in the above passages of the words 'sight' and 'the way' are again cryptic for, as previously related, the doctrinal theme of the Community was called the Way. After a course of instruction on Hellenist thinking, Saul was initiated so that he could clearly see the path to salvation in unity with the Gentiles: 'There fell from his eyes as it had been scales: and he received sight forthwith, and arose, and was baptized' (Acts 9:18).[9]

From this experience, Saul emerged as a fully-fledged Hellenist. At once, he began preaching in Damascus—but there was a problem, for the people could not believe that the man who had come hotfoot to challenge the Messiah was now promoting him instead. The Jews were confused, distrustful and, within a short time, angry to the extent that Saul's life was threatened and the disciples had to spirit him out of the city. Nonetheless, by AD 43 Saul was a fervent evangelist, well enough known under his new name, Paul, to be now associated in the popular mind with Peter. However, a much more insidious problem remained. His conversion had been so traumatic, his change of heart so far-reaching, that Paul regarded Jesus not as an earthly Messiah with an inspiring social message, but as the manifest Son of God—a heavenly power-lord.

Paul's missionary journeys took him to Anatolia (Asia Minor) and the Greek-speaking areas of the eastern Mediterranean. But his dramatically revised version of the Good News was that an awesome Saviour would soon establish a worldwide regime of perfect righteousness—and in this he was aided by ambiguous Old Testament writings such as from the book of Daniel 7:13-14: When written, these texts had nothing whatever to do with Jesus, but they were inspiring enough for Paul and provided the necessary inspiration for his fiery invective.[10] In his excitement, he proclaimed the Wrath of the Lord with all the zeal of an Old Testament prophet—making outrageous claims that gained him unprecedented attention.

> I saw in the night visions, and, behold, one like the Son of man came with the clouds of heaven ....
>
> And there was given him dominion, and glory, and a kingdom, that all people, nations, and languages, should serve him.

In 1 Thessalonians 4:16-17, Paul stated:

> For the Lord himself shall descend from heaven with a shout, with the voice of the

> archangel, and with the trump of God: and the
> dead in Christ shall rise first:
>
> Then we which are alive and remain shall be
> caught up together with them in the clouds, to
> meet the Lord in the air: and so shall we ever
> be with the Lord.

Through Paul's imaginative teaching, a whole new concept of Jesus arose. No longer was he simply the long-awaited Anointed One, the Messiah who would reinstate the Davidic line and free the Jews from oppression in Palestine. He was now the heavenly Saviour of the World!

> ... the image of the invisible God, the firstborn of
> every creature: For by him were all things
> created, that are in heaven, and that are in earth,
> visible and invisible ....
>
> And he is the head of the body, the church ...
> that in all things he might have the preeminence.
> For it pleased the Father that in him should all
> fullness dwell (Colossians 1:15-19).

While James and Peter were individually preaching their less ingenious messages, Paul had strayed into the unfathomable realm of pure fantasy. In his unbridled enthusiasm, he invented an inexplicable myth and uttered a string of self-styled prophecies that were never fulfilled. Yet for all that, it is Paul—not Peter, not James—who dominates the bulk of the New Testament beyond the Gospels. Such was the power of Paul's teaching that the ministering Jesus of the Gospels was transformed into an aspect of Almighty God, and Jesus the dynastic Christ (the royal heir to the House of Judah) was lost to religious history altogether.

Paul's allotted task was to further Hellenic-Jewish instruction among the Gentiles of the Mediterranean coastal lands, and to take Jesus's message to those Jews who lived outside their homeland. But instead, he ignored the root objective and—as was perhaps inevitable—contrived his own cult following. For Paul, the veneration and outright worship of Jesus was sufficient to ensure redemption and entry into the Kingdom of Heaven. All the social values professed and urged by Jesus were cast aside in Paul's attempt to compete with a variety of pagan beliefs.

Throughout the ancient Mediterranean world, there were many religions, whose gods and prophets were supposedly born of virgins and defied death in one way or another. They were all of supernatural origin and had astounding powers over ordinary mortals. To be fair to Paul, he certainly encountered problems that James and Jesus never faced in their native environment. Paul's route to success against such odds was to present Jesus in a way that would transcend even these paranormal idols. But in so doing, he created an image of Jesus so far removed from reality that Jewish society regarded him a fraud. Notwithstanding any of this, however, it was the transcendent Jesus of Paul's invention who later became the Jesus of orthodox Christianity.[11]

The Grail Child

During the early AD 40s, Peter linked up with the newly converted Paul in Antioch, Syria, while James and his Nazarenes remained operative in Jerusalem. A further division in the ranks then became apparent when Simon (the Magus) Zelotes set up a separate base for his esoteric Gnostic sect in Cyprus.[12]

Peter had been Jesus's right-hand man and, as such, he should have become Mary Magdalene's guardian during the years of her separation (symbolic widowhood) but, although Peter had been married himself, he had a low opinion of women and was not

The Roman Empire

prepared to be at the beck and call of a priestess. Paul's opinion of women was even less flattering and he strongly objected to their involvement in matters of religion. The two men, therefore, deliberately excluded Mary from any standing in their new movement and, to ensure her total alienation, they publicly declared her a heretic because she was a close friend of Simon Zelotes' consort, Helena-Salome.

In the course of this, Jesus and Mary once more resumed their married state in December AD 43, six years after the birth of their son. Jesus does not appear to have been too concerned about Peter and Paul's attitude towards Mary, for he knew Peter well enough and was doubtless content to acknowledge Paul's fanaticism, whether he liked it or not. In fact, Jesus seems to have been perfectly happy for his wife to be associated with the Gnostic faction of Simon and Helena (or with the Nazarenes of his brother James), rather than with the new style of sexist ministry that was being promoted by Peter and Paul. After all, Mary (along with Martha) had been the devotional sister of Simon (Lazarus) in Bethany and they were very well acquainted. It was at this time that Mary once more conceived. By the spring of AD 44, Jesus had embarked on a mission to Galatia (in central Asia Minor) with the Chief Proselyte (Head of the Gentile converts), John Mark, perhaps better known as Bartholomew.

During this period, James and his Nazarenes became an increasing threat to Roman authority in Jerusalem. As a direct result, the Apostle James Boanerges was executed by Herod of Chalcis in AD 44 (Acts 12:1-2). Simon Zelotes took immediate retaliatory action and had Herod-Agrippa poisoned,[13] but was then obliged to flee. Thaddaeus, however, was not so fortunate; in trying to escape across the Jordan, he was seized by Chalcis and summarily executed. This placed the expectant Mary in a precarious situation, for Chalcis knew that she was a friend of Simon. She appealed for protection from Paul's one-time student, young Herod-Agrippa II (then aged seventeen), who duly arranged her passage to the Herodian estate in Gaul, where Herod-Antipas and his brother Archelaus had been sent into exile.

Later that year, Mary gave birth to her second son in Provence and there is a specific reference to this in the New Testament: 'The word of God grew and multiplied' (Acts 12:24).[14] This son was the all-important Grail Child and he, after his grandfather, was called Joseph.

Hidden Records and the Desposyni

Having fulfilled his dynastic obligation to father two sons, Jesus was duly released from restrictions and able to lead a normal life once more. From AD 46, his elder son, the nine year-old Jesus II, was schooled in Caesarea. Three years later, he underwent the ceremony of his Second Birth in Provence. In accordance with custom, he would have been symbolically born again from his mother's womb at the age of twelve—his designated First Year as an initiate. In attendance was his uncle James (Joseph ha Rama Theo: 'of Arimathea'), who afterwards took his nephew to the West of England for a time.

In AD 53, Jesus junior was officially proclaimed Crown Prince at the synagogue in Corinth and duly received the Davidic Crown Prince's title of Justus (the Righteous—Acts 18:7).[15] He thereby formally succeeded his uncle, James the Just, as the kingly heir. Having reached the majority age of sixteen, Jesus Justus also became the Chief Nazarite, gaining entitlement to the black robe of that office—as worn by the priests of Isis, the universal Mother Goddess.[16]

His father, Jesus the Christ, went to Rome, via Crete and Malta, in AD 60. Meanwhile, Paul returned to Jerusalem, having travelled extensively with Luke the physician. Once there, however, he was accused of conspiracy against Jonathan Annas, who had been murdered by Governor Felix. The Governor was sent for trial before Emperor Nero in Rome and Paul was obliged to follow. Then, after some time, Felix was acquitted, but Paul remained in custody because of his association with ex-pupil Herod-Agrippa II, whom Nero detested. During this period, Jesus Justus was also in the city (Colossians 4:11).

At about the same time, but far from the perils of Rome, Jesus Justus's younger brother, Joseph, had finished his education at a druidic college and was settled in Gaul with his mother. They were later joined by young Joseph's uncle James, who came permanently to the West, having been hounded out of Jerusalem in AD 62. His Nazarenes had been subjected to brutal harassment by the Romans and the Sanhedrin Council had charged James with illegal teaching.[17] He was, consequently, sentenced to a public stoning and was excommunicated, to be declared spiritually 'dead' by the Jewish elders.[18] The once 'honourable counsellor' of the Sanhedrin and prospective Messiah of the Hebrews thus fell from the very pinnacle of civil and religious grace—an event which has been symbolically portrayed as if he fell bodily from the Temple roof itself.

Having lost all spiritual credibility in the eyes of the law, James reassumed his hereditary style, Joseph *ha Rama Theo,* and made his way westward to join Mary Magdalene and her colleagues in Gaul. Back in Nero's Rome, Peter had arrived to assume responsibility for the Pauline sect, who were by then known as Christians. Nero had developed a passionate hatred for the Christians and, to lessen their number, he instituted a fanatical regime of persecution. His favourite torture was to tie them to stakes in his palace gardens and to fire them as human torches at night.[19] This led to a major revolt by the Christians in AD 64, during the course of which Rome was engulfed by fire. The unbalanced Emperor was the suspected instigator, but he blamed the Christians and had both Peter and Paul put to death.

Before he died, Paul managed to relay a message to Timothy that Jesus was in a place of safety,[20] but he did not say where. It has been suggested by some that Jesus traced Thomas the Apostle's footsteps into India, and he is reckoned to have died at Srinagar, Kashmir, where a tomb has been attributed to him.[21] This resulted from a Kashmiri suggestion in 1894 that Jesus was synonymous with a prophet called Isa, to whom the tomb was originally dedicated — but the evidence, though somewhat intriguing, is far from conclusive in this regard.

Once James (Joseph of Arimathea) had settled permanently in the West, it was not long before Simon Zelotes led most of the Nazarenes out of Jerusalem in AD 65. He took them east of the Jordan and they spread into the region of old Mesopotamia (modern Iraq).

Nero's regime had caused considerable political nervousness and temperatures were raised to dangerous heights in the Holy Land. Early in AD 66, sporadic fighting broke out in Caesarea between the Zealots and Romans. The hostility quickly moved to Jerusalem, where the Zealots gained a number of strategic positions. They held the city for four years until a massive Roman army led by Flavius Titus arrived in AD 70, laying Jerusalem to waste. As Jesus had so rightly predicted many years before, the Temple fell and everything fell with it. Most of the inhabitants were slaughtered; the survivors were sold into slavery and the Holy City was an empty ruin for the next six decades.

In the wake of this destruction, the Jewish nation was in a state of turmoil. Not only did Jerusalem fall, but so too did Qumrân and, in time, the famous last bastion was the mountain fortress of Masada, south-west of the Dead Sea. There, fewer than a thousand Jews withstood repeated sieges by a mighty Roman army, but they were gradually deprived of all supplies and provisions. By AD 74, their cause was hopeless and the garrison commander, Eleazar Ben Jair, organized a programme of mass suicide. Only two women and five children survived.[22]

Various waves of Nazarene refugees fled the Holy Land to perpetuate their tradition in the northern reaches of Mesopotamia, Syria and southern Turkey. The chronicler Julius Africanus, writing in around AD 200, while resident in the city of Edessa (now Urfa, in Turkey, as opposed to Edessa in Greece), recorded details of the exodus.[23] At the onset of the revolt, the Roman governors had caused all the public records in Jerusalem to be burned so as to prevent future access to the details of Jesus's family genealogy. During the Jewish Revolt, all records were fair game to the Roman troops, who were ordered to destroy private records as well—indeed, to destroy any relevant documentary evidence they could find. But, for all that, the destruction was not complete and certain papers remained successfully hidden.

Writing about this purposeful eradication of Messianic documentation, Africanus stated: "A few careful people had private records of their own, having committed the names to memory or having recovered them from copies, and took pride in preserving the remembrance of their aristocratic origins". He described these royal inheritors as the *Desposyni* (Heirs of [or belonging to] the Lord [or the Master]). Throughout the early centuries AD, various *Desposyni* branches were hounded by Roman dictate—first by the Roman Empire and later by the Roman Church. Eusebius confirmed that, in Imperial times, the *Desposyni* leaders became the heads of their sects by way of a 'strict dynastic progression'. But, wherever possible, they were pursued to the death—hunted down like outlaws[24] and put to the Roman sword by Imperial command.

The full truth about this selective Inquisition was certainly concealed, but its mythology and tradition have survived. They have survived by way of Grail lore, the Tarot cards, Arthurian romance, the songs of the Troubadours, Unicorn tapestries, esoteric art and a continued veneration for the heritage of Mary Magdalene. So potent has been the tradition that, even today, the Holy Grail remains the ultimate relic of Quest. But all of this—no matter how enthralling or romantic—is deemed heretical by the orthodox ecclesiastical establishment. Why? Because the ultimate object of the enduring Quest still poses a daunting threat to a Church that dismissed the Messianic succession in favour of a self-styled clerical alternative.

Mary Magdalene

Royal Bride and Mother

Mary Magdalene died in AD 63, aged sixty, at the place now called Saint Baume in southern France.[1] She is described in the New Testament as a woman 'out of whom went seven devils' (Luke 8:2) and later, in the same Gospel, she is said to be a 'sinner'. But in addition to this, she is portrayed in all the Gospels as a favourite and loyal companion of Jesus. However, Luke's descriptions of Mary are again a matter of cryptic styling.

Prior to marriage, Marys were under the authority of the Chief Scribe who, in Mary Magdalene's time, was Judas Sicariote. The Chief Scribe was also the Demon Priest No. 7,[2] and the seven demon priests were established as a formal opposition group to those priests who were the seven lights of the Menorah. It was their duty to supervise the community's female celibates. Upon her marriage, Mary Magdalene was naturally released from this arrangement. Hence, 'the seven demons went out of her' and she was permitted sexual activity on the regulated basis detailed earlier.

As mentioned, her marriage was no ordinary one, and Mary was subject to long periods of marital separation from her husband — periods during which she was ranked not as a wife, but as a 'sister' (in the devotional sense — as a nun might be). In her capacity as a *Sister*, Mary was attached to the Father, Simon Zelotes (Lazarus). Also a *Sister* of the Father was Martha, whose name was similarly titular. Martha meant 'lady', and the difference between Marthas and Marys was that Marthas were allowed to own property, whereas Marys were not. In society, *Sisters* held the same community status as *widows* (*crippled women*),[3] a rank below that of *almah*. Thus, an *almah* (virgin) would marry and move up to the rank of *Mother*, but during her periods of marital separation she would be demoted to below her original unmarried rank.

Mary Magdalene's father was the Chief Priest (subordinate to the High Priest) Syrus the Jairus. The Jairus priest officiated at the great marble synagogue at Capernaum and was ranked quite separately from the Zadok and the Abiathar. It had been an hereditary post from the time of King David, restricted to the descendants of Jair (Numbers 32:41). As 2-Samuel 20:25-26 confirms: 'And Sheva was scribe: and Zadok and Abiathar were the priests: and Ira also the Jairite was a chief ruler about David.'

The first mention of Mary in the New Testament is actually the story of how she was raised from death as Jairus's daughter in AD 17. Being raised (symbolically, from eternal darkness) related either to elevation of status within the Way or, as we have seen, to a release from spiritual death by excommunication. However, since women were not excommunicated, Mary's event was plainly an initiatory raising. First raisings for boys were at the age of twelve and for girls at fourteen. Given that Mary was raised in AD 17, this means that she was born in AD 3 and was therefore nine years younger than Jesus, making her twenty-seven when she entered her marital contract in AD 30.

Having conceived in December AD 32, Mary was aged thirty at her Second Marriage, during which year (AD 33) she bore her daughter Tamar. Four years later she gave birth to Jesus the younger, and in AD 44 (at the age of forty-one) her second son, Joseph, was born. By that time Mary was in Marseilles (Massilia), where the official language was Greek until the 5th century.[4] A fact not generally recognized, but which should perhaps be emphasised, is that the Aramaic-style language of Jesus, the Apostles, and all concerned with Hellenic Judaism was heavily influenced by Greek. The Hebrews, of course, used their own specifically Semitic tongue. This is why terms such as *Alphaeus* and *ha Rama Theo* are combined from both Greek and Hebrew elements. In addition, having been under Roman occupation for so long, this other linguistic culture was to some degree incorporated. Adjustments were also made in respect of the Gentiles (non-Jews) and the Proselytes (Gentile converts to Judaism) so that, within all the variables, there was a mutual understanding.

According to Gnostic tradition, Mary Magdalene was associated with Wisdom (Sophia), represented by the sun, moon and a halo of stars. The female gnosis of Sophia was deemed to be the Holy Spirit, thus represented on Earth by the Magdalene, who fled into exile bearing the child of Jesus. John, in Revelation 12:1-17, describes Mary and her son, and tells of her persecution, her flight into exile and of the continued Roman hounding of the 'remnant of her seed' (her descendants).

And there appeared a great wonder in heaven;
a woman clothed with the sun, and the moon
under her feet, and upon her head a crown of
twelve stars:
And she being with child cried, travailing in
birth, and pained to be delivered.
And there appeared another wonder in
heaven; and behold a great red dragon, having
seven heads and ten horns, and seven crowns
upon his heads.
And ... the dragon stood before the woman
which was ready to be delivered, for to devour
her child as soon as it was born.
And she brought forth a man child ....
And the woman fled into the wilderness,
where she had a place prepared of God ....
And there was war in heaven: Michael and his
angels fought against the dragon ....
And the great dragon was cast out, that old
serpent ....
And they overcame him by the blood of the
Lamb, and by the word of their testimony ....
And when the dragon saw that he was cast
unto the earth, he persecuted the woman
which brought forth the man child.
And to the woman were given two wings of a
great eagle, that she might fly into the
wilderness, into her place ....
And the dragon was wroth with the woman,
and went to make war with the remnant of her
seed, which keep the commandments of God,
and have the testimony of Jesus Christ.

In addition to Mary, other migrants to Gaul in AD 44 included Martha and her maid Marcella. There were also Philip the Apostle, Mary Jacob-Cleophas and Mary Salome-Helena. Their point of disembarkation in Provence was Ratis, which later became known as Les Saintes Maries de la Mer.[5] Despite Mary and Martha's prominence in the Gospel texts, there is no mention at all of them in Acts, nor in any of St. Paul's epistles after their westward departure in AD 44.

The Life of Mary Magdalene by Raban Maar (776-856), Archbishop of Mayence (Mainz) and Abbé of Fuld, incorporates many traditions about Mary dating back well beyond the 5th century. A copy of the Maar manuscript was unearthed at Oxford University in the early 1400s and the work had been cited in the *Chronica Majora* of Matthew Paris, in around 1190. It is also listed in the *Scriptorum Ecclesiasticorum Historia literaria Basilae* at Oxford. Louis XI of France (1461-1483) was insistent on Mary's dynastic position in the royal lineage of France. *Saint Mary Magdalene* by the Dominican friar Père Lacordaire (published after the French Revolution) is a particularly informative work, as is *La Légende de Sainte Marie Madeleine* by Jacobus de Voragine, Archbishop of Genoa (born 1228). Both de Voragine and Maar state that Mary's mother Eucharia was related to the royal house of Israel (that was the Hasmonaean royal house, rather than the Davidic House of Judah).

Another important work by Jacobus de Voragine is the famous *Legenda Aurea* (Golden Legend), one of the earliest books printed at Westminster, London, by William Caxton in 1483. Previously published in French and Latin, Caxton was persuaded by William, Earl of Arundel, to produce an English version from the European manuscripts. It is a collection of ecclesiastical chronicles detailing the lives of selected saintly figures. Highly venerated, the work was given public readings on a regular basis in medieval monasteries and churches. One particular narrative from the *Legenda* is about St. Martha of Bethany and her sister, Mary Magdalene:

> St. Martha, hostess to Lord Jesus Christ, was born into a royal family. Her father's name was Syro, and her mother's Eucharia; the father came from Syria. Together with her sister by inheritance through their mother, Martha came into possession of three properties: the castle Magdalene, and Bethany, and a part of Jerusalem.
>
> After the Ascension of our Lord, when the disciples had departed, she, with her brother Lazarus and her sister Mary, also St. Maxim, embarked in a ship, on which—thanks to its preservation by our Lord—they all came safely to Marseilles. They thereafter proceeded to the region of Aix, where they converted the inhabitants to the faith.

The name Magdalene derives from the Hebrew noun migdal (tower). In practical terms, the statement that the sisters possessed three castles is a little misleading, particularly since Marys (Miriams) were not allowed to own property. The joint heritage actually related to personal status — that is to say they inherited high community stations (castles/towers) of guardianship, as in Micah 4:8[6] — the Magdal-eder (Watchtower of the flock).

The most active Magdalene cult was eventually based at Rennes-le-Château in the Languedoc region.[7] Elsewhere in France there were many shrines set up to Ste. Marie de Madeleine. These included her burial place at St. Maximus, where her sepulchre and alabaster tomb were guarded by Cassianite monks from the early 400s. The enigmatic area of Rennes-le-Château has fascinated many people since it was highlighted in 1982 by Michael Baigent, Richard Leigh and Henry Lincoln in their ground-breaking work *The Holy Blood and the Holy Grail* — along with Henry Lincoln's *The Holy Place*. The astonishing facts of the region's landscspe are no better conveyed, however, than in Chevalier David Wood's landmark cartographic book *Genisis*.

The Cassianite Order has an interesting history. Although St. Benedict is customarily regarded as the Father of Western monasticism, he was actually preceded by John Cassian, who founded his Cassianite monastery in about AD 410 (albeit following innovatory communal endeavours by Martin, Bishop of Tours, and Honoratius, Archbishop of Arles). The significant advance in monastic discipline made by Cassian (to be followed by Benedict and others) was its separation and independence from the organization of the episcopal Church. Cassian denounced the taking of holy orders as a 'dangerous practice', and declared that monks should 'at all costs avoid bishops'. Initially an ascetic hermit in Bethlehem, John Cassian established his twin schools near Marseilles — one for men, and one for women. Hence, Marseilles became a recognized conventual centre: the birthplace of the Candlemas ritual which succeeded the earlier torchlight procession of Persephone of the Underworld. Similarly, the Feast of the Madonna originated at St. Victor's Basilica in Marseilles.

Another important Magdalen seat was that of Gellone, where the Academy of Judaic Studies (the monastery of St. Guilhelm le Désert) flourished during the 9th century. The church at Rennes-le-Château was consecrated to Mary Magdalene in 1059 and, in 1096 (the year of the First Crusade), the great Basilica of St. Mary Magdalene was begun at Vézelay. It was here that St. Francis of Assisi founded the

Franciscan Friars Minor (later the Capuchins) in 1217.[8] It was also at Vézelay in 1146 that the Cistercian abbot St. Bernard of Clairvaux preached the Second Crusade to King Louis VII, Queen Eleanor, their knights, and an assembled congregation of 100,000. Indeed, the enthusiasm of the Crusades was intimately allied to the veneration of the Magdalene.

The Cistercians, Dominicans, Franciscans, and various other monastic Orders of the era thus all followed a lifestyle separate from the episcopacy of the Roman Church. But they shared a common interest in Mary Magdalene. In drafting the Constitution for the Order of Knights Templars in 1128, St. Bernard de Clairvaux specifically mentioned a requirement for 'the Obedience of Bethany, the castle of Mary and Martha'. It is thus evident that the great *Notre Dame* cathedrals of Europe, which were wholly Cistercian-Templar instigated, were dedicated not to Jesus's mother Mary, but to Our Lady, Mary Magdalene.

Scarlet Woman — Black Madonna

Early Christian texts describe Mary Magdalene as 'the woman who knew the all'. She was the one whom 'Christ loved more than all the disciples'; she was the apostle 'endowed with knowledge, vision and insight far exceeding Peter's' and she was the beloved bride who anointed Jesus at the Sacred Marriage (the Hieros Gamos) at Bethany.

Disregarding all this, the Roman Church elected to discredit Mary Magdalene in an attempt to exalt her mother-in-law, Jesus's mother Mary. In order to accomplish this, they made use of ambiguous comments in the New Testament — comments that described the unmarried Magdalene as a 'sinner' (which actually meant that she was a celibate *almah* undergoing assessment in betrothal). The duplicitous bishops decided, however, that a sinful woman must be a whore and Mary was branded as such thereafter.

There is a fascinating parallel between Mary and her fellow migrant Helena-Salome. Because of his dislike for women (especially educated women), Peter had always regarded Helena-Salome as a witch. He paid no heed to the fact that she was close to Jesus's mother and had accompanied her at the Crucifixion. As the consort of Simon Zelotes (Zebedee), Helena had in fact also been the conventual mother of the Apostles James and John Boanerges. Unlike Mary Magdalene, who was attached to the regional Order of Dan, Helena belonged to the tribal Order of Asher, wherein women were allowed to own personal property.[9]

Helena was also a high priestess of the pastoral Order of Ephesus and, as such, was entitled to wear the red robe of the *hierodulai* (Greek:: 'sacred women'). Such highly-ranked females were greatly feared by Peter, for the likes of Helena were a constant threat to his own position. Likewise, the Roman Church did not recognize such cardinal status in women and they were classified as whores and sorceresses. Thus, the once venerated image of the *hierodulai* was transformed and (via medieval French into English) they became 'harlots', to be disparagingly referred to as 'scarlet women'.

Mary Magdalene was a Head Sister of the Nazarite Order (the equivalent of a senior bishop) and was entitled to wear black. In parallel with the early reverence for Mary Magdalene, a cult known as that of the Black Madonna emanated from Ferrières in AD 44.[10] Among the many Black Madonna representations that still exist, one of the finest statues is displayed at Verviers, Liège; she is totally black with a golden sceptre and crown, surmounted by Sophia's halo of stars. Her infant child also wears a golden crown of royalty.

In contrast to the Black Madonna image, it was also common for Mary Magdalene to be portrayed wearing a red cloak, often over a green dress (representing fertility).[11] An example is the famous *Saint Mary Magdalene* fresco by Piero della Francesca, of about 1465, in the Gothic cathedral of Arezzo, near Florence. She is similarly clothed in Botticelli's *Mary at the Foot of the Cross*. The red is intended (like the scarlet of the *hierodulai*) to signify Mary's high clerical status. However, the concept of red-caped women of religious rank infuriated the Vatican hierarchy and, despite the Church's separate veneration of Jesus's mother, it was determined that she should not be dignified with the same privilege. In 1649, the bishops went so far as to issue a decree that all images of Jesus's mother should depict her wearing blue and white only.[12] This had the effect that Jesus's mother Mary, although exalted by the Church was, nevertheless, denied any ecclesiastical recognition within the establishment.

Women were absolutely barred from ordination in the Catholic Church and the general relegation of women (other than Jesus's mother) from any venerable status pushed Mary Magdalene ever further into the background. By the same strategy, Jesus's own physical heirs were totally eclipsed and the bishops were enabled to reinforce their claim to holy authority by means of a self-devised male succession. This was not a Messianic descent from Jesus, as should have been the case, nor even a descent from the *ha Rama Theo* prince, James the Just (brother of Jesus), but a contrived succession from Peter, the headstrong rustic Essene who despised women.

At the same time, the early Church was having to contend with a widespread veneration for the Universal Goddess—particularly in the Mediterranean environment—and this was actually to heighten during the period of clerical squabbling over sexist issues. From prehistoric times, the Goddess had appeared in many guises and had been known by many names, including Cybele, Diana, Demeter and Juno. But however personified, she was always identified with Isis, who was said to be 'the Universal Mother, mistress of all the elements, primordial child of time, sovereign of all things and the single manifestation of all'.

To the ancient Egyptians, Isis was the sister-wife of Osiris, who was the founder of civilization and the judge of souls after death. Isis was specifically a maternal protectress and her cult spread far and wide. She was frequently portrayed holding her child Horus, whose incarnations were said to be the pharaohs themselves. It is a well established fact that the familiar image of the White Madonna is founded upon the depictions of Isis, the nursing mother. It was she too who inspired the mysterious Black Madonna, of whose image there were nearly 200 in France by the 16th century. Some 450 representations have now been discovered worldwide. Even the cherished patron goddess of France, *Notre Dame de Lumière* (Our Lady of Light), has her origins in the Universal Mother.

The image of the Black Madonna and her child has presented a constant dilemma for the Church—especially those statues at notable churches and shrines in continental Europe. In some cases they are black all over, but many have only black faces, hands and feet, although not negroid in character. A few have been overpainted in pale flesh tones to conform with the standard White Madonna representation, whilst many have simply been removed from the public gaze altogether. Some are modestly garbed, but others are displayed with various degrees of prestige and sovereignty, having ornately decorated clothing and crowns.

The Black Madonna has her tradition in Queen Isis and her roots in the pre-patriarchal Lilith. She thus represents the strength and equality of womanhood—a proud, forthright and commanding figure, as against the strictly subordinate image of the conventional White Madonna as seen in Church representations of Jesus's mother. It was said that both Isis and Lilith knew the secret name of God (a secret held also by Mary Magdalene, 'the woman who knew the all'). The Black Madonna is thus also representative of the Magdalene who, according to the Alexandrian doctrine, 'transmitted the true secret of Jesus'. In fact, the long-standing Magdalene cult was closely associated with Black Madonna locations. She is black because Wisdom (Sophia) is black, having existed in the darkness of Chaos before the Creation. To the Gnostics of Simon Zelotes, Wisdom was the Holy Spirit—the great and immortal Sophia who brought forth the First Father, Yaldaboath, from the depths. Sophia was held to be incarnate as the Holy Spirit in Queen Mary Magdalene and it was she who was said to bear the ultimate observance of the Faith.

Magdalene and the Church

From the earliest days of the orthodox Christian movement, all venerators of the female principle were regarded as heretics. Long before the time of Emperor Constantine, Church Fathers such as Quintus Tertullian set the scene against female involvement, stating,

> It is not permitted for a woman to speak in church, nor is it permitted for her to baptise, nor to offer the Eucharist, nor to claim for herself a share in any masculine function— least of all in priestly office.

However, Tertullian was only following opinions expressed by his predecessors, notably Peter and Paul.

In the Gospel of Mary,[13] Peter challenges Mary Magdalene's relationship with Jesus, saying, 'Would he really have spoken privately to a woman, and not freely to us? Why should we change our minds and listen to her?' Again in the Coptic tractate called *Pistis Sophia* (Faith Wisdom),[14] Peter complains about Mary's preaching and asks Jesus to silence her, to stop her undermining his supremacy. Jesus instead rebukes Peter, whereupon Mary later confides, 'Peter makes me hesitate. I am afraid of him because he hates the female race'. Mary had good reason to be wary of Peter, for his attitude was made perfectly obvious on many occasions—as in the Gospel of Thomas.[15] Objecting to Mary's presence among the disciples, 'Simon Peter said unto them, Let Mary leave us, for women are not worthy of life'.

In the Gospel of Philip,[16] Mary Magdalene is regarded as 'the symbol of divine wisdom', but all such texts were excised by the bishops because they undermined the dominance of the male-only priesthood. Paul's New Testament teaching was expounded instead:

> Let the woman learn in silence with all subjection. But I suffer not a woman to teach,

nor to usurp authority over the man, but to be
in silence (1-Timothy 2:11-12).

Such authoritative pronouncements were especially useful because
they actually masked the real issue. The point was that women had to
be excluded at all costs. If they were not, the Magdalene's lingering
presence would be seen to prevail. As the wife of Jesus she was not
only the Messianic Queen but also the mother of the true heirs. There
are, in the Gospels, no less than seven lists of the women who
regularly accompanied Jesus and, in six of these, Mary Magdalene is
the first named, even ahead of his own mother. For centuries after her
death, the Magdalene legacy remained the greatest of all threats to a
fearful Church that had bypassed Messianic descent in favour of a
self-styled Apostolic succession.

In view of the Church's dread of Mary Magdalene, a special new
document was produced, setting out what the bishop's reckoned to be
her position within the scheme of things. Entitled *The Apostolic Order*,
it was the transcript of a presumed discussion between the Apostles
after the Last Supper and it claimed (which the Gospels do not) that
both Mary and Martha were present, thereby defeating part of its own
objective. An extract from the supposed debate reads:

> John said: When the Master blessed the bread
> and the cup, and assigned them with the
> words, This is my Body and Blood, he did not
> offer them to the women who are with us.
> Martha said: He did not offer them to Mary
> because he saw her laugh.

On the basis of this purely imaginary story, the Church decreed that
the first Apostles had decided that women were not to be allowed to
become priests because they were not serious! The essence of this
fabricated conversation was then adopted as formal Church doctrine
and Mary Magdalene was thereafter pronounced a disbelieving
recusant.

Women and the Gospel Selection

The New Testament, as we know it, began to take shape in AD 367,
when an initial selection of writings was collated by Bishop
Athanasius of Alexandria. From this list, certain works were
approved and ratified by the Council of Hippo in AD 393 and the

Council of Carthage in AD 397. There were, however, various criteria which governed the selection—the first being that the canonical Gospels must be written in the names of Jesus's own Apostles. But this ruling appears to have been disregarded from the outset. Although both Matthew and John were Apostles of Jesus, Mark and Luke were not; they are presented in the Acts as being later colleagues of St. Paul. On the other hand, Thomas and Philip were among the original twelve, but the Gospels in their names were excluded! Not only that, but they were sentenced to be destroyed and, throughout the Mediterranean world, these and other books were buried and hidden in the 5th century. Subsequently, the New Testament was subjected to any number of edits and amendments, until the version with which we are now familiar was approved by the extended Council of Trento, in Northern Italy, as late as 1545-63.

Only in recent times have some of the early manuscripts been unearthed, with the greatest of all discoveries being that made in 1945 at Nag Hammadi in Egypt. Although not rediscovered until recent times, the existence of these books had been no secret to historians. Indeed, certain of them, including the Gospel of Thomas, the Gospel of the Egyptians, the Gospel of Truth and others, are mentioned in the 2nd-century writings of Clement of Alexandria, Irenaeus of Lyon and Origen of Alexandria.

What then was the criterion by which the Gospel selection was truly made? It was, in fact, a wholly sexist regulation which precluded anything that upheld the status of women in Church or community society. As mentioned, Peter and Paul's apparent dislike of women was used to set a strategically male dominated scene, but even the quoted statements from these men were chosen very carefully, if not chosen out of context. In St. Paul's Epistle to the Romans, he made particular mention of his own female helpers; Phoebe, for example, whom he called a 'servant of the church' (16:1-2), along with Julia (16:15) and Priscilla, who laid down her neck for the cause (16:3-4). In fact, the New Testament (even in its strategically selected form) is simply alive with women disciples, but the Roman Church bishops elected to ignore them all.

The Church was so frightened of women that a rule of celibacy was instituted for its priests; a rule which became a law in 1138—a rule which persists even today. What really bothered the bishops, however, was not women as such, nor even sexual activity in general terms; it was the prospect of priestly intimacy with women which caused the problem. Why? Because women can become mothers and the very nature of motherhood is a perpetuation of bloodlines—a taboo subject which, at all costs, had to be separated from the necessary image of Jesus.

But, it was not as if the Bible suggested any such thing. In fact, quite the reverse was the case. St. Paul had actually said in his Second Epistle to Timothy (3:2-5) that a bishop should be the husband of one wife and that he should have children, for a man with his own household is better qualified to take care of the Church. Even though, in general terms, the bishops elected to uphold the teachings of Paul in particular, they chose to completely disregard this explicit directive so that Jesus's own marital status could be ignored.

Lady of the Lake

In 633, a mysterious little boat sailed into the harbour of Boulogne-sur-mer in northern France. There was no one aboard, just a 3-foot (c.1 metre) statuette of a Black Madonna and child, together with a copy of the Gospels in Syriac.[17] No one knew where the boat had come from, but it caused quite a stir and its enigmatic occupant (known as Our Lady of the Holy Blood) became the insignia of the Magdalene cathedral of Notre Dame at Boulogne—an object of considerable veneration until it was destroyed in the French Revolution.

The Black Madonna of Boulogne reinforced the connection between Mary and the sea (Latin: *mare*; French: *mer*) in the popular mind and the Mary of the Sea emblem (derived from the cathedral insignia) was used on pilgrims' badges before the time of Charlemagne. Indeed, a version of the device found its way into Scotland before armorial seals were common in Britain. In 11th-century Scotland, Edinburgh's Port of Leith incorporated its own official emblem—a depiction of Mary of the Sea and her Grail Child in a sailing boat protected by a cloud: a reference to James (Joseph of Arimathea) who was once the Cloud—the Leader of the Pilgrims.

For some reason, scholars of heraldry have seen fit to largely ignore the importance of such feminine devices, in just the same way that compilers of family trees and peerage registers have been guilty of dismissing female lineages. This was particularly so during the Georgian and Victorian eras in Britain, the chronicles of which provide the basis for much of the unsatisfactory information available today. Maybe the current onset of the Age of Aquarius will see an end to male-dominated history but, for the time being, the majority of such works are published in the old style and format. Very little research is required, however, to discover that the ideal of *Noblesse*

Uterine (matrilinear inheritance of nobility) was a concept thoroughly embraced throughout the Dark and early Middle Ages.

It is generally stated that the notion of heraldry (the bearing of heraldic arms and family escutcheons) began in the 12th century. This may well be so in Britain, but the British did not invent the concept, as the heralds would once have had us believe.[18] The reputed authorities on the subject, the College of Heralds and the College of Arms, were both established in the late 1300s to control the registers of armsbearers. It was necessary then for a knight to bear a decorated escutcheon so that he might be recognized despite being dressed from head to toe in chain mail and armour. The use of flags and other emblems indicating family or region emanated from earlier times in Flanders and northern France.

However, in spite of this, few in Britain have ever seen an insignia dating from before the 12th century, particularly one that is not of feudal origin. The emblem of the Port of Leith is thus unique in respect of its date, and in respect of its non-feudal, female association.

Archbishop Raban Maar's richly illuminated manuscript of *The Life of Mary Magdalene* consists of fifty chapters bound into six volumes. It tells, among other things, of how Mary, Martha, and their companions left the shores of Asia

> ... and favoured by an easterly wind they travelled on across the [Mediterranean] Sea between Europe and Africa, leaving the city of Rome and all the land of Italy to the right [north]. Then, happily changing course to the right (north), they came to the city of Marseilles in the Gaulish province of Vienne, where the River Rhone meets the coast. There—once they had called upon God, the Great King of all the world—they parted.

The libraries of Paris contain a number of manuscripts even older than Raban Maar's, which bear witness to Mary's mission in Provence. It is specifically mentioned in a hymn of the 600s (republished in the records of the Acta Sanctorum, issued by the Jesuit, Jean Bolland, in the 17th century).[19] Mary's companions, Mary-Salome (Helena) and Mary Jacob (the wife of Cleophas), are said to be buried in the crypt of Les Saintes Maries in the Camargue. Long before the 9th-century church was built, its predecessor was called

Sanctae Mariae de Ratis and near the present main nave is the remains of a sculpture showing the Marys at sea.

Mary Magdalene's association with Gaul has been artistically depicted in two distinct ways: representative and mystical. In some cases she is shown *en voyage* to Marseilles, as in the documented accounts. The most important example of this style of portrayal is perhaps that which has been exhibited at the church of *Les Saintes Maries*: a painting by Henri de Guadermaris. It depicts the Marys' arrival in a boat off the coast of Provence and was shown at the Salon de Paris in 1886. Another famous picture on similar lines is *The Sea Voyage* by Lukas Moser, which forms part of the gold-and-silver-leafed altarpiece, *Der Magdalenenaltar*, at the Katholisches Pfarramt St. Maria Magdalena, Tiefenbronn, in southern Germany.

Edinburgh Port of Leith — *Madonna of the Sea* device

Mary is alternatively portrayed moving above the Earth to receive heavenly enlightenment (as apocryphal romance had her doing on a daily basis), or being carried westward as in the Revelation. A fine example of this style of representation is Mary Magdalene Carried by the Angels. This work of around 1606, by Giovanni Lanfranco, at the Galleria Nazionale di Capodimonte in Naples, shows the naked Magdalene together with three putti soaring above an empty European landscape.

Martha's remains lie buried at Tarascon in the French province of Vienne. Letters patent of Louis XI dated 1482 refer to a visit by the Merovingian King Clovis to this tomb back in the late 5th century. Mary Magdalene's remains were preserved at the Abbey of St. Maximus, some 30 miles (c.48 km) or so from Marseilles. Charles II of Sicily, Count of Provence, disinterred Mary's skull and humerus (upper arm bone) in 1279 in order to have them set in the gold and silver display casings in which they remain today.[20] Some of Mary's other bones and ashes were kept in an urn, but these were vandalized during the French Revolution.

Mary's cave of solitude is to be found nearby at La Sainte Baume. It was this cave which the Sire de Joinville visited in 1254 on returning from the Seventh Crusade with King Louis IX. Afterwards he wrote that they

> came to the city of Aix in Provence to honour the Blessed Magdalene who lay about a day's journey away. We went to the place called Baume, on a very steep and craggy rock, in which it was said that the Holy Magdalene long resided at a hermitage.

Three centuries earlier, Wuillermus Gerardus, Marquis of Provence, made a pilgrimage to the cave, while the lofty grotto church at La Sainte Baume—with its various altars and fine sculpture of Mary Magdalene—has long been a noted place of pilgrimage.

Aix-en-Provence, where Mary Magdalene died in AD 63, was the old town of Acquae Sextiae.[21] It was the hot springs at Aix (Acqs) which gave it its name—*acqs* being a medieval derivative of the Latin word *aquae* (waters). In the Languedoc tradition, Mary is remembered as *la Dompna del Aquae*: the Mistress of the Waters. To the Gnostics (as indeed to the Celts), females who were afforded religious veneration were often associated with lakes, wells, fountains and springs. Indeed, gnosis (knowledge) and wisdom were attributed to the female Holy Spirit which 'moved on the face of the waters' (Genesis 1:2).

Earlier, we saw how the baptismal priests of the Gospel era were described as 'fishers' and, from the moment Jesus was admitted to the priesthood in the Order of Melchizedek (Hebrews 5), he too became a designated 'fisher'. The dynastic line of the House of Judah was thus uniquely established as a dynasty of Priest Kings or, as Jesus's descendants became aptly known in Grail lore, Fisher Kings. The lines of descent from Jesus and Mary Magdalene, which emerged through the Fisher Kings, preserved the maternal Spirit of Aix to become the 'family of the waters' — the House del Acqs.

This family was prominent in Aquitaine — an area with a name that also has its roots in *acquae* ('waters') or *acqs*, as indeed does the town name of Dax, west of Toulouse, which stems from *d'Acqs*.[22] Here, Merovingian[23] kingly branches that evolved from the Fisher Kings became Counts of Toulouse and Narbonne, also Princes of the Septimanian Midi (the territory between France and Spain).

Another family branch, related through the female line, was granted the Celtic Church heritage of Avallon, with Viviane del Acqs acknowledged as the hereditary High Queen in the early 6th century. Subsequently, in Brittany, a corresponding male branch of the Provençal House del Acqs became the Comtes (Counts) de Léon d'Acqs in descent from Viviane I's granddaughter Morgaine.

From the time that Chrétien de Troyes wrote his 12th-century tale of *Ywain and the Lady of the Fountain* — in which the Lady corresponds to *la Dompna del Aquae* — the heritage of Acqs has persisted in Arthurian literature. The *del Acqs* family legacy, which remained central to the Grail theme, was always directly related to the sacred waters and was always associated with Mary Magdalene. Alternatively, the name *du Lac* was used to signify relationship to the Pendragon blood (*lac*, or 'lake', being a red pigment from the eastern dragontree — as in the paint colour Scarlet Lake).[24] In 1484, Sir Thomas Malory's *Morte d'Arthur* used the latter distinction, with Viviane II (Lady of the Fountain and mother of Lancelot del Acqs) duly classified as the Lady of the Lake.

Joseph of Arimathea

The Glastonbury Chapel

In the 1601 *Annales Ecclesiasticae*, the Vatican librarian, Cardinal Baronius, recorded that Joseph of Arimathea first came to Marseilles in AD 35. From there, he and his company crossed to Britain to preach the Gospel. This was confirmed much earlier by the chronicler Gildas III (516-570), whose De Excidio Britanniae stated that the precepts of Christianity were carried to Britain in the last days of Emperor Tiberius Caesar, who died in AD 37. Even before Gildas, such eminent churchmen as Eusebius, Bishop of Caesaria (260-340),[1] and St. Hilary of Poitiers (300-367) wrote of early apostolic visits to Britain. The years AD 35-37 are thus among the earliest recorded dates for Christian evangelism. They correspond to a period shortly after the Crucifixion — prior to the time when Peter and Paul were in Rome and before the Gospels entered the public domain.

An important character in 1st-century Gaul was St. Philip.[2] He was described by Gildas and William of Malmesbury as being the inspiration behind Joseph's assignment in England. The *De Sancto Joseph ab Arimathea* states, 'Fifteen years after the Assumption [that is to say in AD 63], he [Joseph] came to Philip the Apostle among the Gauls'. Freculphus, a 9th-century Bishop of Lisieux, wrote that St. Philip then sent the mission from Gaul to England, 'to bring thither the good news of the world of life and to preach the incarnation of Jesus Christ'.

Upon their arrival in the West of England, Joseph and his twelve missionaries were viewed with scepticism by the native Britons, but were greeted with some cordiality by King Arviragus of Siluria, brother of Caractacus the Pendragon. In consultation with other chiefs, Arviragus granted Joseph twelve hides of Glastonbury land. A hide was an area of land reckoned agriculturally to support one family for one year with one plough — equal in Somerset (the

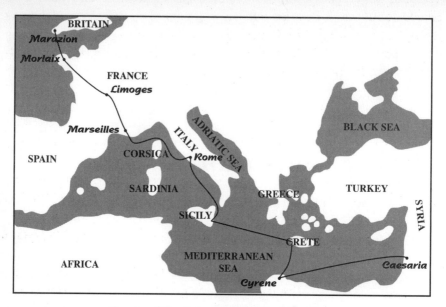

Route of the 1st-century Metal Traders

Glastonbury shire) to 120 acres (*c.*48.5 hectares). Here they built their unique little church in a scale of the ancient Hebrew Tabernacle.[3] These grants remained holdings of free land for many centuries thereafter, as confirmed in the *Domesday Book* of 1086: 'The Church of Glastonbury has its own ville twelve hides of land which have never paid tax'. In Joseph's era, Christian chapels were hidden underground in the catacombs of Rome but, once the wattle chapel of St. Mary was built at Glastonbury, Britain could boast the first above-ground Christian church in the world.[4]

A monastery was subsequently added to the chapel and the Saxons rebuilt the complex in the 8th century. Following a disastrous fire in 1184, Henry II of England granted the community a Charter of Renovation in which Glastonbury was referred to as 'the mother and burying place of the saints, founded by the disciples of our Lord themselves'.[5] A stone Lady Chapel was constructed at that time. Later, the complex grew to become a vast Benedictine abbey, second in size and importance only to Westminster Abbey in London. Prestigious figures associated with Glastonbury included St. Patrick (the first Abbot in the 5th century) and St. Dunstan (Abbot from 940 to 946).

In addition to the accounts of Joseph of Arimathea at Glastonbury, others tell of his association with Gaul and the Mediterranean tin trade. John of Glastonbury (14th-century compiler of *Glastoniensis Chronica*) and John Capgrave (Principal of the Augustinian Friars in England 1393-1464) both quoted from a book found by the Emperor

Theodosius (AD 375-395) in the Jerusalem Pretorium. Capgrave's *De Sancto Joseph ab Arimathea* tells how Joseph was imprisoned by the Jewish elders after the Crucifixion. This is also described in the apocryphal *Acts of Pilate*. The historian, Bishop Gregory of Tours (544-595), similarly mentions the post-Crucifixion imprisonment of Joseph in his *History of the Franks* and, in the 12th century, it was recounted yet again in *Joseph d'Arimathie* by the Burgundian Grail chronicler Sire Robert de Boron.

The *Magna Glastoniensis Tabula* and other manuscripts go on to say that Joseph subsequently escaped and was pardoned. Some years later he was in Gaul with his nephew, Joseph, who was baptised by Philip the Apostle. Young Joseph (Jesus and Mary's second son) is traditionally referred to as Josephes — the name that we shall continue to use in this book in order to distinguish him from his uncle, Joseph of Arimathea.

A good many valuable writings and relics were destroyed in the Glastonbury fire of 1184 and more were lost in the ravages of the Tudor dissolution of the monasteries. In the course of this latter destruction, Abbot Richard Whiting of Glastonbury was murdered in 1539 by the henchmen of King Henry VIII. Fortunately, copies of some important manuscripts were salvaged — one of which (attributed to Gildas III) refers to Joseph of Arimathea as a 'noble decurio'. The 9th-century Archbishop Raban Maar likewise described him as a *noblis decurion*. A Decurio was an overseer of mining estates and the term originated in Spain, where Jewish metalworkers had been operative in the celebrated foundries of Toledo since the 6th century BC.[6] It is not unlikely that Joseph's mining interest was the main reason for the generous land grant by King Arviragus.[7] Joseph was, after all, a well-known metal merchant and artificer in metals: a Master Craftsman (*ho-tekton*), as was his father and the Old Testament characters Tubal-cain and Hiram Abiff — both remembered in modern Freemasonry.

The *De Sancto Joseph* states that Joseph of Arimathea's wattle church of St. Mary was dedicated 'in the thirty-first year after our Lord's Passion' [that is, AD 64]. This conforms with AD 63 as its date of commencement, as given by William of Malmesbury. But, with regard to the fact that the dedication was to St. Mary (often presumed to be Jesus's mother), it has long been a point of debate that a church should have been consecrated to her some fifteen years after her Assumption and centuries before there was anything approaching a Virgin Mary cult. As confirmed in the 12th — 13th-century *Chronicles* of Matthew Paris, however, AD 63 was the very year in which the other Mary — Mary Magdalene — died at St. Baume.

Among the visits Joseph made to Britain, two were of great importance to the Church and were later cited by a number of clerics and religious correspondents. The first (as described by Cardinal Baronius) followed Joseph's initial seizure by the Sanhedrin after the Crucifixion. This visit in AD 35 ties in precisely with an account of St. James the Just in Europe—which is hardly surprising since Joseph of Arimathea and St. James were one and the same. The Rev. Lionel S. Lewis (Vicar of Glastonbury in the 1920s) also confirmed from his annals that St. James was at Glastonbury in AD 35. The second of Joseph's visits followed the AD 62 stoning and excommunication (spiritual death) of James the Just in Jerusalem.[8] Cressy, a Benedictine monk who lived shortly after the Reformation, wrote,

> In the one-and-fortieth year of Christ (that is, AD 35), St. James, returning out of Spain, visited Gaul, Brittany and the towns of the Venetians, where he preached the Gospel, and so came back to Jerusalem to consult the Blessed Virgin and St. Peter about matters of great weight and importance.

The 'weighty matters' referred to by Cressy concerned the necessity for a decision on whether to receive uncircumcised Gentiles into the Nazarene Church. As Jerusalem's first bishop, Jesus's brother James presided at the Council meeting which handled the debate.

A number of old traditions relate to St. James in Sardinia and Spain, but they are often attributed to the wrong St. James. This is mainly because the Apostle James Boanerges (sometimes called St. James the Greater, as distinguished from James of Alphaeus—the Lesser) disappears from the New Testament for a lengthy period.

Misunderstandings, caused by the apparent anomalies and duplicated entries concerning Joseph of Arimathea and St. James the Just, provoked some argument between the bishops at the Council of Basle in 1434. As a result, individual countries decided to follow their different traditions. It is St. Joseph who is most remembered in connection with Church history in Britain, whereas it is as St. James that he is revered in Spain. Even so, the English authorities compromised when linking him with the monarchy and the Royal Court in London became the Palace of St. James.

The bishops' debate followed an earlier dispute at the Council of Pisa in 1409 on the subject of the seniority, by age, of national Churches in Europe. The main contenders were England, France and

Spain. The case was ruled in favour of England because the church at Glastonbury was founded by Joseph/James *'statim post passionem Christi'* (shortly after the Passion of Jesus). Henceforth, the monarch of France was entitled His Most Christian Majesty, while in Spain the appellation was His Most Catholic Majesty. The bitterly contested title of His Most Sacred Majesty was, however, reserved for the King of England.[9] Records of the debate—*Disputatio super Dignitatem Angliae et Galliae in Concilio Constantiano*—state that England won her case because the saint was not only granted land in the West Country by Arviragus, but was actually buried at Glastonbury. The possibility that the other Saint James (Boanerges, or James the Greater) might have visited Spain at some stage was not relevant to the debate.

Having established that Joseph/James was buried at Glastonbury, we ought to look into how it is that the Cistercian *Estoire del Saint Graal* claims that he was buried at the Abbey of Glais in Scotland. This is not as contradictory as it seems, for at the time of Joseph's death the Scots Gaels had not settled in the Western Highlands (Dalriada) but constituted a tribal population of Northern Ireland (Ulster) who had infiltrated the south-west of Britain. The West Country areas settled by the early Scots were often referred to as Scotland (land of the Scots), when the far North of Britain was called Caledonia. Furthermore, the word *glais*—so common in old Scots names—comes from the Irish Goidelic, and means 'stream' or 'rivulet'. The name Douglas, for example, derives from *dubh glais* (dark stream). Early Glastonbury was set amid watery marshland, and was called the Isle of Glais. Thus, Joseph's said burial place at the Abbey of Glais actually referred to the Abbey of Glastonbury.

In the 1st century, mainland Britain (England, Wales and Scotland) was generally known as Albion. The Irish called it Alba—a name which was later restricted to the Scottish North after the Irish Scots had settled in the Western Highlands of Dalriada. By the 900s Alba had been adapted to Albany, and the alternative name, Scotland (or Scotia),[10] emerged about a century later.

Lordship of the Grail

The Joseph distinction (Hebrew: Yosef, meaning 'he shall add') was conferred upon the eldest son of each generation in the Davidic succession. When a dynastic son of the House of Judah (by whatever personal name) succeeded to become the David, his eldest son (the Crown Prince) became the Joseph. If there was no son at the time of a Davidic accession (or if the son was under sixteen years old), then the eldest brother of the David would temporarily hold the Joseph distinction. It would be relinquished to the senior line if and when a son was of age. Added to this was the ha Rama Theo (Arimathea) style of the Divine Highness—equivalent to today's princely title of Royal Highness.

Within the Judaean kingly, priestly, angelic and patriarchal successions, there were numerous dynastic and hereditary titles, along with various distinctions of office and appointment. Thus it was possible for any senior individual to be known by a series of different names according to the context of the moment. As we have seen, Matthew was also Levi in his official capacity. Zacharias was the Zadok and was, therefore, angelically Michael. Jonathan Annas (sometimes called Nathanael) was also James of Alphaeus (the Jacob of the Succession), but additionally he was the Elias. It is simply by virtue of this hierarchical and patriarchal structure that James the Just, brother of Jesus, came also to be known as Joseph of Arimathea (*ha Rama Theo*)—the Joseph (he shall add) of Godly Highness. At different times there were, of course, other Josephs of Arimathea. Now, with these related facts to hand, we should look at the situation from a different perspective—that of pure chronology.

Apart from a few vague descriptive terms, the New Testament gives no real clue as to what Joseph of Arimathea had to do with Jesus's family; neither do the Gospels mention Joseph's age. Outside the scriptures, however, he is often presumed to have been Jesus's mother's uncle. Paintings and picture-books, consequently, portray him as already rather elderly in the AD 30s. That apart, a number of written accounts from a variety of sources record him as coming to Glastonbury thirty years later in AD 63. Furthermore, Cressy's *Church History* (which incorporates the records of Glastonbury monastery) asserts that Joseph of Arimathea died on 27 July AD 82.

If Jesus's mother, Mary, were born in about 26 BC, as is generally reckoned, she would have been aged nineteen (or thereabouts) when Jesus was born. By the time of the Crucifixion she would have been in her middle fifties. If Joseph had been her uncle, he would have been, say, twenty years older than Mary—putting him somewhere in his middle seventies at that point in time. But then, thirty years afterwards (apparently at over 100 years of age) he is reputed to have begun a whole new life as an evangelist and decurio in the West! If that were not enough, the records then claim that he died twenty years later.

Clearly, none of this makes any sense and the hereditary aspect of the Joseph of Arimathea distinction has to be applied. Hence, as established, the Joseph of the Crucifixion era was James the Just, born in AD 1. He died in AD 82, having been formally excommunicated in Jerusalem twenty years earlier.

It is also apparent that Jesus's mother's background and family are not accounted for in the Bible. This is not surprising since the Church interpretation of Mary's heritage is that she was a product of Immaculate Conception. The main sources concerning Mary are not the canonical Gospels but the apocryphal scriptures, *The Gospel of Mary* and the *Protevangelion*. Many of the great artistic depictions of Mary's life and family are based on these, like Albrecht Dürer's famous *The Meeting of Anna and Joachim* (Mary's parents). The most comprehensive work on the subject is customarily accepted to be *La Leggenda di Sant Anna Madre della Gloriosa Vergine Maria, e di San Gioacchino* (The Story of Saint Anna, Mother of the Blessed Virgin Mary, and of Saint Joachim). This work links her parents with the Royal House of Israel, but it does not mention Joseph of Arimathea as her uncle.

It was actually by way of a 9th-century Byzantine concept that the Church first promoted Joseph as Mary's uncle. There is no mention of him in that role beforehand. The concept arose at a time when the cautiously fearful Church councils were debating the approved content of the New Testament. So long as Joseph of Arimathea could be contained as a sideline character in the Davidic structure and, so long as he was not associated with the key Messianic line, his royal descendants could not embarrass the self-styled Apostolic structure of the Roman bishops.

By this strategy, the existence of Jesus and Mary's son, Josephes, was also conveniently disguised in the West. He was generally portrayed as Joseph of Arimathea's son, or sometimes as his nephew (which of course he was). In either role he was no threat to the orthodox scheme of things and, indeed, both definitions of his relationship (son and nephew) had genuine foundation, for he was the heir to the *ha Rama Theo* distinction.

When Jesus became the David, his brother James became the Joseph. This only changed when Jesus the younger was of an age to inherit the title. After the death of Jesus the Christ, his eldest son, Jesus the Justus, became the David. His younger son, Josephes (the new David's brother), then became the Joseph—the designated Crown Prince *ha Rama Theo*. But until that time, while his brother Jesus Justus (called Gais or Gésu in Grail lore) was abroad in Rome and Jerusalem, Josephes' foster-father and legal guardian was his uncle James, the prevailing Joseph of Arimathea.

Later, the firstborn son of Jesus Justus was Galains (called Alain in the Grail tradition).[11] In accordance with the custom of dynastic wedlock, Jesus Justus had first married in September AD 73; his wife was a granddaughter of Nicodemus. The legacy of Davidic kingship (which was to become represented as Lordship of the Grail) was promised to Galains and was, in time, formally passed to him by his uncle and guardian, Josephes. But Galains became a committed celibate and died without issue. Hence, the Grail heritage reverted to Josephes' junior line — to be inherited by his son Josue,[12] from whom the Fisher Kings of Gaul descended.

As previously mentioned, Joseph of Arimathea had been to Britain with Mary's elder son, the twelve year-old Jesus Justus, in AD 49. This event is well remembered in West Country tradition and is evidenced in William Blake's famous song *Jerusalem*. The stories tell of how young Jesus walked upon the Exmoor coast and went to the Mendip village of Priddy. Because those royal feet did indeed 'walk upon England's mountains green' (albeit the son's feet rather than the father's), a stone in memory of his parents, Jesus and Mary Magdalene, was eventually set into the south wall of St. Mary's Chapel, Glastonbury. This stone, which remains on the site of the original 1st-century wattle chapel, is inscribed '*Jesus Maria*' and, in due course (as one of the most venerated relics of the Abbey), it became a prayer station for pilgrims in the Middle Ages. The original chapel was begun in AD 63 (immediately after Mary Magdalene's death) and the old annals[13] state that Jesus personally consecrated the chapel in honour of his mother. It was, therefore, to the Magdalene (not to Jesus the Christ's mother Mary) that the Glastonbury chapel was dedicated by her eldest son, Jesus Justus, in AD 64.

Shield of the Most Worthy

By the time of Mary Magdalene's death in AD 63, her son Josephes had become Bishop of Saraz. In Malory's Morte d'Arthur, Saraz (Sarras) features as the realm of King Evelake, mentioned in the story of Lancelot's son Galahad. The tale begins when Galahad inherits a supernatural shield of the Christ, and encounters the mysterious White Knight:

> Then within a while came Galahad there as
> the white knight abode him by the hermitage,
> and every each saluted other courteously.
> 'Sir', said Sir Galahad, 'by this shield be many
> marvels fallen?'

> 'Sir', said the knight, 'it befell after the passion of Our Lord Jesu Christ thirty-two year, that Joseph of Arimathea, the gentle knight, the which took down Our Lord off the holy Cross, at that time he departed from Jerusalem with a great party of his kindred with him. And so he laboured till that they came to a city that hight Sarras. And at that same hour that Joseph came to Sarras there was a king that hight Evelake, that had great war against the Saracens, and in especial against one Saracen, the which was king Evelake's cousin, a rich king and a mighty, which marched nigh this land, and his name was called Tolleme le Feintes. So on a day these two met to do battle ....'

Saraz was Sahr-Azzah on the Mediterranean coast[14] — perhaps better known as Gaza, the once Philistine centre where Samson met his fate (Judges 16).

There is no record of a King Evelake as such, but the name is a literary variant of the title *Avallach*, as found in quite a number of sovereign and saintly genealogies. It was subject to many different forms, such as *Abalech*, *Arabach* and *Amalach* — but all were ultimately corruptions of the Egyptian-Greek word *Alabarch*. Again, it does not represent a name (neither a forename nor a family name), but a title. St. Jerome (*c.*AD 340-420), translator of the Bible into Latin, stated that Tiberius Alexander, the Procurator of Judaea from AD 46, was the son of Alexander Lysimachus, Alabarch of Alexandria. In essence (although politically applied to magistrates responsible for justice among the Jews), the term 'Alabarch' indicated a community headman (a chief).

The White Knight's tale recounted (as above) that Evelake's Saracen enemy was Tolleme le Feintes (Tholomy the feigned, or false), who is also mentioned in *The Antiquities* of Josephus:

> Tholomy the arch robber, was after some time brought to him bound, and slain; but not till he had done a world of mischief to Idumaea and the Arabians.

The person before whom the bound Tholomy appeared was the Procurator of Judaea, Cuspius Fadus (the predecessor of Tiberius Alexander), who had Tholomy executed in around AD 45.

The White Knight went on to tell how Bishop Josephes informed King Evelake that he would inevitably be killed by Tolleme le Feintes unless he forsook his belief of the old law and believe upon the new law: 'And then there he showed him the right belief of the Holy Trinity'. Evelake was immediately converted, and the Shield of the Most Worthy was presented to him, whereupon he defeated Tolleme.[15] Josephes later baptised King Evelake before setting out to preach the Gospel in Britain.

The strength of the enigmatic white shield lay in its red cross, and in a mystic veil that went before it bearing the image of Jesus. This is reminiscent of the conversion of Emperor Vespasian's son. As narrated in the *Vindicta Salvatoris*, he was cured of leprosy by an ethereal shroud which bore an effigy of the Messiah.[16]

In conclusion, the White Knight related that, following Josephes' instruction, the shield was placed for safe keeping with the holy hermit Nacien. It lay with him in an abbey after his death, to be retrieved eventually by Sir Galahad. Thereafter, in the dying words of Bishop Josephes: 'The last of my lineage shall have it about his neck, that shall do many marvellous deeds'.

In the *De Sancto Joseph* and elsewhere, Nacien (or Nacion) is described not as a hermit, but as a Prince of the Medas. Historically, Prince Nascien of the Septimanian Midi was the 5th-century ancestor of the Merovingian Kings of the Franks, and his descendants also included the 11th-century Seneschals (Stewards) of Dol and Dinan in Brittany. These powerful major-domos were descended from Lancelot's mother, Viviane II del Acqs, dynastic Queen of Avallon, and were progenitors of the most influential of all desposynic strains — the Scots Royal House of Stewart.

Apostolic Missions to the West

A most supportive colleague of Mary Magdalene in Provence was her friend Simon Zelotes who, no longer the active Father, assumed the style given to him by Jesus at his raising — that of Abraham's steward Eliezer, or Lazarus. Under this name he became the first Bishop of Marseilles and his statue is at St. Victor's church. A doorway from the nave of the church leads to a subterranean chapel (located on the site of Lazarus's residence) that was fiercely guarded by the monks in the early days. It was Lazarus — also known as the Great One (Maximus) — who buried Mary Magdalene in her original alabaster sepulchre at St. Maximin in AD 63. Prior to this, he had been in Jerusalem and Antioch for a time and, after Mary's death, he went again to Jerusalem and Jordan before returning to join Joseph of Arimathea.

In Britain, however, Lazarus remained better known by his Apostolic name, Simon Zelotes. Nicephorus (758-829), the Patriarch of Constantinople and Byzantine historian, wrote that

> St. Simon, surnamed Zelotes ... travelled through Egypt and Africa, then through Mauritania and all Libya, preaching the Gospel. And the same doctrine he taught to the peoples of the Occidental Sea and the islands called Britannia.

Around five centuries earlier, in AD 303, Bishop Dorotheus of Tyre had written in his Synopsis de Apostole that 'Simon Zelotes preached Christ through all Mauritania, and Afric the less. At length he was crucified in Britannia, slain, and buried'. The 1601 Annales Ecclesiasticae of Cardinal Baronius also confirm Simon's martyrdom in Britain. He was crucified by the Romans under Catus Decianus at Caistor, Lincolnshire. At the saint's own request, however, his mortal remains were later placed with those of the Magdalene in Provence.

Also associated with Joseph of Arimathea in Britain was Herod-Agrippa's uncle Aristobulus, who had been Mary Magdalene's particular ally when she was afforded protection by the Herodian establishment at Vienne, outside Lyon.[17] Some commentators have suggested that a younger Aristobulus (the second husband of the deadly dancer, Salome) was Mary's confederate, but he was acting as regent for the king in Lesser Armenia at the time. The correct Aristobulus is described in the writings that name him in Britain; they duly refer to him as Arwystli Hen (Aristobulus the Old) and the town of Arwystli in Powys was named after him. He was the brother of Herod-Agrippa I, Herod of Chalcis and of Herodias (the mother of Salome).

The writings of the Roman churchman, Hippolytus (born about AD 160), list Aristobulus as a Bishop of the Britons. Cressy maintains that he was a bishop in Britain ordained by St. Paul himself. The Greek Church Martyrology claims that Aristobulus was martyred in Britain 'after he had built churches and ordained deacons and priests for the island'. This is further confirmed by St. Ado (800-874), Archbishop of Vienne, in the Adonis Martyrologia. Earlier, in AD 303, St. Dorotheus, Bishop of Tyre, wrote that Aristobulus was in Britain when St. Paul sent greetings to his household in Rome: 'Salute them which are of Aristobulus' household' (Romans 16:10). And the Jesuit *Regia Fides* additionally states, 'It is perfectly certain that before St. Paul reached Rome, Aristobulus was away in Britain'. He was, in fact, executed by the Romans at Verulamium (St. Albans)[18] in AD 59.

In addition to being known as Joseph of Arimathea, St. James the Just was called Ilid by the chroniclers of Wales. He was the patron of Llan Ilid in Gwent, having founded a mission at Cor-Eurgain. The *Cwydd to St. Mary Magdalene* in the Gestyn Ceriog refers to Joseph as Ilid, as does the manuscript of *The Sayings of the Wise*. The name Ilid is thought to be a variant of the Hebrew Eli (meaning 'my God' or 'raised up'). The *Achan Sant Prydain* (Genealogy of the Saints of Britain) states that 'there came with Brân the Blessed from Rome to Britain, Arwystli Hen, Ilid, Cyndaf — men of Israel — and Maw or Mawan, son of Cyndaf'. The *Iolo Manuscripts* recount that Ilid was summoned to Britain by Eurgain, the wife of King Caractacus of Camulod, and states, 'This same Ilid was called Joseph in the lections of his life'.

The Silurian Archdruid, Brân the Blessed, was married to Joseph of Arimathea's daughter Anna (Enygeus),[19] who is sometimes loosely referred to as a 'consabrina' of the Blessed Mary (that is Jesus's mother, Mary). Because Joseph has sometimes been wrongly portrayed as Mary's uncle, the word 'consabrina' has often been taken to denote a cousin. In practice, however, the word was very obscure and denoted no more than a junior kinswoman. It was, therefore, the perfect word to use when a genealogical relationship was unspecific, or when it was deemed necessary for it to remain veiled.

In AD 51, Brân was taken hostage to Rome along with Caractacus the Pendragon. Resident in Rome, Gladys, the younger daughter of Caractacus, married the Roman senator Rufus Pudens[20] and thus became Claudia Rufina Britannica (as confirmed by the Roman poet, Martial, in about AD 68). Caractacus' other daughter was St. Eurgen of Llan Ilid (the wife of Salog, Lord of Salisbury). His famed son, Prince Linus, became the first appointed Bishop of Rome.[21] In his Second Epistle to Timothy 4:21 (New Testament), Paul writes: 'Eubulus greeteth thee, and Pudens and Linus, and Claudia, and all the brethren'. Eubulus (*eu-boulos*: 'well advised' or 'prudent') was a variation of Aristobulus (*aristo-boulos*: 'best advised' or 'noblest in counsel').

While in Britain, Joseph of Arimathea's enterprise was maintained by a close circle of twelve celibate anchorites (reclusive devotees). Whenever one died, he was replaced by another. In Grail lore these anchorites were referred to as 'the brethren of Alain (Galains)', who was one of their number. As such, they were symbolic sons of Brân the Patriarch (the Father in the old order—as against the newly styled Bishop of Rome). This is why, in some literature, Alain is defined as the son of Brân (Bron). However, after Joseph's death in AD 82, the group disintegrated—mainly because Roman control had forever changed the character of England.

We have already seen that an amount of confusion reigned because of the various names attributed to Joseph (Joseph of Arimathea, St. James the Just, Ilid, and so forth), but it is clear that certain works of popular folklore have done much to further confuse the issue of descendant lines after his time. These works include the *Bruts*, the *Triads*, the *Mabinogion*, and *Cycles of the Kings*. Historically, they are all important because they are not entirely fictional and most traditions are, by their very nature, based on ancient facts. But these tales are purposefully romantic in construction and, as a result, many sceptical historians have attacked them mercilessly. Equally regrettable is the fact that other writers have been guided rather too wilfully by these semi-fanciful works. Consequently, a good deal of genealogically impossible information is contained in books that appear to stem from authoritative sources.

Unfortunately too, romantic literature pays little heed to correct chronology, and the players concerned are scattered willy-nilly in the adventurous texts. *The High History of the Holy Grail* (*c.*1220) provides a good example in claiming that Perceval (a 6th-century adherent of King Arthur) was the grandnephew of the 1st-century Joseph of Arimathea: 'Good knight was he of right, for he was of the lineage of Joseph of Arimathea, and this Joseph was his mother's uncle'.

The New Christianity

Good King Lucius

In the mid-2nd century, King Lucius, great-grandson of Arviragus, revived the spirit of early disciples in Britain. In so doing, he was popularly held to have 'increased the light' of Joseph's first missionaries and, accordingly, became known as Lleiffer Mawr (the Great Luminary). His daughter, Eurgen, forged the first link between the two key Davidic successions—one from Jesus and the other from James (Joseph of Arimathea)—when she married Aminadab, the great-grandson of Jesus and Mary Magdalene in the line from Josephes, who had become the Nazarite Bishop of Saras (Gaza).

Lucius openly confirmed his Christianity at Winchester in AD 156 and his cause was heightened in AD 177 by a mass Roman persecution of Christians in Gaul. This was enforced especially in the old Herodian regions of Lyon and Vienne, where St. Irenaeus and 19,000 Christians were put to death thirty years later. During the persecution, a good many Gaulish Christians fled to Britain, especially to Glastonbury, where they sought the aid of Good King Lucius. He decided to approach Eleutherius, the Bishop of Rome, for advice (this was, of course, before the days of the Imperial Roman Church). Lucius wrote earnestly to Eleutherius, requesting instruction in Christian government.

The letter in reply, as contained in the *Sacrorum Conciliorum Collectio*, is still extant in Rome. Eleutherius suggested that a good king was always at liberty to reject the laws of Rome, but not the law of God. The following is an extract in translation:

> The Christian believers, like all the people of the kingdom, must be considered sons of the king. They are under your protection .... A king is known by his government, not by whether

> he retains his power over the land. While you
> govern well, you will be a king. Unless you do
> this, the name of the king endures not, and
> you will lose the name of king.[1]

John Capgrave (1393-1464), the most learned of Augustinian friars, and Archbishop Ussher, in his De Brittanicarum Ecclesiarum Primordiis, both recounted that Lucius sent the missionaries, Medway and Elfan, to carry his request for advice to Rome. They eventually returned with the Bishop's emissaries, Faganus and Duvanus (whom the Welsh annals name as Fagan and Dyfan), whose journey was confirmed by Gildas in the 6th century. The Venerable Bede of Jarrow (673-735) also wrote about the King's appeal, which is likewise mentioned in the *Anglo-Saxon Chronicle*.

Fagan and Dyfan reinstated the old order of anchorites at Glastonbury and have since been credited with the second foundation of Christianity in Britain. Following this, the fame of Lucius spread far and wide. He was already celebrated as the builder of the first Glastonbury tower on St. Michael's Tor in AD 167, and now the church at Llandaff was dedicated to him as Lleurwgg the Great.[2]

Even more impressively, Lucius was responsible for founding the first Christian archbishopric in London. A Latin plaque above the vestry fireplace at St. Peter's, Cornhill, in the old City of London, reads:

> In the year of our Lord 179, Lucius, the first
> Christian king of this island now called
> Britain, founded the first church in London,
> well known as the Church of St. Peter in
> Cornhill; and founded there the archiepiscopal
> seat, and made it the metropolitan church and
> the primary church of his kingdom. So it
> remained for the space of four hundred years
> until the coming of St. Augustine .... Then,
> indeed, the seat and pallium of the
> archbishopric was translated from the said
> church of St. Peter in Cornhill to Dorobernia,
> which is now called Canterbury.

The advice given by Bishop Eleutherius in response to Good King Lucius' plea is fascinating, for it is fully in keeping with the underlying principle of service that permeates the Messianic Grail Code. Kings of the Grail dynasties in Britain and France always operated on this basis: they were Common Fathers to the people, never rulers of the lands. (The latter was a particularly feudal and Imperial concept that completely undermined the Code.) They understood, for example, the important difference in being Kings of the Franks as against being Kings of France, or in being Kings of Scots as against being Kings of Scotland. By virtue of this, the Grail monarchs were able to champion their nations rather than champion the clerics and politicians.

From the moment that a national monarchy becomes regulated by Acts of Parliament and Church decree, the styles of King or Queen are worthless. Under such circumstances there is no one left with authority enough to equal that of Church or Parliament and, therefore, no one to act solely on the people's behalf. Grail Kings were defined as Guardians of the Realm and, in this regard, Bishop Eleutherius' advice to Lucius was both profound and enlightened: 'All the people of the kingdom must be considered sons of the king. They are under your protection'.

Saint Michael

The Tor Chapel of St. Michael, Glastonbury, was established by King Lucius, on an ancient pagan site. To this place, the St. Michael ley line runs from St. Michael's Mount, Marazion—through St. Michael's Church, Brentor; St. Michael's Church, Burrowbridge Mump; St. Michael's Church, Othery—onwards to Stoke St. Michael.[3] Recently, the authors Paul Broadhurst and Hamish Miller have released a fascinating book, *The Dance of the Dragon*, which traces the St. Michael/Apollo axis from Ireland, through South West England, France, Italy, Greece and Israel.[4]

St. Michael, to whom so many churches were dedicated, was not a traditional clerical or martyred saint, but corresponds to the Archangel Michael, who is mentioned only once in the New Testament (Revelation 12:7). In his 1st-century work *The Wars of the Jews*, Flavius Josephus confirmed that the Essenes of Qumrân vowed to preserve the names of the angels within their priestly hierarchy. The holder of the angelic style Michael was the Zadokite priest. In descent from the original Zadok of King David's era, the Michael at the time of Jesus was John the Baptist, who had inherited the office from his father, Zacharias.

To that point, the *de jure* Davidic king had always been ranked separately from the angelic priests Michael, Gabriel, Sariel and Raphael. However, both the Zadok and David lines were strictly dynastic, but when John the Baptist died he left no successor. Jesus tried on many occasions to gain recognition as a priest; he even promoted himself visibly as such at what came to be called the Transfiguration. But it was not until the Ascension that his priesthood was formalized, on being carried to the Kingdom of Heaven (the high monastery) to become a high priest (Hebrews 3:1) in the Order of Melchizedek (Hebrews 5:6). His dynastic role then became dually Messianic—that of a Priest King (or as related in Grail lore, a Fisher King). For the first time since the era of David and Zadok, the kingly and angelic titles were conjoined with Jesus being both the David and the Michael:

> Whither the forerunner is for us entered, even Jesus, made an high priest for ever after the order of Melchizedek (Hebrews 6:20).

Fragments of the Prince Melchizedek Document found among the Dead Sea Scrolls indicate that Melchizedek and Michael were one and the same. It is this representation which features in the Revelation when the Archangel Michael (the descending Zadokite power of the Messiah) fights with the dragon of Roman oppression. Similarly, the Qumrân Damascus Document confirms that the styles of Zadok and Melchizedek were equivalent and mutually supportive. In essence, since Zadok was the ultimate high-priestly designation, and since Melchi (or Malchus) meant King, it is apparent that the style of Melchizedek was indicative of Priest-kingship.

Hebrews 7:14 totally dismisses the Gospel-interpreted notion of the Virgin Birth in order to confirm that Jesus's real father was Joseph. It states: 'it is evident that our Lord sprang out of Judah, of which tribe Moses spake nothing concerning priesthood'. It is also explained that the Law concerning priesthood was changed to accommodate Jesus's new archangelic distinction (Hebrews 7:12).

From that time, the dynastic Melchizedek (Melchi-Zadok) succession lay with Jesus's own male line—descending through the Fisher Kings. This was the line of the Davidic *Sangréal*—the Blood Royal of Judah, more romantically known as the Grail Family. In the early days, they were not actual (*de facto*) monarchs but were Priest Kings by right (*de jure*). Not until the 5th century—when the descendant Fisher King Faramund married Princess Argotta, heiress of the Sicambrian Franks—did the Christine line begin its impressive rise to prominence.

It was by no coincidence that St. Michael's presence was recorded in Cornwall in around AD 495, and in Gaul in about 580. Each senior descendant in the Grail line was the dynastic Michael, and the Cornish town of Marazion had Judaic origins—its name (meaning Market Zion) being synonymous with Jerusalem. Across the low-tide causeway from Marazion stands St. Michael's Mount—the location of an early Celtic monastery. This became a Benedictine priory in the 8th century, and was a designated cell of the Abbey of St. Michel in Brittany.

Rise of the Roman Church

In AD 66, the Hasmonaean scion, Flavius Josephus, had been appointed Commander in the defence of Galilee. He had previously trained for the Pharisee priesthood, but accepted military service when the Jews rose up against their Roman overlords. Josephus subsequently became the foremost historian of the era and his writings, *The Wars of the Jews* and *The Antiquities of the Jews*, provide a comprehensive insight into the long and complex history of the nation from the time of the early patriarchs to the years of Roman oppression. In the context of his work it is interesting to note his reference to Jesus.[5] It locates Jesus firmly within the historical fabric of the time, but without any mention of his divinity or of any scriptural motive:

> Now it was at around this time that Jesus emerged—a wise man, if he may be called a man, for he was a worker of marvels. A teacher of such men as receive the truth with pleasure, he drew to him many of the Jews in addition to many of the Gentiles. He was the Christ, and when Pilate—at the suggestion of the principal men among us—had him condemned to be crucified, those that had loved him from the first did not forsake him, for he appeared to them alive again on the third day—just as the godly prophets had foretold about him, and ten thousand other wonderful things about him besides. And the sect of Christians—named after him—are still very much in existence even today.

Josephus' scholarly opus, comprising some 60,000 manuscript lines, was written during the AD 80s when he was in Rome, from where the

Gospel of Mark had emerged a short while before. Although Peter and Paul were executed under Nero's regime, the Gospel writings of the era were not, on the face of it, anti-Roman. Indeed, the early Christians were more inclined to blame the Jews (rather than Pilate) for the persecution of Jesus and, because the Jewish uprising of AD 66-70 had failed, they firmly believed that God had switched allegiance from the Jews to themselves.

Notwithstanding this, the position of Christians within the expanding Roman Empire was hazardous; they were very much a minority group with no legal status. From Nero's crucifixion of Peter to the Edict of Milan in AD 313 (when Christianity was officially recognized), there were no fewer than thirty appointed Christian Bishops of Rome. The first Bishop, installed during Peter's lifetime by Paul in AD 58,[6] was Britain's Prince Linus, the son of King Caractacus. (Linus is sometimes portrayed as if he had been a slave — but this was later Church propaganda and we shall return to the matter because of its particular importance.)

By about AD 120, individual appointments had become the prerogative of group election and candidates had to be citizens of Rome. By the time of Bishop Hyginus (from AD 136), there was little or no connection between the Pauline Christians and the Nazarene followers of Jesus's own Judaic doctrine. The latter had settled mainly in Mesopotamia, Syria, southern Turkey and Egypt — apart from the established movements in Britain and Gaul. In the meantime, the Christians of Rome had been constantly suppressed because their beliefs were thought to challenge the traditional divinity of the Caesars (Emperors). As time passed, the suppression became even more severe, until it once more reached the proportions of Nero's reign and became outright persecution.

The prevailing religion of Imperial Rome was polytheistic (observing many gods) and had emanated largely from the worship of natural deities such as those of the woods and waters. As Rome grew to statehood, the gods of her Etruscan and Sabine neighbours had been incorporated. These included Jupiter (the sky god) and Mars (the god of war). Grecian cults were also embraced and, from 204 BC, the orgies of Cybele (the Asiatic earth goddess) were evident, soon emulated by the hedonistic rituals of Dionysus/Bacchus (the god of wine). As the Roman Empire spread eastwards, so the esoteric cult of Isis, the Universal Mother, was introduced, along with the Persian veneration of Mithras (god of light, truth and justice). Eventually, the Syrian solar religion of *Sol Invictus* (the unconquered and unconquerable Sun) became the all-encompassing belief. Its vision of the sun as the ultimate giver of life enabled all other cults to be subsumed within it, with the Emperor as the earthly incarnation of the godhead.

By the middle of the 2nd century, the original Nazarenes (the followers of Jesus and James's teachings) were unpopular not only with the Roman authorities, but were being severely harassed by the Pauline Christians — particularly by Irenaeus, Bishop of Lyon (born c.AD 120). He condemned them as heretics for claiming that Jesus was a man and not of divine origin as ruled by the new Faith. In fact, he even declared that Jesus had himself been practising the wrong religion and that he was personally mistaken in his beliefs! Irenaeus wrote of the Nazarenes, whom he called *ebionites* (poor), that

> they, like Jesus himself, as well as the Essenes
> and Zadokites of two centuries before,
> expound upon the prophetic books of the Old
> Testament. They reject the Pauline epistles,
> and they reject the apostle Paul, calling him
> an apostate of the Law.

In retaliation, the Nazarenes of the desposynic Church denounced Paul as a 'renegade' and a 'false apostle', claiming that his idolatrous writings should be rejected altogether.

In AD 135, Jerusalem was again crushed by Roman armies — this time under Emperor Hadrian — and the surviving Jews were scattered. Those who remained in Palestine were content (in their despair at such final military defeat) to concern themselves solely with rabbinical law and religion. Meanwhile, the Pauline sect (now quite divorced from its Judaic origins) was becoming ever more troublesome to the authorities.

Having reached the height of its glory in Hadrian's era (AD 117-138), Roman Imperialism began to decline under Commodus. His ineffective rule (AD 180-192) prompted a good deal of disunity which led to many decades of civil war, pitting various generals against each other and against the central government. A conflict arose over who should wear the crown, and opposing sections of the army began to elect their own sovereigns. Emperor Lucius Severus (AD 193-211) managed to restore some order by judicious use of the Praetorian Guard (the Emperor's personal bodyguard), but his discipline did not last for long. Throughout the 3rd century, internal disputes left the borders of the Empire open to attack by Sassanians from Persia and Goths from the Black Sea regions.

In AD 235, the Emperor Maximinus decreed that all Christian bishops and priests should be seized, their personal wealth confiscated and their churches burned. The captives were sentenced to various forms of punishment and slavery, including penal servitude at the lead mines in Sardinia. On arrival, each captive would have one eye removed and the left foot and right knee damaged to restrict movement. The men were also castrated. If that were not enough, they were chained from their waists to their ankles so they could not stand upright and the fetters were permanently welded. Not surprisingly, the majority did not live for more than a few months. In those days, being a Christian was in itself dangerous, but to be a known leader was tantamount to signing a personal death warrant.

By the time of Emperor Decius (AD 249), the Christians had become so rebellious that they were proclaimed criminals and their mass persecution began on an official basis. This continued into the reign of Diocletian, who became Emperor in AD 284. He dispensed with any vestige of democratic procedure and instituted an absolute monarchy. Christians were required to offer sacrifices to the divine Emperor and they suffered the harshest punishments for disobedience. It was ruled that all Christian meeting-houses be demolished and disciples who convened alternative assemblies were put to death. All Church property was confiscated by the magistrates, while all books, testaments and written doctrines of the faith were publicly burned. Christians of any prominent or worthy birthright were barred from public office and Christian slaves were denied any hope of freedom. The protection of Roman law was withdrawn and those who argued with the edicts were roasted alive over slow fires or eaten by animals in the public arena.

Diocletian attempted to counter the persistent aggressions of barbarian invaders by decentralizing control and establishing two separate divisions of the Empire. From AD 293, the West was managed from Gaul, while the East was centred at Byzantium in (what is now) north-western Turkey. But still the assaults continued, in particular new western invasions by the Germanic tribes of Franks and Alamanni, who had previously been held across the Rhine. No longer were the Romans an invading power; they were now themselves the constant victims of insurgency from all sides.

One of the most ruthless of the persecutors under Diocletian was Galerius, governor of the eastern provinces. He ordered that anyone who did not worship the Emperor above all others would be painfully executed. Just before his death in AD 311, however, Galerius issued a surprising decree of relaxation, giving Christians the right to 'assemble in their conventicles without fear of molestation'. After some two and a half centuries of dread and suppression, the Christians entered a new age of conditional freedom.

From AD 312, Constantine became Emperor in the West—ruling jointly with Licinius in the East. By then, Christianity had increased its following considerably and was flourishing in England, Germany, France, Portugal, Greece, Turkey and all corners of the Roman domain. In fact, Christian evangelists were having more success in subduing the barbarians than were the legions of Rome—even in places as far afield as Persia and Central Asia. It took little imagination for Constantine to realize that, while his Empire was falling apart at the seams, there could be some practical merit in his harnessing Christianity. He perceived in it a unifying force which could surely be used to his own strategic advantage.

Although Constantine had succeeded his father, he had a rival for the supreme Imperial rank in the person of his brother-in-law, Maxentius. In AD 312, their armies met at Milvian Bridge (a little outside Rome) and Constantine was victorious. This campaign was the prime moment of opportunity to establish his personal affiliation with Christianity and he announced that he had seen the vision of a cross in the sky, accompanied by the words 'In this sign conquer'. The Christian leaders were most impressed that a Roman Emperor had ridden to victory under their banner.

Constantine then summoned the ageing Bishop Miltiades. The Emperor's purpose was not to join the Faith under the authority of the Bishop of Rome, but to take over the Christian Church in its entirety. Among his first instructions was that the nails from the Cross of Jesus be brought to him—one of which he would have affixed to his crown. His related pronouncement to the bewildered Miltiades was then destined to change the structure of Christianity for all time: 'In the future, We, as the Apostle of Christ, will help choose the Bishop of Rome'. Having declared himself an Apostle, Constantine then proclaimed that the magnificent Lateran Palace was to be the Bishops' future residence.

When Miltiades died in AD 314, he was the first Bishop of Rome in a long succession to die in natural circumstances. Quite suddenly, Christianity had become respectable and was approved as an Imperial religion (in fact, as The Imperial Religion). Constantine subsequently became Caesar of all the Roman Empire in AD 324, thereafter to be known as Constantine the Great.

To replace Miltiades, Constantine (in breach of traditional practice) chose his own associate, Silvester, to be the first Imperial Bishop. He was crowned with great pomp and ceremony—a far cry from the shady back-room proceedings customary to previous Christian ritual. Gone were the days of fear and persecution, but the high price for this freedom was veneration of the Emperor—precisely what the Christian forebears had struggled so hard to avoid. The rank and file had no choice in the matter and the existing priests were quite simply instructed that their Church was now formally attached to the Empire. It was now the Church of Rome.

Silvester was too overwhelmed to perceive the trap into which he was leading the disciples of St. Peter. He saw only the route to salvation offered by Constantine. Although this monumental step gained Christians the right to move openly in society, their hierarchy was now to be encased in gold, ermine, jewels and all the trappings that the Christ himself had decried. Many followers of the Faith were outraged, for their leaders had been seduced and corrupted by the very regime that had been the bane of their ancestors. They declared that the new-found status of acceptability was in no way a victory of conversion; it was an evil cloud of absolute defeat—a profanation of all the principles they had so long held sacred.

Up to that point, the Christian message had been gaining support in all quarters. Those spreading the Gospel knew that Constantine and his predecessors were sorely weakened in the face of the Church's evident gradual success. It was, after all, one of the reasons why Constantine's father had married Britain's Christian Princess Elaine (St. Helena). Silvester and his colleagues in Rome may have considered the new alliance to be a politically sound manoeuvre, but the emissaries in the field viewed it for precisely what it was: a strategic buy-out by the enemy. They claimed that the spiritual message of St. Peter had been subverted by the idolatry of a self-seeking power striving to prevent its Imperial demise. In real terms, the very purpose of Christianity was nullified by the new regime. After nearly three centuries of strife and struggle, Jesus's own ideal had been forsaken altogether—handed over on a plate to be devoured by his adversaries.

Apart from various cultic beliefs, the Romans had worshipped the Emperors in their capacity as gods descended from others like Neptune and Jupiter. At the Council of Arles in AD 314,[7] Constantine retained his own divine status by introducing the omnipotent God of the Christians as his personal sponsor. He then dealt with the anomalies of doctrine by replacing certain aspects of Christian ritual with the familiar pagan traditions of sun worship, together with other teachings of Syrian and Persian origin. In short, the new religion of the Roman Church was constructed as a hybrid to appease all influential factions. By this means, Constantine looked towards a common and unified world religion (*Catholic* meaning Universal) with himself at its head.

Saint Helena

Since the original 1996 publication of *Bloodline of the Holy Grail*, a number of readers have mentioned that the book's portrayal of St. Helena's British royal heritage differs from that generally taught by the Church. It certainly does and, in fact, hers is a good example of how personal histories have been manipulated to suit the strategic interests of the bishops. It is, therefore, worth looking at how the propagandist teaching came about in this regard.

The word 'propagandist' is not used lightly here since the Church teachings concerning St. Helena were actually part of the strategy of the *Congregatio Propaganda Fide*. This specially designated College of the Propaganda of Cardinals was established in 1662 by Pope Gregory XV, and its sole purpose was to 'enforce' Church dogma, through its teachers and approved historians, where it disagreed with traditional or recorded facts.

Prior to that time, published information concerning the birthright of Empress Helena was always obtained from British records. As far as Britain was concerned, it was not until 1776 that the English historian, Edward Gibbon, promoted the Roman fiction of Helena's birth when issuing his *History of the Decline and Fall of the Roman Empire*. This was followed by a vindication in 1779 after his spurious accounts of early Christian development were criticised by academic scholars, but Gibbon had converted to Catholicism in 1753 and was bound to represent Helena in accordance with the official doctrine. According to Gibbon, Helena was born into an innkeeping family from the small town of Naissus in the Balkans. Later, he was obliged to confess that this notion was a matter of conjecture but, notwithstanding this, his original claim has since been slavishly followed by subsequent writers of histories and encyclopedias.

All pre-Gibbon records in Britain relate that Princess Elaine (Greco-Roman: Helen; Roman: Helena) was born and raised at Colchester and she became renowned for her expertise at political administration. Her husband, Constantius, was proclaimed Emperor at York (Caer Evroc). Prior to that, in AD 290, he had enlarged the York archbishopric at Helena's request and was subsequently buried at York. In recognition of Helena's pilgrimage to the Holy Land in AD 326 the church of Helen of the Cross was built at Colchester, where the city's coat-of-arms was established as her cross, with three silver crowns for its arms.

From the time of the Reformation, and especially after the College of Propaganda was instituted, Rome undertook a structured programme of disinformation about many aspects of Church history and this continued with increasing intensity. In practice, however, the revised Roman view about Helena is vague in the extreme, with the various accounts contradicting one another. Many churchmen have put forward the Balkan theory, as repeated by Gibbon; some gave Helena's birthplace as Nicomedia and others cited her as a Roman native.

Quite apart from the British records, the pre-1662 information from Rome also upheld Helena's British heritage — as did other writings in Europe. These included the 16th-century *Epistola* of the German writer, Melancthon, who wrote: 'Helen was undoubtedly a British Princess'. The Jesuit records (even the Jesuit book *Pilgrim Walks in Rome*) state, when detailing Constantine's own birth in Britain: 'It is one of Catholic England's greatest glories to count St. Helena and Constantine among its children — St. Helena being the only daughter of King Coilus'.

The Roman document most commonly cited to uphold the anti-Britain message is a manuscript written in the late 4th century (after Helena's death) by Ammianus Marcellinus — from which the original information concerning Helena (*c*.AD 248-328) has actually gone missing! There is, nevertheless, a spuriously entered margin note from the 1600s, which gives the newly devised Church-approved details on which the Gibbonites and others based their subsequent opinions.

In all of this, the one person that the Church and its dutiful scholars have chosen to ignore is Rome's own Cardinal Baronius, the Vatican librarian who compiled the 1601 *Annales Ecclesiasticae*. In this work, he explicitly stated: 'The man must be mad who, in the face of universal antiquity, refuses to believe that Constantine and his mother were Britons, born in Britain'.

Religion and the Bloodline

The Trinity Debate

From the content of many books about early Christianity, it could easily be imagined that the Roman Church was the true Church of Jesus, whereas other Christ-related beliefs were heretical and ungodly. This is far from the truth; many branches of Christianity were actually far less pagan than the politically contrived Church of Rome. They despised the idols and opulent trappings of the Roman ideal and, for their pains, were accordingly outlawed by Imperial decree. In particular, the esoteric Gnostics were condemned as heathen for insisting that the Spirit was good, but that Matter was defiled. This distinction certainly did not suit the highly materialistic attitudes of the new Church.

There were also those of the Nazarene tradition, who upheld the original cause of Jesus rather than the eccentric and embellished teachings of Paul that were so expediently misappropriated by Rome. These Judaic-Christians of the traditional school controlled many of the principal churches of the Near East during the reign of Constantine. Moreover, they were led by none other than the bloodline descendants of Jesus's own family: the *Desposyni* heirs of the Lord.

In AD 318, a *Desposyni* delegation journeyed to Rome where, at the newly commissioned Lateran Palace, the men were given audience by Bishop Silvester. Through their chief spokesman Joses (a descendant of Jesus's brother Jude), the delegates argued that the Church should rightfully be centred in Jerusalem, not in Rome. They claimed that the Bishop of Jerusalem should be a true hereditary *Desposynos*, while the bishops of other major centres—such as Alexandria, Antioch and Ephesus—should be related. Not surprisingly, their demands were in vain, for Silvester was hardly in a position to countermand the decrees of the Emperor. The teachings of Jesus had been superseded by a doctrine more amenable to Imperial requirement and, in no uncertain terms, Silvester informed the men that the power of salvation rested no longer in Jesus, but in Emperor Constantine!

Given that the Emperors had, for centuries, been revered as deities on Earth and that Constantine had officially claimed Apostolic descent, there was still one significant door left to close. After the visit of the *Desposyni*, he dealt with this very expediently at the Council of Nicaea in AD 325. The Pauline Christians had been expecting a Second Coming of their Messiah, sooner or later, and so Constantine had to demolish this expectation. The mission of Jesus to throw off Roman dominion had failed because of disunity among the sectarian Jews. Constantine took advantage of this failure by sowing the seed of an idea: perhaps Jesus was not the awaited Messiah as perceived! Furthermore, since it was the Emperor who had ensured the Christians' freedom within the Empire then, surely, their true Saviour was not Jesus, but Constantine!

The Emperor knew, of course, that Jesus had been venerated by Paul as the Son of God, but there was no room for such a concept to persist. Jesus and God had to be merged into one entity so that the Son was identified with the Father. It thus transpired, at the Council of Nicaea, that God was formally defined as Three Persons in One: a deity comprising three coequal and coeternal parts—the Father, Son and Holy Spirit (or Holy Ghost). These aspects (persons) of the Trinity bore an uncanny resemblance to the three priestly designations, the *Father*, *Son* and *Spirit*, as used so long before by the Essenes at Qumrân.

There were, though, some bishops who opposed this new dogma. Many of the delegates were Christian theologians of the old school who averred that Jesus was the Son and, furthermore, that the Son had been created in the flesh by God, but he was not himself God. The leading spokesman for this faction was an aged Libyan priest of Alexandria named Arius. But when Arius rose to speak, Nicholas of Myra punched him in the face and that swiftly dealt with the opposition!

The Nicene Creed of the Trinity of God was established as the basis for the new, reformed, orthodox Christian belief. The followers of Arius (thereafter known as Arians) were banished. Some delegates, including Bishop Eusebius of Caesaria, were prepared to compromise, but this was not acceptable and they were compelled to relent fully in favour of the new Creed. And so it was that, with God designated as both the Father and the Son, Jesus was conveniently bypassed as a figure of any practical significance. The Emperor was now regarded as the Messianic godhead—not only from that moment, but as of right through an inheritance deemed reserved for him 'since the beginning of time'.

Within its revised structure, the Roman Church was presumed safe from the emergence of any alternative Christian champion. Indeed, once the historical Jesus had been strategically sidelined, the Christian religion was said to have been named after a man called Chrestus who, in AD 49, had been one of the early protagonists in Rome. There were now only two official objects of worship: the Holy Trinity of God and the Emperor himself—the newly designated Saviour of the World. Anyone who disputed this was declared a heretic and Christians who attempted to retain loyalty to Jesus as the Messianic Christ were proclaimed by the Imperial Church to be heathens.

Meanwhile, it had been customary through the generations for the prevailing Bishop of Rome to nominate his own successor before he died, but his tradition was changed when Constantine proclaimed himself God's Apostle on Earth. It then became the Emperor's right to ratify appointments and the various candidates often came to blows, giving rise to a good deal of bloodshed in the streets. The theory of Apostolic Succession was retained, but the candidature was actually a farce because the Bishops of Rome were, thereafter, selected from the Emperors' own nominees.

In AD 330, Constantine declared Byzantium the capital of the Eastern (Byzantine) Empire, renaming it Constantinople. In the following year he convened a General Council in that city to ratify the decision of the earlier Council of Nicaea. On this occasion the doctrine of Arius (which had gained a significant following in the interim) was formally declared blasphemous. The Emperor's management of the Church was very much a part of his overall autocratic style; his rule was absolute and the Church was no more than a department of his Empire. Silvester might well have been the appointed Bishop of Rome, but his name barely featured in a sequence of events that was instigated by Constantine and forever changed the nature and purpose of Christianity.

Once this form of Roman Christianity had been established as the new Imperial religion, an even more totalitarian edict was to come at the behest of Emperor Theodosius the Great (AD 379-395). In AD 381, a second Ecumenical Council of Constantinople was convened with the purpose of ending the Arian dispute. Theodosius found it difficult to implement his sole divine right of Messianic appointment while the Arians still preached that the Son (Jesus) had been created by God and that the Holy Spirit passed *from* the Father *to* the Son. This concept had to be crushed and Jesus had to be permanently removed from the reckoning.

It was, therefore, decreed by the Church that the doctrine of the Trinity of God must be upheld by all: God *was* the Father, God *was* the Son and God *was* the Holy Spirit. There was to be no more argument!

Decline of the Empire

Throughout this period, the Nazarene tradition was, however, upheld. From the days of the early Jewish revolts, the Nazarenes had retained their religion under the leadership of the *Desposyni*. They flourished in Mesopotamia, eastern Syria, southern Turkey and central Asia. Entirely divorced from the fabricated Christianity of the Roman Empire, their faith was closer to the original teachings of Jesus than any other and had an essentially Jewish base, rather than any idolatrous entanglement with sun worship or other mystery cults. In fact the Nazarenes were the purest of true Christians; their approach to the Trinity was a simple one: God was God and Jesus was a man — an hereditary human Messiah of the Davidic succession. They were absolutely emphatic about this and repudiated any notion that the Blessed Mary was a virgin.

At the same time, there were others who, although prepared to accept the doctrine of the Triune God, still retained a belief in the divinity of Jesus. Their view differed considerably from that of the Nazarenes, for they believed what Paul had said — that Jesus was the Son of God. This gave rise to yet another Creed, which emerged in about AD 390, to become known as the Apostles' Creed. It began, 'I believe in God the Father Almighty and in Jesus Christ, his only begotten Son, our Lord'. This front-line reintroduction of Jesus was hardly conducive to the Saviour status of the Emperor but, within a few years, Rome was sacked by the Goths and the Western Empire fell into decline.

At that point, a new protagonist emerged in the dispute over the Trinity; he was Nestorius, Patriarch of Constantinople from AD 428. In accord with the Nazarenes, Nestorius maintained that the argument over whether Jesus was God or the Son of God was totally irrelevant, for it was plain to all that Jesus was a man, born quite naturally of a father and mother. From this platform, Nestorius stood against his Catholic colleagues, who had brought Jesus back into the picture now that the Empire was failing. They referred to Mary as the *Theotokas* (Greek: 'bearer of God') or *Dei Genitrix* (Latin: 'conceiver of God'). As a result, the Nazarene-Nestorian precept that Mary was a woman like any other was condemned by the Council of Ephesus (AD 431) and she was venerated thereafter as a mediator (or intercessor) between

God and the mortal world. As for Nestorius, he was declared a heretic and banished, but soon found himself among friends in Egypt and Turkey, establishing the Nestorian Church at Edessa in AD 489. It was here that Julius Africanus had previously recorded the Romans' purposeful destruction of the desposynic papers of royal heritage, but had also confirmed the existence of continuing private accounts of lineage – describing the Davidic family sect as maintained by a 'strict dynastic succession'.

From the mid-5th century, the Church of Rome continued in the West, while the Eastern Orthodox Church emerged from its centres at Constantinople, Alexandria, Antioch and Jerusalem. The unresolved debate over the Trinity had driven a wedge firmly between the factions and each claimed to represent the true Faith. The Church of Rome was reformed under the management of an appointed city administration: the Cardinals – a title derived from Latin *cardo* (pivot) – of whom there were twenty-eight appointees stationed at the Vatican.

While the Church of Rome was being restructured, the Western Empire collapsed – demolished by the Visigoths and Vandals. The last Emperor, Romulus Augustulus, was deposed by the German chieftain Odoacer, who became King of Italy in AD 476. In the absence of an Emperor, the prevailing High Bishop, Leo I[1] gained the title of Pontifex Maximus (Chief pontiff or bridge-builder). In the East, however, the story was different and the Byzantine Empire was destined to flourish for another thousand years.

As the might of Rome crumbled, so too did Roman Christianity subside. The Emperors had themselves been identified with the Christian God, but the Emperors had failed. Their religious supremacy had been switched to the Chief Pontiff, but his was now a minority religion in a Christ-related environment of Gnostics, Arians, Nazarenes and the fast-growing Celtic Church.

The Sorcerer Kings

During the latter years of the declining Empire, the greatest of all threats to the Roman Church arose from a desposynic royal strain in Gaul. They were the Merovingian dynasty – male line descendants of the Fisher Kings, with a Sicambrian female heritage. The Sicambrians took their name from Cambra, a tribal queen of about 380 BC. They were originally from Scythia, north of the Black Sea, and were called the Newmage (New Covenant).

The Bibliothèque Nationale in Paris contains a facsimile of the highly reputed *Fredegar's Chronicle* – an exhaustive 7th-century historical work of which the original took thirty-five years to compile. A special edition of Fredegar's manuscript was presented to the illustrious Nibelungen Court and was recognized by the State authorities as a comprehensive, official history. Fredegar (who died in 660) was a Burgundian scribe and his *Chronicle* covered the period from the earliest days of the Hebrew patriarchs to the era of the Merovingian kings. It cited numerous sources of information and cross-reference, including the writings of St. Jerome (translator of the Old Testament into Latin), Archbishop Isidore of Seville (author of the *Encyclopedia of Knowledge*) and Bishop Gregory of Tours (author of *The History of the Franks*).

Fredegar's *Prologue* asserts that his own researches were even more painstaking than those of the writers he cited. Fredegar wrote,

> I have judged it necessary to be more thorough in my determination to achieve accuracy ... and so I have included ... (as if source material for a future work) all the reigns of the kings and their chronology.

To achieve such accuracy, Fredegar, who was of high standing with Burgundian royalty, made use of his privileged access to a variety of Church records and State annals. He tells how the Sicambrian Franks—from whom France acquired its name—were themselves so called after their chief Francio, who died in 11 BC.

In the 4th century, the Sicambrian Franks were in the Rhineland, to which they had moved from Pannonia (west of the Danube) in AD 388 under their chiefs, Genobaud, Marcomer and Sunno. Settling into the region of Germania, they established their seat at Cologne. Over the next century, their armies invaded Roman Gaul and overran the area that is now Belgium and northern France. It was at this stage that Genobaud's daughter, Argotta, married Fisher King Faramund (AD 419-430), who is often cited to have been the true founder of the French monarchy. Faramund was the grandson of Boaz-Anfortas (to whom we shall return) in the direct Messianic succession from Josue's son, Aminadab (in the Christine line), who married King Lucius' daughter Eurgen (in the Arimatheac line).

Faramund, however, was not the only marital partner with a Messianic heritage. Argotta was herself descended from King Lucius' sister, Athildis, who married the Sicambrian chief Marcomer (eighth in descent from Francio) in about AD 130. Thus, the Merovingian succession which ensued from Faramund and Argotta was dually desposynic.

Merovingian Gaul

Argotta's father, Genobaud, Lord of the Franks, was the last male of his line — and so Faramund and Argotta's son, Clodion, duly became the next Lord of the Franks in Gaul. In AD 488, Clodion's son, Meroveus, was proclaimed Guardian at Tournai and it was from him that the line became noted as the mystical dynasty of Merovingians, as they rose to prominence as Kings of the Franks. They reigned not by coronation or created appointment, but by an accepted tradition that corresponded to the Messianic right of past generations.

Despite the carefully listed genealogies of his time, the heritage of Meroveus was strangely obscured in the monastic annals. Although the rightful son of Clodion he was, nonetheless, said by the historian Priscus to have been sired by an arcane sea creature, the *Bistea Neptunis*. There was evidently something very special about King Meroveus and his priestly successors, for they were accorded special veneration and were widely known for their esoteric knowledge and occult skills.[2] The 6th-century Gregory of Tours stated that the Frankish chiefs in the Sicambrian female line of their ancestry were not generally known for their ascetic culture, yet this learned dynasty (from what he called 'the foremost and most noble line of their race') emerged in the ancient Nazarite tradition to become known as the long-haired Sorcerer Kings.

In the Old Testament (Numbers 6:3, 5, 13), Nazarites were Jews such as Samson and Samuel who were bound by strict vows of obligation:

> He shall separate himself from wine and strong drink ....
>
> All the days of the vow of his separation there shall no razor come upon his head: until the days be fulfilled, in the which he separateth himself unto the Lord, he shall be holy, and shall let the locks of the hair of his head grow ....
>
> And this is the law of the Nazarite.

Nazarite vows were binding for specified terms. In the Essene tradition, periods of absolute celibacy were also implemented. The rank of Chief Nazarite was traditionally held by the Davidic Crown Prince, who wore ceremonial black. In this capacity, the royal head of the order had once been Jesus's brother James the Just, and the successive de jure Crown Princes of Judah retained the status and its responsibilities.

Regardless of their ultimately Jewish heritage, the Merovingians were not practising Jews, but neither were other non-Roman Christians whose beliefs had sprung from Judaic origins. The Catholic bishop, Gregory of Tours, described them as 'followers of idolatrous practices', but the priestly Merovingians were not pagan in any sense of being unenlightened. In practice, their spiritual cult was not dissimilar to that of the Druids and they were greatly revered as esoteric teachers, judges, faith-healers and clairvoyants. Although closely associated with the Burgundians, the Merovingians were not influenced by Arianism and their unique establishment was neither Gallo-Roman nor Teutonic. Indeed, it was said to be something entirely new and their culture seemed to appear from out of nowhere.

The Merovingian kings did not rule the land, nor were they politically active; governmental functions were performed by their Mayors of the Palace (Chief Ministers), while the kings were more concerned with military and social matters. Among their primary interests were education, agriculture and maritime trade. They were avid students of proper kingly practice in the ancient tradition and their revered model was King Solomon,[3] the son of David. Their disciplines were largely based on Old Testament scripture but, notwithstanding this, the Roman Church proclaimed them irreligious.

Not only were the Merovingians akin to the early Nazarites, but they retained other customs from biblical times. According to Essene tradition, boys were 'reborn' at the age of twelve when, dressed in a simple robe, they would undergo a ritual re-enactment of birth—a Second Birth (as was mentioned earlier in relation to Jesus Justus). The boy would thus symbolically be born again from his mother's womb and installed in his community position. Merovingian royalty followed a similar practice: kings' sons were granted a hereditary right to dynastic kingship by initiation on their twelfth birthday. There was no need for later coronation. The dynasty was not one of 'created' kings but a succession of natural kings, whose entitlement was automatic by virtue of hallowed appointment. As we have seen, the Merovingians were not only of Christine descent, but were also descended from James (Joseph of Arimathea) through both the sister and daughter of King Lucius.

The Essene custom of Second Birth is evidenced in the Gospels, although in a very obscure manner that was completely misunderstood in translation. In Luke 2:1-12, Jesus's own ceremony of Second Birth was chronologically confused with his actual birth. As in the other Gospels, Luke dates the Nativity (the First or actual birth of Jesus) during the latter reign of Herod the Great, who died in 4 BC. But Luke also states that Cyrenius (Quirinius) was Governor of Syria at the time, and that the Emperor Caesar Augustus had implemented a national census. In reality Cyrenius was never Governor of Syria while Herod was alive; he was appointed to the office in AD 6 when, according to Josephus in the *Antiquities of the Jews*, there was a head-count in Judaea conducted by Cyrenius at the behest of Caesar Augustus. This is the only recorded census for the region; there was none in Herod's time. The census was held twelve years after Jesus's First (actual) Birth—precisely in the year of his Second (initiatory) Birth.

This error was in turn responsible for the chronological confusion that surrounds the story of how Jesus was delayed at the Temple when in Jerusalem with his parents (Luke 2:41-50). The event is reported as occurring when Jesus was twelve years old—but it should actually relate to his designated 'twelfth year'—that is not twelve years after his birth into the world, but twelve years after his birth into the community. At the Passover of that year, Jesus would actually have been twenty-four (or twenty-three in accordance with his official September birthday). At that time, he would have been raised from initiate to manhood, but instead of accompanying his parents to the related celebrations, he stayed behind to discuss his Father's business, with his spiritual Father at that time being the priest Eleazer Annas.

Throughout his childhood Jesus had been associated with brilliant teachers and astronomers—in particular with the philosophical Magi, who were so admired by the Merovingian Kings. In Merovingian times, the three wise Magi of the Nativity were nominated to become the patron saints of Frankish Cologne, having in the meantime been spuriously dubbed Caspar, Melchior and Balthazar.

The Merovingian kings were noted sorcerers in the manner of the Samaritan Magi, and they firmly believed in the hidden powers of honeycomb. Because a honeycomb is naturally made up of hexagonal prisms, it was considered by philosophers to be the manifestation of divine harmony in nature.[4] Its construction was associated with insight and wisdom—as detailed in Proverbs 24:13-14:

> My son, eat thou honey, because it is good ....
> So shall the knowledge of wisdom be unto thy soul.

To the Merovingians, the bee was a most hallowed creature and, having been a sacred emblem of Egyptian royalty, it became a symbol of wisdom. Some 300 small golden bees were found stitched to the cloak of Childeric I (the son of Meroveus) when his grave was unearthed in 1653. Napoleon had these attached to his own coronation robe in 1804. He claimed his right by virtue of his descent from James de Rohan-Stuardo, the natural son (legitimated 1677) of Charles II Stuart of Britain by Marguerite, Duchesse de Rohan. The Stuarts were in turn entitled to this distinction because they, and their related Counts of Brittany, were descended from Clodion's brother Fredemundus—thus (akin to the Merovingians) they were equally in descent from the Fisher Kings through Faramund. The Merovingian bee was adopted by the exiled Stuarts in Europe, and engraved bees are still to be seen on some Jacobite glassware.

When Meroveus's son Childeric died in AD 481, he was succeeded by his fifteen year-old son Clovis. During the next five years, he led his armies southward from the Ardennes, pushing out the Gallo-Romans so that, by AD 486, his realm included such centres as Reims and Troyes. The Romans managed to retain a kingdom at Soissons, but Clovis defeated their forces and the ruler, Syagrius, fled to the Visigoth court of King Alaric II. At this, Clovis threatened war against

Alaric and the fugitive was handed over for execution. By his early twenties, with both the Romans and the Visigoths at his feet, Clovis was destined to become the most influential figure in the West.

At that time the Roman Church greatly feared the increasing popularity of Arianism in Gaul while Catholicism was dangerously close to being overrun in Western Europe, where the majority of active bishoprics were Arian. Clovis was neither Catholic nor Arian and it, therefore, occurred to the Roman hierarchy that the rise of Clovis could be used to their advantage. As it transpired, Clovis aided them quite inadvertently when he married the Burgundian Princess Clotilde at the Black Madonna centre of Ferrières.[5]

Although the Burgundians were traditionally Arian in their beliefs, Clotilde was a Catholic and she made it her business to evangelize her version of the faith. For a time she had no success in promoting the doctrine to her husband, but her luck changed in AD 496. King Clovis and his army were then locked in battle against the invading Alamanni tribe near Cologne and, for once in his illustrious military career, the Merovingian was losing. In a moment of desperation he invoked the name of Jesus at much the same instant that the Alaman king was slain. On the loss of their leader, the Alamanni faltered and fell into retreat, whereupon Clotilde wasted no time in claiming that Jesus had caused the Merovingian victory. Clovis was not especially convinced of this, but his wife sent immediately for St. Remy, Bishop of Reims, and arranged for Clovis to be baptized.[6]

In due allegiance to their leader, around half of the Merovingian warriors followed Clovis to the font. Word soon spread that the high potentate of the West had become a Catholic and this was of enormous value to Bishop Anastasius in Rome. A great wave of conversions followed and the Roman Church was saved from almost inevitable collapse. In fact, were it not for the baptism of King Clovis, the ultimate Christian religion of Western Europe might well now be Arian rather than Catholic. Nevertheless, the royal compliance was not a one-way bargain; in return for the king's agreement to be baptised, the Roman authorities pledged allegiance to him and his descendants. They promised that a new Holy Empire would be established under the Merovingians. Clovis had no reason to doubt the sincerity of the Roman alliance, but he unwittingly became the instrument of a bishops' conspiracy against the Messianic bloodline. With the blessing of the Church, Clovis was empowered to move his troops into Burgundy and Aquitaine. It was calculated that, by virtue of this, the Arians would be obliged to accept Catholicism, but the

Romans also had a longer-term plan in mind—a plan to strategically manoeuvre the Merovingians out of the picture, leaving the Bishop of Rome supreme in Gaul.[7]

Following a succession of military conquests, King Clovis died in Paris at the age of forty-five. He was succeeded by his sons Theuderic, Chlodomir, Childebert and Lothar. At that time, in 511, the Merovingian domain was divided into separate kingdoms. Theuderic succeeded in Austrasia (from Cologne to Basle), based at Metz. From Orléans in Burgundy, Chlodomir supervised the Loire Valley and the west of Aquitaine, around Toulouse and Bordeaux. Childebert succeeded in the region from the Seine across Neustria to Armorica (Brittany), with his capital at Paris; and Lothar inherited the kingdom between the Scheldt and the Somme, with his centre at Soissons. Their decades of combined rule were tempestuous; conflicts continued against the Gothic tribes, and eventually afforded Merovingian penetration into eastern Aquitaine, with Burgundy being fully absorbed into the realm.

Lothar was the last of the four to die, in 561, having previously become overall king. His sons Sigebert and Chilperic succeeded, with the line from Chilperic settling four generations later on Dagobert II, who became King of Austrasia in 674. By then, a council of leading bishops had extended the authority and immunities of the Church, while also reducing the powers of taxation and general administration by the royal house. In consequence, the key provinces of the Merovingian realm were under the immediate supervision of the Mayors of the Palace, who were themselves closely allied to the Catholic bishops. The Roman dismantling of Merovingian supremacy had begun.

The Pendragons

Court of the Fisher Kings

The Sicambrian Franks, from whose female line the Merovingians emerged, were associated with Grecian Arcadia before migrating to the Rhineland. As we have seen, they called themselves the Newmage (the New Covenant), just as the Essenes of Qumrân had once been known.[1] This Arcadian legacy was responsible for the mysterious sea beast—the Bistea Neptunis—as symbolically defined in the Merovingian ancestry. The relevant sea-lord was King Pallas, a god of old Arcadia, whose predecessor was the great Oceanus. In fact, the concept dated back as far as the ancient kings of Mesopotamia, who were said to be born of Tiâmat, the great mother of the primordial salt waters.

The immortal sea beast was said to be ever incarnate in a dynasty of ancient kings, whose symbol was a fish. This became an emblem of the Merovingian kings, along with the Lion of Judah and the *fleur-de-lis*, which was introduced in the late 5th century by King Clovis to denote the royal bloodline of France. Prior to this, the familiar Judaic trefoil had been emblematic of the covenant of circumcision. Both the rampant lion and the *fleur-de-lis* were later incorporated into the royal arms of Scotland.

In Arthurian lore, the Davidic sovereign lineage was represented by the Fisher Kings of the Grail Family and the patriarchal line was denoted by the name Anfortas, a symbolic style corrupted from *In fortis* (Latin: 'In strength'). It was identified with the Hebrew name Boaz, the great-grandfather of David (similarly meaning 'In strength'), who is remembered in modern Freemasonry.

The name Boaz was given to the left-hand pillar of King Solomon's Temple (1-Kings 7:21 and 2-Chronicles 3:17). Its capitals, along with those of the right-hand pillar, Jachin, were decorated with brass pomegranates (1-Kings 7:41-42)—a symbol of male fertility, as identified in *The Song of Solomon* 4:13. It is not by chance that Botticelli's famous paintings, *The Madonna of the Pomegranate* and *The Madonna of the Magnificat*, both show the infant Jesus clutching a ripe, open pomegranate.² Indeed, from 1483 to 1510, Botticelli (more correctly, Sandro Filipepi) was the Nautonnier (Helmsman) of the Prieuré Notre Dame de Sion, an esoteric society with Grail connections. In the Grail tradition of Botticelli's time, the Arcadian sea-lord, Pallas, was manifest in King Pelles: 'My name is Pelles, king of the foreign country and cousin nigh to Joseph of Arimathea'. It was his daughter, Elaine, who was the Grail Bearer of le Corbenic (*le Cors beneicon*: the Body blessed) and the mother of Galahad by Lancelot del Acqs.

Within the traditional Grail stories there is a consistency of names of Jewish, or apparently Jewish, extraction — names such as Josephes, Lot, Elinant, Galahad, Bron, Urien, Hebron, Pelles, Joseus, Jonas and Ban. In almost all of the legends, including Sir Thomas Malory's later 15th-century accounts, accentuated digressions constantly occur in relation to the Fisher Kings. In addition, there are many references to Joseph of Arimathea, King David and King Solomon. Even the priestly Judas Maccabaeus (who died in 161 BC) is featured. Over the years, many have thought it strange that this well-born Hasmonaean hero of Judaea is treated with such high esteem in a seemingly Christian story:

> 'Sir Knight', said he to Messire Gawain, 'I pray you bide ... and conquer this shield, or otherwise I shall conquer you ... for it belonged to the best knight of his faith that was ever ... and the wisest'.
> 'Who then was he?' said Messire Gawain.
> 'Judas Machabee was he ...'.
> 'You say true', saith Messire Gawain, 'and what is your name?'
> 'Sir, my name is Joseus, and I am of the lineage of Joseph of Abarimacie. King Pelles is my father, that is in the forest, and King Fisherman is my uncle'.³

It is known that some of the knights attributed to King Arthur were based upon real characters — particularly Lancelot, Bors and Lionel, who were connected to the del Acqs branch of the Grail Family. But what of the others? The indications are that many had factual origins, although not necessarily from the Arthurian era.

When the majority of Grail romances were written in the Middle Ages, there was little love for the Jews in Europe. Dispersed from Palestine, many had settled in various parts of the West but, owning no land to cultivate, they turned to trade and banking. This was not welcomed by the Christians and so money-lending was prohibited by the Church of Rome. In the light of this, King Edward I had all Jews expelled from England in 1209, except for skilled physicians. In such an atmosphere, it is quite apparent that writers (whether in Britain or continental Europe) would not have found it natural or politically correct to use a string of Jewish-sounding names for local heroes, knights and kings. Yet the names persist, from those of the early protagonists such as Josephes, to that of the later Galahad.

In the early Grail stories, Galahad was identified by the Hebrew name Gilead. The original Gilead was a son of Michael, the great-great-grandson of Nahor, brother of Abraham (1-Chronicles 5:14). Gilead means 'a heap of testimony'; the mountain called Gilead was the Mount of Witness (Genesis 31:21-25) and Galeed was Jacob's cairn, the Heap of the Witness (Genesis 31:46-48). In the footsteps of Bernard de Clairvaux, the Lincolnshire Abbot, Gilbert of Holland, equated the Arthurian Galahad directly with the family of Jesus in the Cistercian *Sermons on the Canticles*. Christian writers would not have exalted men of Jewish heritage to high positions in a chivalric environment unless their names were already known and well established. Evidently, therefore, the characters were based upon some historical foundation, even though their individual time-frames were brought into common alignment for the romances.

Camelot

From around 700 BC, Celtic tribes (keltoi, meaning 'strangers') from Central Europe settled in Britain and, through the Iron Age, their culture developed to an advanced stage until they controlled all of lowland Britain. Over successive centuries, they were joined by further waves of European Celts. The last settlers were the Belgic tribes, who moved into the South-east. The previous inhabitants spread northwards and westwards, establishing such places as Glastonbury in Somerset and Maiden Castle in Dorset. When the Romans arrived in the later BC years, the Celts were driven more generally westwards, despite their ongoing resistance under such formidable leaders as Caractacus and Boudicca (Victoria). The

Romans called the ancient Britons Pretani, a name that derived from the Cymric language of old Wales in which the whole Celtic island was called B'rith-ain, meaning Covenant Land.[4]

The Romans had considerable success in their conquest of Britain, but they could never defeat the Picts of Caledonia in the far north and, because of this, Emperor Hadrian (AD 117-138) had built a great wall across the country to separate the cultures. A majority of Celts south of the wall adapted to the Roman way of life, but their fiery northern cousins kept on fighting, as did the Scots Gaels of Northern Ireland.

In Wales, the early rulers of Powys and Gwynedd descended from Avallach in the line of Beli Mawr (Billi the Great), a 1st-century BC overlord of the Britons. He provides a good example of a character whose time-frame is often confused because of the fables that have grown around him. His grandson was the Archdruid Brân the Blessed (son-in-law of Joseph of Arimathea). By virtue of their historical association, Beli and Brân are often muddled with the earlier brothers Belinus and Brennus (the sons of Porrex), who contended for power in northern Britain in around 390 BC and were regarded as gods in the old Celtic tradition.

More potential confusion arises in that Brân the Blessed is often cited as the father of Caractacus. They were indeed contemporaries in the 1st century AD, but Caractacus' father was Cymbeline of Camulod. The persistent anomaly has fostered no end of complications in books dealing with lineage in the Dark Ages, but the cause is easily explained.

Brân's father, in descent from Beli Mawr, was King Llyr (Lear). Some generations later, however, in a succession from King Lucius, the names were repeated during the 3rd and 4th centuries, when the Welsh chief, Llyr Llediath, was the father of another Brân, father of Caradawc (a variant of the name Caractacus). A further cause of confusion lies in the fact that, as the Archdruid, Brân was the designated patriarchal Father. In symbolic terms, therefore, Brân would indeed have been the 'father' of Caractacus, just as Eleazer Annas and Simon Zelotes were Jesus's spiritual fathers in Judaea.

From the name Beli (or Billi), London's Billingsgate is partly derived. His descendant, Avallach, was the grandson of Joseph of Arimathea's daughter Anna, the wife of Archdruid Brân the Blessed. Joseph's own wife was also called Anna (meaning 'grace').[5] As previously discussed, *Avallach* was a descriptive title and, in the same way, the name *Beli* was also titular — denoting a 'sovereign lord'. As such, it too was dynastically repetitive and was equivalent to the biblical Heli (paternal grandfather of Jesus).

Another descendant of Beli Mawr was King Llud (after whom London's Ludgate was named). He was the progenitor of the kingly houses of Colchester, Siluria and Strathclyde, and his family celebrated key marriages into the lineage of James/Joseph of Arimathea. From among the Welsh princes in the Arimatheac succession emerged the founders and local rulers of Brittany (Little Britain), a Frankish region that had previously been called Armorica ([land] facing the sea). Another very early Davidic line, which progressed through Ugaine Már (4th century BC), maintained the lordship of Ireland as the High Kings (Ard Rí) of Tara.

King Lud's grandson, the mighty Cymbeline (father of Caractacus), was the Pendragon of mainland Britain during Jesus's lifetime. The Pendragon, or Head Dragon of the Island (*Pen Draco Insularis*), was the King of Kings and Guardian of the Celtic Isle. The title was not dynastic; Pendragons were appointed from Celtic royal stock by a Druid council of elders. Cymbeline governed the Belgic tribes of the Catuvellauni and Trinovantes from his seat at Colchester — the most impressive Iron Age fort in the land. Colchester was then called Camulod (Romanized as Camulodunum) — from the Celtic *camu-lot* meaning 'curved light'. This fortified settlement became the later model for the similarly named and seemingly transient court of Camelot in Arthurian romance.[6]

North of Cymbeline's domain, in Norfolk, the people known as the Iceni were ruled by King Prasutagus, whose wife was the famous Boudicca (or Boadicea). She led the great, but unsuccessful, tribal revolt against Roman domination from AD 60 — yelling her famous war-cry *Y gwir erbyn y Byd* (The Truth against the World). It was immediately after this that Joseph of Arimathea came from Gaul to set up his Glastonbury church in the face of Roman Imperialism.

The concept of the dragon — as in Pendragon — in kingly terms emerged directly from the holy crocodile (the *Messeh*) of the Egyptians and from the *Mûs-hûs* of old Mesopotamia. The Pharaohs and Babylonian kings were anointed with crocodile fat and, thereby, attained the fortitude of the *Messeh*, from which stems the Hebrew term, Messiah (Anointed One). The image of the intrepid *Messeh* evolved to become the dragon, which in turn became emblematic of mighty kingship. The Imperial Romans displayed a purple dragon on their standard, and it is this symbol that is depicted in Revelation 12:3, when Michael confronts the 'dragon with seven heads'. As we have seen, the dragon in this instance was Rome: known historically as the City of the Seven Kings (the number of reigning kings before the Republic was formed).

Following the Romans' withdrawal from Britain in AD 410, regional leadership reverted to tribal chieftains. One of these was Vortigern of Powys in Wales, whose wife was the daughter of the previous Roman governor, Magnus Maximus. Having assumed full control of Powys by AD 418, Vortigern was elected Pendragon of the Isle in AD 425 and made good use of the dragon emblem, which subsequently became the Red Dragon of Wales.

By that time, various kingly branches had emerged in the Arimatheac lines from Joseph's daughter Anna, and her husband Brân the Blessed. Among the most prominent of these local kings was Cunedda, the northern ruler of Manau, by the Firth of Forth. In a parallel family branch was the wise Coel Hen who led the 'Men of the North' (the *Gwyr-y-Gogledd*). Fondly remembered in nursery-rhyme as Old King Cole, he governed the regions of Rheged from his Cumbrian seat at Carlisle (the northern *Camu-lot* fortress). Another noted leader was Ceretic, a descendant of King Lucius.[7] From his base at Dumbarton, he governed the regions of Clydesdale. Together with Vortigern, these three kings were the most powerful overlords in 5th-century Britain. Theirs were the families who also bore the most famous Celtic saints and were accordingly known as the Holy Families of Britain.

In the middle AD 400s, Cunedda and his sons led their armies into North Wales to expel unwanted Irish settlers at the request of Vortigern. In so doing, Cunedda founded the Royal House of Gwynedd in the Welsh coastal region west of Powys. The Picts of Caledonia in the far north then took advantage of Cunedda's absence and began a series of Border raids across Hadrian's Wall. An army of Germanic Jute mercenaries, led by Hengest and Horsa, was swiftly imported to repel the invaders but, having succeeded, they turned their attentions to the far south and seized the kingdom of Kent for themselves. Other Germanic Saxon and Angle tribes subsequently invaded from Europe. The Saxons took the south, developing the kingdoms of Wessex, Essex, Middlesex and Sussex, whilst the Angles occupied the rest of the land from the Severn estuary to Hadrian's Wall, comprising Northumbria, Mercia and East Anglia. The whole became known as England (Angle-land) and the new occupants called the Celtic western peninsula Wales (*weallas* meaning 'foreigners').

Because Ireland was separated by sea from the tempestuous British mainland, it became a perfect haven for monks and scholars. Eire-land is said by some to mean 'land of peace', but the ancient name derived more directly from Eire-amhon (father of King Irial of Tara) who married Tamar, the daughter of King Zedekiah of Judah, in about 586 BC. (Eire

England, Ireland and Wales (Celtic and Anglo-Saxon Lands)

was also the name of the Tuatha Dé Danann wife of King Ceathur, who reigned in much the same era.) A unique and indigenous culture thus developed in the form of Celtic Christianity. It emerged primarily from Egypt, Syria and Mesopotamia, with precepts that were distinctly Nazarene. The liturgy was largely Alexandrian and, because Jesus's teachings (rather than his person) formed the basis of the Faith, the Mosaic content of the Old Testament was duly retained. The old Jewish marriage laws were observed, together with the celebrations of the Sabbath and Passover, while the divinity of Jesus and the Roman dogma of the Trinity played no part in the doctrine. The Celtic Church had no diocesan bishops, but was under the direction of abbots (monastic elders) and the whole was organized upon a clan structure, with its activities focused on scholarship and learning.

Cunedda remained in North Wales and, after Vortigern's death in AD 464, he succeeded as Pendragon, also becoming the supreme military commander of the Britons. The holder of this latter post was called the Guletic. When Cunedda died, Vortigern's son-in-law, Brychan of Brecknock, became Pendragon and Ceretic of Strathclyde became the military Guletic. Meanwhile, Vortigern's grandson

Aurelius—a man of considerable military experience—returned from Brittany to lend his weight against the Saxon incursion. In his capacity as a druidic priest, Aurelius was the designated Prince of the Sanctuary of the Ambrius—a holy chamber, symbolically modelled upon the ancient Hebrew Tabernacle (Exodus 25:8—'And let them make me a sanctuary; that I may dwell among them'). The Guardians of the Ambrius were individually styled *Ambrosius* and wore scarlet mantles. From his fort in Snowdonia, Aurelius the Ambrosius maintained the military defence of the West and succeeded as the Guletic when Brychan died.

Saint Columba and Merlin

In the early 500s, Brychan's son (also Brychan) moved to the Firth of Forth as Prince of Manau. There he founded another region of Brecknock in Forfarshire, which the Welsh people referred to as Breichniog of the North. His father's seat had been at Brecon in Wales—and so the northern fortress was similarly called Brechin. Brychan II's daughter married Prince Gabràn[8] of Scots Dalriada (the Western Highlands), as a result of which Gabràn became Lord of the Forth, inheriting a castle at Aberfoyle.

In that era, the Irish Gaels were in dispute with the Brychan house and, under King Cairill of Antrim, launched an assault against Scots Manau in 514. The invasion was successful and the Forth area was brought under Irish rule. Brychan duly called for assistance from his son-in-law, Prince Gabràn, and from the Guletic commander, Aurelius. Rather than attempt to remove the Irish from Manau, the leaders decided to launch a direct sea offensive against Antrim. In 516, Gabràn's Scots fleet sailed from the Sound of Jura with the Guletic troops of Aurelius. Their objective was the castle of King Cairill, the formidable hill-fort at Dun Baedàn (Badon Hill). The Guletic forces were victorious, and Dun Baedàn was overthrown.[9] In 560, the chronicler Gildas III (516-570) wrote about this battle in his *De Excidio Conquestu Britanniae* (The Fall and Conquest of Britain) and the great battle featured in both the Scots and Irish chronicles.[10] Some years after the Battle of Dun Baedàn, Gabràn became King of Scots in 537, with his West Highland court at Dunadd, near Loch Crinan.

At that time, the Pendragon was Cunedda's great-grandson, the Welsh king, Maelgwyn of Gwynedd. He was succeeded in this appointment by King Gabràn's son, Aedàn of Dalriada, who became King of Scots in 574 and was the first British king to be installed by priestly ordination, when anointed by St. Columba.

Born of Irish royal stock in 521, Columba was eligible to be a king in Ireland—but abandoned his legacy to become a monk, attending the ecclesiastical school at Moville, County Down. He founded monasteries in Derry and around, but his greatest work was destined to be in the Western Highlands and islands of Scots Dalriada, having been banished from Ireland in 563. Columba had mustered an army against the unjust King of Sligo, following which he was imprisoned at Tara and then exiled at the age of forty-two. With twelve disciples, he sailed to Iona and established the famous Columban monastery. Later, further north in Caledonia, Columba's royal heritage was well received by King Bruide of the Picts and he attained prominence as a political statesman at the druidic court. With a fleet of ships at his disposal, Columba visited the Isle of Man and Iceland, setting up schools and churches wherever he went—not only in Caledonia and the islands but also in English Northumbria (Saxonia).

At that time, the Scottish Lowlands (below the Forth) consisted of thirteen separate kingdoms. They bordered on the Northumbrian realm to the south and on the Pictish domain to the north. Although geographically outside Wales, the regions of Galloway, Lothian, Tweeddale and Ayrshire were all governed by Welsh princes. One of these dynastic regions above Hadrian's Wall was that of the *Gwyr-y-Gogledd* (Men of the North), whose chief was King Gwenddolau.

Shortly before Aedàn's kingly ordination by Columba, King Rhydderch of Strathclyde had killed King Gwenddolau in battle near Carlisle. The battlefield sat between the River Esk and Liddel Water, above Hadrian's Wall. (It was here, at the Moat of Liddel, that the Arthurian tale of *Fergus and the Black Knight* was set). Gwenddolau's chief adviser (the Merlin of Britain) was Emrys of Powys, the son of Aurelius. On Gwenddolau's death, however, the Merlin fled to Hart Fell Spa in the Caledonian Forest and then sought refuge at King Aedàn's court at Dunnad.

The title of Merlin (applied to the Seer to the King) was long established in the Druid tradition. Prior to Emrys, the appointed Merlin was Taliesin the Bard, husband of Viviane I del Acqs. At his death in 540, the title passed to Emrys of Powys, who was the famous Merlin of Arthurian tradition. Merlin Emrys was an elder cousin of King Aedàn and was, therefore, in a position to request that the new king take action against Gwenddolau's killer. Aedàn, therefore, complied and duly demolished Rhydderch's Court of Alcut at Dumbarton.

In those days the most important urban centre in the north of the Britain was Carlisle. It had been a prominent Roman garrison town and, by AD 369, was one of the five provincial capitals. In his *Life of St. Cuthbert*, Bede refers to a Christian community in Carlisle long before the Anglo-Saxons penetrated the area. A little south of Carlisle, near Kirkby Stephen in Cumbria, stands the ruin of Pendragon Castle. Carlisle was also called Cardeol or Caruele in Arthurian times and it was here that Grail writers such as Chrétien de Troyes located King Arthur's second royal court. *The High History of the Holy Grail* refers specifically to Arthur's court at Carlisle, which also features in the French *Suit de Merlin* and in the British tales, *Sir Gawain and the Carl of Carlisle* and *The Avowing of King Arthur*.

The supreme office of Pendragon endured for 650 years, but through all that time the one Pendragon who never existed was Uther Pendragon, the legendary father of King Arthur. At least, he certainly did not exist under that name, although Arthur's father was indeed a renowned Pendragon, as we shall see.

King Arthur

The Historical Warlord

It is often claimed that the first quoted reference to Arthur comes from the 9th-century Welsh monk, Nennius, whose *Historia Brittonum* cites Arthur at numerous identifiable battles. But, Arthur was recorded long before Nennius in the 7th-century Life of St. Columba. He is also mentioned in the Celtic poem *Gododdin*, written in about 600.

When King Aedàn of Dalriada was installed by St. Columba in 574, his eldest son and heir (born in 559) was Arthur. In the *Life of St. Columba*, Abbot Adamnan of Iona (627-704) related how the Saint had prophesied that Arthur would die before he could succeed his father. Adamnan further confirmed that the prophecy was accurate, for Arthur was killed in battle a few years after Columba's own death in 597.

The name Arthur is generally reckoned to derive from the Latin *Artorius*, but this is quite incorrect. The Arthurian name was purely Celtic, emerging from the Irish *Artur*. The 3rd-century sons of King Art were Cormac and Artur. Irish names were not influenced by the Romans and the root of the name Arthur can be found as far back as the 5th century BC, when Artur mes Delmann was King of the Lagain.

In 858, Nennius listed various battles at which Arthur was victorious. The locations included the Caledonian Wood north of Carlisle (*Cat Coit Celidon*) and Mount Agned — the fort of Bremenium in the Cheviots, from which Anglo-Saxons were repelled. Also featured was Arthur's battle by the River Glein (Glen) in Northumbria, where the fortified enclosure was the centre of operations from the middle 500s. Other named Arthurian battlegrounds were the City of the Legion (Carlisle) and the district of Linnuis — the old region of the Novantae tribe, north of Dumbarton, where Ben Arthur stands above Arrochar at the head of Loch Long.

To place Arthur in his correct context, it is necessary to understand that such apparent names as Pendragon and Merlin were actually titles. They applied to more than one individual over the course of time. Arthur's father, King Aedàn mac Gabràn of Scots, became Pendragon by virtue of the fact that he was Prince Brychan's grandson. In this line, Aedàn's mother, Lluan of Brecknock, was descended from Joseph of Arimathea. There never was an Uther Pendragon, even though he was grafted into English charts of the era in 16th-century Tudor times. The name Uther Pendragon was invented in the 12th century by the romancer Geoffrey of Monmouth (later Bishop of St. Asaph) and the Gaelic word *uther* (or *uthir*) was simply an adjective meaning 'terrible'. Historically, there was only ever one Arthur born to a Pendragon: he was Arthur mac Aedàn of Dalriada.

On his sixteenth birthday in 575, Arthur became sovereign Guletic (commander) of the British forces and the Celtic Church accepted his mother, Ygerna del Acqs, as the High Queen of the Celtic kingdoms. Her own mother (in the hereditary lineage of Jesus and Mary Magdalene) was Viviane I, dynastic Queen of Burgundian Avallon. The priests, therefore, anointed Arthur as High King of the Britons following his father's ordination as King of Scots. At the time of her conception of Arthur by Aedàn, Ygerna (Igraine) was, however, married to Gwyr-Llew, Dux of Carlisle. The *Scots Chronicle* records the event as follows:

> Becaus at ye heire of Brytan was maryit wy
> tane Scottis man quen ye Kinrik wakit, and
> Arthure was XV yere ald, ye Brytannis maid
> him king be ye devilrie of Merlynge, and yis
> Arthure was gottyn onn ane oyir mannis
> wiffe, ye Dux of Caruele.

In the *Historia Regum Britanniae* (History of the Kings of Britain) by Geoffrey of Monmouth (c.1147), Gwyr-Llew, the Dux of Caruele (Warlord of Carlisle), was literally spirited away to the southern West Country to become Gorlois, Duke of Cornwall.[1] This adjustment of the facts was deemed necessary because Geoffrey's Norman patron was Robert, Earl of Gloucester. The *Historia* was funded by Norman money, with an express requirement to cement King Arthur into the English tradition, even though he did not feature in the *Anglo-Saxon Chronicle*.

Although presented as a factual account, Geoffrey's work was known to be inaccurate in many respects. The historian William of

Malmesbury called it 'dubious stuff' and William of Newburgh went even further, stating, 'Everything that the man took pains to write concerning Arthur and his predecessors was invented'.

Many were particularly baffled by Geoffrey's Duke Gorlois of Cornwall because there were no dukes in 6th-century England. The early title of *Dux* was quite different from that of the later ducal nobility; it was a strictly military distinction and held no feudal tenure of land ownership. Another anomaly was the assertion by Geoffrey that the 6th-century Arthur had been born at Tintagel Castle—but there was no castle at Tintagel until the first Earl of Cornwall built one in the early 12th century. Previously there had been only a ruined Celtic monastery on the site.

Another misappropriation of the Pendragon's son was manifest in Wales and the tradition persists today. There actually was an Arthur in 6th-century Wales—in fact, he was the only other royal Arthur of the era, but he was not the son of a Pendragon and he was not the Arthur of Grail lore. This other Arthur was installed as Prince of Dyfed by St. Dubricius in 506, even though he and his forebears were enemies of the native Welsh. He was descended from disinherited Déisi royalty, expelled from Ireland in the late 4th century. When the Roman troops left South Wales in AD 383, the Déisi leaders came from Leinster to settle in Dyfed (Demetia). Arthur, Prince of Dyfed, features as a notorious tyrant in *The Lives of the Saints* (in the tales of Carannog and others) and he is generally portrayed as a troublesome regional interloper.

In Arthurian romance, the confusion between the Scots and Welsh Arthurs arose mainly because of the Merlin connection. As we have seen, Merlin Emrys was the son of Aurelius. But Aurelius' wife was Arthur of Dyfed's sister, Niniane. Aurelius had married her in an effort to curtail the Déisi invasions of Powys, but his strategy was short-lived. This, of course, meant that Merlin Emrys was Arthur of Dyfed's nephew while, at the same time, he was a cousin to the Pendragon Aedàn mac Gabràn and was the appointed guardian of Aedàn's son, Arthur of Dalriada.

According to the 10th-century *Annales Cambriae* (Annals of Wales), Arthur perished at the Battle of Camlann—but to which Arthur do the annals refer? Certainly not to Arthur of Dalriada for he was recorded in Scotland after that event. The 15th-century *Red Book of Hergest* (a collection of Welsh folk-tales) states that the Battle of Camlann was fought in 537, and the probable location was Maes Camlan, south of Dinas Mawddwy. If so, then it is quite possible that Arthur of Dyfed fought there. He was renowned for leading incursions into both

Gwynedd and Powys. What is certain, however, is that Arthur of Dalriada fought a later battle at Camelon, west of Falkirk. The *Chronicles of the Picts and Scots* refer to this northern conflict as the Battle of Camelyn. He also fought subsequently at Camlanna (or Camboglanna) by Hadrian's Wall—the battle which led to his demise.

As for Geoffrey of Monmouth, he decided to ignore all the geographical locations, siting his fanciful battle by the River Camel in Cornwall. Geoffrey also associated the Irish battle of Badon Hill (Dun Baedàn) with a battle at Bath, because the latter place had once been known as Badanceaster.

In the *Life of Saint Columba*, Abbot Adamnan related that, in the late 500s, King Aedàn of Scots had consulted St. Columba about his due successor in Dalriada, asking, 'Which of [my] three sons is to reign: Arthur, or Eochaid Find, or Domingart?' Columba replied,

> None of these three will be ruler, for they will fall
> in battle, slain by enemies; but now if thou hast
> any other younger sons, let them come to me.

A fourth son, Eochaid Buide, was summoned and the saint blessed him, saying to Aedàn, 'This is thy survivor'. Adamnan's account continues:

> And thus it was that afterwards, in their season, all
> things were completely fulfilled; for Arthur and
> Eochaid Find were slain after no long interval of
> time in the Battle of the Miathi. Domingart was
> killed in Saxonia; and Eochaid Buide succeeded to
> the kingdom after his father.

The Miathi (as mentioned by Adamnan) were a tribe of Britons who settled in two separate groups, north of the Antonine and Hadrian Walls respectively. The Antonine Wall extended between the Firth of Forth and the Clyde estuary. Hadrian's Wall traversed the lower land between the Solway Firth and Tynemouth. In 559, the Angles had occupied Deira (Yorkshire) and had driven the Miathi northwards. By 574, the Angles had also pushed up into Northumbrian Bernicia. Some of the Miathi decided to stay by the lower Wall and make the best of it, while others moved further north to settle beyond the upper Wall.

The main stronghold of the northern Miathi was at Dunmyat, on the border of modern Clackmannanshire, in the district of Manau on the Forth. Here, they had cast their lot with the Irish settlers, which made them none too popular with the Scots and Welsh. Despite King Cairill's 516 Badon Hill defeat in Antrim, the Irish remained boisterously obstructive in Manau. Consequently, the Guletic forces made another incursion into Ulster in 575.

This second assault at Dun Baedàn is the one mentioned by Nennius, who rightly described Arthur's presence, whereas the Gildas account relates to the earlier 516 battle and correctly gives Ambrosius Aurelius as the commander. Nennius gives Arthur rather more credit than his due, however, for on this second occasion the Scots were defeated and Arthur's father, King Aedàn, was obliged to submit to Prince Baedàn mac Cairill at Ros-na-Rig on Belfast Lough.[2]

Following King Baedàn mac Cairill's death in 581, Aedàn of Scots finally managed to expel the Irish from Manau and the Forth. Later, in 596, Arthur's cavalry drove the Irish out of Scots Brecknock. King Aedàn was present at the battles, but Arthur's younger brothers Brân and Domingart were killed at Brechin on the Plain of Circinn.

In confronting the Irish at Manau, the Guletic troops also had to face the Miathi Britons. They were successful in driving many of them back to their southern territory, but those who remained when the Guletic troops departed had to contend with the Picts, who promptly moved into their domain. By the end of the century, the Picts and Miathi were united against the Scots, whom they met at the Battle of Camelyn, north of the Antonine Wall. Once again the Scots were victorious and the Picts were driven northwards. Afterwards, a nearby ironworks foundry construction was dubbed *Furnus Arthuri* (Arthur's Fire) to mark the event. It was a long-standing attraction and was not demolished until the 18th-century Industrial Revolution.

Three years after Camelyn, the Scots faced the southern Miathi and the Northumbrian Angles. This confrontation was a protracted affair fought on two battlegrounds—the second conflict resulting from a short-term Scots retreat from the first. The forces initially met at Camlanna, an old Roman hill-fort by Hadrian's Wall. Unlike the previous encounter, however, the Battle of Camlanna was a complete fiasco for the Scots. Falling for a diversionary tactic by the Miathi, the Scots allowed the Angles to move behind them in a concerted north-westerly push towards Galloway and Strathclyde. The unlucky definition of a *Cath Camlanna* has been applied to many a lost battle thereafter.

Only a few months earlier, the Angle king, Aethelfrith of Bernicia, had defeated King Rhydderch at Carlisle, thereby acquiring new territory along the reaches of the Solway. The Dalriadan forces under

Aedàn and Arthur were therefore under some pressure to intercept and halt the Angles' northward advance. They were said to have assembled immense forces, drawn from the ranks of the Welsh princes and they even gained support from Maeluma mac Baedàn of Antrim, the son of their erstwhile enemy. By that time, the Irish were themselves daunted by the prospect of an Anglo-Saxon invasion.

Modred and Morgaine

It is important to note that King Aedàn was a Celtic Church Christian of the Sacred Kindred of St. Columba. Indeed, the Dalriadans were generally associated with the Sacred Kindred, which was distinctly grounded in the Nazarene tradition, but incorporated some customary druidic and pagan ritual.

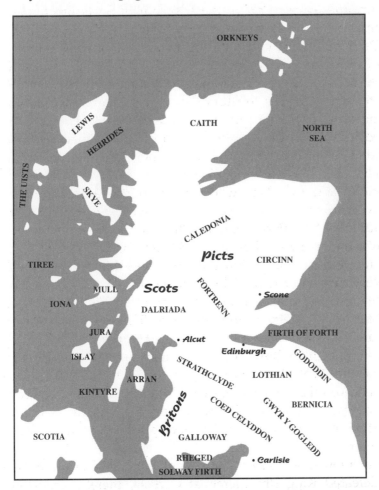

Early Scotland (Caledonia and Dalriada)

Arthur, however, became obsessed with Roman Christianity, to the extent that he began to regard his Guletic cavalry as a holy army. This disposition led to considerable disturbance within the Celtic Church for Arthur was, after all, destined to be the next King of Scots. The elders were particularly worried that he might try to implement a Romanized kingdom in Dalriada and it was on this account that Arthur made an enemy of his own son Modred, Archpriest of the Sacred Kindred. Modred was an associate of the Saxon King Cerdic of Elmet (the West Riding of Yorkshire) and Cerdic was allied to Aethelfrith of Bernicia. It was not difficult, therefore, to persuade Modred to oppose his father on the battlefield and to ally himself with the Angles in his bid to save the Scots kingdom from losing its ancient druidic heritage.

And so it was that, when the Scots faced the Angles and Miathi at Camlanna in 603, Aedàn and Arthur found themselves not only against King Aethelfrith, but also against their own Prince Modred. The initial affray at Camlanna was short-lived and the Celtic troops were obliged to chase after the Angles, who had swept past them. They caught up again at Dawston-on-Solway (then called Degsastan in Liddesdale) and the *Chronicles of Holyrood* and *of Melrose* refer to the battle site as Dexa Stone. Archpriest Modred's appearance with the invaders severely downcast the Celtic spirits and it was here that Arthur (aged forty-four) fell alongside Maeluma mac Baedàn.

The battle, which began at Camlanna and ended at Dawston, was one of the fiercest in Celtic history. The *Tigernach Annals* call it 'the day when half the men of Scotland fell'. Although Aethelfrith was victorious, heavy losses were sustained by all. His brothers Theobald and Eanfrith were slain, along with all their men and King Aedàn fled the field having lost two sons, Arthur and Eochaid Find, along with his grandson, Archpriest Modred.

Aethelfrith never reached Strathclyde, but his success at Dawston enabled the Northumbrian territory to be extended northwards to the Firth of Forth, incorporating the Lothians. Ten years later, in 613, Aethelfrith besieged Chester and brought Cumbria fully under Angle control. This drove a permanent geographical wedge between the Welsh and the Strathclyde Britons. The Mercian Angles then pushed westwards, forcing the Welsh behind what was eventually to be the line of Offa's Dyke, while the Wessex Saxons encroached beyond Exeter, annexing the south-west peninsula.

In time, the once conjoined Celtic lands of Wales, Strathclyde and Dumnonia (Devon and Cornwall) were totally isolated from each other and the Kindred of St. Columba blamed it all on Arthur. He had failed in his duties as Guletic and High King. His father, King Aedàn of Dalriada, died within five years of the Camlanna disaster, which was said to have opened the door to the final conquest of Britain by the Anglo-Saxons. The days of Celtic lordship were done and, after more than six centuries of tradition, Cadwaladr of Wales (twenty-sixth in line from Joseph of Arimathea) was the last Pendragon.

In the wake of Arthur's defeats at Camlanna and Dawston (jointly called *di Bellum Miathorum*: the Battle of the Miathi), the old kingdoms of the North existed no more. The Scots, who were physically separated from their former allies in Wales, perceived that their only route towards saving the land of Alba (Scotland) was to become allied with the Picts of Caledonia. This was achieved in 844, when Aedàn's famed descendant, King Kenneth MacAlpin, united the Picts and Scots as one nation.[3] The records of Kenneth's installation support his truly important position in the family line by referring to him as a descendant of the Queens of Avallon.

Had Modred survived he would undoubtedly have become Pendragon, for he was a great favourite of the Druids and the Celtic Church. Arthur's mother, Ygerna, was the elder sister of Morgause, who married Lot of Lothian, the ruler of Orkney. Lot and Morgause were the parents of the Orkney brothers Gawain, Gaheries and Gareth. Morgause was also, (like Ygerna) a younger sister of Viviane II, the consort of King Ban le Benoic,[4] a desposynic descendant of Faramund and the Fisher Kings. Viviane and Ban were the parents of Lancelot del Acqs.

On the death of her first husband, the Dux of Carlisle, Ygerna married Aedàn of Dalriada, thereby legitimating Arthur before his titles were bestowed. By way of this union, the lineages of Jesus and James/Joseph of Arimathea were combined in Arthur for the first time in about 350 years—which is why, despite his shortcomings, he became so important to the Grail tradition.

Arthur's maternal grandmother, Viviane I, was the dynastic Queen of Avallon, a kinswoman of the Merovingian kings. His aunt, Viviane II, was the official Keeper of Celtic Mysticism and this heritage fell, in due course, to Ygerna's daughter, Morgaine. Arthur was married to Gwenhwyfar of Brittany, but she bore him no children. On the other hand, he did father Modred by Morgaine. Old Registers, such as the *Promptuary of Cromarty,* suggest that Arthur also had a daughter called Tortolina, but she was actually his granddaughter (the daughter of Modred). Arthur's half-sister Morgaine (alternatively known as Morganna or Morgan le Faye) was married to King Urien of Rheged and Gowrie (Goure)[5] who, in Arthurian romance, is called Urien of

Gore. Their son was Ywain, founder of the Breton House de Léon d'Acqs, who held the rank of Comte (Count). In her own right, Morgaine was a Holy Sister of Avallon and a Celtic High Priestess. She is referred to in Royal Irish Academy texts as 'Muirgein, daughter of Aedàn in Belach Gabráin'.

Writers have sometimes considered Arthur's sexual relationship with his half-sister Morgaine to be incestuous, but this was not the way it was regarded in Celtic Britain. At that time, the anciently perceived dual nature of God prevailed, as did the equally ancient concept of the sacred sister-bride. In this regard, the prayer of the Celts began, 'Our Father-Mother in the heavens' and, in conjunction with this, specifically defined rites were performed to denote the mortal incarnation of the dual 'male-female' entity. As the earthly manifestation of the goddess Cerridwin, Morgaine represented the female aspect, while Arthur, as her half-brother from the same mother, was her true male counterpart in the established tradition of the pharaohs.

At the May festival of Beltane, Arthur was apprehended as a god in human form and was obliged to participate in a ritual of sacred intercourse between the twin aspects of the incarnate Father-Mother. In view of Arthur and Morgaine's presumed divinity during this rite, any male offspring from the union would be deemed the Celtic Christ and would be duly anointed as such. By virtue of this, although Arthur was destined to become the prominent subject of romantic history, it was his son Modred who held the highest spiritual position; he was the designated Christ of Britain, the ordained Archpriest of the Sacred Kindred and an anointed Fisher King.

In his maturity, Arthur upheld the Roman tradition, but it was Archpriest Modred who strove to amalgamate the old Celtic teachings with those of the Christian Church, treating both Druids and Christian priests on an equal basis. It was this essential difference between father and son that drove them against each other. Arthur became significantly Romanized, whereas Modred upheld religious toleration in the true nature of Grail kingship. Despite the extraordinary success of Arthur's early career, his eventual Catholic leaning caused him to betray his Celtic Oath of Allegiance. As High King of the Britons he was supposed to be the Defender of Faith but, instead, he imposed specific ritual upon the people. When he and Modred perished in 603, Arthur's death was not mourned by the Celtic Church, but he will never be forgotten. His kingdom fell because he forsook the codes of loyalty and service. His ultimate neglect facilitated the completion of the Saxon conquest and his knights will roam the wasteland until the Grail is returned. Contrary to all myth and legend, it was the dying Archpriest Modred (not Arthur) who was carried from the field by his mother Morgaine's Holy Sisters.

The Holy Sisters

In Geoffrey of Monmouth's *Historia*, Morgan le Faye's nine Holy Sisters are cited as guardians of the Isle of Avalon. As far back as the 1st century, the geographer Pomponius Mela had similarly written of nine mysterious priestesses living under vows of chastity on the Isle of Sein, off the Brittany coast near Carnac. Mela told of their powers to heal the sick and foretell the future, in much the way that Morgaine del Acqs was a Celtic High Priestess with prophetic and medicinal powers. The Roman Church, however, would not tolerate such attributes in a woman and, because of this, the Cistercian monks were obliged to transform Morgan le Faye's image in the Arthurian Vulgate Cycle.

The Cistercians were closely identified with the Knights Templars of Jerusalem and Grail lore was born directly from the Templar environment. The Counts of Alsace, Champagne and Léon (with whom writers like Chrétien de Troyes were associated) all had affiliations with the Order, but the Catholic Church still held sway in the public domain. Consequently, women were afforded no rights to fulfil any ecclesiastical or sacred function and, to this end, from the middle 1200s, Morgaine (dynastic heiress and Celtic holy sister of Avallon) was portrayed as Morganna the malevolent sorceress. In the English poem *Gawain and the Green Knight* (written in around 1380), it is the jealous Morganna who transforms Sir Bercilak into the Green Giant in order to frighten Guinevere.

In a manner similar to the matriarchal practice of the Picts, Morgaine's Avallonian dynasty was perpetuated in the female line. The difference was that the Queens' daughters held the senior positions, rather than their sons — thus the honour was eternally female in concept. Originating from the same lineage of Jesus, the nominal Queens of Avallon, in Burgundy, emerged alongside the Merovingian kings, while other important offshoots were the male lines of the Septimanian and Burgundian royal successions.

Morgaine's son Ywain (Eógain) founded the noble house of Léon d'Acqs in Brittany and the later arms of Léon bore the black Davidic Lion on a gold shield (in heraldic terms: 'Or, a lion rampant, sable'). The province was itself so named because *léon* was Septimanian —

Spanish for 'lion'. The English spelling appeared in the 12th century as a variant of the Anglo-French *liun*. Until the 14th century, the Scots Lord Lyon, King of Arms, was still called the *Léon Héraud*.

In some books, it is suggested that Ywain's son, Comte Withur de Léon d'Acqs (often corrupted to d'Ak), is synonymous with Uther Pendragon because of the similarity of their first names. But actually Withur was a Basque name, derived from the Irish *Witur*, whose Cornish equivalent was *Gwythyr*. It was not related to *Uther* which, as previously mentioned, derived from a Gaelic adjective meaning 'terrible'. The Comité (County) of Léon was established in about 530 at the time of the Breton King Hoel I. He was of Welsh Arimatheac descent and his sister Alienor was Ywain's wife.

At that time, there were two levels of authority in Brittany. In the course of a protracted immigration from Britain, Breton Dumnonia had been founded in 520, but it was not a kingdom as such. There emerged a line of kings such as Hoel, but they were not Kings of Brittany, they were Kings of the immigrant Bretons. Throughout this period, the region remained a Merovingian province and the local kings were subordinate to Frankish authority by appointed Counts styled the *Comites non regis*. The supreme Frankish Lord of Brittany 540-544 was Chonomore, a native of the Frankish State with Merovingian authority to oversee the development of Brittany by the settlers. Chonomore's forebears were Mayors of the Palace of Neustria and he was the hereditary Comte de Pohor. In time, the descendants of Ywain's aunt Viviane II became overall Counts of Brittany.

Brittany features prominently in Arthurian romance. At Paimpont, about 30 miles (*c*.48 kilometres) from Rennes, is the enchanted Forest of Broceliande, from which stretches the Valley of No Return, where Morganna confined her lovers. Also to be found are the magic Spring of Barenton and Merlin's Garden of Joy, although most of the stories of Broceliande were actually transposed from far earlier accounts of the historical Merlin Emrys in the Caledonian Forest of Scotland.

Isle of Avalon

As indicated in Geoffrey of Monmouth's romance, Avalon was traditionally associated with the magical Otherworld. It was here that the legendary Arthur was tended by the maidens in his eternal abode. Morgan le Faye promised to heal Arthur's wounds if he would remain on the Isle and nothing was ever said of his death. The implication was, therefore, that Arthur might one day return.

When Geoffrey wrote his story, he was clearly unaware of the furore it would cause. Not only was the the account inaccurate in many respects, but he had suggested a possible Second Coming of the King. This, along with the sacred powers he attributed to women, was quite unacceptable to the Roman Church and the later writer, Sir Thomas Malory, took a route of compromise. He simply had Bedevere place the wounded Arthur in a barge full of women who would transport him to Avalon. Then Bedevere walked through the forest and came upon a chapel in which Arthur's body had been interred.

Although Geoffrey's Avalon was based on the Otherworld of Celtic tradition (A-val or Avilion), his interpretation was more related to Classical writings about the Fortunate Islands, where the fruit was self-tending and the people immortal. In mythological terms, such places were always 'beyond the western sea'. At no point did any of the early writers identify a location for the mystic Isle; it did not have to be anywhere in particular — certainly not within the mortal domain, for its enchantment was that of an eternal paradise. In literal terms, however, it was associated with the history of Burgundian Avallon and the Ladies of the Lake — the Viviane queens of the House del Acqs.

All of this changed in 1191, when the Isle of Avalon was suddenly identified with Glastonbury in Somerset. The definition of this inland location as an island was justified on the basis that Glastonbury stood amid watery marshland and the nearby lake-villages of Godney and Meare dated from about 200 BC. Nevertheless, because of the geographical anomaly, the name Vale of Avalon became a popular alternative. Prior to this date there had been no recognized connection between Arthur and Glastonbury, except for a passing mention by Cardoc of Llancarfan.[6] He wrote, in 1140, that the Abbot of Glastonbury had been instrumental in Gwynefer's release from King Melwas of Somerset, but he did not suggest that Glastonbury was Avalon — neither did anyone else.

What happened in 1191 was that the monks of Glastonbury made use of Arthurian tradition in a manner that would truly impress today's marketing specialists. Some writers have since labelled their actions an outright fraud, while others have tried to make the case that the monks were themselves deluded by circumstance. Whatever the truth of the matter, they not only saved their Abbey from extinction, but gave birth to a whole new Glastonbury tradition. The Abbey had been badly damaged by fire in 1184 and King Henry II began to fund the reconstruction. When he died in 1189, his son Richard I came to the throne, but he was more concerned with applying Treasury resources to the Holy Land Crusade. As a result, the Glastonbury funding was terminated, leaving the Abbot and his monks penniless. So what did they do but dig a hole between a couple of Saxon monuments south of the Lady Chapel where, to the amazement of all, they found the supposed remains of King Arthur and Queen Guinevere!

Some 16 feet (*c.*4.8 metres) below ground, in a hollowed oak canoe, they unearthed the bones of a tall man, along with some smaller bones and a tress of golden hair. Such a find was of little consequence in its own right, but the monks were in luck, for not far above the log coffin there was said to have been a leaden cross embedded in stone. Upon the cross was inscribed *Hic Iacet Sepultus Inclytus Rex Arthurius In Insula Avallonia Cum Uxore Sua Secunda Wenneveria* (Here lies interred the renowned King Arthur in the Isle of Avalon with his second wife Guinevere). Not only had they found Arthur's grave but they had also conveniently found written proof that Glastonbury was the Isle of Avalon!

However, the Roman Church officials were far from happy that Guinevere was described as the king's second wife and it was asserted that the inscription was obviously incorrect.[7] This posed something of an immediate problem but, soon afterwards the legend reappeared, miraculously changed in spelling and format. This time it dispensed with Guinevere altogether, so that it was far more in keeping with requirement: *Hic Iacet Sepultus Inclitus Rex Arturius In Insula Avalonia* (Here lies interred the renowned King Arthur in the Isle of Avalon).

Quite why the monks should have dug in that particular spot is unclear—and even if they did find the bones as stated, there was nothing to associate them with King Arthur. The identification came only from the inscription on the leaden cross, yet the Latin was plainly of the Middle Ages, differing from Arthurian Latin to the extent that today's English differs from that of Tudor times.

Whatever the facts, the monks' purpose was well served and, following a successful publicity campaign, pilgrims flocked in their thousands to Glastonbury. The Abbey was substantially enriched with their donations and the complex was rebuilt as planned. As for the alleged bones of Arthur and Guinevere, they were deposited in two painted chests and placed in a black marble tomb before the high altar.

The entombed remains proved to be such a popular attraction that the monks determined to benefit further from their new-found tourist trap. It was apparent that if Arthur's bones created such a stir, then the relics of a saint or two would have a significant impact. So they took to their spades once more and, very soon, other discoveries were announced: the bones of St. Patrick and St. Gildas, along with the remains of Archbishop Dunstan, which most people knew had lain at Canterbury Cathedral for 200 years!

By the time of Henry VIII's dissolution of the monasteries, Glastonbury Abbey was boasting dozens of relics, including a thread from Mary's gown, a sliver from Aaron's rod and a stone that Jesus had refused to turn into bread. At the dissolution though, the Abbey's days of monastic activity were done and the said relics disappeared without trace. Since that time, no one has seen the supposed bones of Arthur and Guinevere; all that remains is a notice marking the site of the tomb. To many people, nonetheless, Glastonbury will always be associated with Avalon. Some prefer Geoffrey's idea of Tintagel, while others stake their claims on Bardsey or Holy Island. Yet, apart from the reality of Avallon in Burgundy, it is plain that the Celtic Otherworld was a mythical realm, with a tradition dating back beyond record.

If the mystic Isle existed within the mortal plane, then it was akin to that eternal paradise which the pre-Goidelic Fir Bolg tribe called Arunmore. From Connacht in Ireland, the Fir Bolg installed their King Oengus mac Umóir, on the timeless island haven in the ancient days BC. It was to this place that the warriors fled after their defeat by the Tuatha Dé Danann at the legendary battle of Magh Tuireadh.[8] The Enchanted Isle was said to lie in the sea between Antrim and Lethet (the stretch of land between the Clyde and the Forth). Arunmore was the Isle of Arran, the traditional home of Manannan, the sea-god. Arran was also called Emain Ablach (the place of apples)[9] and this association was perpetuated in the *Life of Merlin*, which referred specifically to the *Insula Pomoru* — the Isle of Apples.

Intrigue Against the Bloodline

The Evolving Church

Having been separated from the Byzantine Church, the Church of Rome developed the theme of the Apostles' Creed sometime after the year 600. Passages were incorporated that are still familiar today: God became 'the maker of heaven and earth' and, in a thoroughly non-biblical portrayal, Jesus (having suffered under Pontius Pilate) 'descended into hell', before rising on the third day. The Creed also, at this time, introduced the concept of the Holy Catholic Church and the Communion of Saints.

During the 6th and 7th centuries, the supposedly heretical Nestorian belief spread into Persia, Iraq and southern India—even as far east as China, where missionaries arrived at the Imperial Court of the T'ang Emperor T'ai-tsung in 635. He was so inspired by the new doctrine that he had the Nestorian Creed translated into Chinese and sanctioned the building of a commemorative church and monastery. Nearly a century and a half later, in 781, a monument in honour of Nestorius was erected at Sian-fu.

In the meantime, the Arians—who also denied Jesus's divinity—had gained a very strong foothold in European society. Christian history generally uses the term 'barbarian' to describe Arians such as the Goths, Visigoths (West Goths), Ostrogoths (East Goths), Vandals (Wends), Lombards and Burgundians, but the description refers to no more than cultural differences; it does not mean these peoples were heathen ruffians. The open hostility of the said barbarians towards Rome and Byzantium was no more barbaric than the Romans' own savage empire-building and was, for the most part, more defensive than aggressive. Although once wholly pagan (as indeed were the Romans themselves), these tribes had, in large measure, become followers of Arius during the 4th century. From Spain and Southern France, through to the Ukraine, most of Germanic Europe was Arian Christian in the 600s.

Madonna of the Magnificat—Sandro Botticelli (1445-1510).
Jesus clutches the ripe, open pomegranate of fertility.

Conquest of Jerusalem by the Romans—Nicolas Poussin (1594-1665).
Invasion by the troops of General Titus in AD 70.

Sposalizio della Vergine—The betrothal of Mary and Joseph—Raphael (1483-1520).
A younger than normally portrayed Joseph, despite the conventions of his depiction.

The Last Supper—Jean-Baptiste de Champaigne (1631-81).

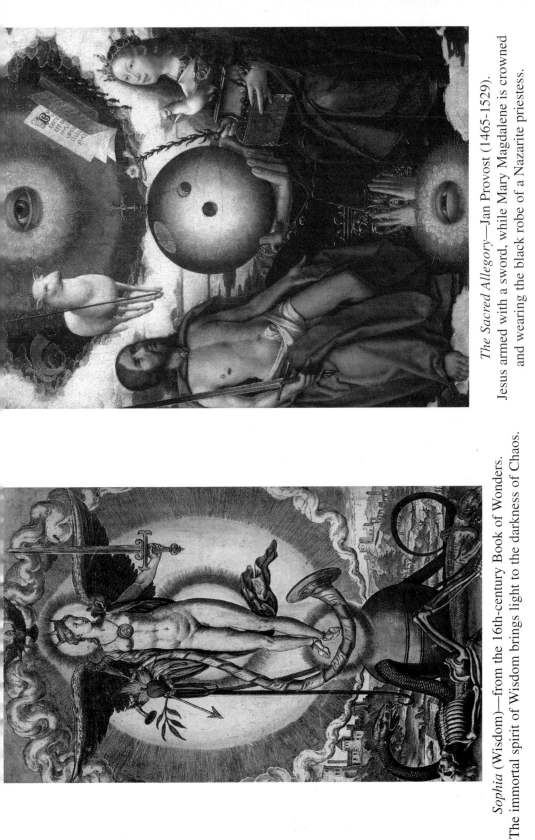

Sophia (Wisdom)—from the 16th-century Book of Wonders.
The immortal spirit of Wisdom brings light to the darkness of Chaos.

The Sacred Allegory—Jan Provost (1465-1529).
Jesus armed with a sword, while Mary Magdalene is crowned and wearing the black robe of a Nazarite priestess.

Mary Magdalene in Provence—Nertherlandish, 16th century.
Mary wears the red cape of the sacred hierodulai, as denied by the Roman Church.

Christ at the House of Mary and Martha—Tintoretto, c.1575.
Mary Magdalene anoints the feet of Jesus at the Hieros Gamos.

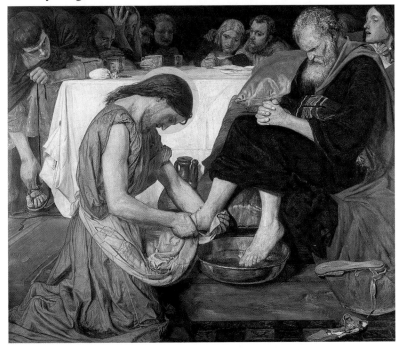

Jesus Washing Peter's Feet at the Last Supper—Ford Maddox Brown, c.1865.
Embodiment of the Grail Code of Service.

Leap of Faith—Sir Peter Robson, 1996.
Allegory of the Crucifixion and Resurrection.

The Rest on the Flight into Egypt (detail)—Gerard David, 1510.
A defiance of the 'blue and white only' regulation concerning Mary, showing a glimpse of cardinal red and the grapes of the Grail vine.

The Wine Press—John Spencer Stanhope, 1864.
Jesus: "I am the true vine" (John 15:1).

Mary Magdalene Carried by the Angels—Giovanni Lanfranco (1582-1647).
Allegory of the expectant Mary's AD 44 flight into Europe.

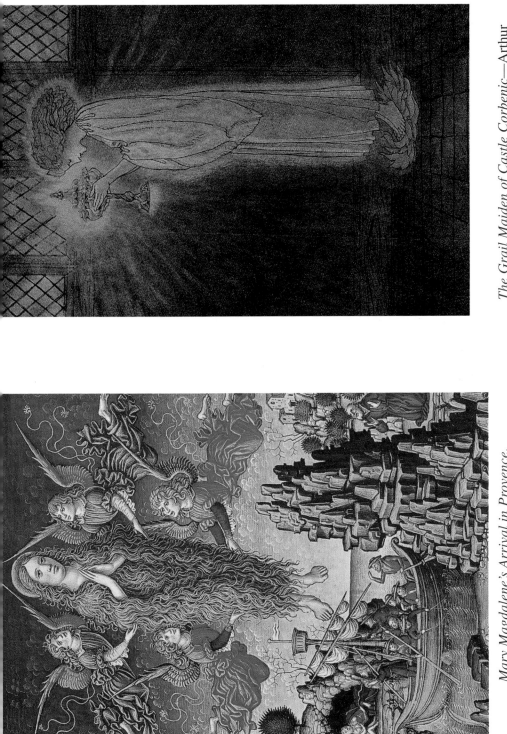

The Grail Maiden of Castle Corbenic—Arthur Rackham (1867-1939).

Mary Magdalene's Arrival in Provence. From the 1490 *Sforza Book of Hours.*

King Clovis of the Merovingian Franks—William H. Rainey (1852-1936).

Sir Galahad—The Quest—Arthur Hughes, 1870.

The Accolade—Edmund Blair-Leighton, 1901.
Grail Queen and Sir Knight of the Splendid Way.

Bloodline of the Holy Grail

Allegory of the conflict between the Grail Church
and the Imperial Roman establishment.

Joan of Arc and the Sword of Deliverance—Dante Gabriel Rossetti, 1863.
Integration of the Grail's lily symbolism is apparent.

The Birth of Venus—Sandro Botticelli, c.1485.
Incorporating the Aphrodite scallop shell of Marie de la Mer.

'Y gwyr erbyn y Byd'—Truth Against the World—Sir Peter Robson, 1996.
The battle cry of Queen Boudicca.

The Arthurian Round Table—Walter Crane (1845-1915).

Galahad, Bors and Perceval are fed with the Sanct Grael—
Dante Gabriel Rossetti (1828-82).

Another doctrine which had, to some extent, become associated with the Nestorians and Arians was a remnant of the 4th-century cult of Priscillian of Avila. His alternative Christian movement had begun in north-western Spain and had made significant inroads into Aquitaine. Fundamental to the Priscillian belief — which came out of Egypt, Syria and Mesopotamia — was the mortality of the Blessed Mary, as against her semi-divine image in the Roman Church. Priscillian had been executed in AD 386 at Trier (north of Metz), although his body was later transferred for burial in Spain.[1]

In view of these widespread alternatives to orthodox Christianity, it is quite apparent that the Catholic Church was far from paramount in the West. Catholicism was surrounded and infused with various other forms of the faith. However, they were generally based on Judaic traditions, rather than on the Pauline concept which had been adopted and revised by Rome. With the exception of some spiritually-based factions within the Gnostic movement, they retained beliefs akin to the *Desposyni* tradition, promoting the Nazarene doctrine of Jesus's own humanity and preaching his message rather than venerating his person.

In parallel with the ceremonial structure of the Roman Church, a scholarly sect evolved on the fringe of Catholicism. It was a monastic movement (fronted by Martin of Tours) which denied the episcopacy and was based on ancient Egyptian and generally Eastern concepts. The Essene society at Qumrân had lived a solemn, regulated existence — a style of religious discipline that had been perpetuated in desert regions. This same austere seclusion, essential to the monastic existence whether applied to small communities or ascetic hermits (*eremoi*), was entirely appropriate to a life of study and contemplation.

The monastic pioneer St. Martin (*c.*AD 316-397) is perhaps best remembered for dividing his cloak to share it with a naked beggar. Originally from Pannonia, Martin was a successful soldier in the Imperial Army before he settled in Poitiers and established Gaul's first great monastery at Marmoutier. In about AD 371 he was appointed Bishop of Tours, but continued his monastic existence. Later he was to become a patron saint of France.

One of the early missionaries from Europe to the British Isles was St. Germannus d'Auxerre, who visited Britain in the 5th century, and was the teacher of Ireland's St. Patrick. The son of a Celtic church deacon, Patrick had been captured as a boy by pirates. After some time in slavery, he had escaped to Gaul, where he was trained as a missionary at the monasteries of Lérins and Auxerre. Then in AD 431 he returned to Britain, and began his mission in Northumbria.

Patrick's teachings were different in many respects from those of Rome, and his writings indicate a distinct tendency towards Arian and Nestorian traditions. He was not at all popular with the Catholic Church—indeed, its governors stated definitively that he was quite unsuited to the priesthood. Patrick relied solely on the scriptures for his teaching. He had no time for the contrived authority of Roman bishops, for he was much more concerned with the fraternity of the opposing Celtic Church.

One of the foremost figures in the establishment of European monasteries was St. Benedict (c.AD 480-544). Initially a native of Spoleto in Italy, Benedict took up residence in a remote forest-cave near Rome. He later found a far more congenial retreat on the beautiful Monte Cassino (a prominent hill between Rome and Naples) at what was in fact an old temple site of Apollo. The pagan location was hardly to the liking of the Catholic bishops, but Benedict was soon joined by a large following of disciples, from whose number emerged Gregory the Great, Bishop of Rome 590-604.[2] In a fairly short space of time, the Benedictine group attained some considerable influence in political affairs—especially in their efforts to reconcile the Goths with the warlike Lombards of Italy.

The Order of St. Benedict promoted pious reverence, the strict observance of prayer times, and common ownership within a monastic environment of learning under the supervision of a resident abbot. In due course Benedict founded twelve monasteries, each housing twelve monks, and is generally regarded as the Father of monastic orders in Western Christendom. From those early times, the Benedictines were largely responsible for maintaining high standards of education, and of sacred art and music in Europe. This era of the evolving Benedictine Order marks the beginning of what is sometimes called the Age of Saints—an age which, in the Roman Catholic tradition, may be said still to be in progress.

While the Roman Church was busily concerned with dogma and ecclesiastical structure, the Celtic Church was showing an interest in the hearts and minds of the people. By 597, Celtic Christianity was so widespread that Bishop Gregory of Rome sent the Benedictine monk, Augustine, to England specifically to establish the Roman Church more firmly in that country. His arrival was deliberately timed to follow the death that year of the prominent Father of the Sacred Kindred, the gentle St. Columba. Augustine began his work in South-eastern England—in Kent to be precise—where the local King Aethelbert's wife was already a confirmed Catholic. In 601, Augustine was proclaimed the first Archbishop of Canterbury and, two years later, he attempted to become Primate of the Celtic Church as well. However, such an endeavour could only fail against an establishment that remained far more Nazarene than Roman. Indeed, Augustine's plan was not for a unification of Churches, but for the strategic subjugation of a traditional Church which Rome had declared more or less heretical.

It was not until 664, at the Synod of Whitby in North Yorkshire, that Rome achieved the first doctrinal victory over the Celtic Church. The main debate concerned the date of Easter, for the Chief Pontiff of the day had decided that Easter should no longer be formally associated with the Jewish Passover. Against all prevailing custom and against all Celtic tradition, the Catholic bishops succeeded in getting their own way—so displacing for all time the historic Jewish and Celtic ties. Traditionally, however, Britain's Easter festival was not a Passover celebration in the Jewish style, neither was it anything to do with Jesus. Easter (in both name and season) actually represented Eostre, the goddess of Spring, whose feast-day was observed long before any association with Christianity.

Following the Synod, the Catholic Church increased its strength in Britain, but the Celtic Church could not be suppressed without an open declaration of war against Ireland. However, the days of Roman Imperialism were over and no army that the Roman Church could muster would ever defeat the fierce troops of the Irish kings. The Celtic Church, consequently, remained very active in Britain and the Sacred Kindred of St. Columba eventually became the ecclesiastical seat of the Kings of Scots.

Through all this, the Bishop of Rome's biggest problem was his inability to gain supremacy over the royal houses of Celtic Britain. Rome had seen a measure of potential success with the conversion of King Arthur, but Arthur had been killed and the Druid style Nazarene heritage remained firm through the successors of his half-brother Eochaid Buide. Shortly after Eochaid's accession, Bishop Boniface IV adopted the new Roman style of Pope (Papa) in 610, as an alternative to being called a 'bridge-builder' (pontiff). This was a blatant and positive attempt to compete with the long-standing Celtic distinction of Father, inherited from the Essene tradition. But when the new papal supremacy was tested on Dianothus, Abbot of Bangor, he responded that neither he nor his colleagues recognized any such authority. They were prepared, he said, to acknowledge the Church of God, 'but as for other obedience, we know of none that he whom you term the Pope (or Bishop of Bishops) can demand'. A local letter written to the Abbot of Iona in 634 referred unequivocally to St. Patrick (the prevailing Father) as 'Our Pope'.

Over the centuries, various attempts were made to deny the priestly and patriarchal heritage of the Celtic Church (which was more than authoritative enough to cause concern in the Vatican).[3] Roman Catholic holy orders were supposed to rely on Apostolic Succession, but no such succession could be proved, for the Apostle Peter (on whom the succession supposedly hinged) had never held any formal office. The first appointed Bishop of Rome was Britain's Prince Linus (son of Caractacus the Pendragon) and, as recorded in the Church's own *Apostolic Constitutions*, Linus began the true succession, having been installed by St. Paul during Peter's lifetime in AD 58.

Later, in AD 180, Irenaeus, Bishop of Lyon, wrote, 'The Apostles having founded and built up the Church at Rome, committed the ministry of its supervision to Linus'. In attempts to veil the royal heritage of Linus, he has often been portrayed as if he were a lowly slave, but this has not removed the thorn from the Church's side and, because of it, the papal doctrine has to be considered 'infallible' when emanating from the throne. Without this doctrine, the whole concept of a structured progression of high bishops in Apostolic succession from Peter would collapse, since Peter was never a Bishop of Rome, neither of anywhere else.

Bishop Theodosius attempted to forge an Apostolic link in 820, when he announced that the remains of James Boanerges (St. James the Greater) had been unearthed at Compostela in Spain. In 899 the resultant shrine to Sant Iago (St. James) became a great cathedral, later to be destroyed by the Moors in 997, and rebuilt in 1078. But it was common knowledge from the New Testament that James Boanerges (the brother of John) was executed in Jerusalem by Herod of Chalcis in AD 44 (Acts 12:2). Therefore, the bones that had been discovered (if genuinely belonging to a James at all) were more likely those of the disciple James Cleophas, who came to the West with his wife Mary Jacob on the Magdalene voyage. Even this is something of a remote possibility, however, and it has been not unconvincingly suggested that the relics and the later heritage of Santiago di Compostela more likely belong to Priscillian of Avila.

Schism in Christianity

Rome's final split with the Eastern Church occurred in 867, when the latter announced that it maintained the true Apostolic Succession. The First Vatican Council disagreed and so Photius, Patriarch of Constantinople, actually excommunicated Pope Nicholas I of Rome!

This led to a whole new round of argument about the definition of the Trinity. The Catholics of Western Christendom decided to ratify what was called the *Filioque Article*, which had been introduced at the Council of Toledo in 598. It declared that the Holy Spirit proceeded 'from the Father and *from* the Son' (Latin: *filioque*). The Eastern Church claimed otherwise, stating that the Spirit proceeded 'from the Father *through* the Son' (Greek: *dia tou huiou*). It was a somewhat intangible and quite extraordinary point of theological dispute, but it was apparently good enough to split formal Christianity down the middle. In reality, of course, it was simply a trivial excuse to perpetuate the debate over whether the Church should be politically managed from Rome, or from Constantinople. The final result was the formation of two quite distinct Churches from the same original.[4]

As time progressed, the Eastern Church changed relatively little. From its primacy at Constantinople, it continued to adhere strictly to scriptural teachings and its focus of worship became the Eucharist (Thanksgiving) ritual with bread and wine.

Catholicism, on the other hand, underwent numerous changes: new doctrines were added and old concepts were amended or further substantiated. From the 12th century, seven Sacraments were deemed to embody the grace of God in a person's physical life (though not all were necessary for individual salvation). They were classified as: baptism, holy communion, confirmation, confession and penance, ordination to holy orders, the solemnization of matrimony and the anointing of the seriously ill and dying (the Extreme Unction or Last Rites). It was further decreed that the bread and wine of the Communion were actually transformed, upon consecration, into the physical body and blood of Jesus (the doctrine of Transubstantiation).

Inasmuch as Constantine's Roman Church had commenced as a hybrid, so too was the structure to remain composite. New methods and ideologies were introduced to maintain efficient control of congregations from a distance in an expanding Catholic society. In this way, Roman Catholicism evolved in a strictly regulated fashion and some doctrines that seem today to be traditional are actually quite recently implemented features. It was not until Victorian times that certain aspects of the Catholic creed (hitherto only implied) were determined as explicit items of faith. The doctrine of the Immaculate Conception, for instance, was not formally expressed until 1854, when Pope Pius IX decreed that Mary, the mother of Jesus, was herself conceived free from Original Sin. Mary's Assumption into Heaven was not defined until the 1950s by Pope Pius XII, whilst Pope Paul VI did not proclaim her Mother of the Church until 1964.

Such decrees were themselves rendered possible by the ultimate assertion of authority — that of 'papal infallibility'. The dogma to this effect was proclaimed at the First Vatican Council in 1870 and stated, in a way that brooked no opposition, that 'the Pope is incapable of error when defining matters of Church teaching and morality from his throne'!

Control of Religious Art

The Roman Catholic Church was not only concerned with retaining control over historical records and romantic literature. Indeed, the bishops set their sights against anything that appeared contrary to their dogmatic notions and, to this effect, an orthodox correctness was implemented and regulated throughout the creative sphere. That the Madonna should be depicted only in blue and white has already been mentioned, but there were other rules which governed sacred art in general. Some artists, such as Botticelli and Poussin, successfully introduced symbolic elements into their works — elements that the uninitiated would not comprehend but, in general terms, the art of much of Europe was constrained by strict Vatican guidelines.

From the earliest days of the Roman Church, the male relatives of Jesus had posed a problem, but this was successfully countered when they were pushed into the background of Church tradition while Mary, the mother of Jesus, was brought to the fore. The unfortunate Joseph (father of Jesus and James and the true link in the royal succession) was deliberately sidelined, while the cult of the Virgin Mother grew out of all proportion. By way of this considered strategy, public knowledge of the continuing bloodline of Judah was conveniently suppressed.

Rules were laid down by the Church as to who might be portrayed in art and how.[5] Anne (Anna), the mother of Mary, was seldom introduced into paintings with her daughter because her presence would detract from Mary's divine status. If Anne's visible attendance was essential, she was placed in a subordinate position. Francesco da San Gallo's *Saint Anne and the Madonna* provides a good example of how the mother is seated behind her daughter. Cesi's *The Vision of Saint Anne* shows Anne kneeling before a vision of Mary. Leonardo da Vinci's *The Virgin and Child with Saint Anne* is cleverly contrived to position the adult Mary on her mother's knee, thereby keeping the Madonna to the fore. Similarly, Anne stands behind her daughter in Pietro Perugino's *The Family of the Virgin*.

From Taddeo Gaddi's *Joachim Rejected from the Temple*

Mary's husband, Joseph, and her father, Joachim, were generally confined to inferior or background positions within pictorial artwork. Both characters created problems because their paternal functions were contrary to the purported Immaculate Conception and Virgin Birth. As early as the fresco paintings of Taddeo Gaddi (died 1366), it was preferred to reduce Joachim's status by showing him at his least dignified. He was often, therefore, portrayed being ejected from the Temple by the High Priest Issachar, having presumed to offer a feast-day lamb although he was not yet a father. In Michelangelo's The Holy Family, Mary is raised on a central throne, while her husband Joseph leans over a background balustrade, seemingly contemplating some unrelated matter.

The Church would gladly have denied that the Blessed Mary ever married, but artists could not escape the directness of the Gospels. Nevertheless, there was no room for any suggestion of physical attachment between Joseph and Mary. Joseph was, for that reason, generally depicted as being considerably older than his wife — balding and taking little interest in his family, as in Ghirlandajo's *The Adoration of the Shepherds* (c.1485). The famous *Doni Tondo* by Michelangelo

(1504) similarly features a very bald and white-bearded Joseph, as does Caravaggio's *The Rest on the Flight into Egypt*. Indeed, Joseph was not infrequently shown as positively infirm, leaning uncomfortably on a crutch, while Mary remained always beautiful and serene, as in Paolo Veronese's *The Holy Family*.

When Joseph was advanced to sainthood in his own right in 16th-century Spain, things changed a little to his benefit. Yet by means of subtle symbolism he was still portrayed only as Jesus's foster-father, and often held a white lily to express the purity of his relationship with Mary. Raphael's renowned *Sposalizio* (depicting the marriage of Mary and Joseph), falls into this category—displaying a lily atop Joseph's baton, even though allowing him to be a younger man than was usual.

From *The Nativity* by Lorenzo di Credi

Just as the lily was the accepted symbol of Mary's virginity, so the rose was the symbol of her beauty. She was often depicted holding a rose, or in a rose garden, as in the Madonna of Cesare di Seso, and The Madonna of the Rose Bush by Martin Schoen. The two concepts both derive from *The Song of Solomon* 2:1—'I am the rose of Sharon and the lily of the valleys'. From very early on the lily was called the fleur de Marie, and it was for this reason that the gladiolus lily (in its Judaic fleur de lis form) was adopted by the Merovingian kings to signify their Messianic descent in France.

Joseph's necessary presence was a cause of some difficulty for artists depicting the Nativity. But the difficulty was overcome in such paintings as Alessandro Moretto's 16th-century *The Nativity* by showing him as elderly with a supportive staff. Sometimes Joseph even appears to be in his dotage, or asleep, as in Lorenzo di Credi's portrayal. One way or another, this kingly descendant of the House of David was, time after time, reduced to being a superfluous onlooker (as in Hans Memling's *The Adoration of the Magi*) and he was seldom permitted to be a part of any relevant action. Moreover, in such pictures as Van Dyck's *Repose in Egypt*, Joseph seems hardly capable of any action—being more ready to collapse at Mary's feet and to join her father, Joachim, on the official road to oblivion.

Enter the Carolingians

By the mid-7th century, Rome was in a position to begin dismantling the Merovingian succession in Gaul—a plan which, as we saw earlier, was contrived at the baptism of King Clovis. In 665, the Mayor of the Austrasian Palace (akin to a Prime Minister) was firmly under papal control. When King Sigebert II died, his son Dagobert was only five years old—at which point Mayor Grimoald took action. To begin, he kidnapped Dagobert and had him conveyed to Ireland, to live in exile among the Scots Gaels. Then, not expecting to see the young heir again, Grimoald told Queen Immachilde that her son had died.

Prince Dagobert was educated at Slane Monastery, near Dublin, and he married the Celtic Princess Matilde when he was fifteen. Subsequently, he went to York under the patronage of St. Wilfred. But then Matilde died and Dagobert decided to return to France, much to the amazement of his mother. In the meantime, Grimoald had placed his own son on the Austrasian throne, but Wilfred of York and others spread word of the mayoral treachery and the House of Grimoald was duly discredited. Having secondly married Gizelle de Razès, a niece of the Visigoth king, Dagobert was reinstated in 674 (after an absence of nearly twenty years) and the Roman intrigue was thwarted—but not for long.[6]

Dagobert II's reign was short but effective; his major success was in centralizing the Merovingian sovereignty, but the Catholic movement set itself firmly to negate his Messianic heritage because it overshadowed the supremacy of the Pope. Dagobert's jealous enemies included his own powerful Mayor, Pepin the Fat of Heristal. Two days before Christmas 679, Dagobert was hunting near Stenay in the Ardennes when he was confronted by one of Pepin's men and lanced to death—impaled to a tree. The Church of Rome was quick to approve the assassination and immediately passed the Merovingian administration in Austrasia to the ambitious Mayor.

Pepin the Fat was, in due course, succeeded by his illegitimate son, the well-known Charles Martel (the 'Hammer') who gained recognition by turning back the Moorish invasion near Poitiers in 732. He then sustained the Roman endeavour by gaining control of other Merovingian territories. When Martel died in 741, the only Merovingian of any notable authority was Dagobert II's nephew, Childeric III. Martel's son, Pepin the Short, was the Mayor of Neustria. Up to that point (except for the Grimoald affair), the Merovingian monarchy had been strictly dynastic; hereditary succession was an automatic and sacred right—a matter in which the Church had no say whatsoever. But that tradition was destined to be overturned when Rome grasped the opportunity to 'create' kings by papal authority. In 751, Pepin the Short, in league with Pope Zachary, secured Church approval for his own coronation as King of the Franks in place of Childeric. To facilitate this, a fraudulently prepared document was produced, which decreed that the Pope was Christ's personally appointed representative on Earth, and that only he had the right to appoint kings. The document was called the *Donation of Constantine*, and was said to have been written and signed by Emperor Constantine 400 years earlier. As has been proven many times, from the Renaissance onwards, the *Donation* (as discussed at length in *Realm of the Ring Lords*) was a blatant forgery. However, it enabled the Church's long-awaited ideal to come to fruition and, from that time onwards, kings were endorsed and crowned only by self-styled Roman prerogative.

So Pepin became king with the full blessing of the Pope, and Childeric was deposed. The pledge of allegiance made by the Roman Church, in AD 496, to King Clovis and his descendants was broken. After two and a half centuries, the Church was suitably geared to usurp the ancient legacy of the Merovingian bloodline and to take control of the Frankish realm by installing its own kings. Childeric was publicly humiliated by the bishops. His hair (kept long in the Nazarite tradition) was cut brutally short and he was incarcerated in a monastery, where he died four years later. Thus began a new dynasty of French kings, the Carolingians—so named after Pepin's father, Charles (Carolus) Martel.[7]

The official histories of the era were, not surprisingly, compiled by Vatican scribes, or by others who operated by Vatican authority. The inevitable result was that accounts of Dagobert's life were suppressed to the point of his non-existence in the chronicles. Not for another thousand years were the true facts of his existence to be made public once more. And only then did it become apparent that Dagobert had a son called Sigebert, who was rescued from the mayoral clutches in 679. Following his father's murder he was removed to his mother's home at Rennes-le-Château in Languedoc. By the time of Childeric's deposition, Sigebert (effectively Sigebert III) had become the Count of Razès, succeeding his maternal grandfather, the Visigoth, Bera II. In time, the deposed Merovingian line from Sigebert included the famous crusader, Godefroi de Bouillon, Defender of the Holy Sepulchre.

King of the Jews

After their defeat by Charles Martel in the 730s, the Islamic Moors retreated to the city of Narbonne in the South of France, which became their base for further military resistance. This posed a difficult and prolonged problem for Pepin the Short, who duly sought assistance from the Jews of Narbonne. He finally gained their support — but at a price. The Jews agreed to deal with the problem if Pepin guaranteed the setting up of a Jewish kingdom within the territory of Burgundy — a kingdom that would have at its head a recognized descendant of the Royal House of David.[8]

Pepin agreed and the Jews defeated the Moors from within the city. The Jewish kingdom of Septimania (the Midi) was then established in 768, from Nimes to the Spanish frontier, with Narbonne as its capital. The previous governor of the region was the Merovingian, Theuderic IV (Thierry), who had been ousted from power in Neustria and Burgundy by Charles Martel in 737. Theuderic (known to the Moors as Makir Theodoric) was married to Pepin the Short's sister Alda. It was their son, Count Guilhelm de Toulouse, who then acceded to the new throne as the King of Septimania in 768. Guilhelm was not only of Merovingian lineage, but was a recognized Potentate of Judah, holding the distinction of Isaac in the patriarchy.

Pepin's son, Charles, was the ruler who became known as Charlemagne the Great. As King of the Franks from 771 and Emperor of the West from 800, Charlemagne was pleased to confirm Guilhelm's entitlement to dynastic sovereignty in Septimania. The appointment was also upheld by the Caliph of Baghdad and, reluctantly, by Pope Stephen in Rome. All acknowledged King Guilhelm of the House of Judah to be a true bloodline successor of King David. Guilhelm was particularly influential at the Carolingian Court and he had an illustrious military career. In spite of his prominent position, Guilhelm was greatly influenced by St. Benedict's monastic asceticism and founded his own monastery at Gellone. In

791 he instituted his famous Judaic Academy of St. Guilhelm and was later featured by the Holy Grail chronicler Wolfram von Eschenbach.

By his wife Guibourg, Guilhelm's eldest son and heir was Prince Bernard of Septimania; his other sons were Heribert, Bera and Theodoric. Bernard became Imperial Chamberlain and was second in authority to the Carolingian Emperor. He was the leading Frankish statesman from 829 and married Charlemagne's daughter Dhuada at the Imperial Palace of Aix-la-Chapelle in June 824. They had two sons: William (born November 826) and Bernard (born March 841). William became a prominent military leader and Bernard II held the reins of Aquitaine, to rival King Louis II in power and influence within the region.

More than 300 years later, the Davidic succession was still extant in the Spanish Midi, although the notional kingdom had ceased to function as a separate State within a State. In 1144 the English monk, Theobald of Cambridge, stated (when initiating a charge of ritual murder against the Jews of Norwich):

> The chief men and rabbis of the Jews who dwell in Spain assemble together at Narbonne, where the Royal Seed resides, and where they are held in the highest esteem.

In 1166, the chronicler, Benjamin of Tudela, reported that there were still significant estates held by the prevailing Davidic heirs:

> Narbonne is an ancient city of the Torah[9] .... Therein are sages, magnates and princes, at the head of whom is Kalonymos, son of the great Prince Todros of blessed memory, a descendant of the House of David, as stated in his family tree. He holds hereditaments and other landed properties from the rulers of the country, and no one may dispossess him'.

The Holy Roman Empire

King Charlemagne greatly expanded the Frankish territories, and by harassing the Saxons also became King of the Lombards. In 800 he was crowned Emperor of the West by Pope Leo III. By this strategy the Church of Rome inaugurated a new Imperial dominion—a dominion in control of territory that comprised much of Western and Central Europe. Charlemagne's successor was Louis I (the Pious), at whose death in 840 the unity of the Empire was undermined by his rebellious sons. Then, after three years of strife, the kingdom was split into three at the 843 Treaty of Verdun. The Middle Kingdom included Italy, Lorraine and Provence. In the West was France, and in the East Germany.

Apart from Charlemagne — who established France as an Imperial and cultural domain — the Carolingians were largely incompetent rulers. Their nobles became semi-independent, while the Norsemen (Normans) were allowed to invade Northern France and establish Normandy. The last Carolingian king was Louis V (the Feckless). He was succeeded by Hugh Capet, the Duke of France, in 987, and thus began the new Capetian dynasty, which was to reign until 1328.

When the Capetians succeeded to the throne of France, the elective Imperial title passed to the German kings of Saxon lineage and, from the 11th century onward, the Emperors were mainly of the Hohenstaufen succession. In due course they became so powerful that they were contending with the papacy for overall supremacy in Europe. The main dispute began in 1075 as an argument — called the Investiture Controversy — over exactly who had the primary right to invest bishops in return for their pledges of loyalty.

In the context of this ongoing struggle against Vatican domination, the supporters of the anti-Roman Hohenstaufens became known as Ghibellines (after their castle at Waiblingen). Their pro-Roman rivals were known as Guelfs (or Guelphs, after Welf, Duke of Bavaria). The Ghibellines held their position of prominence until the Hohenstaufens were militarily defeated by a papal alliance in 1268. From that time the Empire became the Holy Roman Empire, and the emergent Emperors were invariably Habsburgs — a family that originated in 10th-century Switzerland. From 1278, the Habsburgs were the rulers of Austria, and from 1516 they also inherited the Spanish crown. For five centuries they were the most prominent of all European houses, and they governed the Holy Roman Empire, almost continuously, until it was abolished in 1806.

Temple of the Grail

Legacy of the Sangréal

Of all Arthurian themes, the most romantic is that of the Holy Grail yet, because of the Grail's enduring tradition, there is a lingering uncertainty about its place in time. Its champions have been portrayed in the 1st century, in the Arthurian period and in the Middle Ages. In essence, the Grail is timeless.

The Grail has been symbolized by many things: a chalice, a platter, a stone, a casket, an aura, a jewel and a vine. It is sought by some and seen by others. It is sometimes tangible, with appointed guardians and maidenly bearers, but is often ethereal, appearing in a variety of guises including that of Jesus himself. Its powers include those of rejuvenation, knowledge and provision. Just as Jesus was a healer, teacher and provider, so too is the Grail. In name it has been the *Graal*, the *Saint Graal*, the *Seynt Grayle*, the *Sangréal*, the *Sankgreal*, the *Sangrail*, the *Sank Ryal* and the *Holy Grail* but, however defined, its spirit remains at the very centre of achievement.

Despite a background that is both romantic and sacred, Grail lore remains an unproclaimed heresy, having been associated with pagan tradition, blasphemy and unholy mysteries. Moreover, the Roman Church has openly condemned the Grail because of its strong female associations—particularly with the ethos of Courtly Love (*Amour Courtois*) in the Middle Ages. The romantic notions of Chivalry and the songs of the Troubadours were despised by Rome because they placed womanhood on a pedestal of veneration, contrary to Catholic doctrine. To a far greater extent though the Church's reluctance to accept the *Sangréal* tradition derives from the Grail Family's specifically defined Messianic lineage.

In its most popular role, the Holy Grail is identified as the cup used by Jesus at the Last Supper. After the Crucifixion, it was supposedly filled with Jesus's blood by Joseph of Arimathea. This concept first arose in the 12th century, but its perpetuation was largely due to Alfred, Lord Tennyson's *Holy Grail*, published in 1859.

It was Sir Thomas Malory who first used the words *Holy Grayle* in his 15th-century adaptation of the French *le Saint Graal*. Malory referred to 'the holy vessel', but also wrote of the *Sankgreal* as being 'the blessed blood of Christ', with both definitions appearing in the same story. Apart from such mentions, Malory gave no description of the Grail—only that it appeared at Camelot 'covered in white samite' (a fine silk). It was seen by Lancelot in a vision and eventually achieved by Galahad. In Malory's account, the Grail champions are Bors, Perceval, Lancelot and his son Galahad. The last described as 'a young knight of kings' lineage and of the kindred of Joseph of Arimathea, being the grandson of King Pelles'.

Medieval tradition related that Joseph of Arimathea brought the Holy Grail to Britain, while even earlier European lore told how Mary Magdalene originally brought the *Sangréal* into Provence. It is a significant fact that, prior to the 15th century, the majority of Grail romances came out of continental Europe. Even such tales as the Welsh *Peredur* derived from European texts. The Celtic legends of Ireland and Wales featured magic cauldrons, and it was partly because of these that the Grail came to be perceived as a cup or

Medieval France

chalice. However, the notion was not inappropriate, for it was only to be supposed that the royal blood must have been conveyed in a vessel of some kind.

The earliest written account of *le Seynt Graal* comes from the year 717, when a British hermit called Waleran saw a vision of Jesus and the Grail. Waleran's manuscript was referred to by Heliand, a French monk of the Abbey of Fromund, in around 1200; also by John of Glastonbury in the *Cronica sive Antiquitates Glastoniensis Ecclesie*, and later by Vincent of Beauvais in his 1604 *Speculum Historiale*. Each of these texts relates how Jesus placed a book in Waleran's hands. It began:

> Here is the Book of thy Descent.
> Here begins the Book of the Sangréal.

In the public domain, the literary Grail did not appear until the 1180s, at which stage it was described simply as a 'graal'; it was neither explained as a holy relic, nor associated with the blood of Jesus. In his *le Conte del Graal — roman de Perceval*, Chrétien de Troyes states:

> A damsel came in with the squires, holding between her two hands a graal .... And as she entered ... there was such a brilliant light that the candles lost their brightness. After her came a damsel holding a dish of silver. The graal which preceded her was of refined gold, and it was set with precious stones of many kinds .... The youth [Perceval] watched them pass, but he did not dare to ask concerning the graal and whom one served with it.

On this first occasion, at the castle of the wounded Fisher King, the graal is not described as a cup, neither is it associated with blood. But later in the story Chrétien explains:

> Do not think that he [the Fisher King] takes from it a pike or a lamprey, or a salmon; the holy man sustains and refreshes his life with a single mass wafer. So sacred a thing is the graal, and he himself is so spiritual, that he needs no more for his sustenance that the Mass wafer which comes with the graal.

If Chrétien's graal was big enough to accommodate a large fish, it was clearly not a cup in this context, but a sizable tureen. Its mystery, however, lies in the fact that it served just a single Mass wafer. Elsewhere in Chrétien's work, there is mention of a hundred boars heads served on graals while, in around 1215, the Abbot of Froidmont, centring upon this explanation, described a graal as a deep dish used by the rich.

Up to that point, there was no link between the Fisher King's graal and the traditional *Sangréal*. But, in the 1190s, the Burgundian writer, Sire Robert de Boron, changed this with his poem *Joseph d'Arimathie – roman de l'Estoire dou Saint Graal*. He redefined Chrétien's Fisher King (previously contemporary with King Arthur) as Bron (a kinsman by marriage of Joseph of Arimathea) and reclassified the relic as *le Saint Graal*: a 'chalice of holy blood'.

According to de Boron, Joseph obtained the Passover cup from Pilate and collected Jesus's blood when removing him from the cross. He was imprisoned by the Jews, but managed to pass the cup to his brother-in-law Hebron, who travelled to the Vales of Avaron. There he became Bron the Rich Fisher. Bron and his wife Enygeus (Joseph's sister) had twelve sons, eleven of whom married, while the twelfth, Alain, remained celibate. Meanwhile, Joseph joined the family abroad and constructed a table to honour the Graal. At this table there was a particular seat called the *Siege Perilous*. It represented the seat of Judas Iscariot and was reserved especially for Alain. In later stories it was to be the virgin knight Galahad for whom the *Siege Perilous* was reserved at the Round Table of Camelot.

At about the same time as de Boron's *Joseph d'Arimathie*, another related work appeared by a writer known as Wauchier. It was very much a continuation of Chrétien's account but, in this tale, the Graal acquired a different aspect, performing a physical role:

> Then Gawain saw entering by the door the rich Graal, which served the knights and swiftly placed bread before each one. It also performed the butler's office: the service of wine, and filled large cups of fine gold, and decked the tables with them. As soon as it had done this, without delay it placed at every table a service of food in a large silver dish. Sir Gawain watched all this, and marvelled much how the Graal served them. He wondered sorely that he beheld no other servant, and hardly dared to eat.

In some respects, Wauchier's version brought the Chrétien and de Boron stories together. King Arthur's knights were featured, but the author also recounted the tradition of Joseph of Arimathea. He explained that Joseph's lineal descendant was Guellans Guenelaus, the deceased father of Perceval and that, in keeping with previous texts, Perceval's mother was a widow.

The story known as the *Perlesvaus,* or the *High History of the Holy Grail,* is a Franco-Belgian work dating from about 1200. It is very specific about the importance of Grail lineage, asserting that the *Sangréal* is the repository of royal heritage, thereby reiterating the important dynastic principle of Waleran's 8th-century manuscript. In the *Perlesvaus,* the Grail is not defined as a material object, but as a mystic aura that contains various images of Messianic significance. In this work, the *Corpus Christi* of Chrétien's Mass wafer emerges as the continuing presence of the Christ.

In respect of the cup symbolism, the *Perlesvaus* states:

> Sir Gawain gazes at the Grail, and it seems to
> him that there is a chalice within it, although
> at the same time there is not one.

Gawain, Lancelot and Perceval are all featured in the Perlesvaus and the paramount question is 'Whom does the Grail serve?' Only by asking this question can Perceval heal the groin wound of the Fisher King and return the barren Wasteland to fertility. In the Perlesvaus, the Fisher King (Priest King) is called Messios, denoting his Messianic standing. Other accounts refer to the Fisher King Anfortas (effectively the same name as King David's great-grandfather Boaz, both meaning 'In strength' — thereby identifying the Davidic lineage). Alternatively, the Fisher King is sometimes called Pelles (from Pallas, the ancient Bistea Neptunis of the Merovingian ancestry).[1]

Not the least important feature of the *Perlesvaus* is its evident reference to the Knights Templars. On the Island of the Ageless, Perceval comes to a glass hall, to be met by two Masters. One acknowledges his familiarity with Perceval's royal descent. Then, clapping their hands, the Masters summon thirty-three other men who are 'clad in white garments', each bearing 'a red cross in the midst of his breast'. Perceval also carries the red cross of the Templars upon his shield. The tale is basically Arthurian, but it is set in a later period, at a time when the Holy Land is in the hands of the Saracens.

Also from the early 1200s comes a most important Grail romance called *Parzival*, by the Bavarian knight Wolfram von Eschenbach. Once again a Templar association is evident, for the Knights of the Templeise are portrayed as guardians of the Temple of the Grail, located on the Mount of Salvation (Munsalvaesche). Here, the Fisher King officiates at the Grail Mass and is specifically depicted as a Priest King in the style of Jesus, the Merovingians and the Kings of Scots. Munsalvaesche has long been associated with the mountain fortress of Montségur in the Languedoc region of southern France.

Wolfram stated that Chrétien's Grail story was wrong, giving his own source as being Kyôt le Provenzale, a Templar attaché who wrote of an early Grail manuscript from Arabia. It was by the learned Flegetanis, whom he said was

> A scholar of nature, descended from Solomon,
> and born of a family which had long been
> Israelite until baptism became our shield
> against the fire of hell.

As with the *Perlesvaus*, Wolfram's *Parzival* lays great stress on the importance of Grail lineage. Wolfram also introduced Perceval's son Lohengrin, the Knight of the Swan. In the Lorraine tradition, Lohengrin was the husband of the Duchess of Brabant (Lower Lorraine). *Parzival* explains that Perceval's father was Gahmuret (as against Guellans in the Wauchier account) and that the Fisher King of Perceval's day was Anfortas, son of Frimutel, son of Titurel. The Fisher King's sister, Herzeylde, was Perceval's mother: the 'widow lady' of tradition. Expounding at length on the various mystical attributes of the Grail, the text names its bearer as the Queen of the Grail Family, Repanse de Schoye, declaring:

> She was clad in the silk of Arabia, and she
> bore, resting on a green silk cloth, the
> perfection of earthly paradise, both roots and
> branches. It was a thing men call the Grail,
> which surpassed every earthly ideal.

Despite the reference to roots and branches, the Grail is said to be a 'stone of youth and rejuvenation'. It is called Lapsit Exillis (sometimes Lapis Elixis) — a variant of Lapis Elixir, the alchemical Philosophers' Stone. Wolfram explains:

> By the power of that stone the Phoenix burns
> to ashes, but the ashes speedily restore him to
> life again. Thus doth the Phoenix moult and
> change its plumage, after which he is bright
> and shining as before.

At the Fisher King's sacrament of the Eucharist, the Grail Stone records the names of those called to its service—but it is not possible for everyone to read those names:

> Around the end of the stone, an inscription in
> letters tells the name and lineage of those, be
> they maids or boys, who are called to make
> the journey to the Grail. No one needs to erase
> the inscription, for as soon as it has been read
> it vanishes.

In very similar terms (the relevance of which is fully explained in *Genesis of the Grail Kings*), the New Testament (Revelation 2.17) states:

> To him that overcometh will I give to eat of
> the hidden manna [divine food, as in the
> Eucharist], and will give him a white stone,
> and in that stone a new name written, which
> no man knoweth saving he that receiveth it.

Wolfram (who also wrote of Guilhelm de Gellone, King of Septimania) said that the original Flegetanis manuscript was held by the House of Anjou, a noble house that was closely allied with the Templars. He also claimed that Perceval was himself of Angevin blood. In *Parzival*, King Arthur's Court is set in Brittany, while in another work Wolfram located the Grail Castle in the Pyrenees. He also made specific mention of the Countess of Edinburgh (Tenabroc) as being among the Grail Queen's retinue.

The Cistercian *Vulgate Cycle* of around 1220 contains the *Estoire del Graal*, the *Queste del Saint Graal* and the *Livres de Lancelot*, as well as other tales of Arthur and Merlin. In these, the descriptions of the Grail are largely influenced by Chrétien and de Boron, while the earlier 'Graal' spelling is reinstated. In the *Estoire*, the story of Joseph of Arimathea is extended to include his time in Britain, while his heir, Bishop Josephes of Saraz, is identified as the head of the Grail fraternity. Bron (de Boron's Rich Fisher) reappears as the *Estoire's*

Fisher King. The Graal, meanwhile, has become the miraculous *escuele* (dish) of the Paschal Lamb. In both the *Estoire* and the *Queste*, Grail Castle is symbolically called 'le Corbenic' (the Body Blessed).[2] The *Queste* identifies Galahad as being 'descended from the high lineage of King David' but, more importantly, it specifically notes his descent in the succession from King Solomon.

The *Livres de Lancelot* (which feature Gawain in the first instance) go on to expand the story of Galahad, detailing him as the son of Lancelot by the daughter of Pelles. She is the Grail princess Elaine le Corbenic and Pelles is the son of the wounded Fisher King, whereas in Malory's later account Pelles is himself the King.

King Arthur certainly received mentions in the early Grail literature, but it was not until the 13th-century *Vulgate Cycle* that he was fully established in this regard. However, after the Holy Land fell in 1291, the Grail legends slipped from the public arena. It was not until the 15th century that Sir Thomas Malory revived the theme with his tale of *The Sankgreal: The Blessed Blood of Our Lord Jesus Christ*.

The Philosophers' Stone

We have already seen that Jesus and Mary Magdalene's younger son, Josephes, attended a druidic college. Educational institutions of the kind were internationally renowned; there were no fewer than sixty such colleges and universities in Europe, boasting a total attendance of more than 60,000 students. The Druid priests were not part of the Celtic Church but were an established, cohesive element in the structure of Gaelic society in Gaul, Britain and Ireland. They were described by the writer Strabo, in the 1st century BC, as 'students of nature and moral philosophy'.[3] He continued,

> They are believed to be the most just of men,
> and are therefore entrusted with judgements in
> decisions that affect both individuals and the
> public at large. In former times they arbitrated
> in war, able to bring to a standstill opponents
> on the point of drawing up in line of battle;
> murder cases have very frequently been
> entrusted to their adjudication.

The Sicilian, Diodorus, another writer of the time, described the Druids as great 'philosophers and theologians, who are treated with special honour'. The Druids were in addition said to have been both exceptional statesmen and divine seers.[4] One ancient text states that

> The Druids are men of science, but they are also men of God, enjoying direct intercourse with the deities and able to speak in their name. They can also influence fate by making those who consult them observe positive rules or ritual taboos, or by determining the days to be chosen or avoided for any action that is contemplated.

In later times the Roman Church looked for the slightest excuse to denounce the Druid priests and the monks of the Celtic Church, finding the mark of sin even in their hairstyles. Both priests and monks wore long, flowing hair from the back of their heads, with the fronts of their heads shaved across from the temples. The emergent Roman clergy, however, adopted an alternative tonsure: a circlet of short hair around an otherwise cleanshaven head, representative of a holy crown. According to Rome, the Celtic hairstyle was the heretical symbol of the Magians, and they condemned it as 'the tonsure of Simon Magus'.[5]

When Diodorus wrote of the Britons in the 1st century BC, he referred to the works of the Greek writer Hecataeus from three centuries before, and accordingly called them Hyperboreans (people from beyond the North Wind). He told how the god Apollo visited a Hyperborean temple 'every nineteen years—the period over which the return of the stars to the same place in the heavens is accomplished'. This 19-year astronomical cycle was used by the Druids for calendar calculation, as confirmed by the old Calendar of Coligny found in the French Department of Ain, north of Lyon, in 1897.[6]

The Calendar—a fragmented bronze tablet—dates from the 1st century AD and is the longest document to be unearthed in Gaul. It gives a table of 62 consecutive months (about five solar years), each month having either 29 or 30 days. Also intercalated is the alternative lunar calendar of thirteen months per solar year. The days of each month are related to each other, with inherent dark and light periods, and annotated as to auspicious and inauspicious days. Altogether, the Coligny Calendar indicates a significant competence in astronomical science, akin to that of the ancient Babylonians.

Astronomy was of prime importance to the Druids, who were said to 'have much knowledge of the stars and their motions, of the size of the world and of the earth, and of natural philosophy'. They believed also in reincarnation (the transmigration of souls) — an aspect of ancient Pythagoreanism. As long ago as the 6th century BC, Pythagoras founded one of the earliest mystery schools. Within this environment was developed a model of the universe that was correctly based on the fact that the Earth revolves around the Sun (the heliocentric principle). But even as long afterwards as the 16th century, the Polish astronomer Nicholas Copernicus was threatened with excommunication, and worse, for his belief in this concept. On presenting his theory, Copernicus suffered an onslaught of abuse from the Catholic Church, which insisted that the Earth was the centre of the universe. To the earlier Druids, with their advanced knowledge of heavenly bodies, the very idea of an Earth-centred universe would have been unthinkable.

In common with the Samaritan Magi of the Qumrân era, the Druids were practitioners of advanced numerology and healing. During the Gospel period, the Essenes of Qumrân were especially interested in the mathematics which governed the order of the cosmos. Their culture was to a large extent dominated by Pythagorean thought, inherited through the Magi of West Manasseh — a sect founded by Menahem in 44 BC. A successor of Menahem as Head of the Magi was Mary Magdalene's colleague Simon (the Magus) Zelotes, whose Gnostics were said to possess a unique and esoteric wisdom (called *Sapientia*) that transcended Christianity.

A Gnostic document, found at Chenoboskion in Egypt and known as the *Treatise of Hermes Trismegistus*, states:

> It is thus by degrees that the adepts will enter
> into the way of immortality, and will attain to
> a conception of the Ogdoad, which in turn
> reveals the Ennead.

The Ogdoad ('eightfold') corresponds to the heaven of the stars, outside the individual heavens of the planets, and the Ennead ('ninefold') refers to the great outer heaven of the universe. The separate heaven of Earth itself was called the Hebdomad ('sevenfold'). To the Gnostics the heavens were strictly stratified areas of space surrounding the Earth, the planets and the stars. Even though the heavens were subject to their own mythology, the logical understanding of the Gnostics bore little relation to the cosmological principle of the later Roman Church, which for centuries insisted that the Earth was flat, and that Heaven was simply 'above'.[7] (Some schools even suggested that Heaven — also flat — was supported above the Earth by invisible pillars.)

Hermes Trismegistus was the Greek Neoplatonists' name for Thoth, the Egyptian god revered as the founder of alchemy and geometry. Following the teachings of Plato (c.429-347 BC), the Neoplatonists[8] claimed that the human intellect was not related to the material world, and that individual spirituality would increase in relation to one's contempt for earthly values. The relevance of Hermes was that his special knowledge was held to represent the Lost Wisdom of Lamech (seventh in succession from Eve's son Cain — Genesis 4:18-22). Just as Noah saved various life forms from the great Flood, so Lamech's three sons, Jabal, Jubal and Tubal-cain, preserved the ancient wisdoms of creative science, carved upon two stone monuments: the Antediluvian Pillars. One son was a mathematician, the second a mason, and the third a metalworker. Hermes discovered one of the pillars, transcribing its sacred geometry onto an emerald tablet that was inherited by Pythagoras, who also discovered the second pillar.

The association of the sacred knowledge of the cosmos with an emerald tablet is reminiscent of Wolfram's *Parzival*, in which the Grail is identified as a stone and likened to an emerald jewel. Moreover, an inscription from the emerald tablet of Hermes appears on some *Temperance* Tarot cards:

> Visit the interior parts of the earth; by rectification thou shalt find the hidden stone.

Through association with the enigmatic Stone, the Grail has been identified with alchemy — the science of concentrating vital currents and life forces. At the time of the Catholic Inquisition, alchemists were careful to veil their art behind symbols of metallurgy — claiming they were attempting only to turn base metals into gold. Indeed, the alchemists were metallurgists of the highest order, but, in philosophical and metaphysical terms, they were rather more concerned with the transformation of the worldly person (lead) into a spiritually illuminated person (gold). Just as gold was tried and tested in the fire, so the human spirit was tried in the crucible of life — and the agent for this illumination was perceived as the Holy Spirit.[9]

Not surprisingly, this doctrine of human perfectibility through enlightenment was deemed heretical by the Church whose teachings it superseded. Although founded on a Judaeo-Christian base, the

Grail tradition was likened to alchemy, and was therefore itself regarded as a heresy. The hidden stone was described in the alchemical *Rosarium Philosophorum* in terms of geometry:

> Make a round circle of the man and the woman, and draw out of this a square, and out of the square a triangle. Make a round circle, and you will have the stone of the philosophers.

Like the Philosophers' Stone, the Grail has been identified as the key to knowledge and the sum of all things. In its nominal form as the Graal, the etymological root stems from the old Mesopotamian term Gra-al — said to be the 'nectar of supreme excellence'. It stems likewise from the Celtic word gar, meaning 'stone', so that gar-al is the cup of the stone.[10] As we have seen, the priesthood of Jesus was that of Melchizedek (Hebrews 5:6-7), who is portrayed in the northern doorway of Chartres Cathedral. Here, at the Door of the Initiates, Melchizedek is the host of Abraham (in accordance with Genesis 14:18-20) and he bears a cup which holds the hidden manna (spiritual nourishment, or daily bread) of the sacred stone.

The Guild of Masons, who built Chartres and other French cathedrals, were called the Children of Solomon. Hiram Abiff, the architect of King Solomon's Temple, was a Hermetic alchemist — described as 'an artificer in metals'. His ancient forerunner was Tubal-cain (Genesis 4:22), the son of Lamech and the teacher of all who followed. In Freemasonry, Hiram Abiff is identified as the Son of the Widow, and in Grail lore the constant epithet of Perceval is precisely the same. The original Widow of the Grail bloodline was Ruth the Moabite (heroine of the Old Testament book of Ruth), who married Boaz to become the great-grandmother of David. Her descendants were called Sons of the Widow.

The underlying principle of Hermes Trismegistus was 'As above, so below', which denotes that the harmony of earthly proportion is representative of its universal equivalent — in other words, that earthly proportion is the mortal image of cosmological structure.[11] From the smallest cell to the widest expanse of the galaxies, a repetitive geometric law prevails, and this was understood from the very earliest of times.

The Grail Hallows

Vessel and the Vine

In its representation as a stone or jewel the Holy Grail is the repository of spiritual wisdom and cosmological knowledge, signifying 'fulfilment'. As a dish or platter it carries the Mass wafer of the Eucharist or the Paschal Lamb and symbolizes the ideal of 'service'. Its most popular representation as a chalice containing the blood of Jesus is, however, a purely female image. To the Church, sacred vessels had pagan associations and Grail imagery was thus moved into the convenient wings of mythology.

In the pagan tradition, the Grail was likened to the mystical cauldrons of Celtic folklore: the horns of plenty, which held the secrets of provision and rebirth. The father of the Irish god-kings, Dagda of the Tuatha Dé Danaan, had a cauldron that would only cook for heroes. Likewise, the horn of Caradoc would not boil meat for cowards. The pot of the goddess Ceridwen contained a potion of great knowledge and the Welsh gods, Matholwch and Brân, possessed similar vessels.[1] The similarity of the name Brân to that of Bron the Rich Fisher has often been cited, with the suggestion that perhaps one derived from the other.

The vessel of mystery to the ancient Greeks was the *Krater*. (In mundane contexts, a krater was a stone bowl for mixing wine.[2]) In philosophical terms, the Krater contained the elements of life and Plato referred to a krater which contained the light of the sun. Alchemists similarly had their own vessel from which was born Mercurius, the *filius philosophorum* (son of the philosophers) — a divine child who symbolized the wisdom of the *vas-uterus*, while the Hermetic vessel itself was called the 'womb of knowledge'. It is this uterine aspect of the enigmatic vessel that is so important in Grail science.

The medieval *Litany of Loretto* went so far as to describe Jesus's mother Mary as the *vas spirituale* (spiritual vessel). In esoteric lore, the womb was identified as the 'vessel of life' and was represented by a cup or chalice. Prehistoric shrines dating from 3500 BC associate the figure with the womb of the Mother Goddess.[3] The reverse male symbol was a blade or horn, ordinarily symbolized as a sword, although its most powerful representation was in the fabulous mythology of the Unicorn. In Psalm 92:10 we read, 'My horn shalt thou exalt like the horn of an unicorn'. Along with the Lion of Judah, the legendary Unicorn remained synonymous with the anointed kingly line of Judah, to emerge in the heraldic arms of Scotland. The Holy Grail became likened to a vessel because it was said to carry the perpetual blood of Jesus and, just as the kraters and cauldrons contained their various secrets, so too was the blood of Jesus (the *Sangréal*) held to be contained within a cup.

In *Parzival*, it is said of the Grail Queen that 'she bore ... the perfection of earthly paradise, both roots and branches'. According to the New Testament Gospel of John 15:5, Jesus said, 'I am the vine, ye are the branches'. Psalm 80:8 reads, 'Thou hast brought a vine out of Egypt: thou hast cast out the heathen, and planted it'.

The lineage of the Merovingian kings was called the Vine, and the Bible classifies the descendants of Israel as a Vine—the line of Judah being described at some length as the Lord's cherished plant (Isaiah 5:7). Indeed, some artistic portrayals of Jesus show him in a wine-press, accompanied by the statement 'I am the true vine' (John 15:1). Some Grail emblems and watermarks depict a chalice containing clusters of grapes—the fruit and seeds of the vine.[4] From the grape comes wine—and the wine of the Eucharist is the eternal symbol of the Messianic bloodline.

In the original Grail legends there were constant references to the Grail Family, the Grail dynasty and the custodians (or guardians) of the Grail. Quite apart from legend, the Knights Templars of Jerusalem were indeed the Guardians of the *Sangréal*. The associated Prieuré Notre Dame de Sion became allied to the Merovingian bloodline in particular and it was the Merovingian descendant Godefroi de Bouillon, Duke of Lower Lorraine, who was installed as Defender of the Holy Sepulchre and King of Jerusalem in 1099.

Cups and stones aside, the importance of the Grail exists in its definition as the *Sangréal*. From this came *San Greal* = *San Graal* = *Saint Grayle* = *Holy Grail*. More correctly, it was the *Sang Réal*—the Blood Royal, carried by the uterine Chalice of Mary Magdalene. It was she who inspired the *Dompna* (Great Lady) of the Troubadours—who were so callously treated by the Inquisition—and they called her the Grail of the World.

As detailed in medieval literature, the Grail was identified with a family and a dynasty. It was the desposynic Vine of Judah, perpetuated in the West through the blood of Jesus. This lineage included the Fisher Kings and Lancelot del Acqs. It descended to the Merovingian Kings of France and the Stewart Kings of Scots, incorporating such reputed figures as Guilhelm de Gellone and Godefroi de Bouillon.

In descent from Jesus's brother James/Joseph of Arimathea, the Grail Family founded the House of Camulod (Colchester) and the Princely House of Wales. Notable in these lines were King Lucius, Coel Hen, Empress Helena, Ceredig Gwledig and King Arthur. The divine legacy of the *Sangréal* was perpetuated in the sovereign and most noble houses of Britain and Europe and it is still extant today.

Having established that the Vine represents the Messianic bloodline, it follows that the Vineyard is the place where that vine will flourish. About two centuries after the Council of Constance in 1417, Archbishop Ussher of Armagh (the 17th-century compiler of Bible chronology) commented on the Council records. From these he quoted 'Immediately after the passion of Christ, Joseph of Arimathea ... proceeded to cultivate the Lord's Vineyard, that is to say, England'.[5]

It is apparent from the annals of saintly genealogy and bardic pedigree that the Messianic line of the *Sangréal* came into Britain from 1st-century Gaul. In the Lord's Vineyard the line flourished to become the Princely House of Wales and from this early root stemmed the *Gwyr-y-Gogledd* chiefs of the northern regions.

In parallel, another branch of the Vine conjoined with the great kings of Camulod and Siluria. It was by no chance that Prince Linus, son of Caractacus, became the first Bishop of Rome. Neither was it a fluke of circumstance that Helena (Princess Elaine of Camulod), daughter of Britain's Coel II, married Emperor Constantius.[6] By way of this alliance Rome was attached to the Judaean royal succession which it had tried so hard to suppress by other means. St. Helena's son was Constantine the Great and, having a Celtic Christian mother[7] of a desposynic line, he was not slow to proclaim himself the true Messiah, even though his father's predecessors had been savage persecutors of the Christian movement.

The Rod of Jesse

Despite their said discovery of the bones of Arthur and Guinevere even the inventive monks of Glastonbury did not produce anything purporting to be the Holy Grail — if only because it had never been defined as a Christian relic prior to their digging escapades. Although de Boron was soon to identify the Saint Graal as the chalice of the Last Supper, the monks had never heard of it as such; there was no Holy Grail mentioned in the Bible, nor in any other orthodox scripture. Moreoever, because the Grail legends emanated mainly from outside England, there was nothing of substance to link the Grail with Glastonbury — apart from the connection with Joseph of Arimathea.

And so, not to be outdone, the monks announced the discovery of a pair of cruets that were said to have been buried with Joseph. They had previously been mentioned (in around 540) by King Maelgwyn of Gwynedd, the uncle of St. David, who wrote:

> Joseph had with him in his sarcophagus two
> white and silver cruets filled with the blood
> and sweat of the prophet, Jesus.

The cruets are portrayed in stained-glass windows at St. John's Church, Glastonbury, at Langport Church in Somerset, and in a rood-screen portrait at Plymtree, Devon — but they were never put on public display, if indeed they ever existed. Hence, this lack of visible accreditation gave rise a few centuries later to a new Glastonbury tradition — one that was more amenable to the common gaze: the enchanted Thornbush.[8] In 1520, local literature described a bush on Wearyall Hill that bore fresh leaves and blossoms at Christmas time as well as in May. The bush was destroyed during the Cromwellian Civil War (1642-1651), but shoots from it were replanted in the area, and each plant flowered again in the same way. Botanical experts discerned that the shrub was not native to England, and seemed to be of Levantine origin — in consequence of which a new Somerset mythology began.

In 1716 a local innkeeper asserted that the unusual thorn plant sprang from the staff of Joseph of Arimathea, which he had planted to blossom at Christmas (not that the December festival had been relevant in Joseph's day. It was nearly 300 years later that Constantine adjusted the date of Jesus's birthday to comply with the Yuletide solstice). The notion that Joseph's rod should burst into flower in this way derived originally from a prophetic verse in Isaiah (11:1), which reads: 'And there shall come forth a rod out of the stem of Jesse [the father of David], and a branch shall grow out of his roots'. In some Church artwork and apocryphal writings, the budding staff of the royal bloodline is depicted in the hand of Jesus's father, Joseph.

It was not until Alfred, Lord Tennyson's 19th-century *Idylls of the King* that Glastonbury was specifically linked with the Holy Grail. The unusually reddish water of Glastonbury's Chalk Well (actually tinted red by iron oxide) was ready-made for association with the blood of Jesus. It was duly renamed Chalice Well, and the water's colour was said to derive from the contents of the Grail chalice which Joseph had buried nearby. The famous lid of the well shaft, complete with Celtic-style ironwork, was designed by the architect Frederick Bligh Bond after World War I. Notwithstanding the assortment of saintly and Arthurian mementoes at Glastonbury (some real and some contrived), Joseph of Arimathea's personal association with Britain remained historically much better attested. It was a subject of debate at various European Church Councils, with the English able to claim a Christian connection long before any at Rome. At the Council of Pisa in 1409 there was even an argument about whether Joseph or Mary Magdalene had come to the West first. These days it would be astonishing if the Church were to admit that Mary or Joseph ever came at all.

Tarot and the Grail

The mysterious blood-tipped white lance that generally accompanied the Grail in the legends was said to be the weapon that pierced the groin of the Fisher King. It was identified with the biblical spear of Longinus, which drew the blood of Jesus at the Crucifixion. The lance, along with a cup, sword and dish (or platter), constituted the Hallows of Grail Castle.[9]

Many readers have asked about the nature of Longinus since, although his name is generally well known as that of the centurion with the spear, it is not actually mentioned in the Gospels. It comes, in fact, from the apocryphal *Acts of Pilate* 15:7 (sometimes called the *Gospel of Nicodemus*), which was omitted from the New Testament. In practice though, Longinus was not a proper name at all; it was the Latinized form of the Greek word Longynx, which meant 'spearman' or 'lancer'.

Following Pope Gregory IX's first Catholic Inquisition of 1231, Grail lore was condemned by the Church. It was not denounced outright as a heresy, but all material related to it was suppressed. As a result, the tradition moved towards underground symbolism — particularly that of the Tarot cards.[10] These emerged from northern Italy, Marseilles and Lyon in the 1300s. Some of the most refreshing work to emerge in recent years concerning the Tarot, and concerning graphic symbolism in general, comes from the American author, Margaret Starbird. Her writings in this regard are fully in accord with the precepts of Grail tradition.

The four suits of the Tarot's Minor Arcana were the Swords, Cups, Pentacles and Batons (or Wands). These corresponded with the Sword, Cup, Platter and Lance of the Grail Hallows. Eventually they became redefined as the Spades, Hearts, Diamonds and Clubs that are used in playing card decks today. The Spade was originally a blade (the male symbol); the Heart was the chalice of the alternative Church (the female symbol); the Diamond was a valuable Pentacle disc (also representing a dish or platter of service), and the Club (denoting the continuing Davidic lineage) was depicted as the sprouting Rod of Jesse.

From the earliest times, the symbols and had been used to identify the sacred unity of the bridal chamber. The V-shaped symbol of the female Chalice and upturned V of the male Blade (gender opposites) were brought together (one above the other) in the familiar X-sign. This was the original holy Sign of the Cross, and was used as the mark of baptism and initiation long before the time of Jesus. As confirmed in the Dead Sea Scrolls, it was placed on the foreheads of those who cried for Jerusalem (Ezekiel 9:4), and was granted at the highest degree of Community initiation into the Sanctuary.

By way of later Roman influence, a new cross was devised — the upright Latin cross of St. Peter's Church, with its high crosspiece. The esoteric Christians retained their former X, however, perceiving the Latin cross as representative of Roman torture. And so the original became a sign of heresy in the eyes of Rome. This heretical image has been perpetuated to this day as being associated with flesh and the devil — as in X-rated movies. Indeed, its anti-establishment significance has been indoctrinated in schools through the simple process of using x to mean 'wrong'.[11]

Even though St. Peter's cross was Latinized, the tradition of his brother Andrew was maintained by the original X-glyph: the St. Andrew's cross. Andrew was crucified at Patras near the Black Sea, where he had worked among the Scythians before they began their westward movement to Ireland and Caledonia. As a result, he became the patron saint of Scotland, and his cross became the famous national Saltire. Rome was not happy about the reappearance of this ancient esoteric device, and a covering story was contrived to the effect that Andrew perished on an X-shaped cross.

A compromise cross was later devised — the familiar non-cruciform, non-esoteric, upright centred cross. This became the cross of Saint George, whose cult was brought to the West by the Crusaders. Following the 1864 Geneva Convention, it became the symbol of the International Red Cross agency—a colour reversal of the Swiss flag.

The powers of the Pope's inquisitors were increased in 1252, when torture, secret trials and death by burning were authorized. In Spain, the persecution of heretics was aimed particularly at apostate Jews and Muslims from 1478. Pope Paul III's Roman Inquisition against Protestants began in 1542. The 'underground stream' of the Grail retained its identity by way of secret watermarks and outline symbols. Because of its simplicity, the X-symbol was widely used— sometimes very openly and cleverly. In Botticelli's *Madonna of the Pomegranate,* an angel wears a red ribboned X on his chest. In his *Madonna of the Book* (1483), Mary wears a red X on her bodice, while the baby Jesus holds three miniature golden arrows. These were the esoteric symbols of the Three Shafts of Enlightenment—a motif of Hermetic alchemists.

The secrets of the Tarot were held in the 22 trump cards—the Major Arcana. The word 'trump' in this context derives from the old French *trompe,* corresponding to the trumpet that figuratively split Peter's Church. The Tarot trumps have been called *The Book of Thoth,* an

Tarot Cards—*The World* and *The Tower*

expression of the secret wisdom. The Church of Rome condemned the minor suits, but expressly banned the trumps because they were deemed blasphemous. In truth there was nothing anti-Christian about the playing cards, although they were undoubtedly anti-establishment. The Christianity of the Tarot was that of old Grail lore, not that of Catholicism. The fact that gypsies and others subsequently used the Tarot cards for divination was quite incidental to their original purpose — but it was through this secondary use that Church propaganda managed to foist an abiding sinister image onto the Tarot deck.

Modern playing cards still retain the *Joker* from the Tarot. He is a fool but, even so, the Joker always wins. His legacy is from 1-Corinthians:

> The Lord knoweth the thoughts of the wise,
> that they are vain. Therefore, let no man glory
> in men (3:20-21).
> We are fools for Christ's sake (4:10).

A literary representation of the Joker is apparent in Perceval, the simple man who succeeds where the more accomplished fail. Other Tarot figures have made their mark in the world at large. Not the least of these is the female symbol of Justice. She is the star-maiden Virgo, with her two-edged sword and the scales of Libra. The portrayal actually has more to do with discrimination than with justice — showing Nature's balance and harmony on the one hand, while the other wields the spike of judicial authority. The original card depicted the tenuous position of the Grail Church against the severity of the Roman Inquisition, and it was known as the Magdalene Card.

Other cards associated with Mary Magdalene were *The Tower*, *The World*, and *Strength*. In the Grail tradition, *The Tower* (or House of God) represented the *Magdal-eder* (the Watchtower of the Flock, as in Micah 4:8), and it was not unlike a chess Castle (or Rook). Being struck by lightning, or otherwise mysteriously assaulted, *The Tower* symbolized the plight of the esoteric Church against the merciless Roman establishment.

The spirit of Mary Magdalene was also manifest in *The World*. Standing or dancing within an oval wreath, and either naked or clothed, the woman held a sceptre or other mark of sovereignty. Some cards showed her above an encircled landscape. The portrayal was similar to the soaring, hair-enveloped Magdalene in the 1490 *Sforza Book of Hours*.

The *Strength* card normally depicted a woman in charge of a lion, or supporting a broken pillar. Some cards had both images. The former was the Lion of Judah, and the latter was the Pillar of Boaz ('In strength') from Solomon's Temple. Either way, the woman was the governess and mainstay of the royal succession:

> And thine house and thy kingdom shall be established for ever before thee: thy throne shall be established for ever (2-Samuel 7:16).

In some early decks, a Grail design was incorporated within this card, and the woman was identified with Mary Magdalene. The depiction represented the continuation of the Davidic line as in Psalm 89:4: 'Thy seed will I establish for ever, and build up thy throne to all generations'.

Guardians of the Sacred Relic

The Crusader Knights

From the onset of the 8th-century Carolingian dynasty in France, the Church implemented a new territorial dominion, fronted by its puppet-kings, across western and central Europe. This became the Holy Roman Empire, which persisted until its termination in 1806. During this period, Imperial history was compiled by Vatican scribes, or by those who operated by Vatican authority. The inevitable result was that accounts of the murdered Merovingian King Dagobert were suppressed to the point of his non-existence in the chronicles. Not for another thousand years did the true facts of his life become generally known, and only then in the 17th century did it become apparent that Dagobert had a son called Sigebert, whose descendants included the famous crusader, Godefroi de Bouillon, Defender of the Holy Sepulchre.

By the time of the Norman conquest of Britain in 1066, the Merovingians of Gaul had been formally ignored for some 300 years. During their reign, however, they had established a number of governmental customs which prevailed thereafter. One of the Merovingian innovations was a system of regional supervision by chief officers called *Comtes* (Counts). As deputies of the Kings, the Counts acted as chancellors, judges and military leaders. They were not unlike the Celtic Earls of Britain, although the nature of both titular groups became changed to incorporate land tenure during feudal times.

In the 11th century, the Counts of Flanders and Boulogne emerged at the very forefront of Flemish society. Given Godefroi de Bouillon's Davidic inheritance through the Merovingians, it was fitting that he (a brother of Count Eustace III of Boulogne) should become the designated King of Jerusalem after the First Crusade. This military venture was sparked in 1095 by the Muslim seizure of Jerusalem, subsequent to which Pope Urban II raised a formidable army, led by the best knights in Europe. It was particularly inspired by Peter the Hermit who led an ill-fated Peasants' Crusade of men, women and children across Europe to regain the Holy Land. The majority did not reach their destination, and thousands were massacred *en route* by outlaws and wayward soldiers of the Byzantine Empire. In the esoteric Tarot cards, the Hermit (an allusion to Peter) is portrayed with a lantern lighting the way.

In the wake of the Hermit's misfortune, Pope Urban's army was coordinated by Adhemar, Bishop of Le Puy, and in the vanguard was Robert, Duc de Normandie, together with Stephen, Comte de Blois, and Hugh, Comte de Vermandois. The Flemish contingent was led by Robert, Comte de Flandres, and included Eustace, Comte de Boulogne, with his brothers Godefroi de Bouillon and Baldwin. The South of France was represented by Raymond de St. Gilles, Comte de Toulouse.

At that point, Godefroi de Bouillon was Duke of Lower Lorraine. He had succeeded to the title through his famous mother, St. Ida, from whom he gained the castle and lands of Bouillon—estates which he mortgaged to the Bishop of Liège in order to fund his Holy Land campaign. By the time the First Crusade was under way, Godefroi had become its overall commander and, on its eventual success in 1099, he was proclaimed King of Jerusalem. In the event, he preferred not to use the dignity of King, assuming instead the alternative distinction, Defender of the Sacred Sepulchre.

Of the eight Crusades, which persisted until 1291 in Egypt, Syria and Palestine, only Godefroi's First Crusade was to any avail, but even that was marred by the excesses of irresponsible troops who used their victory as an excuse for wholesale slaughter of Muslims in the streets of Jerusalem. Not only was Jerusalem important to the Jews and Christians, but it had become the third Holy City of Islam, after Mecca and Medina. As such, the city sits at the heart of continuing disputes today.

The Second Crusade to Edessa, led by Louis VII of France and the German Emperor Conrad III, failed miserably. Then, around a hundred years after Godefroi's initial success, Jerusalem fell again to the mighty Saladin in 1187. This prompted the Third Crusade under Philip Augustus of France and Richard the Lionheart of England, but they did not manage to win back the Holy City. The Fourth and Fifth Crusades centred on Constantinople and Damietta. Jerusalem was reclaimed briefly after Emperor Frederick II's Sixth Crusade, but was finally conceded to the Sultan of Egypt in 1244. Louis IX then led the

Seventh and Eighth Crusades, but fell short of reversing the situation. By 1291, Palestine and Syria were firmly under Muslim control, and the Crusades were over.

During this crusading era, various knightly Orders emerged, including the Ordre de Sion (Order of Sion),[1] founded by Godefroi de Bouillon in 1099. Others were the Knights Protectors of the Sacred Sepulchre and the Knights Templars. Godefroi de Bouillon died in 1100, soon after his Jerusalem triumph, to be succeeded as King by his younger brother, Baldwin of Boulogne. After eighteen years, Baldwin was followed, in 1118, by his cousin, Baldwin II du Bourg. According to the orthodox accounts, the Knights Templars were founded in that year as the Poor Knights of Christ and of the Temple of Solomon. They were said to have been established by a group of nine Frenchmen, who took vows of poverty, chastity and obedience, and swore to protect the Holy Land.

The Frankish historian, Guillaume de Tyre, wrote at the height of the Crusades (in around 1180) that the function of the Templars was to safeguard the highways for pilgrims. But, given the enormity of such an obligation, it is inconceivable that nine poor men succeeded without enlisting new recruits until they returned to Europe in 1128. In truth, there was a good deal more to the Order than is conveyed in Guillaume's account.

The Knights were in existence for some years before they were said to have been founded by Hugues de Payens, a cousin and vassal of the Comte de Champagne. Their function was certainly not highway patrol and the King's chronicler, Fulk de Chartres, did not portray them in that light at all. They were the King's front-line diplomats in a Muslim environment and, in this capacity, they endeavoured to make due amends for the actions of unruly Crusaders against the Sultan's defenceless subjects. The Bishop of Chartres wrote about the Templars as early as 1114, calling them the *Milice du Christi* (Soldiers of Christ). At that time, the Knights were already installed at Baldwin's palace, which was located within a mosque on the site of King Solomon's Temple. When Baldwin moved to the domed citadel on the Tower of David, the Temple quarters were left entirely to the Order of Templars.

Hugues de Payens was both the founder and first Grand Master of the Order. His second in command was the Flemish knight Godefroi Saint Omer, while another recruit was André de Montbard, a kinsman of the Count of Burgundy. In 1120 Fulk, Comte d'Anjou (father of Geoffrey Plantagenet) also joined the Order, and he was followed in 1124 by de Payen's liege lord, Hugues, Comte de Champagne. The

Knights were evidently far from poor, and there is no record of these illustrious noblemen policing the Bedouin-infested highways for the benefit of pilgrims.

The task of ministering to the pilgrims was actually performed by the Hospitallers of St. John of Jerusalem. The separate Knights Templars were a very select and special unit. They had sworn a particular oath of obedience — not to the King or to their leader, but to the Cistercian Abbot, St. Bernard de Clairvaux (died 1153),[2] who was related to the Comte de Champagne. Indeed, it was on land donated by the Comte that Bernard built the Cistercian monastery of Clairvaux in 1115. It was St. Bernard who rescued Scotland's failing Celtic Church and rebuilt the Columban monastery on Iona.[3] It was St. Bernard who (from 1128) first translated the sacred geometry of King Solomon's Masons, and it was St. Bernard who preached the Second Crusade at Vézelay to King Louis VII and a congregation of 100,000. At Vézelay stood the great Basilica of St. Mary Magdalene and St. Bernard's Oath of the Knights Templars required the 'Obedience of Bethany — the castle of Mary and Martha'.[4]

There is no coincidence in the fact that Chrétien de Troyes' 12th-century work, *le Conte del Graal*, was dedicated to Philippe d'Alsace, Comte de Flandres. Nor was it by chance that Chrétien was sponsored and encouraged in his undertaking by Countess Marie and the Court of Champagne. Grail lore was born directly out of this early Templar environment, and the *Perlesvaus* portrayed the Knights as the wardens of a great and sacred secret. Wolfram's *Parzival* defined them as the Guardians of the Grail Family.

Sanctuary of the Ark

Deep beneath the Jerusalem Temple site was the great stable complex of King Solomon, which had remained sealed and untouched since Bible times. The enormous underground shelter was described by a Crusader as 'a stable of such marvellous capacity and extent that it could hold more than 2000 horses'.[5] To open up this capacious repository was the original secret mission of the Knights Templars, for it was known by St. Bernard to contain the wealth of Old Testament Jerusalem, including the Ark of the Covenant which, in turn, held the greatest of all treasures: the Tables of Testimony.[6]

One might well ask why these relics from the time of Moses became the objects of such a guarded mission fronted by a Cistercian abbot and the flower of Flemish nobility. Today's Church-approved writings state that the tablets of Moses bore the Ten Commandments etched into stone by God Himself—yet the substance of these well-known decrees of moral discipline hardly constituted any sort of secret. In fact, the tablets sought by the Knights were uniquely important, for they bore far more than the familiar Commandments. Inscribed on them were the Tables of Testimony—the cosmic equation: the divine law of number, measure and weight. The mystical art of reading the inscriptions was achieved by the cryptic system of the Qabala.

The Ten Commandments were something else altogether. They were the precepts that God firstly delivered to Moses and the people on Mount Sinai (Exodus 20 to 23), accompanied by a series of verbal ordinances. Then, God said to Moses (Exodus 24:12),

> Come up to me into the mount, and be there:
> and I will give thee tables of stone, and a law,
> and commandments which I have written;
> that thou mayest teach them.

There are three quite separate items listed here: tables of stone; a law; commandments. God further stated, 'And thou shalt put into the ark the testimony which I shall give thee' (Exodus 25:16). Later, in Exodus 31:18, 'he gave unto Moses ... two tables of testimony, tables of stone.'

The original tablets were broken by Moses when he cast them to the ground (Exodus 32:19). Afterwards, God said to Moses (Exodus 34:1),

> Hew thee two tables of stone like unto the
> first: and *I will write* upon these tables the
> words that were in the first tables, which thou
> brakest.

Subsequently, God verbally reiterated the Commandments, and said to Moses, 'Write thou these words', whereupon Moses 'wrote ... the words of the covenant, the ten commandments' (Exodus 34:27-28).

There was a positive distinction made between the Tables of Testimony (written by God) and the Ten Commandments (separately written by Moses). For centuries the Church has implied that the Covenant of the Ten Commandments was the important part of this package, in consequence of which the truly important Tables of Testimony have been strategically ignored.

Conventual Blood Cross of the Knights Templars

Onwards from Exodus 25, precise instructions for the Ark's construction are set down in great detail. Similarly, the methods for its transportation are given, along with the specifications for clothes and footwear to be worn by the bearers and overseers. The design and materials for the Tabernacle, in which the Ark was to be kept, are in addition thoroughly described, as is the composition of the altar within. Notwithstanding all this, Exodus 37-40 continues to give a full account of how these instructions were followed to the letter, so repeating everything again. There was no room for any mistakes, nor any deviation from blueprints laid down. All the building work was entrusted to Bezaleel, the son of Uri Ben Hur of Judah.

When constructed precisely in compliance with the Old Testament descriptions, the Ark is discovered to be not only an elaborate coffer but an electrical condenser—built of resinous wood, and double-plated inside and out with gold. The facts have been stated many times by scientists and theologians alike. The individual plates when negatively and positively charged can produce several hundred volts—sufficient even to kill a man. Uzzah discovered this to his cost when he touched the Ark (2-Samuel 6:6-7 and 1-Chronicles 13:9-10). Moreover, the Ark also emerges as an effective transmitter of sound, by way of which Moses was said to have communicated with God (Exodus 25:22).

The Ten Commandments were, and are, written, spoken, discussed and taught. They have never been a secret to anyone—unlike the Tables of Testimony. These precious tabulations were placed in the self-protecting Ark, to be guarded by the Levites. Following the Ark's dramatic transportation across Jordan and through Palestine (Joshua and 1-Samuel), it was taken to Sion (Jerusalem) by David. His son, King Solomon, had the Temple built by the Master-Mason Hiram Abiff, and the Ark was lodged in the Holy of Holies. Access was forbidden, except for ritual inspection by the High Priest alone once a year.

Apart from a few items of passing reference, that is the last the Bible has to tell about the Ark of the Covenant. Rumour suggested that the Ark was removed to Ethiopia (Abyssinia), but Revelation 11:19 indicates that it remained in the Temple of Heaven. Undoubtedly, the Ark and the Tables were the prized possessions of Jerusalem, but when Nebuchadnezzar of Babylon destroyed the Temple (in around 586 BC), neither was listed in the schedule of plunder.

At that time, the High Priest of Jerusalem was Hilkiah, whose son was Jeremiah the prophet (Jeremiah 1:1), who was also the captain of the Temple Guard. Prior to Nebuchadnezzar's invasion, Hilkiah instructed Jeremiah to have his men secrete the Temple treasures in the stables beneath — including the Ark of the Covenant. This was duly done, with the Guard forming an elite Order of the Temple so as to retain the record of the sacred hoard. Hence, when St. Bernard and de Payens established their Order more than 1500 years later, their appointed Knights knew precisely what they were seeking, and where.

Bloodline of the Holy Grail readers have often enquired about when precisely the Order of the Temple of Jerusalem was founded, since there is an amount of controversy as to whether it was in or before the generally given year of 1118. In reality, however, it can be said that the 12th-century establishment was actually a reconstituting of the Order, for it was originally founded by Hilkiah and Jeremiah long before in 586 BC.

By 1127, the Templars' search was over. They had retrieved not only the Ark and its contents, but an untold wealth of gold bullion and hidden treasure, all of which had been safely stowed below ground long before the Roman demolition and plunder of AD 70. It was not until 1956 that confirmatory evidence of the Jerusalem hoard came to light at Manchester University. The deciphering of the Qumrân *Copper Scroll* was completed that year and it revealed that an 'indeterminable treasure', along with a vast stockpile of bullion and valuables, had been buried beneath the Temple.

In the light of the Templars' overwhelming success, Hugues de Payens received a summons from St. Bernard to attend a forthcoming Council at Troyes. It was to be chaired by the papal ambassador, the Cardinal Legate of France. Hugues and a company of knights duly left the Holy Land with their auspicious find and St. Bernard announced that the Jerusalem mission had been fulfilled. He wrote,

> The work has been accomplished with our help, and the Knights have been sent on a journey through France and Burgundy, under the protection of the Count of Champagne, where all precautions can be taken against all interference by public or ecclesiastical authority.[7]

The Champagne Court at Troyes was well prepared for the cryptic translation work to follow and, in readiness, the Court had long sponsored an influential school of Qabalistic studies. The Council of Troyes was held in 1128, at which time St. Bernard became the official Patron and Protector of the Knights Templars. In that year, international status as a Sovereign Order was conferred upon the Templars and their Jerusalem headquarters became the governing office of the capital city. The Church established the Knights as a religious Order and Hugues de Payens was formally installed as Grand Master.

As distinct from the Templar Cross (red on white), the Hospitallers of Saint John used a different colour scheme (silver on black) in the same design. Their pilgrims' hospital in Jerusalem was founded before the Crusades in about 1050. After the fall of Acre, which ended the Crusades in 1291, the Hospitallers were forced to leave Palestine. They went to Rhodes and Cyprus, adding secular and military ventures to their activities, and from 1530 they were established as the Knights of Malta. An offshoot, chartered in 1888, created Britain's St. John Ambulance Association, which still uses the same badge.

After the Council of Troyes, the Templars' rise to international prominence was remarkably swift. They became engaged in high-level politics and diplomacy throughout the western world and were advisers to monarchs and parliaments alike. Just eleven years later, in 1139, Pope Innocent II (another Cistercian) granted the Knights international independence from obligation to any authority save himself. Irrespective of kings, cardinals or governments, the Order's only superior was the Pope. Even prior to this, however, they were granted vast territories and substantial property across the map from Britain to Palestine. The *Anglo-Saxon Chronicle* states that when Hugues de Payens visited England's Henry I, 'the King received him with much honour, and gave him rich presents'. The Spanish King,

Alfonso of Aragon, passed a third of his kingdom to the Order and the whole of Christendom was at their feet.

Notre Dame

When news spread of the Templars' incredible find, the Knights became revered by all and, notwithstanding their Jerusalem wealth, large donations were received from all quarters. No price was too high to secure affiliation and, within a decade of their return, the Templars were probably the most influential body the world has ever known. Nevertheless, despite the prodigious holdings of the Order, the individual Knights were bound to a vow of poverty. Whatever his station in life, every Templar was obliged to sign over title to his possessions—yet still the sons of nobility flocked to join the Order. Being so well funded, the Templars established the first international banking network, becoming financiers for the Levant and for practically every throne in Europe.

Just as the Order grew to high estate, so too did the Cistercians' fortune rise in parallel and, within twenty-five years of the Council of Troyes, they could boast more than three-hundred abbeys. But that was not the end of it, for the people of France then witnessed the most astounding result of the Templars' knowledge of the universal equation. City skylines began to change as the great *Notre Dame* cathedrals, with their majestic Gothic arches, rose from the earth. The architecture was phenomenal—impossible, some said. The pointed ogives reached incredible heights, spanning hitherto insurmountable space, with flying buttresses and thinly ribbed vaulting. Everything pulled upwards and, despite the thousands of tons of richly decorated stone, the overall impression was one of magical weightlessness.

By referencing the Tables of Testimony, the cosmic law and its sacred geometry were applied by the Templar masons to construct the finest holy monuments ever to grace the Christian world. At the northern door of *Notre Dame de Chartres* (the Gate of the Initiates), a relief carving on a small column depicts the Ark of the Covenant undergoing transportation. The inscription translates to: 'Here, things take their course; you are to work through the Ark'.[8]

The cathedrals were all built at much the same time, even though some took more than a century to complete in their various stages.[9] *Notre Dame* in Paris was begun in 1163, Chartres in 1194, Reims in 1211 and Amiens in 1221. Others of the same era were at Bayeux, Abbeville, Rouen, Laon, Evreux and Etampes. In accordance with the Hermetic principle 'As above, so below', the combined ground-plan of the *Notre*

Dame cathedrals replicates the Virgo constellation.[10] Of all these, *Notre Dame de Chartres* is said to stand on the most sacred ground.

Notable among the authorities on the history of Chartres is Louis Charpentier, whose research and writings have done much to increase the understanding of Gothic architecture in general. He tells that at Chartres the telluric earth currents are at their highest and the site was recognized for its divine atmosphere even in druidic times. So venerated is the location of Chartres that it is the only cathedral not to have a single king, bishop, cardinal, canon, or anyone interred in the soil of its mound. It was a pagan site, dedicated to the traditional Mother Goddess—a site to which pilgrims travelled long before the time of Jesus. The original altar was built above the 'Grotte des Druides', which housed a sacred dolmen[11] and was identified with the Womb of the Earth.

One of the greatest mysteries of Gothic architecture is the stained glass used in the cathedral windows. This first appeared in the early 12th century, but disappeared just as suddenly a hundred years later. Nothing like it had ever been seen before, and nothing like it has been seen since. Not only is the luminosity of Gothic glass greater than any other, but its light-enhancement qualities are far more effective. Unlike the stained glass of other architectural schools, its interior effect is the same whether the light outside is bright or dim. Even in twilight, this glass retains its brilliance way beyond that of any other.

Gothic glass also has the unique power to transform harmful ultra-violet rays into beneficial light, but the secret of its manufacture was never revealed, although it was known to have been a product of Hermetic alchemy. Those employed to perfect the glass were Persian philosophical mathematicians such as Omar Khayyam, whose adepts claimed their method incorporated the *Spiritus Mundi*—the cosmic breath of the universe. Only very recently, as detailed in *Genesis of the Grail Kings*,[12] has the secret manufacturing process become known—a process which has stunning implications way beyond the glass itself.

Throughout the Gothic cathedrals works of architectural art abound, depicting biblical history and the Gospel stories, in which much attention is given to the life of Jesus. Some of the work currently visible was added after the 1300s, but during the true Gothic era there was not one portrayal of the Crucifixion. On the basis of pre-Gospel writings discovered in Jerusalem, the Templars denied the Crucifixion sequence as described in the New Testament and, for that reason, never depicted the scene. The 12th-century window in the West front

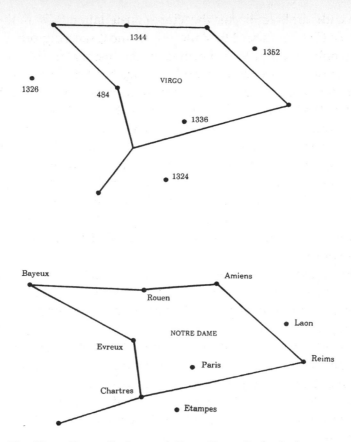

The Virgo Constellation and *Notre Dame* Cathedrals.
(Based on a diagram by Louis Charpentier)

of Chartres includes a medallion of the Crucifixion, but this was transferred from elsewhere at a later date—probably from St. Denis, just north of Paris. There are similarly inherited windows at other *Notre Dame* cathedrals.

In addition to the Jerusalem bullion, the Templars also found a wealth of ancient manuscripts in Hebrew and Syriac, providing first-hand accounts that had not been edited by any ecclesiastical authority. In the light of these, it was widely accepted that the Knights possessed an insight which eclipsed orthodox Christianity—an insight which permitted them the certainty that the Church had misinterpreted both the Virgin Birth and the Resurrection. They were nevertheless highly regarded as holy men, and were firmly attached to the Cistercian popes of the era.

In times to follow, however, the once revered knowledge of the Templars caused their persecution by the popes of other Orders, and by the savage Dominican friars of the Inquisition. It was at that point in the history of Christianity that the last vestige of free thinking disappeared. Neither special knowledge nor access to truths counted for anything against the hard new party line of Rome. So too did all traces of the female aspect disappear, with only the Blessed Mary left to represent all womankind. In practice, her semi-divine Virgin-Madonna status was so far removed from any reality that she represented no one. But despite this, a ray of hope has prevailed, for another female light shines from the cathedrals of *Notre Dame*, wherein the veneration of Mary Magdalene remains central to the theme. The beautiful Magdalene window at Chartres has an inscription which reads 'Donated by the Water-carriers' — the Aquarians. Mary was the bearer of the Holy Grail and she will undoubtedly become more prominent as the great new inspiration of the Aquarian Age — the age of renewed intellect, wisdom and the Universal Law of the Ark.

Brotherhood of the Third Degree

The Notre Dame cathedrals and major Gothic constructions were mainly the work of the Children of Solomon — a guild of masons instructed by St. Bernard's Cistercian Order. St. Bernard had translated the secret geometry of King Solomon's masons who, under their own master, Hiram Abiff, were denoted by degrees of knowledge and proficiency. Solomon had specifically approached King Hiram of Tyre for the assistance of Hiram Abiff, an architect and metalworker, skilled in sacred geometry.[13] Even though Tyre was a renowned centre of Goddess worship, Hiram Abiff became the chief designer and Master Mason for the Temple of Jehovah. By virtue of this, he was destined to become a key symbolic figure in later Freemasonry.

Other masonic brotherhoods of medieval France were the Children of Father Soubise, and the Children of Master Jacques.[14] When the 14th-century Dominican-led Inquisition against the Templars was in full swing, these guilds were equally at risk. Being practitioners of the Masonic Craft, they held privileged information concerning the workings of sacred geometry and Universal Law according to their attained degrees. There were three such degrees: Apprentice Companion, Attained Companion, and Master Companion — just as there are now three degrees in the mainstream of modern speculative Freemasonry. This is why, following the Inquisition of the Templars, a severe interrogation to extract the most vital or the most secret information is often called the Third Degree.

Although modern Freemasonry is said to derive from the medieval guilds of Europe, the Craft had far more distant origins. Carvings on the Egyptian obelisk in Central Park, New York, have been identified as masonic symbols from the time of Pharaoh Tuthmosis III (*c*.1468-1436 BC).[15] He was the great-great-grandfather of Moses. Tuthmosis (heir of Tuth/Thoth) was the founder of an influential secret society of scholars and philosophers, whose purpose was to preserve the sacred mysteries. In later times, the Samaritan Magi were members of the Order, being attached to the Egyptian Therapeutate, an ascetic community at Qumrân. It was from Egypt that Moses (Akhenaten) introduced the concept of temple worship to the Israelites when he created the Tabernacle at Sinai. Similarly, the very notion of priesthood was Egyptian—inherited originally from ancient Sumer. Prior to the Tabernacle of Moses, the Jewish patriarchs had used simple outside stone altars as places of reverence and sacrifice—such as those erected by Noah (Genesis 8:20) and Abraham (Genesis 22:9).

A second Egyptian obelisk from the Temple of the Sun (known for some obscure reason as Cleopatra's Needle—relating to Cleopatra VII, although it predated her by more than a thousand years) stands on the Thames Embankment in London. It is 68 feet 6 inches (20.88 metres) high[16] and weighs 186 tons. The two granite obelisks were originally entrance pillars to the Temple at Heliopolis, but were moved to Alexandria in 12 BC, then to London and New York in 1878 and 1881 respectively.

In line with the Egyptian practice of placing free-standing pillars at temple entrances, Hiram Abiff introduced the same theme at the porch of King Solomon's Temple in Jerusalem. The pillars, with their rounded capitals, were akin to the designs of Tyre goddess worship, and were also similar to the fertility symbols dedicated to Astarte in Canaan. The Jerusalem pillars were called Jachin and Boaz (1-Kings 7:21 and 2-Chronicles 3:17). They were built hollow in order to serve as repositories for the archival and constitutional rolls of Masonry. Moreover, although the Temple was dedicated to Jehovah and designed primarily to house the Ark of the Covenant, its construction was not limited to the Hebrews' masculine principle of God: it was constructed largely in keeping with traditional custom and incorporated both the male and female geometric energies.

The Temple was completed in seven years, at the end of which time Hiram was murdered and placed in a shallow grave. His death is said to have come about through his refusal to impart the Master Mason's secrets to the unenlightened workers. Today, the symbolized slaying of Hiram features significantly in the Third Degree ceremony of Freemasonry; the candidate is struck down and raised again from the darkness of his grave by use of the Master Mason's secret grip.

Modern Freemasonry is speculative rather than operative, but even in Hiram's day the society of artificers to which he belonged had its own lodges, symbols and passwords. One evident symbol was the ascia (the mason's trowel), an emblem used by the Pythagoreans and Essenes. It is also found in the catacombs of Rome, where portrayals of masonic initiation were painted in the tombs of the persecuted Innocenti.

Slaughter in Languedoc

West-north-west of Marseilles, on the Golfe du Lion, stretches the old province of Languedoc where, in 1208, the people were admonished by Pope Innocent III for unchristian behaviour. In the following year, a papal army of 30,000 soldiers descended upon the region under the command of Simon de Montfort. They were deceitfully adorned with the red cross of the Holy Land Crusaders, but their purpose was very different. They had, in fact, been sent to exterminate the ascetic Cathari sect (the Pure Ones) who, according to the Pope and King Philippe II of France, were heretics. The slaughter went on for thirty-five years, claiming tens of thousands of lives and culminating in the hideous massacre at the seminary of Montségur, where more than 200 hostages were set up on stakes and burned alive in 1244.[17]

In religious terms, the doctrine of the Cathars was essentially Gnostic; they were notably spiritual people, who believed that the spirit was pure but that physical matter was defiled. Although their convictions were unorthodox in comparison with the avaricious pursuits of Rome, the Pope's dread of the Cathars was actually caused by something far more threatening. They were said to be the guardians of a great and sacred treasure associated with a fantastic and ancient knowledge. The Languedoc region was substantially that which had formed the 8th-century Jewish kingdom of Septimania and was steeped in the traditions of Lazarus (Simon Zelotes), whilst the inhabitants regarded Mary Magdalene as the Grail Mother of Christendom.[18]

Like the Templars, the Cathars were expressly tolerant of the Jewish and Muslim cultures. They also upheld the equality of the sexes[19] but, for all that, they were condemned and violently suppressed by the Catholic Inquisition (formally instituted in 1233) and were charged with all manners of blasphemy and sexual deviance. Contrary to the charges, the witnesses brought to give evidence spoke only of the Cathars' Church of Love and of their unyielding devotion to the ministry of Jesus. They believed in God and the Holy Spirit, recited the Lord's Prayer and ran an exemplary society with its own welfare system of charity schools and hospitals. They even had the Bible translated into their own tongue, the *langue d'oc* (hence the regional name), and the non-Cathar population equally benefited from their altruistic efforts.

In practical terms, the Cathars were simply non-conformists, preaching without licence and having no requirement for appointed priests or the richly adorned churches of their Catholic neighbours. St. Bernard had said that 'No sermons are more Christian than theirs and their morals are pure' — yet still the papal armies came, in the outward guise of a holy mission, to eradicate their community from the landscape.

The edict of annihilation referred not only to the mystical Cathars themselves, but to all who supported them — which included most of the people of Languedoc. At that time, although geographically a part of France, the region was actually an independent State. Politically, it was more associated with the northern Spanish frontier, having the Count of Toulouse as its overlord. Classical languages were taught, along with literature, philosophy and mathematics. The area was generally quite wealthy and commercially stable, but all this was to change in 1209 when the papal troops arrived in the foothills of the Pyrenees. In allusion to the Languedoc centre at Albi, the savage campaign was called the Albigensian Crusade[20] — at least that is what we are generally told. However, the name has a far more important implication. Albi was, in fact, a variant of the old European word *ylbi* (a female elf) and the Cathars referred to the Messianic *Sangréal* as the *Albi gens*: the 'Elven bloodline'.

Of all the religious cults that flourished in medieval times, Catharism was the least menacing and the fact that the Cathars were associated with a particular ancient knowledge was no new revelation; Guilhelm de Toulouse de Gellone, King of Septimania, had established his Judaic Academy more than four centuries earlier. However, this fact (along with the notion that the Cathars held an unsurpassed treasure more historically meaningful than the root of Christianity) led Rome to only one conclusion: the Ark, the Tables of Testimony and the Jerusalem manuscripts must be hidden in Languedoc. This, it was felt, was enough to blow the lid off the fundamental concept of the orthodox Roman Church. There was only one solution for a desperate and fanatical regime — and so the word went out: 'Kill them all!'

Kingdom of the Scots

Persecution of the Templars

The pseudo Crusade ended in 1244, but it was to be another sixty-two years before Pope Clement V and King Philippe IV were in a position to harass the Knights Templars in their bid for the arcane treasure. By 1306 the Jerusalem Order was so powerful that Philippe IV of France viewed them with trepidation; he owed a great deal of money to the Knights and was practically bankrupt. He also feared their political and esoteric might, which he knew to be far greater than his own. With papal support, King Philippe persecuted the Templars in France and endeavoured to eliminate the Order in other countries. Knights were arrested in England, but north of the Border in Scotland the papal Bulls were ineffective. This was because King Robert the Bruce and the whole Scottish nation had been excommunicated for taking up arms against Philippe's son-in-law, King Edward II of England.[1]

Until 1306, the Knights had always operated without papal interference, but Philippe managed to change this. Following a Vatican edict forbidding him to tax the clergy, the French king arranged for the capture and murder of Pope Boniface VIII. His successor, Benedict XI, also met his end in very mysterious circumstances, to be replaced in 1305 by Philippe's own candidate, Bertrand de Goth, Archbishop of Bordeaux, who duly became Pope Clement V. With a new Pope under his control, Philippe drew up his list of accusations against the Knights Templars. The easiest charge to lay was that of heresy, for it was well known that the Knights did not hold to the established view of the Crucifixion and they would not bear the upright Latin cross. It was also known that the Templars' diplomatic and business affairs involved them with Jews, Gnostics and Muslims.

On Friday 13 October 1307, Philippe's henchmen struck and Templars were seized throughout France. Captured Knights were imprisoned, interrogated, tortured and burned. Paid witnesses were called to give evidence against the Order and some truly bizarre statements were obtained. The Templars were accused of a number of assorted practices deemed unsavoury, including necromancy, homosexuality, abortion, blasphemy and the black arts. Once they had given their evidence, under whatever circumstances of bribery or duress, the witnesses disappeared without trace. But, despite all this, the King did not achieve his primary objective, for the treasure remained beyond his grasp. His minions had scoured the length and breadth of Champagne and Languedoc but, all the while, a majority of the hoard was hidden away in the Treasury vaults of Paris.

Kingdom of the Scots

At that time, the Grand Master of the Order was Jacques de Molay. Knowing that Pope Clement V was a pawn of King Philippe, Molay arranged for the Paris hoard to be removed in a fleet of eighteen galleys from La Rochelle. Most of these ships sailed to Scotland[2] (and some to Portugal), but Philippe was quite unaware of this and negotiated with various monarchs to have the Templars generally pursued outside France. Subsequently, Philippe forced Pope Clement to outlaw the Order in 1312 and, two years later, Jacques de Molay was burned at the stake.

Edward II of England was reluctant to turn against the Knights but, as Philippe's son-in-law, he was in a difficult position. Thus, on receiving an outright instruction from the Pope, he complied with the rule of the Inquisition. Many Templars were arrested in England, while their lands and preceptories were confiscated and subsequently passed to the Hospitallers of St. John.

In Scotland, however, the story was very different: the papal Bull was totally ignored. Long before, in 1128, Hugues de Payens had first met King David I of Scots soon after the Council of Troyes, and St. Bernard de Clairvaux had integrated the Celtic Church with his wealthy Cistercian Order. King David granted Hugues and his Knights the lands of Ballantradoch, by the Firth of Forth (now the village of Temple), and they established their primary seat on the South Esk. The Order was then promoted and encouraged by successive kings, particularly William the Lion. Considerable tracts of land were passed to the Knights—especially around the Lothians and Aberdeen—and the Templars also took possession of property in Ayr and Western Scotland. A large contingent fought at Bannockburn in 1314, following which they became very prominent in Lorne and Argyll. From the time of Robert the Bruce, each successive Bruce and Stewart heir was a Knight Templar from birth and, by virtue of this, the Scots royal line comprised not only Priest Kings but Knight Priest Kings.

Banquo and Macbeth

From the time of the usurped Merovingians, the most significant reigning dynasty in the desposynic succession was Scotland's Royal House of Stewart, whose heritage was part Scots and part Breton. In respect of their Scottish ancestry, one of the most important characters was Banquo, the 11th-century Thane of Lochaber.

From the time when Kenneth MacAlpin united the Picts and Scots in 844, the individual Kings of Scots inherited their crowns by way of Tanist descent in accordance with Pictish custom. Although the Scots maintained their kingship by succession through the male line, the Pictish tradition had been matrilinear. An arrangement was therefore devised by which Pictish princesses married Scots kings, thus maintaining the *status quo*, but the descent was not set in one family line. Kings were selected in advance from sons, nephews and cousins in parallel lines of descent from a common source. In this particular case, the common source was King Kenneth. The great advantage of this selective arrangement was that minors never achieved the crown, as happened to Scotland's detriment in later times after the system was discarded.

Following nearly 200 years of alternating Tanist succession in the Scots descent, a furious dispute arose when the tradition was discarded by King Malcolm II. Instead of correctly affording the kingship to his younger cousin, Boede of Duff (Dubh), he decided that his own immediate offspring should inherit the crown. The problem was that Malcolm had no son, but he did have three daughters, of whom Bethoc, the eldest, was married to Crinan, Archpriest of the Sacred Kindred of St. Columba.[3] Like Columba himself, Crinan was descended from the Tir Conaill royalty of Ireland. Malcolm's second daughter, Donada, was married to Findlaech MacRory, Mormaer of Moray, while Olith (the youngest) was married to Sigurd II, Norse Prince and Jarl (Earl) of the Orkneys. An additional complication was caused because King Malcolm's sister Dunclina was married to Kenneth of Lochaber who, through the structure of Tanistry, had a secondary claim to the crown as a cousin of Boede in descent from Kenneth MacAlpin.

The sons of these various marriages were each and all in the running for kingship when Malcolm II died in 1034 and, among these sons, the heir with the closest right to succession was Dunclina's son, Banquo (Banchu), Thane of Lochaber. Yet, in accordance with Malcolm's wishes, the son of his eldest daughter, Bethoc, succeeded as King Duncan I. Being also the son and hereditary heir of Archpriest Crinan (who was slain by Vikings in 1045), Duncan became Scotland's first Priest King in the style of the earlier Merovingians of Gaul. This concept of the monarch as both the sovereign representative and the religious patriarch remained at the core of Scots culture thereafter.

Prior to Malcolm's death, a revolt against the planned succession had been instigated by Gruoch, senior daughter of the logical Tanist, Boede of Duff, who had no living son. Consequently, King Malcolm slew Boede, thereby leaving Gruoch with a significant sovereign claim by the rule of Tanistry. At this, she mustered fierce opposition against the King, who responded by killing her husband, Gillacomgen of

Moray. Gruoch (who was pregnant at the time) fled to the protection of her cousin-in-law Macbeth, the son of Donada and Findlaech. Then, shortly afterwards in 1032, she married her protector and was henceforth Lady Macbeth.

When Malcolm II died in 1034, Gruoch persuaded Macbeth to challenge his cousin Duncan's succession. She was not alone in her resentment of Duncan and a series of riots ensued, led by various Clan chiefs. Not even the influential Banquo of Lochaber, a captain in Duncan's army, could contain the riots. A military council was therefore convened at which Macbeth gained control of the King's troops, managing to subdue the revolt. He thus became more popular than the King himself, further elevating the ambitions of Lady Macbeth, who knew the crown was within her husband's grasp. But what of King Duncan? The truth of his demise in 1040 is still uncertain. History relates that he was killed in an affray at Bothnagowan (Pitgaveny, near Elgin), whereas romantic literature tells that he was murdered in Macbeth's castle. Whatever the case, Macbeth duly became King south and west of the Tay, while his cousin Thorfinn of Caithness (the son of Olith and Sigurd) ruled the rest of Scotland.

For seventeen years Macbeth ran an orderly realm, while his wife hosted a popular court. At the beginning, however, Thane Banquo endeavoured to regain the crown for Duncan's son, Malcolm Canmore, Prince of Cumbria. In the course of the dispute, Macbeth slew two of Banquo's sons and arranged for Banquo and his eldest son, Fleance, to be ambushed. Banquo was killed in the fight, but Fleance escaped to the castle of Prince Gruffyd ap Llewelyn of Gwynedd (North-west Wales). There he became the first husband of Gruffyd's daughter Nesta, with whom he remained for some time. Then, following his eventual death, Nesta married Osbern Fitz Richard de Léon.

Throughout Macbeth's reign, Malcolm persisted with his claim, gaining the support of Thorfinn and, in 1057, their combined armies forced Macbeth's retreat at Lumphanan. Conceding absolute defeat, Lady Gruoch Macbeth committed suicide and, soon afterwards, Macbeth was slain. Thorfinn was also killed in the battle and his widow, Ingibjorg, was obliged to marry Malcolm Canmore. Despite his victory, Malcolm did not accede to the crown immediately, for the Macbeth party was still in control and placed Lady Gruoch's son Lulach (by her first husband Gillacomgen) on the throne. A few months later, however, Lulach was slain at Strathbogie and, in 1058, Malcolm III Canmore was proclaimed King of Scots.[4]

The accounts of Macbeth, Lady Macbeth and Banquo have been treated very sparingly by historians, but their legendary status lives on in William Shakespeare's popular play based on the *Chronicles of Englande, Scotlande and Irelande* by Raphael Holinshed (died 1580). Shakespeare's *Macbeth* was written nearly six centuries after the historical event. Therefore, when constructing the prophecies of the three weird sisters, the playwright already knew precisely what had followed in history. On consulting their auguries early in the play, the witches inform Macbeth that he will be King. They also tell Banquo that, although he will never reign, he will beget a line of future kings — as indeed he did.

The High Stewards

The name Stewart derives from the 'Steward' distinction, as used in the Middle Ages in Scotland. The early Stewarts became Kings of Scots in 1371 and the royal branch later adopted the French corrupted name Stuart (as did some other branches also). From their earliest days it was known that the Stewarts were descended from Banquo of Lochaber and their descent through this noble Thane (ultimately from King Alpin, the father of Kenneth I) was listed in all relevant genealogies. It was also a fact, however, that the Stewarts emerged from the 11th-century Seneschals (Stewards) of Dol in Brittany.[5] In sovereign terms, their conjoined legacies were of enormous significance, for their Scots lineage was of the Arimathea succession, while their Breton inheritance was that of Jesus himself, through the Fisher Kings.

Fesse Chequey of the High Stewards of Scotland

The pre-Scotland forebear of the Breton line was Alan, Seneschal of Dol and Dinan, a contemporary of Banquo and Macbeth in the second quarter of the 11th century. Alan's sons were Alan and Flaald (hereditary Stewards of Dol) and Rhiwallon (Lord of Dol). The senior son, Alan (Alanus Siniscallus), was a commander in the First Crusade and appears in the Cartulary of St. Florent as a benefactor of the Abbey. His brother Flaald (Fledaldus) was the Baron of St. Florent and married Aveline, the daughter of Arnulf, Seigneur de Hesdin of Flanders. The third brother, Lord Rhiwallon, became Abbot of St. Florent de Saumur in 1082.

Certain peerage registers cite Aveline as the wife of Flaald's son, Alan, but such entries are incorrect.[6] Alan Fitz Flaald was born with the 'de Hesdin' title inherited from his mother Aveline (Ava). She is described in the *Cartulary of St. George, Hesdin*, as being of an age to consent to her father's gifting of English estates to the Priory in 1094. When Seigneur Arnulf (the brother of Count Enguerrand de Hesdin) joined the Crusade in 1090, Aveline became his deputy and heiress in England. She was styled *Domina de Norton* (Lady of Norton) and her son was Alan Fitz Flaald de Hesdin, Baron of Oswestry in the reign of King Henry I. Alan married Adeliza, the daughter of Sheriff Warine of Shropshire,[7] thereby inheriting that same office. He also founded Sporle Priory in Norfolk as a cell of St. Saumur.

Alan the Steward's sons were William and Jordan Fitz Alan. William succeeded to the Oswestry and Shropshire titles after the death of his cousin Alan and, from him, the Fitzalan Earls of Arundel descended. Jordan inherited the hereditary Stewardship of Dol and also the lands of Tuxford, Burton and Warsop in England. Alan also had a daughter, Emma, who married Walter, Thane of Lochaber — the son of Fleance (son of Banquo) and Princess Nesta of Gwynedd. Their son, Alan of Lochaber, married his cousin, Adelina of Oswestry (the daughter of Alan Fitz Flaald) and they were the parents of Walter Fitz Alan (died 1177), who became the first High Steward of Scotland.

Some published charts of Stewart genealogy mistakenly identify Walter the High Steward with his grandfather Walter, Thane of Lochaber. The mistake arose because an alternative form of the name Alan was Flan and this became confused with Fleance, the name of the son of Banquo.[8]

It was actually the latter Walter Fitz Alan who was appointed to the Scots Grand Stewardship of King David I (1124-1153). Walter arrived in Scotland in about 1138 and was granted lands in Renfrewshire and East Lothian by King David I. On becoming the High Steward of

Scotland, Walter gained the highest of conferred positions and was also made Chancellor of Treasury Revenues. This latter office gave rise to the *Fesse Chequey* in the armorial bearings of the Stewarts: the 'chequey' represents the chequered (or checked) table that was used for monetary calculation and from this derived the term Exchequer, as applied to the State Treasury Department.

During the reign of David's grandson, Malcolm IV, Walter founded the Cluniac Paisley Priory and was appointed Commander of the King's Army. In 1164 the Renfrew coast was invaded by 160 Norse warships of the mighty Somerled, Thane of the Isles. The ships contained more than 6000 warriors bent on conquest but, once ashore, they were defeated by a much smaller force under the command of Walter's Household Knights. In the Library of Corpus Christi College, Cambridge, there is a manuscript by the monk William of Glasgow, which gives an eyewitness account of the 1164 Battle of Renfrew. He states that Somerled was killed early in the fight, following which the invaders were routed with heavy slaughter. The battle is also described in the *Chronicles of Man, of Holyrood* and *of Melrose.*

Of all the Scots kings, young Malcolm IV (known as The Maiden) was the weakest, as he proved by giving away the long-prized territories of Cumbria to Henry II of England. He then went to Toulouse at the age of fourteen and spent most of his remaining ten years abroad. It was just as well for Scotland that Walter the Steward was there to manage political, military and financial affairs in the King's stead.

Malcolm IV was succeeded by his brother William in 1165; he was a much stronger character, nicknamed the The Lion. A while after his accession, William sought to regain Northumberland and Cumberland from Henry II at Alnwick in 1174. By that time, King Henry of England was married to Eleanor of Aquitaine (the former wife of Louis VII of France), but their sons (with Eleanor's approval) sided with William of Scots in the Cumbrian dispute, standing against their father on the battlefield. In the event, William was defeated and captured, following which he was obliged to sign the Treaty of Falaise, recognizing the English King as Lord Paramount of Scotland. William was thereafter held in custody and, once more, Walter the High Steward took the reins.

Walter Fitz Alan died in 1177 and was succeeded by his son Alan as the 2nd High Steward. In 1189, Alan joined the Third Crusade with Henry II's son and successor, Richard I *Coeur de Lion* (the Lionheart). Before leaving for the Holy Land with Alan, King Richard declared the Treaty of Falaise null and void, reaffirming Scotland's right to independence. Alan the Steward died in 1204 and his son Walter became 3rd High Steward to William's son and heir, Alexander II. This Walter was the first to use the name Stewart, and it was he who raised Paisley Priory to the status of an Abbey in 1219. By 1230 he was Justiciar North of the Forth as well as Chancellor.

The succeeding King Alexander III became one of Scotland's most impressive monarchs although, in the early days, his reign was subject to the partial regency of the 4th High Steward, Walter's son Alexander. At that time the Norse invaders were proving troublesome once more and, in 1263, the fleet of the Norwegian King Haakon arrived at Clydeside. They were defeated at the Battle of Largs by Scots forces under the command of Alexander Stewart, who was rewarded with the Lordship of Galloway.

King Alexander III married Margaret, the daughter of Henry III Plantagenet of England and, in order to keep the peace with the King of Norway, their daughter, Princess Margaret of Scotland, was married to the future King Eric II. Unfortunately, she died in childbirth soon afterwards — two years before the death of her father, who left no surviving sons. This meant that the sole heiress to the Kingdom of Scots was Alexander's granddaughter, the Maid of Norway, who was then only three years old. And so the 5th High Steward, Sir James (Alexander Stewart's son), became Regent in Scotland.

The Scots were then concerned that their nation might come under rule from Norway. The Bishop of Glasgow approached the Maid's uncle, King Edward I of England, for advice in the matter but, in view of Plantagenet aspirations towards control of Scotland, Edward's response was predictable. He suggested that Margaret, Maid of Norway, should be married to his own son Edward Caernarvon and that she should be brought up at the English Plantagenet court. From that moment, Edward I considered his suggestion to be a positive betrothal, but the Scots did not think of it as a binding agreement. Four years later, however, it was decided to bring the young heiress to Scotland in any event.

In September 1290, Margaret, the seven year-old Queen of Scots, set sail for her sovereign land — only to die suddenly and mysteriously when her ship reached Orkney. In the aftermath of this tragedy Sir James Stewart endeavoured to keep the peace, but the emergent Wars of Succession and Independence were destined to plague Scotland for many years.

Robert the Bruce

The three main contenders for Margaret's inheritance were John Comyn (in descent from King Donald Ban), John Balliol (in descent from Prince David, Earl of Huntingdon) and Robert Bruce, Lord of Annandale (in another descent from Prince David). Bruce was the initial favourite, but Edward I of England proclaimed himself Lord Paramount of Scotland in view of the supposed betrothal of his son. He gained permission from a few Scots nobles to adjudicate and, by political manoeuvre, took control of the nation's key fortresses. Then, with a specially appointed committee, whom he called 'the wisest in England', Edward made his selection. The Plantagenet council was insistent that the new King of Scots must be prepared to rule under the King of England. Robert Bruce was the Scots' own choice, but he refused to submit to Edward, stating,

> If I can get the aforesaid kingdom by means of
> my right and a faithful assize, well and good.
> But if not, I shall never, in gaining that
> kingdom for myself, reduce it to thraldom'.

John Balliol, on the other hand, agreed to the requirement and thereupon became the appointed King, swearing the necessary oath:

> I, John, King of Scotland, shall be true and
> faithful to you, Lord Edward, by the grace of
> God, King of England, the noble and superior
> Lord of the Kingdom of Scotland, the which I
> hold and claim to hold of thee.

Balliol gained the throne in 1292, at which time the High Steward was still Sir James Stewart. Sir James was himself a supporter of Robert Bruce and a stern opponent of King Edward and Balliol. Edward compelled Balliol to provide money and troops for the English army — a move that stirred many to form a martial resistance movement under the Paisley-born knight Sir William Wallace. With the support of James Stewart, Wallace achieved some initial success, whereupon Edward deposed Balliol in 1296 and began to rule Scotland himself. Wallace won a good victory at Stirling in 1297, after which he was proclaimed Warden of Scotland but, in the following year, he was defeated by Edward's longbowmen at Falkirk. In 1305 he was captured and executed by the English, who impaled his head on London Bridge and sent the rest of his body in pieces to cities in Scotland and the North.

From that time, a new leader took up the Scots cause. He was Robert the Bruce, the succeeding heir of Robert Bruce the contender. Irrespective of the presumed Plantagenet interest, the Scots crowned Robert I Bruce in 1306. Then, when Edward II invaded Scotland in 1314, Bruce defeated him at Bannockburn and declared his nation's independence.

The Royal House of Stewart

Sir James Stewart died within three years of Bruce's coronation and was succeeded by his son Walter Stewart, the 6th High Steward. Walter had commanded the left wing of the Scots army at Bannockburn and been knighted by Bruce on the battlefield. Then, in the following year, Walter married King Robert's daughter Marjorie. Some months later Robert went to Ireland, leaving Walter Stewart as his Regent in Scotland, but Marjorie then died in a riding accident, still within a year of her marriage. At the time of her death she was pregnant, but her unborn son Robert was saved by caesarian operation and, in time, became the 7th High Steward. By the age of nineteen, Robert was the Regent for Bruce's son, King David II, holding the office until David was of age in 1341.

Soon afterwards, Edward III Plantagenet began the Hundred Years' War with France. David decided to take up the French cause, but was defeated and captured by the English at Nevill's Cross in 1346. He was held in custody for eleven years, during which time Robert the High Steward took charge in Scotland. King David was eventually freed in 1357, but not before he had come to an arrangement with Edward III. Addressing the Scottish Parliament, David announced that, should he die without issue, the crown of Scotland would pass to the King of England, but the response echoed loud and clear: 'So long as one of us can bear arms, we will never permit an Englishman to reign over us'. From that moment, David was disregarded by the Scots and, when he died without an heir in 1371, the people decided to make their own choice for his successor.

There was only one man who could possibly succeed—the man who had been running Scotland for years and whose ancestors had been deputy kings for six generations. He was Robert Stewart, the 7th High Steward.

On 26 March 1371, the Royal House of Stewart was founded by King Robert II. For the first time since the 6th-century Arthur mac Aedàn of Dalriada, the key Grail successions of Britain and Europe had conjoined in Scots royalty and the Stewarts' ancient legacy of kingship was fulfilled.

The Age of Chivalry

War and the Black Death

The 14th century was a period of great strife and general disorder in Britain and continental Europe. It was a century not only of continual wars but also of plagues, one of which claimed the lives of nearly one-third of England's population. During the latter 1200s the Scots had been continually harassed by the House of Plantagenet, but in 1314 Robert the Bruce defeated the English invaders at Bannockburn. Subsequently, in 1328, Scotland's independence was formally recognized by Edward II at the Treaty of Northampton.

Soon afterwards, England was at war with France. The struggle was sparked by a dispute between Edward II and the French king, to whom Edward (who was also the Duke of Aquitaine) was technically a vassal in respect of certain properties in France. Edward refused to acknowledge the primary authority of the French Crown in this regard, whereupon (in 1324) King Charles IV of France seized some of Edward's territories in Gascony. In retaliation, Edward threatened to cease trading with Flanders, and formed an alliance with the Duke of Burgundy. The irony was that Edward II was married to the French king's sister, Isabella, who became so unpopular in England because of the dispute that in 1325 she returned to France. There, she and her English lover, Roger Mortimer, Earl of March, plotted the overthrow and murder of Edward II in 1327.

The following year, Charles IV (the last of the Capetian succession) died, and a new dynasty began under his cousin the Duke of Valois, who became Philip VI. But Philip's inheritance was challenged by the new King of England, Edward III. In consequence of his father's assassination (instigated by his own mother), Edward declared that he was himself the true King of France, being the grandson of Isabella's father Philip V. In 1330 Edward III had Mortimer executed, and confined Isabella to a convent. Then in 1346 he took his bowmen to

Crecy and mowed down the serried ranks of French knights with a hail of arrows. So began the Hundred Years' War, which had hardly got under way when England was struck by the Black Death in 1348.

In that very same year—amid the general turmoil of battle and plague—the Age of Chivalry was born. Tradition has it that in 1348 King Edward noticed some of his courtiers laughing when the Countess of Salisbury dropped her garter in their presence. Apparently, Edward picked up the item and affixed it to his own leg, saying, *'Honi soit qui mal y pense'* (Shame to him who sees wrong in it). From this small beginning emerged the Order of the Garter, taking the King's chance comment as its motto (alternatively, and badly, translated as Evil to him who evil thinks). Edward, whose jousting tournaments became widely renowned, selected twenty-four knights with whom to inaugurate the Order. The romantic tradition of King Arthur's Round Table was his model for knightly equality, and a Code of Chivalry was drawn up whereby knights were required to serve God and the King, to do battle for their good names, and to respect and defend the honour of ladies. (This subject is covered more fully in the companion book, *Realm of the Ring Lords.*[1])

Edward III's eldest son was Edward, Prince of Wales (designated by later historians the Black Prince because of the colour of his armour). At Crecy he won three plumes (feathers), along with the motto *Ich dien* (I serve), and these have since become emblems of the Princes of Wales. For eight years, the Black Prince ruled Aquitaine, where he was ruthless and greatly feared. In England, however, he was a noted exponent of chivalry, and his reputation introduced an element of high romance into a bleak period of long-term war and disease.

Arthurian Romance

The romantic legends of King Arthur, which provided a model for the Age of Chivalry, had little to do with the historical Arthur—a Celtic Ard Rí (High King) and warlord, whose Guletic warriors gained a fearsome reputation in the 6th century. Nonetheless, Grail lore had brought Arthur into the public domain and, when England's Noble Order of the Garter was founded by Edward III in 1348, Arthur's cavalrymen were updated to become gallant armoured champions of the day. The great 18 foot (*c.*5.5 metres) oak Round Table of the Plantagenet era now hangs in Castle Hall, Winchester. It has been carbon-dated to about the reign of Henry III (1216-1272), but its symbolic Arthurian paintwork was a later addition, probably designed in the Tudor reign of King Henry VIII.

We have already considered the historical Arthur in a previous chapter,[2] but it is appropriate now to look at the legendary Arthur who so inspired the Age of Chivalry – the Arthur whose story was born when Geoffrey of Monmouth produced his colourful *Historia Regum Britanniae* in about 1147. Commissioned by the Norman Earl of Gloucester, Geoffrey transposed Arthur mac Aedàn of Scots Dalriada into an English West Country environment. He also transformed Gwyr-Llew, Dux of Caruele, into Gorlois, Duke of Cornwall, while inventing Uther Pendragon and introducing various other themes to suit the feudal requirement. Amid all this, one of Geoffrey's most romantic introductions was Arthur's magic sword, Caliburn, which had been forged on the Isle of Avalon.

In 1155, the Jersey poet Robert Wace composed the *Roman de Brut* (Story of Brutus). This was a poetical version of Geoffrey's *Historia*, based upon a tradition that civilization in Britain was founded in around 1130 BC by Prince Brutus of Troy.[3] A copy of Wace's poem, which included the very first reference to the Knights of the Round Table, was presented to Eleanor of Aquitaine. In this notable work, Geoffrey's Queen Guanhumara[4] appeared more correctly as Gwynefer (from the Gaelic *Gwen-hwyfar*: 'fair spirit') and Arthur's Caliburn was renamed Excalibur.[5]

In about 1190, the Worcestershire priest Layamon compiled an English version of Wace's poem but, prior to this, a more exciting romance emerged from France. Its author was Chrétien (Christian) de Troyes, whose mentor was Marie, Countess of Champagne. Chrétien transformed Arthur's already adventurous tradition into thoroughly inspired legend and gave Gwynefer the more poetic name of Guinevere. His five related tales appeared in about 1175 and it was in his tale of Lancelot, entitled *Le Chevalier de la Charrette*, that Camelot first appeared as the royal court. Chrétien moved in aristocratic circles and such stories of his as *Yvain – le Chevalier au Lion* were based on a number of noble characters from 6th to 11th-century Léon. The distinctive heraldic arms of the Comtes de Léon d'Acqs incorporated a black lion on a golden shield and they were accordingly known as Knights of the Lion.

It was at this stage that continental European writers began amalgamating Arthurian literature with the lore of the Holy Grail. At the request of Count Philippe d'Alsace, Chrétien commenced his famous tale of Perceval in *Le Conte del Graal* (the Story of the Grail). But Chrétien died during the course of this and the work was concluded by other writers.

Next on the Arthurian scene was the Burgundian poet Robert de Boron. His verses of the 1190s included *Joseph d'Arimathie – roman l'Estoire dou Saint Graal.* However, unlike Chrétien's story of the *Sangréal*, de Boron's was not contemporary with King Arthur. In essence it was more concerned with the time-frame of Joseph of Arimathea.

From about the same era came an anonymous manuscript entitled *Perlesvaus*. This work had Templar origins and declared that Joseph of Arimathea was Perceval's great-uncle. Then, in about 1200, emerged the tale of *Parzival*, a detailed and expanded story of the Grail Family by the Bavarian knight Wolfram von Eschenbach.

King Arthur was brought more fully into the picture by a series of five stories from the period 1215-1235, which became known as the *Vulgate Cycle*. Written by Cistercian monks, these works featured Lancelot's son Galahad, whose mother was the Fisher King's daughter, Elaine le Corbenic. Arthur's greatest knight, Perceval, also remained a central character. The *Vulgate Cycle* retained Wace's Excalibur as Arthur's sword and established the theme of his obtaining it from the Lady of the Lake. At this stage, the story of Arthur's drawing a sword from a stone had nothing whatever to do with Excalibur. This stemmed from a quite separate incident in Robert de Boron's *Merlin* and it was not until the 19th century that Excalibur and the stone were brought together.

Throughout this period of Franco-European lore, King Arthur had little prominence in Britain except for brief appearances in such works as the 13th-century *Black Book of Carmarthen*. Geoffrey of Monmouth had claimed that the Welsh town of Carmarthen was named after Merlin (as *Caer Myrddin*: Seat of Merlin) but, in fact, the name had nothing whatever to do with Merlin; it derived from the Roman name for the settlement, *Castra Maridunum*.

The English poem *Arthour and Merlin* appeared in the latter 1200s and, from Wales in around 1300, came the *Book of Taliesin*, which featured Arthur in the supernatural Otherworld. He also made appearances in the *White Book of Rhydderch* (c.1325) and the *Red Book of Hergest* (c.1400). The Welsh *Triads* included some Arthurian references, as did the *Four Branches of the Mabinogi* which, in the 19th century, were translated from Welsh into English by Lady Charlotte Guest under the revised title of *The Mabinogion*.

Not until the 15th century—around 800 years after the time of the historical Arthur—did all the legends consolidate into the general format that we know today. This occurred in the collected writings of Sir Thomas Malory of Warwickshire. They were printed in 1485 under the title *Morte d'Arthur* (Death of Arthur). Being one of the first books published in print by William Caxton, Malory's Arthurian cycle was acknowledged as the standard work on the subject, although it has to be said that it was not an original account of anything. The work was commissioned by Margaret Beaufort of Somerset, the mother of the man who, by force of arms in that very year, became King Henry VII, the first of the reigning House of Tudor.

It was also during that same period that Uther Pendragon and Arthur began to appear in newly assembled genealogies and there was an express reason for this. When Henry VII (son of Edmund Tudor of Richmond) usurped the Plantagenet throne of Richard III, his only claim to succession was through his mother, a great-great-granddaughter of Edward III. In order to present his own Tudor heritage in a favourable light, Henry commissioned new genealogies to show an impressive descent from the princely House of Wales. However, in preparing these charts, the genealogists sought to add a spark of intrigue and, for good measure, the names of Uther and Arthur were introduced into a related Cornish line.

Malory's famous tales were a compilation of the most popular traditions from various sources. All the familiar names were brought into play and, to appease Henry Tudor, Camelot was located at Winchester in Hampshire. In addition, the old tales were greatly enhanced and many new story lines were conceived. Not the least of these was the love affair between Lancelot and Guinevere. Chivalric principles were central to Malory's portrayal, even though he was himself a criminal of some renown, having been imprisoned for theft, rape, cattle rustling, debt, extortion and the attempted murder of the Duke of Buckingham. At various stages between 1451 and 1470, he was held under lock and key in the cells of Coleshill, Colchester Castle, Ludgate, Newgate and the Tower of London.

Malory settled Arthur firmly into the Middle Ages and his characters forsook their Celtic garb for suits of shining armour. He entitled his inspired work *The Whole Book of King Arthur and His Noble Knights of the Round Table*. In all, there were eight interlaced stories: *The Tale of King Arthur*, *The Noble Tale of King Arthur and Emperor Lucius*, *The Noble Tale of Sir Lancelot du Lake*, *The Tale of Sir Gareth*, *The Book of Sir Tristram de Lyonesse*, *The Tale of the Sangréal*, *The Book of Sir Lancelot and Queen Guinevere* and *The Most Piteous Tale of the Morte Arthur*.

From the days of Thomas Malory, the Arthurian legends became an integral part of British heritage. They achieved a great revival with the birth of 19th-century Romanticism — a largely nationalistic movement which appealed to the Victorians' nostalgia for a lost Golden Age. During this era the Poet Laureate, Alfred, Lord Tennyson, wrote his famous *Idylls of the King* and Arthurian themes were very apparent in the striking paintings of the Pre-Raphaelite Brotherhood.

Merrie Englande

The turbulent medieval times have often been referred to as the age which saw the flowering of Merrie Englande—a tag that persists despite the severe plagues and hardships of the era. In truth, the description had little to do with the fact that England was 'merry'. The description derives rather more precisely from Mary Jacob (St. Mary the Gypsy), who had come to Western Europe with Mary Magdalene in AD 44. Alongside the veneration of the Magdalene, the cult of Mary the Gypsy was widespread in England during the Middle Ages. The name Mary is an English form (based on a Greek variant) of the Egyptian name Mery, meaning 'beloved' (Hebrew: Miriam). As we have seen, the name had long been associated with the sea (Latin: mare; French: mer) and with water in general—as in a mere or pool. Consequently, Mary the Gypsy was identified with the goddess Aphrodite, who was said to have been born from the sea foam.

Mary Jacob (the wife of Cleophas, according to John 19:25) was a 1st-century priestess and is sometimes referred to as Mary the Egyptian. Her Oath of Wedlock was called the *Merrie* (again from 'beloved')—whence probably derives the English verb 'to marry'. Outside Catholic doctrine, the Holy Spirit was considered to be female and was always associated with water. Often depicted with a fish-tail, St. Mary was a traditional merri-maid (mermaid) and was given the attributive name Marina. She is portrayed alongside Mary Magdalene (*la Dompna del Aquae*) in a window at the Church of St.Marie in Paris. As Maid Marian, her cult is incorporated in the Robin Hood legends, while Mary Magdalene's incarnation appears in the Celtic tradition as Morrigan, the Great Queen of Fate. The individual identification of the two Marys is often confusing because both are associated with Provence and the sea.

In the early days of Christianity, Emperor Constantine banned the veneration of Mary the Gypsy, but her cult continued and was introduced into England from Spain. Mary Jacob-Cleophas had landed at Ratis (*Saintes Maries de la Mer*) together with Mary Magdalene and Mary Helena-Salome, as detailed in *The Acts of Magdalene* and the ancient MS *History of England* in the Vatican Archive. Her most significant emblem was the scallop shell, depicted so effectively along with her Aphrodite status in Botticelli's famous painting, *The Birth of Venus*. Even today, the Compostela pilgrims carry the shells of the aphrodisiac fish to the supposed St. James's tomb at Santiago. Mary the Gypsy — sacred harlot and love cultess — was ritually portrayed by the Anglo-Saxons as the May Queen and her dancers, Mary's Men, still perform their rites under the corrupted name of Morris Men in English rural festivities. Another reference to Mary's Men is found in the rebellious Merrie Men of the Greenwood legends.[6]

Scotland and the Grail

Many of the Scottish families so often accredited with Norman descent are actually of Flemish origin.[7] Their ancestors were actively encouraged to emigrate to Scotland during the 12th and 13th-century reigns of David I, Malcolm IV and William the Lion. A policy of purposeful settlement was implemented because the Flemings were very experienced in trade, agriculture and urban development, with their strategic arrival in Scotland being quite unlike the unwanted Norman invasion of England. Such families as Balliol, Bruce, Comyn, Douglas, Fleming, Graham, Hay, Lindsay and many others all have their heraldic origins in Flanders. In recent years some excellent in-depth research has been conducted in this field by the heraldic historian Beryl Platts.

The Engrailed Cross of St. Clair

There were few Normans of note in medieval Scotland, but one Norman family who did achieve great prominence from the 11th century was that of St. Clair. Henri de St. Clair was a Crusader with Godefroi de Bouillon. More than two centuries later, his descendant (also Henri de St. Clair) was a commander of the Knights Templars at the Battle of Bannockburn. The St. Clairs (who eventually became the

Sinclair Earls of Caithness) were of Viking heritage through both the Dukes of Normandy and the Jarls (Earls) of Orkney. Following the Inquisition of the Templars and their settlement in Scotland, the St. Clairs became Scots Ambassadors to both England and France. Henry de St. Clair (son of Henri the Crusader) was a Privy Councillor and his sister, Richilde, married into the de Chaumont family, who were kin to Hugues de Payens, the original Grand Master of the Templars.

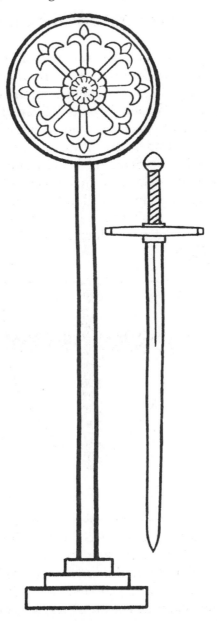

Sword and Chalice of the Holy Grail

The Templar legacy of the St. Clairs is particularly apparent just south of Edinburgh, near to the original Templar centre at Ballantradoch. Here, in the village of Roslin, stands the 15th-century Rosslyn Chapel which, at first glance, resembles a miniature Gothic cathedral with its pointed-arch windows and climbing buttresses topped with elaborate pinnacles. Closer inspection reveals, however, that it is actually a strange combination of Nordic, Celtic and Gothic styles.

The St. Clairs received the Barony of Roslin from Malcolm III Canmore in 1057 and, in the following century, they built their castle in the vicinity. Deep beneath this fortress, it is said that the sealed vaults still contain some of the Templar treasure brought from France during the Catholic Inquisition. When the Templar Fleet escaped from the coast of Brittany in 1307, the majority of ships and their valuable cargo went to Scotland by way of Ireland and the Western Isles.[8] Some went to Portugal, however, where the Templars became reincorporated as the Knights of Christ. The famous Portuguese navigator Vasco da Gama, who pioneered the Cape route to India in 1497, was a Knight of Christ, while the earlier Prince Henry the Navigator (1394-1460) was the Order's Grand Master.

In addition to the French evacuees, Scotland also received the Templars who escaped from England, where their headquarters from 1185 had been at Temple, south of Fleet Street in London. Since their 14th-century proscription, the site has been occupied by two Inns of Court: the Inner Temple and Middle Temple. Nearby stands the 12th-century round church of the Templars, while Temple Bar, the Westminster gateway to the City, stood between Fleet Street and the Strand.

From the time that Roslin came into St. Clair possession, prominent family members were buried there, with the exception of Rosabelle, the wife of Baron Henri the Crusader. She was drowned off the coast to leave a haunting memory, as recalled by Sir Walter Scott during the 19th century. In his *The Lay of the Last Minstrel*, he wrote,

> And each Sinclair was buried there,
> With candle, book and knell;
> But the sea-caves rung,
> And the wild winds sung
> The dirge of lovely Rosabelle.

Throughout their early years, the St. Clair Barons of Roslin were of the highest ranking Scots nobility and they were numbered among the closest confederates of the kings. In the 13th century, Sir William de St. Clair was Sheriff of Edinburgh, Lothian, Linlithgow and Dumfries, while also appointed Justiciar for Galloway. King Alexander III additionally selected him as foster-father to the Crown Prince of Scotland.

Following the death of Robert the Bruce in 1329, a later Sir William de St. Clair, set out with Bruce's heart in a silver casket.[9] Along with Sir James Douglas and two other knights, he was to bury the casket in Jerusalem but, on reaching Andalusia in southern Spain, the party was confronted by the Moorish cavalry. Seeing no way out, the four men charged the invincible foe and were duly slain. The Moors were so impressed with the knights' courage that they returned the casket to Scotland, where Bruce's heart was later buried at Melrose Abbey.

It was a descendant William Sinclair, Earl of Caithness, Grand Admiral and Chancellor of Scotland, who founded Rosslyn Chapel in 1446. The family of St. Clair (having adapted their name to Sinclair in the late 1300s) were by then the eminent guardians of the Kings — the *Sangréal* (Blood Royal) — in Scotland. Five years earlier, King James II Stewart had also appointed William to the post of Hereditary Patron and Protector of Scottish Masons. These were not speculative freemasons but operative, working stonemasons, proficient in the application of mathematics and architectural geometry. William was thus able to call upon the finest craftsmen and builders in the country. Once the Rosslyn foundations were laid, building work commenced in 1450 and the Chapel was completed in 1486 by William's son Oliver. It was meant to be part of a larger collegiate church, but the rest was never built, although the foundations are still discernible.

In spite of its age, the Chapel is in remarkable condition (though currently undergoing extensive repair) and is still in regular use. The building is 35 feet x 69 feet (c.10.7 metres x 21 metres), with a roof height of 44 feet (c.13.4 metres). Many hundreds of stone carvings adorn the walls and ceilings. They tell stories from the Bible and depict numerous Masonic symbols and examples of Templar iconography. There are swords, compasses, trowels, squares and mauls in abundance, along with various images of King Solomon's Temple. Rosslyn Chapel provides such an unusually stimulating visual and spiritual experience as to commend itself to visitors. The historian and biographer Andrew Sinclair has written at length about the history of Rosslyn and the Sinclairs, imparting a detailed account of the Sinclair fleet's transatlantic voyage in 1398, long before the supposed discovery of America by Christopher Columbus. Indeed, there are various original American corn-cob carvings at Rosslyn, which confirm the fact.

Apart from the Judaic and esoteric carvings, the Christian message is also evident, with an assortment of related depictions in stone. Also, there are constant traces of Islam and the whole is strangely bound within a pagan framework of winding serpents, dragons and woodland trees. Everywhere, the wild face of the Green Man peers from the stone foliage of the pillars and arches, symbolizing the constant earth forces and the life-cycle. And all of this is enveloped in a vast array of fruits, herbs, leaves, spices, flowers, vines and the emblematic plants of the garden paradise. Inch for inch, Rosslyn is probably the most extravagantly decorated church in the country, although not one crafted image can be construed as being art for art's sake. Every carving has a purpose and each purpose relates to the next while, despite the seeming ambiguity of the scene, an almost magical harmony reigns throughout.

The name St. Clair derives from the Latin, *Sanctus Clarus*, meaning Holy Light and, above all else, Rosslyn is the ultimate Chapel of the Holy Grail, with the mystical quest paramount in its imagery. The Knights Templars were the Guardians of the Grail Family and the family shield of St. Clair bore an engrailed (scalloped) black cross upon silver to denote its bearer as a Knight of the Grail. At Rosslyn and elsewhere in Scotland, wall carvings and tombs of the Grail Knights bear the emblem of a tall-stemmed Chalice with the bowl face-forward. In its bowl, the Rosy Cross (with its *fleur-de-lis* design) signifies that the *vas-uterus* contains the Blood Royal.

The Stone of Destiny

Not only were the Grail Knights and Templars appointed Guardians of the Stewart Sangréal in Scotland, they also became protectors of the Stone of Destiny (the Stone of Scone). This most sacred of Scots treasures had been brought to Scotland from Ireland by Fergus Mór mac Erc (the first King of Dalriada) in the 5th century, having originally been carried to Ireland from Judah in about 586 BC. The venerated holy relic was said to be the anointed Stone of the Covenant, known as Jacob's Pillow (Genesis 28:18-22), on which Jacob laid his head and saw the ladder reaching up to Heaven at Beth-el. In a dream, God promised Jacob that his seed would generate the line of kingship to follow — the line which in due course became the Davidic succession.

When the Jews were persecuted by Nebuchadnezzar of Babylon, Mattaniah, the son of King Josiah (and a direct descendant of David), was installed in Judah. Known as King Zedekiah, he acceded to the throne of Jerusalem in 598 BC. Twelve years later Jerusalem fell to Nebuchadnezzar, whereupon Zedekiah was taken to Babylon and blinded (Jeremiah 39:6-7, 52:10-11). His sons were murdered, but his daughter Tamar was removed to Ireland (via Egypt and Spain) by the prophet Jeremiah, son of the Jerusalem high priest Hilkiah. He also brought the Stone of the Covenant, which became known as *Lia Fáil* (Stone of Destiny).[10] In Latin it was the *Saxum Fatale.*

Princess Tamar (Teamhair/Tea) gave her name to Tara, the seat of the High Kings of Ireland, and she married Eire-amhon, Prince of Scythia—father of Ard Rí (High King) Irial, ancestor of Ugaine Már (Ugaine the Great). Subsequently, over a millennium, Irial's successors were installed in the presence of the sacred Stone. The Irish heritage then progressed into Scotland, where the relic of Judah became synonymous with the Kings of Dalriada. King Kenneth I MacAlpin (844-859) later moved the Stone to Scone Abbey when he united the Scots and the Picts. By the time of William the Lion (died 1214), the Stone of Destiny bore witness to nearly a hundred coronations in sovereign descent from King Zedekiah.

On declaring himself Overlord of Scotland in 1296, Edward I of England stole what he thought was the Stone of Destiny. What he actually got was a piece of sandstone from a monastery doorway, which has since rested beneath the Coronation Throne at London's Westminster Abbey. This piece of rubble is 26 inches long by 11 inches deep (*c.*66 x 28 cm) and weighs about 335 lbs (*c.*152 kg). Royal seals of the early Scots kings depict a much larger installation rock, but this rock was not the sacred Stone of Destiny—no more than is the medieval masonry prize of King Edward. The real Stone of Destiny is said to be smaller, more naturally rounded, and is of inscribed black basalt, not of hand-cut sandstone. It was hidden by the Cistercian Abbot of Scone in 1296, and it has remained hidden ever since. The Columban tradition tells that, on secreting the Stone, the Abbot prophesied that one day the Michael would return to his inheritance. It is of importance to note that the X-sign, which became so hated by the Roman Church, was identified with the archangel Michael (Melchizedek)[11] onwards from Old Testament times. The heritage of St. Michael was the dynasty of high Zadok priests—a heritage that prevailed in the continuing Messianic line. The relationship of St. Andrew with the Saltire was a later development.

It is hardly surprising that the Scots authorities never attempted to retrieve the bogus stone from England. Even Robert the Bruce declined to accept it in 1328 at the Treaty of Northampton. After some young Scots removed the Westminster stone across the Border on

Christmas Day 1950, it was duly returned to London without any undue excitement. In relation to the real Stone, The Rev. J. MacKay Nimmo of St. Columba's Church, Dundee, has since stated, "When Scotland achieves self-government, the Stone will reappear .... Until then, we will continue to guard this ancient symbol of our national identity".[12]

The recent Parliamentary return of the sham artifact to Scotland is, therefore, of no consequence whatever. Furthermore, even if one accepts the symbolism of the Westminster stone as being emblematic of Scottish nationhood, it has not been returned into Scots ownership. It is intended simply that the Crown officers will keep it in Scotland instead of in London, with the proviso that it will be carried back for future Westminster coronations. In short, with the stone now on display in Edinburgh Castle, this constitutes a thoroughly empty gesture which openly perpetuates the coercive ideal of King Edward I by confronting the Scots with a daily reminder of their subjugated historical position.

Joan of Arc

During the 1400s, when Rosslyn Chapel was being built, the Grand Helmsman of the Prieuré Notre Dame de Sion was René d'Anjou. He was the Count of Bar, Provence, Piedmont and Guise; also Duke of Calabria, Anjou and Lorraine. Additionally, he was a titular King of Jerusalem, being a scion of Godefroi de Bouillon's House of Lorraine. In his capacity as Helmsman, René was succeeded by his daughter Yolande, whose own successors in this regard included Botticelli and Leonardo da Vinci. René's other daughter, Margaret, married King Henry VI of England.

It was René d'Anjou who gave Christopher Columbus his first ship's commission, and it is from René that the familiar Cross of Lorraine derives. The cross, with its two horizontal bars, became the lasting symbol of Free France and was the emblem of the French Resistance during World War II. Among René's most prized possessions was a magnificent Egyptian cup of red crystal, which he obtained in Marseilles. It was said to have been used at the wedding of Jesus and Mary Magdalene, bearing the later inscription (translated):

> He who drinks well will see God. He who quaffs at a
> single draught will see God and the Magdalene.[13]

René d'Anjou's literary work, entitled Battles and the Order of Knighthood and the Government of Princes, exists today in the translation of the Rosslyn-Hay Manuscript in the library of Lord William Sinclair. It is the earliest extant work of Scottish prose and its leather-bound oak cover bears the names 'Jhesus—Maria—Johannes' (Jesus—Mary—John). Similarly, a mason's inscription at Melrose Abbey reads, 'Jhesus—Mari—Sweet Sanct John'.[14]

St. John (Jesus's 'beloved disciple') was greatly venerated by the Grail Knights and Templars. He was the inspiration for the Hospitallers of Saint John of Jerusalem and Britain's later St. John Ambulance Association. It is significant that the New Testament Gospel of John makes no mention of the Virgin Birth, only of Jesus's Davidic descent. More importantly, it gives the New Testament's only account of the historically significant wedding at Cana (John 2:1-11). Interestingly, the Rosslyn manuscript symbolizes St. John by way of a Gnostic serpent and a Grail emblem.

Among René d'Anjou's colleagues was the famous Maid of Orléans, Jeanne d'Arc (Joan of Arc). Born in 1412, Joan was the daughter of a Domrémy farmer in the Duchy of Bar. In the following year Henry V (probably the most power-crazed of all English monarchs) became King of England. He was described by his own nobles as a cold, heartless warmonger, even though historical propaganda has since conferred upon him the mantle of a patriotic hero. At the time of his accession, the Plantagenet war against France had subsided, but Henry decided to revive Edward III's claim to the kingdom of France. This he did on the basis that Edward's mother of a whole century before was the daughter of King Philippe IV.

Henry V, with 2,000 men-at-arms and 6,000 archers, swept through Normandy and Rouen, defeating the French at Agincourt in 1415. He was subsequently proclaimed Regent of France at the Treaty of Troyes. With the aid of the faithless French Queen Isabau, Henry then married the French King's daughter, Katherine de Valois, and set a course towards overthrowing her brother, the Dauphin, who was married to René d'Anjou's sister Mary. It transpired, however, that Henry V died two years later, as did King Charles VI of France. In England the heir to the throne was Henry's infant son, whose uncles—the Dukes of Bedford and Gloucester—became Overlords of France. The French people were somewhat concerned about their future prospects, but all was not lost for along came the inspired Joan of Arc. In 1429 she appeared at the fortress of Vaucouleurs, near Domrémy, announcing that she had been commanded by the saints to besiege the English at Orléans.

At the age of seventeen, Joan departed for the Royal Court at Chinon, along with the Dauphin's brother-in-law, René d'Anjou. Once at Chinon on the Loire, she proclaimed her divine mission to save France from the invaders. At first the Court resisted Joan's military ambitions, but she gained the support of Yolande d'Aragon, who was the Dauphin's mother-in-law and the mother of René d'Anjou. Joan was then entrusted with the command of more than 7000 men, including the prestigious Scots Royal Guard of the *Gendarmes Ecossais* and the most prominent captains of the day. With René d'Anjou at her side, Joan's troops destroyed the blockade at Orléans and overthrew the English garrison. Within a few weeks the Loire Valley was again in French hands and, on 17 July 1429, Charles the Dauphin was crowned at Reims Cathedral by Archbishop Regnault of Chartres.

Less than a year after her success, the Maid of Orléans was captured while besieging Paris and the Duke of Bedford arranged for her trial by Pierre Cauchon, Bishop of Beauvais, who condemned her to life imprisonment on bread and water. When Joan refused to submit to rape by her captors, the Bishop pronounced her an ungrateful sorceress and, without further trial, she was burned alive in the Old Market Square at Rouen on 30 May 1431.

When the Dauphin was crowned at Reims, the brave shepherdess of Lorraine had stood alongside the new King with her now famous banner, which bore the names '*Jhesus – Maria*': the same as on the sacred stone at the Glastonbury Chapel ('*Jesus – Maria*');[15] as repeated (along with St.John) in the Rosslyn-Hay manuscript ('*Jhesus – Maria*') and as etched at Melrose Abbey ('*Jhesus – Mari*') — the names which at all times relate to the marriage of Jesus and Mary Magdalene, and to the perpetual Bloodline of the Holy Grail.

America Before Columbus

It was mentioned above that Christopher Columbus was sponsored by René d'Anjou, while another of his patrons was Leonardo da Vinci, who was well connected with prominent families such as the Medicis. However, there was a good deal more to Columbus' own family background than the history books generally tell. He is, of course, best known as the official discoverer of America, but he was not the first to make the voyage, as is made apparent in Rosslyn Chapel.

Columbus (the son of Domenico Colombo and Suzanna Fontanarossa) was born in Genoa, Italy, in 1451. Having entered service with the Captain of Porto Sancto in Madeira, he married the

Captain's daughter, Felipa Perestrello, in 1478. Subsequently, he approached the Portuguese Court with the concept of reaching Asia by sailing westwards. His appeal for funding was rejected by King John II, who contracted Ferman Dulmo to explore the Atlantic in accordance with Columbus' suggestion.[16]

Columbus made a secondary approach to the Spanish monarchs, King Ferdinand II of Aragon and his wife Queen Isabella of Castile. However, since the Portuguese scheme was under way, Columbus was rejected yet again. In 1492, Dulmo returned, but with no report of any new lands. Columbus then confronted Ferdinand and Isabella once more, and this time he won their support. On 3 August 1492, he set sail from Palos with three small ships — the *Niña*, the *Pinta* and the *Santa Maria*.

Eight months later, Columbus returned to Barcelona, but not with the anticipated silks and spices from the East. Instead, he was accompanied by six brown-skinned natives bearing pearls, strange fruits, gold, and exotic birds. He had discovered an exciting New World across the sea, and the Pope declared that these rich lands belonged to Spain. The name America did not emerge for another five years. It derived from the Florentine navigator, Amerigo Vespucci,who sailed to the south continental mainland in 1497.

Upon his return, Columbus related that he had landed on Watling Island (now San Salvador in the Bahamas). He had also visited Hispaniola (Haiti and the Dominican Republic) and Cuba. Ferdinand and Isabella were delighted, and their hero was offered a seat at the Spanish Court. His second voyage (1493-96) took him to Guadaloupe, Antigua, Puerto Rico and Jamaica. The third voyage of 1498 saw Columbus in Trinidad, and on the mainland of South America. Then, in 1499, the colonists of Haiti revolted against his presuned command of their affairs. Consequently, a new Spanish governor was installed, and Columbus was shipped back to Europe in chains. His last voyage in 1502-04 concerned the coastal exploration of Honduras and Nicaragua but, despite his hour of glory, he died in poverty two years later at Valladolid. Columbus was buried at Seville and in 1542 his remains were removed to Hispaniola.

This exciting piece of maritime history is well enough known. What is not so well known is the fact that the New World discovery was no accident. Columbus was fully armed with detailed navigational charts before he set sail. They had been drawn up on previous Atlantic crossings, and were vouched for at the Spanish Court by John Drummond, whose grandfather had been to America in 1398. Drummond was related to the Drummond Earls of Perth, where the records confirm that he was with Ferdinand and Isabella in 1492. Both Columbus and Drummond had lived on the Island of Madeira. Drummond's father, John (The Scot) Drummond, had settled there in 1419, along with Columbus' father-in-law, Bartholomew Perestrello.

John the Scot's father was Sir John Drummond of Stobhall, Justiciar of Scotland. Sir John's sister, Anabella, was the wife of King Robert III Stewart of Scots. Sir John's own wife was Elizabeth Sinclair, whose nephew, William Sinclair, was the founder of Rosslyn Chapel. Elizabeth's father, Henry Sinclair, Baron of Roslin, Earl of Orkney, led a successful trans-Atlantic expedition, nearly a century before Columbus—and even he was not the first.

Henry Sinclair's Norse ancestors had explored the Atlantic as far back as the 10th century. In Hauk's *Book of the Icelandic Saga* (extant copy dated 1320), Leif Ericsson is detailed as having crossed the Atlantic to Wineland the Good in 999. Indeed, the Orkney sailors had reached land to the West within Henry's own lifetime. Their reports claimed that the natives of a far away place called Estotilands sowed corn and exported furs and sulphur to Greenland.

Estotilands was the place eventually called Nova Scotia (New Scotland) in Canada. The Orkney sailors also told of a southern country called Drogio. The natives of Drogio ran naked in the hot winds but, across the sea, the people were very refined. Their land was rich in gold, and they had cities and great temples to their gods. These various accounts were all confirmed when voyagers travelled to the Caribbean Islands, and onwards to Florida, and Mexico—the home of the Aztec indians. In complete disregard of these early discoveries, tradition has it that the Aztec empire was not explored until the Spanish conquistador, Hernán Cortéz, arrived there in 1519.

From 1391, the master of Sinclair's fleet was the Venetian sea captain, Antonio Zeno. The Zenos were among the oldest families of Venice, and were noted Admirals and Ambassadors from the 8th century. Before Sinclair and Zeno made their own passage across the Ocean, Henry drew up a contract with his daughter, Elizabeth, and her husband, Sir John Drummond. The deed was sealed at Roslin on May 13th 1396. It empowered Sir John and Elizabeth to claim Henry's Norwegian lands if he and his sons should perish in the expedition.[17]

In May 1398, the Sinclair fleet set sail. There were twelve warships and a hundred men—some of whom had made the voyage before. Their first port of call was Nova Scotia, where they landed at Cape Blomidon in the Bay of Fundy. Even today, the Micmac indians tell of the incoming ships of the great god Goolscap, who taught them about the stars, and how to fish with nets. On his return home to Venice, Antonio Zeno wrote that, at this place, he had seen streams of pitch running into the sea, and a mountain that issued smoke from its base. Nova Scotia is certainly very rich in coal, and there are exposed coastal seems of pitch where the coal brooks run at Asphalt. Nearby, the greasy underground residues often smoulder beneath the hills of Cape Smokey. At Louisburg on Cape Breton, there is a primitive canon, found in 1849. It is of the Venetian type used by Zeno, and of a style that was quite obsolete by the time of Columbus.

From Nova Scotia, Sinclair continued south towards the land of Drogio. Evidence of the journey can be seen at Massachusetts and Rhode Island. At Westford, Massachusetts, where one of Henry's knights died, the grave is still discernible. Punched into a rock ledge is the seven-foot effigy of a 14th-century knight wearing a basinet, chain-mail and a surcoat. The figure bears a sword of the 1300s, and a shield with Pentland heraldry. The knight's sword is broken below the hilt—indicative of the customary broken sword that would have been buried with the knight—the same as was laid before Perceval in Grail lore.

At Newport, Rhode Island, is a well preserved two-storey medieval tower. Its construction (an octagon within a circle, and eight arches around) is based on the circular model of the Templar churches. Similar remains are to be found at the 12th-century Orphir Chapel on Orkney. The Newport architecture is Scottish, and its design is reproduced at the St. Clair Church, Corstorphine, where Henry Sinclair's daughter has her memorial. Rhode Island was not officially founded until 1636, but its founding was no chance event. At the Public Records Office in London, a text dated four years earlier describes the 'rounde stone towre' at Newport. It proposed that the tower be used as a garrison for the soldiers of Sir Edmund Plouden, who colonized the area.

More than fifty years after the Sinclair expedition, Christopher Columbus was born into the Age of Discovery in Europe. In Portugal, he became a Knight of Christ in the revised Templar Order, as did his famous contemporaries, Vasco da Gama, Bartolomeu Dias and Ferdinand Magellan. He also belonged to the Order of the Crescent (founded by René d'Anjou)—also known as the Order of the Ship. The Crescent knights were particularly concerned with matters of navigation, but had been condemned by the Church for insisting that the world was round!

Through John Drummond and others, Columbus knew precisely where he was heading—and it was not to Asia. Maps of the transatlantic New World were already in existence within his Templar circle. In particular, he had access to the new Globe of the World, which was completed in 1492 — precisely the year that he set sail. This was produced by the Nuremberg cartographer, Martin Behaim. He was a navigational business partner of a certain John Affonso Escorcio — an alias of the man who was better known as John Drummond.

Heresy and Inquisition

The Hammer of Witches

Following the persecution of the Knights Templars and their allies, the Holy Office of the Catholic Inquisition continued its work mainly in France and Italy. The Pope's appointed Inquisitors were essentially Dominican Black Friars and Franciscan Grey Friars. Their power was considerable and they gained a terrible reputation for their cruelty. Torture had been granted papal sanction in 1252 and the trials were all held in secret. Victims who confessed to heresy were imprisoned and burned, whilst those who made no such confession were given exactly the same punishment for their disobedience.

By the 15th century, the Inquisition had lost some of its momentum, but new impetus was gained in Spain from 1480, when the wrath of the Spanish Inquisition was largely directed against Jews and Muslims. The Grand Inquisitor was the brutal Dominican, Tomâs de Torquemada, senior confessor to Ferdinand II and Queen Isabella. A few years after its implementation, however, the Spanish Inquisition set its sights towards another apostate cult. The resultant oppression was to last for more than two centuries — not only in Spain, but throughout Christian Europe. The unsuspecting prey were described as 'the most diabolical heretics who ever conspired to overthrow the Roman Church'.

In 1484, two Dominicans, Heinrich Kramer and James Sprenger, published a book called the *Malleus Maleficarum* (the Hammer of Witches). This evil but imaginative work gave full details of what was perceived to be the hideous new threat posed by practitioners of satanic magic. The book was so persuasive that, two years later, Pope Innocent VIII issued a Bull to authorize the suppression of this blasphemous sect.[1] Up to that point, the cult known as witchcraft had not really constituted a threat to anyone, resting mainly in the continuation of pagan ritual and fertility rites by the peasant classes.

In real terms, it was little more than the vestige of a primeval belief in the divine power of natural forces, focused above all on Pan, the mischievous Arcadian god of the shepherds. Pan was traditionally portrayed with the legs, ears and horns of a goat, but the creative Dominicans had other ideas about the pipe-playing Horned One. They blackened his image so that he was seen to correspond to the Devil himself and the friars invoked a passage from the ordinances of Exodus 22:18-19, which stated,

> Thou shalt not suffer a witch to live. Whosoever lieth with a beast shall surely be put to death.

Then, by means of a blatant misapplication of the Bible text, they condemned the Pan cultists firstly as witches and, secondly, as people who performed hideous revels with a familiar animal. Since the Inquisitors were all men, it was determined that witchcraft must be a form of depravity linked to the insatiable wantonness of women!

The English word 'witch' derives from an ancient variant of 'willow' — the tree of the Triple Moon Goddess (maiden, woman and hag). Willow worshippers were said to possess supernatural powers of divination (as graphically portrayed by the three witches of William Shakespeare's *Macbeth*) — and this enabled the Church to include all manner of magicians and fortune-telling gypsies within its loose classification of Witchcraft. Indeed, the revised definition was so all-embracing that just about anybody who did not conform precisely to the orthodox dogma was under suspicion as a practitioner of the black arts. (This subject is covered in depth in *Realm of the Ring Lords*.[2])

Although some generally anti-establishment characters were caught in the ever widening net as a method of circumventing courtroom trial, the organized witch-hunts were, for the most part, directed against the defenceless rural classes. The unfortunate victims were either strangled, drowned, or burned alive, having been accused of venerating the devil at nocturnal orgies and of consorting with evil spirits. Meanwhile, those of the privileged class who possessed true esoteric skills and Hermetic knowledge were obliged to conduct their business in the secrecy of their lodges and underground clubs.

Protestant Revolt

During the early years of this persecution, the Dominican monk, Johann Tetzel, implemented a lucrative scheme to replenish the Vatican coffers. The scheme concerned the forgiveness of sins, which had hitherto been expiated by means of penances such as fasting, repetition of the rosary and other acts of repentance. Tetzel's concept replaced these traditional penalties with Indulgences — formal declarations of guaranteed absolution, which were available for cash. Approved by papal decree, the sale of Indulgences soon became a source of considerable revenue for the Church.

For centuries, the orthodox clergy and its associated monastic Orders had suffered a series of outrageous measures imposed by an avaricious hierarchy that was becoming ever more corrupt. Through it all, they had upheld successive Vatican dictates with as much loyalty as they could muster, but the trading of Christian salvation for money was more than some could tolerate. The practice was, therefore, openly challenged. In October 1517, an Augustinian monk and professor of theology at the University of Wittenberg, Germany, nailed his written protest to the door of his local church — an act of formal objection that was destined to split the Western Church permanently in two. On receiving a papal reprimand, he publicly set fire to it and was excommunicated for his pains. His name was Martin Luther and his fellow protesters became known as Protestants.

Luther's attempt to reform a particular Church practice actually gave rise to a much larger scale Reformation movement and the establishment of an alternative Christian society outside Vatican control. In England, the most significant consequence of the ensuing Reformation was the formal rejection of the Pope's authority and his replacement as Head of the English Church by the Tudor King Henry VIII. This was, in due course, followed by the establishment of the independent Church of England under Queen Elizabeth I, who was excommunicated by Rome in 1570. Scotland's formal secession from a somewhat limited vestige of papal control occurred in 1560 under the influence of the Protestant reformer John Knox.

It was by no chance that Martin Luther's protest gained support in some very influential circles, for Rome had many enemies in high places. Not the least of these enemies were the Knights Templars and the underground Hermetic societies, whose esoteric crafts had been condemned by the Catholic Inquisition. The truth was not so much that Luther gained the support of others, but that he was the willing instrument of an already active movement which endeavoured to dismantle the rigid international domination of the Pope.

The Protestant split with Rome facilitated an environment of democratic free-thinking, which culminated in the achievements of Britain's Royal Society and fuelled the cultural and intellectual ideals of the Renaissance. Indeed, the High Renaissance movement of 1500-

1520 set the perfect scene for Luther's stand against the politically motivated bishops. This was the age of the individual and of human dignity; it was the age when Leonardo da Vinci, Raphael and Michelangelo developed the harmony of classical art to its highest form; it was the age in which the excitement of pagan-orientated scholarship re-emerged in a burst of colour to cross new frontiers of science, architecture and design. Above all else, the Reformation countered all aspirations to recreate the supreme lordship of Imperial Rome.

Ever since the Catholic Church had ousted the Merovingian kings in the 8th century, there had been a calculated move to reflect earlier glories through the contrived Holy Roman Empire. But the Reformation undermined all of this as the nations of Europe polarized and divided. Germany, for instance, separated into a predominantly Protestant north and a Roman Catholic south. As a result, the Spanish Inquisition against Jews and Muslims was extended to include Protestants as well. Initially, they were hounded mainly in the Low Countries, but then, in 1542, an official Roman Inquisition against all Protestants was established by Pope Paul III. Not surprisingly, the Protestants took up arms.

The powerful Catholic Habsburgs, who governed Spain and the Empire, took the brunt of the Protestant retaliation. They suffered a devastating blow when King Philip II's Spanish Armada was scattered to the winds in 1588. They were additionally plagued by the lengthy Protestant Revolt in the Netherlands from 1568, and by the Thirty Years' War in Germany from 1618 — a conflict that began when the Bohemian Protestants rebelled against Habsburg rule from Austria. They offered their crown instead to the German Prince Friedrich V, Elector Palatine of the Rhine. He was the nephew of the French Huguenot leader, Henri de la Tour d'Auvergne, Duc de Bouillon. On his acceptance of the Bohemian honour, however, the wrath of the Pope and the Holy Roman Emperor descended and the lengthy war was begun. During the strife, Bohemia's cause was joined by Sweden, along with Protestant France and Germany. In time, the Imperial territories were severely depleted, to the extent that the Emperor retained purely nominal control in the Germanic states.

In 1562, the French Protestants (Huguenots) rose against their own Catholic monarchy and the ensuing civil struggles (which lasted until 1598) became known as the 'Wars of Religion'. The House of Valois was then in power, but the contemporary Regent of France was the Florentine Catherine de Medici. She was the niece of Pope Clement VII and was largely responsible for the notorious St. Bartholomew's

Day Massacre of 24 August 1572. On that ill-fated day more than 3,000 Huguenots were slaughtered in Paris, while another 12,000 were killed elsewhere in France. This clearly delighted Pope Gregory XIII, who sent a personal note of congratulation to the French court!

Prominent in the Wars of Religion was the noble French family of de Guise. Although they were leaders of the Catholic Holy League, the members of this family were no friends of the ruling Valois dynasty. In fact, they disputed the legitimacy of the Valois succession, and claimed their own right to the throne by virtue of descent from the Emperor Charlemagne through the House of Lorraine.[3] This posed something of a problem for the Scots troops in France because, following their active part in Joan of Arc's victory at Orléans, they had for some time provided an elite bodyguard for the House of Valois. The Scots Guard of the *Compagnie Gendarmes Ecossais* had no religious obligation to either Catholics or Protestants, but they did have a binding allegiance to the Valois kings by way of their formal incorporation.[4]

Their dilemma was caused because King James V Stewart had been married to Mary de Guise, and the current Queen Mary of Scots was their daughter. But in 1558 she had married Catherine de Medici's eldest son, the Valois Dauphin, François. And so the unfortunate Scottish soldiers were caught in the middle of the French conflict — obliged in honour to support the House of Valois against that of de Guise, although they had previously led the army of Mary de Guise's brother, François, to retrieve Calais from the English in 1558. Indeed, as well as being a Valois bodyguard, they were also traditional supporters of the de Guise senior House of Lorraine. All things considered, the Guard was truly placed in a difficult situation.

The Scots' problem of balancing this conflict of interests was finally solved when the Valois dynasty became extinct. From 1589 France began two centuries of rule by the succeeding House of Bourbon, to whom the Scots Guard had no formal commitment.

From the early days of the Frankish kings, the papal administrators had managed to displace any powerful institution that threatened the evolving Holy Roman Empire. But, quite suddenly, it had been confronted by an unforeseen opponent — a revised and generally more acceptable image of itself — a parallel, independent Christian Church. Moreover, this opposition movement was upheld by the same victims of persecution and proclaimed heresy that the Vatican had thought suppressed. In the newly enlightened Age of Reason, the Protestants emerged under the unified banner of the Red (Rosy) Cross — an emblem incorporated in Martin Luther's own personal seal.

The Rosicrucians (as they were styled) preached liberty, fraternity and equality. They were the constant challengers of tyrannical oppression and, in time, were destined to be instrumental in both the American and French Revolutions. Following the Reformation, the Rosicrucian Order was largely responsible for the establishment of a new spiritually aware environment. People discovered that the Apostolic history of the Roman bishops was an outright fraud and that the Church had deliberately sabotaged the story of Jesus. It also became apparent that the Rosicrucians (like the Cathars and Templars before them) had access to an ancient knowledge which held more substance than anything promulgated by Rome.

Against the weight of this onslaught, Rome's only defence was to continue with its well-tried declarations of heresy. Threats of violence were issued against anyone who opposed the Catholic doctrine. In fact, a new charge had to be found—a charge that was not so lightweight as that of heresy, which had sufficed in the past. The opposers of Catholicism, in whatever form, were therefore specifically defined as devil worshippers and the Hammer of Witches Inquisition was implemented against an imagined satanic conspiracy fronted by sorcerers. The problem was that nobody really knew who these presumed sorcerers were—and so a series of ludicrously tragic trials and tests was devised to root them out. In the midst of all of this, the harsh Puritan sect became politically allied to the Roman strategy, implementing their own witch-hunts in England and America. Over a period of some 250 years, more than a million innocent men, women and children were murdered by the delegated authority of the witch-finders.

Order of the Rosy Cross

In 1614 and 1615, two tracts known as the *Rosicrucian Manifestos* emerged from Germany. They were the *Fama Fraternitatis* and the *Confessio Fraternitatis*. These were followed in 1616 by an associated romance called *The Chemical Wedding*, written by the Lutheran pastor Johann Valentin Andreae. The earlier Manifestos were by related authors, if not also by Andreae, who was a senior official of the Prieuré Notre Dame de Sion. The publications announced a new age of enlightenment and Hermetic liberation in which certain universal secrets would be unlocked and made known. In view of the advent of the Stuarts' scientific Royal Society a few decades later in Britain, the prophecies were correct enough but, at the time, they were veiled in allegory. The writings centred on the travels and learning of a mysterious character named Christian Rosenkreutz, a Brother of the Rosy Cross. His name was plainly designed to have Rosicrucian significance and he was depicted wearing the apparel of the Templars.

The action of *The Chemical Wedding* takes place in the magical Castle of the Bride and Bridegroom—a palace filled with lion effigies, where the courtiers are students of Plato. In a setting worthy of any Grail romance, the Virgin Lamplighter arranges for all present to be weighed on the scales, while a clock tells the motions of the heavens and the Golden Fleece is presented to the guests. Music from strings and trumpets is played throughout and all is cloaked in an atmosphere of chivalry, with knights in Holy Orders presiding. Beneath the castle stands a mysterious sepulchre bearing strange inscriptions, while outside in the harbour lie twelve ships of the Golden Stone flying their individual flags of the Zodiac. Amid this curious reception, a fantasy play is conducted to tell the compelling story of an unnamed princess who, cast ashore in a wooden chest, marries a prince of similarly obscure background and thereby causes a usurped royal heritage to be restored.

When combined with the two earlier publications, *The Chemical Wedding's* Grail significance was blatantly obvious. The Church, therefore, wasted no time in bringing the full weight of its condemnation against the *Manifestos*. The setting was mythical, but to illustrate the scene the Rosicrucians only ever used one actual castle in their depictions: the Castle of Heidelberg, the abode of the Palatine Lion—the home of Prince Friedrich of the Rhine and his wife, Princess Elizabeth Stuart, the daughter of King James VI of Scots (James I of England).

Notwithstanding the Rosicrucian awakening of the Reformation, the Brotherhood of the Order of the Rosy Cross had a very ancient history, dating back to the Egyptian Mystery School of Pharaoh Tuthmosis III (*c*.1468-1436 BC). The old teachings were furthered by Pythagoras and Plato, to later find their way into Judaea through the ascetic Egyptian Therapeutate, which presided at Qumrân in the days before Jesus. Allied to the Therapeutate were the Samaritan Magi of West Manasseh, at whose head was the Gnostic leader Simon (Magus) Zelotes, a lifelong confederate of Mary Magdalene. The Samaritan Magi, whose representatives were apparent at the Nativity, were founded in 44 BC by Menahem, a Diaspora Essene and the grandfather of Mary Magdalene. Menahem's descent was from the priestly Hasmonaeans—the family of Judas Maccabaeus, who is so revered in the Arthurian Grail story of Gawain.

The 'beloved disciple', John Mark (sponsor of the Gospel of John and also known as Bartholomew), was a specialist in curative healing and remedial medicine, attached to the Egyptian Therapeutate (cognate in name with the English adjective 'therapeutic'). It was because of this that John became the revered saint of the Knights Hospitallers of Jerusalem. John Mark was the disciple to whom Jesus entrusted the care of his mother at the Crucifixion: 'And from that hour the disciple took her unto his own' (John 19:27). Some Bibles — including the King James Authorized Version — erroneously add an extra word (generally in *italics*): '... unto his own *home*'. But the word 'home' was not applicable to the original Gospel text. John was, in fact, appointed as Mary's paranymphos (personal attendant) and those defined as 'his own', unto whom he took Mary, were the nurses of the Therapeutate. (A *paranymphos* was, strictly speaking, one who ceremonially conducted a bride to her bridegroom.)

The symbol of the Therapeutate healers was a serpent — the same as is shown (along with the Rosy Cross Grail emblem) to denote St. John in the Rosslyn-Hay Manuscript of King René d'Anjou. The Gnostic Serpent of Wisdom is used as part of the caduceus[5] insignia of many international medical associations today. It was because of John's particular closeness to Jesus's family that he recognized the true significance of the sacred wedding feast at Cana. The kingly dynasty of Jesus was of great merit, but so too was the Hasmonaean and royal heritage of Mary Magdalene. She was the original *Notre Dame des Croix*, the bearer of the Messianic vase, the Lady of the Light — and it is in her Chalice that the Rosy Cross of the *Sangréal* is always found.

Among the notable Rosicrucian Grand Masters was the Italian poet and philosopher Dante Alighieri, author of *The Divine Comedy* in around 1307.[6] One of Dante's most avid students was Christopher Columbus who, in addition to his patronage by the Spanish court, was sponsored by Leonardo da Vinci, a member of René d'Anjou's Order of the Crescent (a revival of an earlier crusading Order established by Louis IX). Another prominent Grand Master was Dr. John Dee, the astrologer, mathematician, Secret Service operative and personal adviser to Queen Elizabeth I. Also, the lawyer and philosophical writer Sir Francis Bacon, Viscount St. Albans, was Grand Master in the early 1600s. Under King James VI (I) Stuart, Bacon became Britain's Attorney General and Lord Chancellor. Because of the continuing Inquisition, he was greatly troubled by the prospect of large-scale Catholic settlement in America, as a result of which he became particularly involved with Britain's own transatlantic colonization, including the famous *Mayflower* voyage of 1620. Among Bacon's Rosicrucian colleagues was the noted Oxford physician and theological philosopher Robert Fludd, who assisted with the English translation of the King James Authorized Version of the Bible.

In 1307, the Rosicrucians had been formally inaugurated in Scotland by King Robert the Bruce, who selected certain Templars and Hospitallers to be founders of the *Elder Brethren of the Rosy Cross*. The Order was inherited by his descendants of the Royal House of Stewart and, by the time of Britain's 17th-century Stuart era, the Rosicrucians were inextricably linked with the scientific Royal Society. This academy included masters and academics such as Robert Boyle and Sir Christopher Wren, who were prominent within the Order of the Rosy Cross. The aims and ambitions of the Order, along with the eminent scholars Sir Isaac Newton, Robert Hooke, Edmond Halley and Samuel Pepys, were straightforward: to advance the study and application of ancient science, numerology and cosmic law. Rosicrucians also undertook to encourage the ideals of the Egyptian Therapeutate by promoting international medical aid for the poor. It is not in the least coincidental that the most influential agency in the field of emergency relief throughout the world (as established by the Geneva Convention of 1864) is identified by its familiar Red Cross.

By the time of King Charles I, the Rosicrucian Order was well established in a number of countries, including Britain, France, Germany and Holland. The work of the Order progressed very well for a time, irrespective of papal condemnation issued by way of decrees from the Vatican. Against this background of progress, however, a new enemy was setting its sights towards the scholarly fraternity — an enemy whose pernicious endeavour was to blight spiritual and technological advancement for a good time to come. The Puritans had arrived.

It is a sad fact that often when the actions of one malicious regime are suppressed, another of equal iniquity is created in its stead. Such was the case with the separation of Henry VIII's English Church from Rome. It took little time for Henry to close the monasteries and sell their land to the merchant classes — but it was not as if the cultured monks of England bore any real affinity to the episcopal Catholic Church. Similarly, in establishing the Protestant Anglican Church (the Church of England), Henry's daughter, Queen Elizabeth I, was quick to force her absolute control on the Catholics of Ireland. She sold Ulster to the London Guilds, whose merchants compelled the Irish to become their servants or leave their homeland.

Henry VIII did not become a Protestant, as is often suggested; in fact he had expressly denounced Martin Luther in his writings. What he did was to sever the English branch of the Church from papal control. This facilitated his divorce from Catherine of Aragon (the daughter of Ferdinand and Isabella of Spain). It also enabled him to gain access to Church wealth and property in England. When the Council of Protestant Reformists took the reins after his death, the people were not happy, but they were even less happy when Mary Tudor married Philip of Spain and began to burn Protestants in England. *Bloody Mary* died before a great public revolt could take place, and her half-sister Elizabeth calmed the furore by creating the Protestant Anglican Church. It was her fear that Ireland might be used to launch a Spanish invasion of England that prompted her actions, but a short-term end rarely justifies a long-term means, and the sad repercussions of Elizabeth's assault are still being felt today.

Whatever the motives of Henry and Elizabeth, their efforts greatly increased the power of the merchant classes, who joined forces with the Dutch Protestants to suppress Spain's international commercial pretensions. King Philip II's response was the great Armada, but this was successfully repelled with the considerable help of inclement weather. England emerged as a religiously independent nation with the Anglican Church firmly at its helm—but a good deal had changed since Martin Luther had made his stand well over a century before.

The Anglican Church, with its own episcopal structure, became no more tolerant of other denominations than had been the Church of Rome. By the time of Charles I Stuart (1625-1649) it had become positively antagonistic towards anyone who dared to question its dogma. As an ironic repeat of Templar history, the Rosicrucian scientists, astronomers, mathematicians, navigators and architects became victims of the pernicious Protestant establishment. The Anglican clerics called them pagans, occultists and heretics, just as the Roman Church had done before. In truth, the downfall of King Charles I had far more to do with his religious toleration and his association with these great men of advanced learning than orthodox history books will ever tell.

If the occult scientists of high society were persecuted by their own national Church, there was little hope for the practitioners of old lore in the lower strata—those who had been called witches by the Inquisition. They lived in fear of the Protestant extremists just as they had lived in fear of the Catholics. And the Protestant sect that came closest to the Inquisition's fanaticism was the very sect which split from the Anglican episcopacy in order to become more religiously 'pure'. What these Puritans achieved, however, was to become intolerant bigots, devoid of any spiritual intellect. Indeed, they were so undemocratic in their beliefs that their parliamentary head was a brutal despot who put even Tomâs de Torquemada in the shade. It was during the years of Oliver Cromwell's savage Protectorate, from 1649, that the Royal Society was forced to go underground as the *Invisible College*. Not until after the 1660 Stuart Restoration did the brilliant Rosicrucians appear openly once more, with King Charles II as the Society's patron and sponsor.

House of the Unicorns

The Union of Crowns

Scotland's Royal House of Stewart arose from a marital union of the hereditary lines of Jesus and his brother James — springing from the Merovingians' own source on the one hand, and from the Celtic Kings of Britain on the other. The Stewarts emerged, therefore, as a truly unique Grail dynasty and have long been known as the House of Unicorns. We have already seen that the horn of the Unicorn was symbolically equivalent to the blade in Grail lore, and both were equally representative of the 'male', as against the 'female' chalice.

Along with the Davidic Lion of Judah and the Franco-Judaic *fleur-de-lis*, the desposynic Unicorn was incorporated in the Royal Arms of Scotland. The Unicorn was considered to correspond to the virile Jesus, and was related to the Messianic anointing imagery of Psalm (Sacred song) 92:10. Indeed, the mystic beast was among the foremost symbols of the Albigensian Cathars, who were so hideously persecuted by the early Inquisition. In medieval legend the Unicorn was always associated with fertility and healing, and Renaissance tapestries portray his head in the lap of the royal bride. This alludes to the ancient ritual text of the Sacred Marriage (the *Hieros Gamos*): 'The king goes with lifted head to the holy lap',[1] as originally expressed in the poetic rite of old Mesopotamia — the land of Noah and Abraham.

The Cathars believed that only the Christine horn of the Unicorn could purify the false doctrines that flowed from the Roman Church, and in this regard the revered creature was often portrayed with his horn dipped into a stream or a fountain. Other depictions show the Unicorn trapped within an enclosed garden — confined, but very much alive. The seven tapestry panels of *la Dame à la Licorne* at the Cluny Museum in Paris were originally from medieval Lyon. The seven Flemish *Hunt of the Unicorn* panels in the Cloisters of the Metropolitan Museum, New York, come from 16th-century Languedoc, and show the Unicorn being chased and persecuted. When captured, he is sacrificed, but is then seen alive and well in the garden of the bride. This is a direct replication of the story of Jesus.

The mythological symbolism of the Unicorn was central to the so-called heresies of Provence that were so brutally condemned by the Church. It was by no chance that the fabulous beast of the Grail bloodline found his place as guardian of the Lion in the Arms of Scotland, along with the X-sign of male and female unity — the well-known Saltire, popularly identified as the cross of St. Andrew.

When Robert II Stewart (grandson of Robert the Bruce) founded the Scottish Royal House in 1371, the succession was entailed on his heirs in the Scots Parliament. The Plantagenet Houses of York and Lancaster subsequently battled for dominion in England, but lost out to the Tudors. In France, the Valois dynasty fought constant wars against rival claimants, and were succeeded by the Bourbons. But through all of this the Stewarts maintained their uninterrupted dynastic position. (The full story of the Royal House of Stewart is related in HRH Prince Michael of Albany's *The Forgotten Monarchy of Scotland*.)

The Heraldic Unicorn

Before the High Stewards became Kings of Scots, their family branches were well positioned in terms of noble status, and as time progressed they acquired titles in Lorne, Innermeath, Atholl, Lennox, Doune, Moray and elsewhere. By the late 16th century the name Stewart had become Stuart in the royal line—a change that occurred by way of French association through the Stewart Seigneurs d'Aubignie and Mary Queen of Scots' first marriage to the Dauphin, since there was no 'w' in the French alphabet.

Following the childless death of Elizabeth Tudor of England, the Scottish and English Crowns were united in 1603. James VI of Scots was the great-grandson of James IV and Henry VIII's sister Margaret. He was therefore deemed to be Elizabeth's closest living relative, and was therefore invited to succeed. In actual fact, England had a suitable heir to the throne in Edward Seymour, Lord Beauchamp, by descent from Henry VII's daughter Mary. Nevertheless, although many were happy enough to recognize a legitimate parallel succession from Henry VII, others were far from content that the King of Scots had become King of England. They did not object to the crowns being united, but they would have preferred a reverse situation, so that an English monarch governed Scotland. As a result, one of history's greatest political conspiracies was set against James and the Stuart kings. When James VI of Scots arrived in London to become also James I of England, he was confronted by two immediate problems. The first was related to religion. Both Scotland and England were established as Protestant nations, but James had experienced a Presbyterian upbringing whereas England was Anglican. The second difficulty was that the Westminster administration was wholly English, and Scots born before James's 1603 accession were debarred from government office. This meant that he had at least sixteen years to face before any Scotsman could appear at Westminster!

After many failed attempts to gain control of Scotland, the English Parliament had discovered a strategic route to Scottish possession— one that may well have been devised before James was invited to succeed. Once James was settled on the united thrones, a solution to the long-standing ambition was in place: (a) future Kings of Britain would remain based in London, thereby restricting Scottish influence even in the affairs of Scotland; (b) Westminster could eventually dissolve the traditional Scottish Three Estates Parliament; (c) at an appropriate time, the Stuarts could be discredited and deposed, and (d) a puppet monarch of Westminster's own choosing could then replace the Scottish succession. The perceived outcome of this strategy would be Scotland's overall subjection to English rule—an ambition which had prevailed since the Plantagenet days of Edward I. And that is precisely what happened from 1688 when King James VII (II) was usurped and sent into exile by Church and parliamentary conspirators.

Earlier, in 1560, the austere Presbyterian Kirk (regulated by elders rather than bishops) had become the National Church of Scotland. South of the Border, the Anglican Church had existed since Elizabeth I authorized the *Thirty-nine Articles* of the English doctrine in 1563. So when the Stuarts succeeded as overall monarchs of Britain, they were expected to uphold two major Churches, each without offence to the other. It was an impossible task—particularly since the King was supposed to be Head of the Church of England. In order to achieve a compromise, the Stuarts founded the Scottish Episcopal Church, which introduced a like structure of Protestant bishops in parallel with the Anglican equivalent. But the kings then had a third Church to uphold, and this made things even more difficult. Over and above this, there was another complication. In addition to being Kings of Britain, the Stuarts were also Kings of Ireland (the Irish Free State was not established until 1921), and therefore had responsibilities towards the Irish people, who were traditionally Catholic.

Elizabeth I had ruled without much parliamentary consultation, and had put the Crown into considerable debt. King James was in consequence obliged to implement higher taxation. However, in approving this measure, Parliament insisted that he could not rule in the autocratic Elizabethan style. In fact they put forward a series of restrictions which left the King with hardly any individual powers at all. James responded, declaring that by Scots tradition he was not answerable to Parliament but to God and the nation. It was his duty, he maintained, to uphold Scotland's Written Constitution on behalf of the people, and to take constitutional stands against Parliament and the Church if and when the need arose. But unlike Scotland, England had no Written Constitution (as is still the case), and the people had nothing to protect their rights and liberties. All that existed was a feudal tradition which vested the power of the land in the wealthy upper classes.

Throughout the Stuart era, religious differences between rival factions of the Christian Church were very much to the fore. In enforcing the Acts of Uniformity in respect of the *Book of Common Prayer*, James VI (I) upset the Catholics and prompted the Gunpowder Plot to blow him up in Parliament. Conversely, in introducing his Authorized Version of the Bible, he caused the Protestants to assert that he was siding with Rome. There was no way in which the Stuart king could satisfy the Anglicans, the Presbyterians, the Episcopalians and the Catholics without being thoroughly tolerant of them all. The problem was that the Anglican Parliament did not react well to such toleration, especially when it was extended to include Jews as well.

When James's son Charles I acceded to the throne, his immediate concern was the discriminatory nature of the Westminster Parliament. The ministers were so wrapped up in religious and territorial wrangling that they had forgotten all about managing the country. Charles therefore dissolved the troublesome Parliament in 1629 and instituted his own new administration. By so doing he gained considerable popularity; he also managed to balance the national budget for the first time in centuries. Within six years he was more favourably accepted than any monarch since Henry VII (1485-1509) — but as the dogmatic Puritans rose to power, so Charles's reign collapsed.

The high-minded doctrines of the Anglican bishops had become thoroughly disliked by large sectors of the community. Not surprisingly, therefore, the people were quick to follow instead their local Puritan preachers who denounced the episcopacy altogether. King Charles did all he could to salvage the Anglican reputation, but succeeded only in alienating many potential supporters. During the ongoing struggle with Spain, Charles allied himself with France by marrying Henri IV's daughter, Henrietta Maria, and this upset both the Anglican Church and the Puritans, for Henrietta Maria was a Catholic.

Civil War

After eleven years of self-sufficiency, Charles was obliged to recall his Parliament in 1640. This followed severe problems with the Scottish Kirk, whose non-episcopal elders had been offended by the Archbishop of Canterbury's attempt to enforce the Anglican prayer book in Presbyterian Scotland. At Westminster the Puritan ministers promptly impeached Archbishop Laud for treason, and he was subsequently beheaded along with King Charles's deputy, Viscount Strafford. The Puritans then set about abolishing the King's council of the Star Chamber, and drew up the Grand Remonstrance — a list of complaints against the King himself.

Having smoothed over the Scottish problem, Charles was then confronted by further troubles the following year in Ireland. There, the Catholics were reacting violently against the presence of British Protestants who were being encouraged to migrate in their thousands to Ulster. King Charles endeavoured to raise an army to quell the insurgency, but Parliament refused him the finance, thinking that Charles might turn the army upon themselves. Then in 1642, when Charles tried to arrest five MPs for obstructive behaviour, the gates of London were locked firmly against him — and the result was civil war.

In Nottingham the King mustered a force of Royalist Cavaliers, while Oliver Cromwell — an ambitious country MP — assumed command of the Parliamentary forces. His cavalry met the Royalists at Edgehill, but the battle ended indecisively. Unlike the colourful Cavaliers, the Westminster party were indeed puritanical, especially with their severely short haircuts which caused them to be dubbed Roundheads. Simultaneously, Cromwell's breast-plated troopers were given the nickname Ironsides.[2]

Following Edgehill, the Roundheads established the *Solemn League and Covenant* with the Scottish Kirk, promising to introduce Presbyterianism into England if the Kirk would supply additional soldiers. This, along with a fee of £30,000 a month (equivalent to around £2,000,000 a month in today's terms), was sufficient to win the Kirk's support — and it was as a direct result that Cromwell defeated the Royalists at Marston Moor in 1644.

In the following year, Parliament's New Model Army defeated Charles again at Naseby. Only at this stage, however, did the Kirk's soldiers discover the true nature of their fellow Puritans. They had previously seen them simply as other non-episcopal Protestants, akin to their own Presbyterian society — but now their eyes were opened. It was reported that the Roundheads slaughtered all the Irish women found in the Royalist camp after the Battle of Naseby, and they mutilated the English women with knives. They took the Scotsmen prisoners, gouged out their eyes, cut off their ears, and nailed down their tongues. In the South, people had supported the Puritan cause in large number, but now this seemingly temperate sect was seen in a new light as an army of fanatical persecutors — to rival the savage Catholic Inquisitors of the Holy Office in Europe. These same Puritan fanatics were soon destined to pursue their own erstwhile supporters with a vengeance, in their effort to root out witches and sorcerers!

It was only a matter of time before King Charles was forced to surrender, and in 1646 he was handed into Parliamentary custody at Newark. Later that year he began negotiations with the sorely embarrassed Presbyterian Kirk. The elders recognized that in siding with the Puritans they had actively assisted in the downfall of their own royal dynasty (unlike the Scots Episcopalians who had remained loyal to the Crown). But it was too late to make amends, and although a Scots army was mustered against Cromwell, he defeated it at Preston in August 1648. Early in the following year, King Charles I was tried at Westminster Hall, and beheaded in Whitehall on 30 January 1649. The Puritan army thereafter swept through Ireland, killing thousands of innocent citizens — an atrocity for which the unfortunate English people as a whole were blamed.

With no king to consider, Parliament established an interim period of Commonwealth, and in 1650 Cromwell defeated the late king's son Charles, Prince of Wales, at Dunbar. Irrespective of this, the Scots crowned Charles II at Scone on 1 January 1651, and he faced Cromwell's troops again at Worcester. He lost once more, however, but managed to escape to France.

Some two years later, in 1653, Oliver Cromwell terminated both his Parliament and the Commonwealth. Appointing himself Lord Protector, he then ruled by military force alone, and his Protectorate was far more severe than any regime that had ever gone before. At his order, the Anglican prayer book was forbidden, along with any forms of celebration at Christmas or Easter. Property was sequestrated, education was constrained, and freedom of speech was terminated. Adultery was punished by death, and single mothers were imprisoned. Sports and entertainment were pronounced blasphemous, inns were closed, meetings were prohibited, and punitive fines were imposed at will by the soldiers. Those who dared to pray at all prayed for 'a speedy return to the protection of the Common Law'.

When Oliver Cromwell died in 1658, his despotic legacy fell to his son Richard. Fortunately, he was not possessed of his father's ambition, with the result that it was not long before Charles II was invited back to his kingdoms. The Restoration of Charles Stuart to the throne thus occurred in 1660, eleven years after the execution of his father.

Charles proved to be a skilful and popular king. He reformed the Anglican Church and maintained a society wherein all religious denominations were equally accepted. Yet, despite these achievements, the Anglican politicians and clergy pursued their imperious course. No matter what the king thought, they had no intention of showing any forbearance towards other religious persuasions, particularly not to the Jews or the Catholics. Moreover, because Charles was married to the Portuguese Catherine of Braganza, they insisted that he must have leanings toward the Church of Rome. Parliament therefore passed the restrictive 1673 and 1678 *Test Acts*, precluding anyone other than Anglicans from holding governmental or public office.

The Invisible College

It is no secret — although perhaps not the most widely known fact — that the early development of Masonic lodges in Britain was directly allied to the House of Stuart. Emanating from the archetypal grading of medieval stonemasons by degrees of proficiency, a symbolic concept of ritualized Masonry evolved during the reign of Charles I. The earliest inductions into Free (or speculative) Masonic lodges were recorded in about 1640. The movement was largely concerned with the structured acquisition of knowledge in unexplained science, much of which had been preserved in Scotland since the time of the original Templars and Cistercian monks.

In Stuart England, the early Freemasons of Charles I and Charles II were men of philosophy, astronomy, physics, architecture, chemistry and generally advanced learning. Many were members of the country's most important scientific academy, the Royal Society, which had been styled the *Invisible College* after it was forced underground during the Cromwellian Protectorate. The Society was established under Charles I in 1645, and incorporated under Royal Charter by Charles II in 1662 after the Restoration. Early Fellows of the Society included Robert Boyle, Isaac Newton, Robert Hooke, Christopher Wren and Samuel Pepys.

One only has to consider the accomplishments of the Royal Society to realize that, like the early Templars, they were endowed with very special knowledge. The natural philosopher Robert Boyle (1627-1691) was a noted alchemist, a student of Nostradamus, and a leading authority on Grail lore. Boyle supported the mathematical astrologer Galileo Galilei in his avowal of the Copernican heliocentric principle of the solar system. He made many discoveries concerning the properties of air, and formulated the notable *Boyle's Law.*[3] His colleague, the physicist Robert Hooke (1635-1703), invented the hair-spring, the double air-pump, the spirit level, and the marine barometer. Also in the fraternity was the astronomer and geometrician Edmond Halley, who calculated the motion of celestial bodies and accurately predicted the future regular appearances of Halley's Comet.

Isaac Newton (1642-1727) was one of the greatest scientists of all time, renowned in particular for announcing the *Law of Gravity* and the definitions of orbital force. He was a noted alchemist, a refiner of the calculus, deviser of the Laws of Motion, and inventor of the reflecting telescope. One of Newton's foremost studies concerned the structure of the ancient kingdoms, and he claimed the pre-eminence of the Judaic heritage as an archive of divine knowledge and numerology. Newton was wholly conversant with Universal Law, sacred geometry, and Gothic architecture. Although he was a deeply spiritual man, and an authority on early religion, he openly rejected the Trinity dogma and the divinity of Jesus, maintaining that the New Testament had been distorted by the Church before its publication. Not only was Newton the President of the Royal Society but he was also a Helmsman of the Prieuré Notre Dame de Sion.

The original Order of Sion had been inaugurated by the Knights Templars to accommodate Jews and Muslims within their Christian organization and, until 1188, they shared the same Grand Master. Although the early Templars had a Christian affiliation, they were noted exponents of religious toleration, which enabled them to be influential diplomats in both the Jewish and Islamic communities. However, their liberal association with Jews and Muslims was denounced as heresy by the Catholic bishops, and was instrumental in the Knights' excommunication by the Church of Rome in 1306.

From 1188, the Order of Sion had been restructured, and evolved to pursue a more specific course of loyalty to the Merovingian lineage of France. The Templars, on the other hand, were especially concerned with supporting the emergent Stewart succession. In practice, the two operated in close association because they were essentially concerned with the same root bloodline.

Another prominent Royal Society member was Sir Christopher Wren (1632-1723) — the architect of St. Paul's Cathedral, the Royal Exchange, Greenwich Hospital (the Royal Naval College), the Royal Greenwich Observatory and numerous other churches, halls and monuments. He was also an acclaimed mathematician and professor of astronomy. Wren was Grand Master of the esoteric Order of Rosicrucians. So too had been Robert Boyle and the Lord Chancellor, Sir Francis Bacon. Other Rosicrucian Grand Masters included Benjamin Franklin (1706-1790), who distinguished between positive and negative electricity, and Thomas Jefferson, the third President of the United States of America (1801-1809).

Modern historians have an unfortunate habit of extolling certain virtues of such great and learned men while paying no attention to the root sources of their wisdom. They are explicitly described as artists, scientists, politicians or whatever, but from Leonardo to Newton, and from Newton to Franklin, their common interests were Hermetic alchemy and the Sacred Craft. In fact their various revelations were not necessarily first-time discoveries; they were more the products of studying cosmic laws and equations of very ancient origin. As an organized group, the men were able to assist each other with translation, experiment and development. The story of Newton and the falling apple may well add a little memorable humour to the *Law of Gravity*, but Newton admitted the true source of inspiration to have been Pythagoras' *Music of the Spheres*, dating from the 6th century BC.

In Britain, and during their later exile, the Stuart kings were at the very forefront of Scottish Rite Freemasonry, which was founded on the most ancient of all arcane knowledge and Universal Law. Their Breton heritage was closely allied to the noble families of Boulogne and Jerusalem, and their background was largely Templar inspired. It should come as no surprise, therefore, that it was under Charles I and Charles II (who posed such a problem to the narrow-minded Puritans and the Anglican Church) that the *Invisible College* of the Royal Society emerged—a college that within a brief period of Stuart patronage revealed some of the greatest scientific discoveries of all time.

Liberty of Conscience

Jacobites

In religious terms it is quite impossible to classify the early Stuarts within any specific denomination; they were simply Christians. Yet, one by one, they were the victims of individual Church jealousies, with each opposing faction seeking to further its own ambition against the others. Not until King Charles II's brother and successor James VII (II) declared his personal Catholicism could any Stuart king be individually labelled in such a way. Nonetheless, despite his personal leaning, it is quite apparent that King James was the most religiously tolerant king in the history of Britain. He not only refrained from imposing his persuasion but did quite the opposite — he issued a written Declaration for Liberty of Conscience, proposing the ideal of religious freedom for all:

> It is our constant sense of opinion that Conscience ought not to be constrained, nor people forced in matters of mere religion. It has ever been contrary to our inclination — as we think it is to the interest of governments which it destroys, by spoiling trade, depopulating countries and discouraging strangers. And finally, that it never obtained the end for which it was employed ....
>
> We do likewise declare that it is our royal will and pleasure that, from henceforth, the execution of all, and all manners of, penal laws (in matters ecclesiastical) for not coming to the Church, or not receiving the sacrament, or for any other nonconformity to the religion established, or by reason of the exercise of

religion in any manner whatsoever, be immediately suspended; and the further execution of the said penal laws is hereby suspended .... And to the end that, by the Liberty hereby granted, the Peace and Security of our Government in the practice thereof may not be endangered, we have thought fit, and do hereby straitly charge and command all our loving subjects, that we do freely give them leave to meet and serve God after their own way and manner.

In issuing this Declaration of 4 April 1687, James endeavoured to dispel all bigotry in favour of sympathetic indulgence. What he failed to recognize was that neither he nor the people were at liberty to make decisions in this regard. By that time, two operative political groups (parties) had evolved at Westminster, and they were each denoted by a nickname foisted upon them by the other. They were the Whigs (rustlers) and the Tories (thieves) — the latter of whom were the natural inheritors of the Royalist position. The Whigs were essentially those of the wealthy land-owning establishment, and when James issued his Declaration the Whigs were in the majority. They not only condemned the King but had him formally deposed for daring to acknowledge the alternative faiths of the Catholics, Presbyterians, Jews, Quakers and others. They centred their argument on James's toleration of Catholics although his forbearance in relation to the Jewish faith would realistically have been a more likely target for committed Anglican Christians. It is evident therefore that his persecution had little to do with matters of religion; it was more precisely concerned with the fact that the King challenged the right of Parliament to impose its will upon the people.

This, of course, brings us back to where our book began — with the notion of Service. In essence, King James was acting fully in accordance with the Grail Code — a code that obliges those in authority, whether in elected or hereditary positions, to concern themselves not with the powers of their positions but with the duties' of those positions.

In attempting to grant religious equality, King James endeavoured to override the restrictive 1673 and 1678 *Test Acts*, which bound those in public office to communion with the Church of England. The *Test Acts* were eventually repealed in 1828-29 to the benefit of Catholics. Later, in 1858, the clauses were also relaxed in favour of Jews. In

Britain today, all religious denominations (Christian or otherwise) are afforded the right to worship according to their conscience – precisely as King James VII (II) conceived over 300 years ago. Few would now claim that James was wrong in his tolerant outlook; he was simply ahead of his time.

Not all of the Anglican hierarchy were in opposition to King James, however. His supporters included Archbishop Sancroft of Canterbury, and the Bishops of Bath and Wells, Ely, Gloucester, Norwich, Peterborough, Worcester, Chichester, and Chester. When James was deposed, they were all deprived of their sees and incumbencies. History has since been manipulated to suggest that James was displaced because he was a Catholic. In truth he was deposed to guarantee power to a Parliament that was not elected by a democratic vote of the people.

On James's departure, the throne was jointly offered to the Dutch Stadholder (chief magistrate), William of Orange, and his wife (James's daughter) Mary. But at that stage, strict new rules were introduced. The 1689 *Bill of Rights* stated that future monarchs could reign only with Parliamentary Consent, and that MPs should be freely elected. In fact, MPs of the era were certainly not freely elected. Only a very limited number of male property-owners who enjoyed high incomes were allowed to vote, and the House of Commons was far from characteristic of the populace it was supposed to represent.

Although Queen Mary was a Protestant, the ministers were concerned about William's own relationship with Rome. Holland was the chief northern province of the then independent Netherlands, but had previously been attached to the Holy Roman Empire, and it was known that William's army largely consisted of Catholic mercenaries. It was for this reason that the *Act of Settlement* was passed in 1701 to secure the throne of Britain for Protestants alone – an Act that remains binding today, even though it was passed in the Commons by a majority of only one vote!

After King James's deposition, the House of Lords determined that because there was a legal compact between the King and the people, the throne was 'not vacant' (although not technically occupied either). It was suggested that a regency was the best way to preserve the kingdom during the remainder of James Stuart's lifetime.

But the Dutch invader, William of Orange, assembled a London Convention Parliament on 26 December 1688. With his armed guards stationed in and around the House, he declared that he had no intention of becoming a Regent – neither would he consent to sharing in government. His declaration was so forceful that there was an immediate fear of war, and many thought he would seize the Crown regardless. A panic conference ensued between the Lords and the Commons, resulting in a revised decision that perhaps the throne was vacant after all![1]

At this time of writing, the present Prince of Wales is faced with a personal dilemma in matters of religion and the Church. Ever since Tudor times English monarchs have been designated Defenders of the Faith — that is the Anglican Protestant faith. HRH Prince Charles has stated, however, that as a prospective king in these cosmopolitan times, he would prefer to be classified simply as a Defender of Faith — meaning Faith in general, of whatever persuasion. There are significant echoes here of the unfortunate King James VII (II) and his *Declaration for Liberty of Conscience*. Yet very little has changed in the past 300 years. British monarchs are still invested as Heads of the Church of England, and the current Anglican hierarchy are as protective and separatist as their 17th-century predecessors. Despite the fact that the United States of America and other Western nations have formal Written Constitutions to uphold individual rights and liberties, the British still have no such protection. By virtue of this, Parliament and the Church retain ultimate dominion over the monarchy (and thus over the people) as long as the *Bill of Rights* and the *Act of Settlement* prevail.

When William III and Mary II acceded jointly to the British throne, an ambiguous Stuart legacy was inherent. Mary was the daughter of King James VII (II) by his first wife, Anne Hyde of Clarendon. William (whose father was William of Nassau) was the son of King Charles I's daughter Mary. However, despite these apparent links, the Scots were not satisfied at the loss of their rightful dynastic king. In 1689 (the year after James's deposition) there came the first Jacobite Rising. Viscount Graham of Claverhouse, Grand Prior of the Knights Templars in Scotland (and known as *Bonnie Dundee*), led a force of Highlanders against the Government troops at Killiecrankie on 27 July. Although the Scots' attempt was successful, Viscount Dundee was mortally wounded in the battle. On 18 August the Highlanders were less fortunate at Dunkeld. Then on 1 July 1690 King William's Orangemen defeated James VII's restitutional troops at the Battle of the Boyne in Ireland.

Amid all this, the Campbells and some other Scottish clans decided to win favour with the new monarchs by aiding the Government's suppression of the Jacobite loyalists (they were called Jacobites because the name James derives from the Latin *Jacobus/Jacomus*, being originally Jacob in Hebrew — hence they were Jacob-ites). King

William instructed that all Highland Chiefs should swear an Oath of Allegiance to him, but the majority were reluctant to comply; their kings had always sworn fealty to the nation, rather than the reverse. In order to force the issue, Sir John Dalrymple, Secretary of State for Scotland, was empowered to persecute one reluctant clan as an example to the others. He chose the MacDonalds of Glencoe, who had failed to meet the Oath of Allegiance deadline of 1 January 1692. The ageing MacDonald chief, MacIain, had actually tried to swear his Oath at Fort William on 30 December, but no Crown officer was present, and as a result he did not manage to comply until 6 January — almost a week late.

Unlike some other clans, the MacDonalds had no military strength and were easy prey. Their settlement nestled between the towering mountains of Glencoe, which constituted more of a geographical trap than a natural fortress. On 1 February Dalrymple sent two companies of Argyll's Regiment, under Robert Campbell of Glenlyon, to exterminate the unsuspecting clan. Arriving in the guise of a peaceful mission, the soldiers took lodging with the hospitable families for many days. Then, on the bitter morning of 13 February, they cut down every MacDonald they could find, sparing neither the women, the elderly, nor the young. Not surprisingly, the dreadful Glencoe Massacre had an opposite effect to that intended. Instead of intimidating the clans into supporting the new regime, it caused them to form a strong Jacobite confederacy against the ruthless Dutchman and his Government.

Treaty of Union

When Queen Anne succeeded William III in 1702, the majority of Scots showed no enthusiasm, even though she was the late Queen Mary's sister. Anne had openly deserted her father, King James, to support her brother-in-law William of Orange. She was anathema to the Stuarts and had never visited Scotland. In 1706, Anne announced her intention to dissolve the Scottish Parliament. On receipt of the declaration, however, the Scots ministers responded that such an action was illegal under Scots law. They cited their Written Constitution, the 1320 Declaration of Arbroath, which stated that, if a monarch should

> make us or our kingdom subject to the King of
> England or the English, we should exert
> ourselves at once to drive him out as our

enemy and a subverter of his own rights and
ours, and make some other man, who was
well able to defend us, our King.

It was clear that Anne's plan would fully subject the realm to English
domination from Westminster. But although the Scots could not drive
out the English Queen, they were afforded the legal right to introduce
a Bill of Security (1706), by virtue of which, in accordance with the
Constitution, they were not bound to accept Anne's chosen heir. In
this they retained the liberty to elect a Scots sovereign from a royal
line other than one chosen by England. That Anne would have to
choose an heir, rather than give birth to one, was meanwhile
becoming ever more apparent. She actually conceived eighteen times,
but only five children were born alive, of whom one alone survived
infancy, and even he died at the age of eleven. In the event, her own
nominated choice of successor was the German Electress, Sophia.

It transpired that Anne got her way despite the *Bill of Security*. She
proposed commercial restrictions on the Scots and threatened a large-
scale military invasion. In March 1705 Westminster passed the *Alien
Act*, which stated that the Scots must accept Sophia of Hanover as
Anne's nominated successor or all trade between the North and South
would cease: the importation of Scottish coal, linen and cattle into
England would be forbidden, and there would conversely be no
continued export of English goods into Scotland.

From 1 May 1707 the Scottish Parliament was adjourned, and the
Crowns of Scotland and England became one as Westminster took
control of the newly conjoined kingdom of Great Britain under the
terms of the *Treaty of Union*. Regardless of this, the Scottish
Covenanters ignored the imposed regime; they formally renounced
Queen Anne and proclaimed her half-brother, James Francis Edward
Stuart, the true King of Scots. He was the son and heir of James VII (II)
by his second wife Mary d'Este de Modena. James VIII (like his father
before him) was a Catholic, but the Presbyterian Covenanters cared
nothing for the individual religion of their king. Unlike the English
system, the Scots monarchs were not Heads of any national Church.
Both the Presbyterians and Episcopalians were far more concerned
with preserving their traditional royal house outside English
supremacy.

Following the *Treaty of Union*, the Scots were allowed to keep their
own Kirk, along with their separate legal system. However, various
Parliamentary measures were introduced to disadvantage the Scots in
relation to the English.[2] But the Scots were not alone at the mercy of

the regulatory powers; the English people had suffered William and Mary's rapacious taxing of light and air since 1695. This taxing of each individual window above six in every house worth more than five pounds a year was retained for 156 years. Even today the bricked up, tax-saving windows of many old houses are still to be seen, particularly in the rural areas.

By the time of Queen Anne's death in 1714, her nominee Sophia of Hanover had also died. The Whig ministers therefore installed Sophia's son George, Elector of Hanover, on the throne of Britain – in spite of loud protests from the Tory benches. Much to the convenience of the Whig oligarchs, King George I spoke only German, and spent most of his time abroad. The reins of national administration were held mainly by his Lord of the Treasury, Robert Walpole. He became the first effective Prime Minister, and developed the undemocratic idea of the Cabinet (an inner circle of ministers who meet privately outside the House to control Government policy). From that time, not only did the people have no say in matters of their own government, but nor did the majority of MPs, who were subsequently regulated by the Whips (so named after the deputies of Hunt Masters) in accordance with Cabinet (or Shadow Cabinet) requirement.

Outside Scotland, many Westminster Tories and their supporters had sought to replace Anne with James Francis Edward Stuart. He was the rightful heir to the Scots succession, and had been their titular King James VIII since 1707. Nevertheless, the Whigs strategically ignored James because he refused to be tied to the Anglican Church. Scottish and English royalists made an attempt to gain the Crown for James Stuart in 1715, but their limited revolt was unsuccessful, and so James returned across the water to continue his French exile at St. Germain-en-Laye, near Paris.

Bonnie Prince Charlie

In 1727 George II of Hanover succeeded his father as King of Britain. The next significant Jacobite Rising took place eighteen years later, in 1745, when Charles Edward Stuart (Bonnie Prince Charlie) challenged Britain's German succession. The Scottish clergy were wholly supportive. On Sunday 24 September of that year, the Episcopal Church symbolically crowned King Charles III at the Abbey of Holyrood House. Representatives of the Catholic and Presbyterian Churches were also present to witness and approve the event.

Despite the fact that James VIII was still alive, he had formally transferred his interests to his son by Declaration on 23 December 1743:

> We esteem it for our service, and for the good of our kingdoms and dominions, to nominate and appoint, as we hereby nominate, constitute and appoint, our dearest son, Charles, Prince of Wales, to be sole Regent of our kingdoms of England, Scotland and Ireland, and of all our other dominions during our absence.

Prince Charles was eager to restore Parliament and the Constitution. He was similarly determined that the English should be afforded identical rights of political and religious freedom. In his first Proclamation, issued in Edinburgh on 9 October 1745, Charles Edward stated,

> With respect to the pretended Union of the two nations, the King cannot possibly ratify it since he has had repeated remonstrances against it from each kingdom.

Soon after his figurative coronation, Charles was invested as Grand Master of the Order of the Temple of Jerusalem — and on taking his vow, he declared,

> You may be sure that when I truly come into my own I will raise the Order to what it was in the days of William the Lion.

From successful beginnings at the Battle of Prestonpans, the Scots marched southwards. Having advanced at speed all the way to Derby, they were quite unaware of the panic that had seized London and the House of Hanover. George II had even loaded the Crown Jewels onto a Thames barge in readiness for a quick getaway to Germany. The politicians hastily put out a barrage of propaganda to convince English and Welsh Jacobites that Charles would never reach the capital — and it worked; the Prince's anticipated reinforcements did not materialize.

Because the Scots had not yet confronted King George's main force under the Duke of Cumberland, Lord George Murray persuaded the clan chiefs that a strategic retreat was in order. Back in Scotland, he said, they could regroup and meet Cumberland on their own territory. After a few skirmishes on the way, and a Jacobite success at Falkirk, the Scots finally met Cumberland's massive army on Culloden Moor, near Inverness, on 16 April 1746. But despite all their previous success, the Scots were too tired and hungry to perform well. Bad judgements were made, and they were thoroughly defeated.

Ironically, had it not been for the ministerial propaganda in the South, the Highlanders could actually have marched from Derby and seized the capital with ease. 'Your ancestor was quite wrong', said the later King George V to Murray, Duke of Atholl. 'The Jacobite army should have continued straight on to London, and a Stuart would be today's King of Scotland and England, with each country having its own Parliament'.

Character Assassination

For the majority of people in Britain, James VII's objective of religious freedom for all was a very welcome innovation. It appealed greatly to their sense of individual liberty. It was therefore seen as imperative by the Whigs that, to preserve their own dominion, they should denigrate the memory of King James and the Stuarts. Their attack was launched on a thoroughly personal level — aimed at first towards James's wife, Queen Mary d'Este. She was the daughter of Alfonso IV, Duke of Modena, but the Hanoverians decided to portray her as an illegitimate child of the Pope!

There was not much that could be said against James's brother and immediate predecessor, Charles II — he was too well regarded in the popular mind — but James VI (I) and Charles I were other good targets. The Cromwellian annals were scoured for suitably critical content. James VI had been known to all as the British Solomon, but the Whigs renamed him the Wisest Fool in Christendom. His unfortunate intestinal illness was used to create the impression that he was a vulgar glutton, and the most common of all Puritan witch-hunting charges was laid against him, that of sexual deviancy.

Those things apart, the widespread popularity of Prince Charles Edward Stuart was an enormous threat to George II, and so he became the main object of the Hanoverian thrust. While the Duke of Cumberland pursued his violent subjugation of the Highlands after Culloden, the *Bonnie Prince* was portrayed in England as a treacherous warmonger, and labelled as a dangerous usurper — even though it was his own family that had been usurped. Before long, the whole scene was set against the *de jure* King of Scots. He was described as a drunk and a woman-hater; his various offspring (apart from Charlotte of Albany) were excluded from the British history books, as indeed were his numerous lady companions, except for one childless marriage to Princess Louise de Stolberg and his relationship with Charlotte's mother, Clementina Walkinshaw. Indeed, his eventual fits of asthma and epilepsy made it very easy for the image of drunkenness to be sustained.

Establishment based history in England still portrays the Prince as a troublesome pawn of Rome, but he was certainly not that. His rapport with the Pope was far from amicable, and he formally converted to the Anglican Protestant faith at the age of 29. Subsequently, he wrote,

> In order to make my renunciation of the Church of Rome the most authentic .... I went to London in the year 1750, and in that capital did then make a solemn abjuration of the Romish religion, and did embrace that of the Church of England.

Following Charles Edward's death in 1788, various accounts of his life were compiled from Hanoverian sources. There are now any number of published biographies, in large measure adapted from one another. Whether intentionally or otherwise, these biographies are generally founded on the contrived reports of the Hanoverian propaganda machine. Scotland, however, has retained her own legacy of pride in the Bonnie Prince. The registers of Europe similarly convey a very different image of Charles Edward and his legitimate descendants; they depict a resolute royal bloodline that was strategically veiled by the British Government until recent times.

The English now await the prospect of HRH Charles, Prince of Wales, becoming their King Charles III of the House of Windsor. At the same time, many Scots pursue a dogged course towards renewed independence. A first possible step in this latter regard has been the recent reinstatement of the Scottish Parliament—albeit still subordinate to Westminster. Scotland already has a traditional Written Constitution which could be re-implemented, if not bettered in an independent environment—and that Constitution gives the nation the right to choose its own monarch while also rejecting overlordship from England.

If the present HRH Charles, Prince of Wales, does become King of Britain, it is unlikely that Nationalist Scots would readily accept a second Charles III. Following the coronation of his mother, Queen Elizabeth II, the Scots rightly protested that they never had an Elizabeth I since Elizabeth Tudor had reigned in England but not in Scotland.

The prevailing Royal House is therefore faced with a considerable dilemma. Just as it once changed its German family name in 1917 from Saxe-Coburg-Gotha to Windsor in order to appease the British nation during World War I, it might perhaps be obliged to consider taking a further such diplomatic step. Just as Prince Charles's grandfather Albert, Duke of York, became King George VI, it is entirely possible that Britain's next king is crowned not as Charles III but as George VII. Alternatively, given that Parliament and the Church hold the trump cards, Prince Charles might somehow be bypassed altogether — particularly if he does not satisfy Anglican requirement with regard to the Defence of the Faith. These are, of course, speculative notions, but it will be interesting to see what happens.

The Sangréal Today

The Bloodline Conspiracy

These days it is generally understood that establishment history is largely based on recorded propaganda. It was originally compiled to suit the political needs of the era when written, rather than necessarily being an accurate record of events. In short, it is generally a slanted version of the truth. For example, the English historical version of the 1415 Battle of Agincourt understandably differs from that of the French viewpoint. Similarly, the Christian perception of the Crusades is not necessarily shared by the Muslims. There are at least two sides to most histories.

In 1763 the journalist John Wilkes accused George III's Government of misrepresenting facts in a King's speech. Today such challenges are common enough, but Wilkes was seized and flung into the Tower of London. In those days there was no freedom of speech or opinion, yet during that same period of constraint a vast amount of Government-approved history was produced.

Gradually, over the years of the 20th century, the official registers of nobility have been revised to correct a multiplicity of errors in past editions. But many of the errors (some still not fully corrected) were not mistakes as such in the first place—they were purposeful misrepresentations.[1] As a direct result of Hanoverian (Georgian and Victorian) policy, for instance, it has long been claimed in Britain that the Stuart succession became extinct while in exile. British history books are pretty well unanimous in stating that Charles Edward Stuart had no wife at his death, and no legitimate male offspring. But they are quite wrong and the continental European records tell a very different story.[2]

According to doctrinal English opinion, the present heir to the Royal House of Stuart is Franz, Duke of Bavaria, who is said to inherit the Scottish honours by virtue of the Last Will and Testament of

Charles Edward's younger Catholic brother, Cardinal Henry, *de jure* Duke of York. This Will supposedly nominated Charles Emmanuel IV of Sardinia as the Stuart successor. By way of marriages in the female line of descent from Charles Emmanuel's brother, Victor Emmanuel I, the present Franz of Bavaria succeeds his father, the late Duke Albrecht, relying (in this regard) on a somewhat tenuous ancestry back to Henrietta, a daughter of Charles I. The fact is, however, that Cardinal Henry Stuart's Will did not name Charles Emmanuel as his successor. This is a complete fantasy that has made its way into the history books, but was originally a purposely contrived deception on the part of Georgian politicians — a deception perpetuated by the later Victorian ministers.

From the time that the Elector of Hanover began his reign as King George I of Britain in 1714, it became politically expedient to suppress or veil a good deal of information about certain families while enhancing the lineage of others. The House of Stuart came under particular attack in order to justify the incoming German succession. Even today, history books repeat the nonsense contrived contemporarily and afterwards to discredit the Scots dynasty and its associated families. The fabrications are so well ingrained that they are destined to prevail for as long as historical authors continue to copy from one another.

Charles Edward Stuart was married in 1772 to Princess Louise Maximilienne, the daughter of Gustavus, Prince de Stolberg-Guedern. In 1784, however, papal dispensation for divorce was obtained following Louise's affair with the Italian poet Vittorio, Count Alfieri. Louise had been declared barren by the doctors, and after a few years of marriage she left Charles in 1780 to take up residence with her lover. The divorce is frequently described as the end of married life for Charles Edward — but it was not.

The Stuart archives in Rome and Brussels reveal that in November 1785 Charles was married again — to the Comtesse de Massillan at the Santi Apostoli in Rome. She was Marguerite Marie Thérèse O'Dea d'Audibert de Lussan — a cousin by descent from Charles's grand uncle, King Charles II. Until 1769 she had been a ward of her own grand uncle, Louis Jacques d'Audibert, Archbishop of Bordeaux. Marguerite's paternal grandmother Thérèse, Marchesa d'Aubignie, was the daughter of James de Rohano Stuardo, Prince of Boveria, Marquis d'Aubignie. He was the natural son (legitimated 1667) of King Charles II and Marguerite, Duchesse de Rohan. On her mother's side, Marguerite de Massillan was descended through the Comtes de Lussan.

In November 1786 the 37 year-old Countess gave birth to a son, Edouard Jacques Stuardo (Edward James Stuart), who became known as Count Stuarton. Although no secret in Europe, news of Charles Edward's legitimate son and heir was immediately suppressed by the Hanoverian Government at Westminster. He has consequently since been totally neglected by academic historians in Britain.

In that same month Charles Edward's daughter, Charlotte of Albany (born 1753 by Clementina Walkinshaw of Barrowfield), met with King George III's brother William, Duke of Gloucester, at the house of Prince Santa Croce in Rome. Concerned about the strength of her own position as Charles Edward's legitimated offspring, Charlotte informed Gloucester of the royal birth and sought his advice. The Duke confided that Charlotte's status was probably safe enough, but his main concern was a letter that had been sent to her father by King George III in 1784. It suggested that Charles Edward could return to Britain from exile as the Count of Albany (Scotland). Charles had declined the invitation, but the matter was now complicated by the newborn son who might well choose otherwise on becoming the second Count Stuarton in due course.

When Prince Charles Edward died, a contrived substitution of Wills enabled knowledge of both the marriage and the birth to be concealed from the British public—a concealment that was perpetuated through the Hanover-Saxe-Coburg era.

In 1784 Charles had made a Will nominating his brother Cardinal Henry, *de jure* Duke of York, as his royal heir, while Charlotte of Albany was to be the sole estate beneficiary. This is well enough documented in the historical biographies, but what those accounts fail to mention is that this was not Charles's final Testament. It was superseded by another before his death. Not only was the fact of this later Will concealed by the Georgian Parliament, but so too was the reason for its existence.

In order to stabilize King George III's position, his politicians thought it expedient to end the problem of Stuart popularity in Britain by having the Scottish line declared extinct—particularly since the Jacobites had been so instrumental in the American War of Independence (1775-1783). An enormous number of deprived Scots had emigrated to America following the brutal Highland Clearances after Culloden. They had not managed to regain their independence at home, but continued their cause from across the Atlantic, thereby aiding their fellow Americans to secure their own freedom from Hanoverian control.

On 30 January 1788 the *de jure* King Charles III (fondly remembered as *Bonnie Prince Charlie*) died, aged 67, at the Palazzo Muti in Rome. Shortly before his death he wrote his Last Will and Testament. This was witnessed on 13 January 1788 by the Dominican Father O'Kelly and the Abbé Consalvi, both of whom were executors. The Will stated that Charles's son and daughter, Edward and Charlotte, were to be co-heirs of the estate; his son Edward was to succeed to the Royal Honours on his 16th birthday, and Cardinal Henry was to be temporary Regent in the meantime.

Following Charles Edward's demise, however, his ambitious brother Henry wasted no time in proclaiming himself King Henry I of Scots (IX of England). To support this claim he produced not Charles's Will of 1788 but his earlier Will of 1784—which suited Britain's Government since Cardinal Henry was not likely to have any children. Both O'Kelly and Consalvi were party to the intrigue in return for rapid promotion within the Church. Soon afterwards, the former became Dominican Procurator, while the Abbé was raised to the Cardinalate. Charlotte of Albany was provided with a home in Frascati, and the Palazzo Muti was retained for Marguerite de Massillan and Prince Edward. Also involved in the scheme was the Abbé James Placid Waters, Procurator of the Benedictines in Rome.

By declaring himself King de jure, Henry sought to nullify the immediate Regency clause in his brother's Will. But in January 1789 Henry made his own Will in which he redressed his selfish strategy for the future: all his possessions and heritable status were bequeathed to Prince Edward James—that is, 'to my nephew, Count Stuarton'. Both Cardinal Ercole Consalvi and Cardinal Angelo Cesarini were privy to the Will and were executors, as attested in their memoirs.

As it happened, Henry subsequently lost a great deal of his wealth in the French Revolution and during the Napoleonic advance into the Papal States. In 1799 he became a pensioner of the British Crown at the rate of £5,000 per annum (about £250,000 per annum in today's terms)—but in return he was required to rewrite his Will. At a joint meeting between Prince Edward, Comtesse Marguerite, and the Pope, a suitable rewording was agreed. The new Will was made in 1802, but the inheritance still rested with Prince Edward. The revised document simply substituted the words 'to my nephew, Count Stuarton' with 'in favour of that Prince to whom it descends by virtue of *de jure* blood relationship'.

When Henry Stuart died in July 1807, King George and the British Parliament decided that the second Will was actually less appropriate than the former. They therefore ignored the 1802 document and reverted to Henry's original Will of 1789—but the press stated that Henry had made his bequest to his relation Count Stuarton (meaning, of course, Edward James). However, no one in England thought to enquire who this relation, Count Stuarton, might be. An example of a typical press report is that of the *Gentleman's Magazine*, September 1807:

> He [Henry] possessed before 1798 a very valuable collection of curiosities at his villa, where many scarce tracts and interesting manuscripts concerning the unfortunate House of Stuart were among the ornaments of his library. In his Will, made in January 1789, he had left the latter to his relation Count Stuarton; but they were all, in 1798, either plundered by the French and Italian Jacobins at Rome, or confiscated by the French Commissaries for the libraries or museums in Paris.

In fact, the library manuscripts had not been purloined by those accused; some are at the Vatican, some are in Roman libraries, and others were withheld by the British Government. In any event, according to the Memoirs of Henry's executors, Cardinals Cesarini and Consalvi (at the Bibliothèque National, Paris), Henry's library collection was of small relevance as an individual bequest since he bequeathed all he owned to his 'nephew, Count Stuarton'.

That apart, and having dealt with the first hurdle, the Hanoverian ministers then produced Henry's amended 1802 Will. By virtue of its malleable nature, the wording ('in favour of that Prince to whom it descends by virtue of *de jure* blood relationship')[3] was strategically implemented in favour of Charles Emmanuel IV, ex-King of Sardinia. He had recently abdicated to join the Jesuit Order, and so the Stuart legacy passed very conveniently to a potentially childless monk! Charles Emmanuel duly wrote to King George's Parliament denouncing the nomination because he knew the Stuarts to be alive and well. Indeed, having lived with him in Sardinia from 1797, Marguerite and her son Edward were then resident at his house by the Corso in Rome. The correspondence was nevertheless ignored at Westminster, and the whole issue was put under wraps in Britain. History now records the diverted Stuart succession as having progressed from Sardinia, through Modena, into Bavaria. The reality is that the legitimate Royal House of Stuart (Stewart) exists today, and has long been actively interested in European constitutional management.

In 1809 a dispute over sovereign loyalties arose between two sons of George III. It became known as the War of the Brothers. Prince Edward, Duke of Kent (the father of Queen Victoria), was a Freemason, while his brother Prince Augustus Frederick, Duke of Sussex, was a Knight Templar. Edward's problem was that his brother's Templar colleagues were Stuart supporters, so he therefore endeavoured to sway their allegiance to the reigning House of Hanover. In the event he failed, but compromised by creating a Templar-styled branch within the existing Masonic structure. This fell under the protectorate of Kent, and followed the English *York Rite* of Freemasonry, while the original Templars pursued the *Scottish Rite* under the protectorate of Prince Edward James Stuart, 2nd Count of Albany.

While the exiled Stuarts were in France and Italy, they were deeply involved with the general growth and dissemination of Freemasonry, and they were patrons of the exported *Scottish Rite*, which had higher degrees and held more profound mysteries than other Masonic systems. Prominent in this movement was Charles Edward's cousin and mentor, the Comte de St. Germain. The Stuarts' involvement was firmly based on established rights and privileges, with a desire to initiate brethren into the true antiquity and pedigree of the Craft.

In England, the inherent secrecy of the club-like lodges provided the perfect facility for undercover intrigue against the Whigs and the German succession. Throughout the land, the Jacobite societies and Tory lodges became closely entwined — as a result of which they became prime targets for Whig Intelligence, whose high-ranking Secret Service operatives duly infiltrated the fraternities. In later years English Freemasonry has dispensed with political intrigue to become more concerned with allegorical representation and the codes of brotherly love, faith and charity. In Europe, however, many scientifically-based intellectual lodges of the traditional style are still extant.

In 1817 a Dr Robert Watson purchased in Rome some of Cardinal Henry's documents concerning the Stuart dynasty. He paid £23.00 sterling (equivalent to about £610.00 today), and prepared to publish the contents. But, before he had a chance to do this, the files were seized by the papal police and passed to London so that their contents would not become known. Some time later, the doctor received a payment from Westminster for having been deprived of his property.

Not content with this, Watson pursued his right to the papers—only to be found dead (supposedly having committed suicide) in 1838. The papers have never since appeared in the public domain. The *Jacobite Peerage Register* of 1904 records that this was done specifically to avoid their content becoming known to Charles Emmanuel of Sardinia.

Along with Cardinal Henry, the Abbé Waters also lost his possessions and became a pensioner of King George. Waters, an executor for Charlotte of Albany, was the custodian of various other Stuart papers—his guardianship of which constituted the route to his future Hanoverian income. In 1805 the Abbé was obliged to pass them over to the British Government. At length, some were deposited at Windsor Castle, where they remain today. As for the rest, their whereabouts are conveniently unknown.

By virtue of these documentary acquisitions, the way was deemed clear for Prince Edward James to be totally excluded from historical records in Britain. But this was not the case in continental Europe, where he is well documented in papers held by the Stuart Trustees, and features in the writings of René, Vicomte Chateaubriand, Abbé James Waters, Princess Caroline Murat and others. Although the Stuarts have been ignored by the British authorities since the death of Cardinal Henry, the descendants of Prince Edward James, Count Stuarton, 2nd Count of Albany, have been actively engaged in social, political, military and sovereign affairs for the past two centuries. They have often advised Governments on constitutional and diplomatic matters in an effort to promote the ideals of public service and religious toleration, as upheld by their own reigning house, and they have been particularly concerned with matters of trade, welfare and education.

In 1888 Prince Edward's grandson, Charles Benedict James Stuart, 4th Count of Albany, was scheduled to visit Britain. He was due to attend a grand Stuart Exhibition at the New Gallery, London. It was sponsored by the Order of the White Rose and the main organizers were Bertram, Earl of Ashburnham, and Melville Massue, Marquis de Ruvigny. But the Exhibition was wholly undermined by Hanoverian agents and Prince Charles Benedict was found murdered in Italy.

There was no display in 1888 after all, but a rather different Exhibition was held the following year. Instead of being in honour of the Stuarts as was planned, it was promoted to celebrate the bicentenary of the Whig Revolution which had deposed James VII (II) and the Stuarts in 1688. The Exhibition's new patron was Queen Victoria herself, and the event was used as a cover to obtain even more valuable documents of Stuart heritage. Having been ousted from their patronage, Lord Ashburnham and the Marquis de Ruvigny directed their future interests towards the chivalric societies of Europe—the Order of the Realm of Sion, the Knights Protectors of the Sacred Sepulchre, and the Order of the Sangréal.

In spite of Queen Victoria's efforts to suppress Stuart popularity, there was a significant Jacobite revival in the late 1800s. The Queen's advisers therefore sought to emphasize her tenuous claim to Stuart descent to the exclusion of the Stuarts' own Scottish heritage. As a result, Thane Banquo and the Scots line from King Alpin disappeared from the Hanoverians' readjusted Stuart registers. The Lord Lyon, King of Arms, subsequently wrote, 'The traditional account of the descent of the family from Banquo, Thane of Lochaber, and through him from the ancient Kings of Scotland, is now generally discredited'. From that time, the Stuarts' Breton line was brought wholly to the fore—but why anyone should have to discredit one line of a descent in order to promote another is beyond ordinary understanding.

Subsequent members of the Scots Royal Family were prominent in the Belgian Resistance during World War II. Hubert Pierlot, Prime Minister of Belgium, was a close friend of the Stewarts, who had reverted to the original spelling of their name in 1892. In that year they had moved to the Château du Moulin in the Belgian Ardennes, where they lived until 1968. This castle had originally been given to the family in 1692 by King Louis XIV. As recently as 1982, the City of Brussels honoured the Stewarts with a grand reception. Then, on 14 December 1990, the Brussels Registrars signed, sealed and authenticated an updated Charter of the Royal House of Stewart, detailing the complete family descent from the time of Robert the Bruce down to date.

Today, there are several lines descended from Prince Edward James, 2nd Count of Albany. They include the Counts of Derneley and the Dukes of Coldingham. Foremost, however, in the main line of legitimate descent from Charles Edward Stewart and his son Edward James is the present 7th Count of Albany: Prince Michael James Alexander Stewart, Duc d'Aquitaine, Comte de Blois, Head of the Sacred Kindred of St. Columba, Knight Grand Commander of the Order of the Temple of Jerusalem, Patron Grand Officer of the International Society of Commission Officers for the Commonwealth, and President of the European Council of Princes.[4]

The senior Stewart descent goes all the way back to King Arthur's father, King Aedàn of Scots, on the one hand, and to Prince Nascien of the Septimanian Midi on the other. Their Scots descent traces further back through King Lucius of Siluria to Brân the Blessed and

James/Joseph of Arimathea, while the Midi succession stems from the Merovingians' male ancestral line through the Fisher Kings to Jesus and Mary Magdalene. Conjoining the lines from their 1st-century points of departure, the descent is in the succession of the Royal House of Judah. This is a truly unique line of sovereign lineage from King David in one of the key descents which comprise the *Bloodline of the Holy Grail*.

The Crown of America

Beneath the streets of Rome, the catacombs of the pagan era hold the remains of more than six-million Christians. Laid in a single row the passages would extend for 550 miles (880 kilometres). Ironically, the later fanaticism of the Inquisitions accounted for more than a million additional lives because the victims were supposedly 'not' Christian!

Through the centuries, millions of Jews have been persecuted and killed as a result of anti-Semitism initiated by the early Christian Church. This was managed mostly under cover of the accusation of deicide, and it ran completely out of control during the holocaust of the early 1940s. Additionally, tens of millions of Soviet Russian lives were lost during Stalin's brutal dictatorship—an autocratic totalitarianism that despised religion in any form. Vast numbers such as these are beyond the bounds of practical imagination, but their memory cannot be confined to savage regimes of the past. Worldwide religious feuds continue just as in the days of old, and the ethnic cleansing of the Inquisition is still apparent today.

In theory, Communism was introduced to fulfil a socialist ambition, but the dream soon died as the giant machine rose to power by military oppression. Capitalism, on the other hand, is equally ruthless because it venerates balance-sheets above the welfare of people. As a result, millions are condemned to starve to death in the poorer regions while vast food mountains stockpile elsewhere. Even in the United States, where the Constitution promotes the ideals of liberty and equality, we see an ever-widening gap between the privileged and subordinate groups. Rich communities are now barricading themselves within walled environments, while the welfare systems of the West are crumbling into bankruptcy.

History has proved many times over that absolute rule by monarchs or dictators is a road to social disparity. Yet the democratic alternative of elected government has often proved similarly inequitable. Even elected parliaments can become egotistic and dictatorial in a world where those entrusted to serve regard themselves instead as the masters. Additionally, in countries such as Britain that have a multi-party political structure, the people are regularly faced with the rule of ministers empowered by a minority vote. In such circumstances, who is there to champion the rights of individuals? Trade unions, some might say—but quite apart from being politically biased in themselves, such organizations are still subject to governmental control. Although they may have a weight of membership, they have no final authority to equal that of Parliament. As far as the judicial system is concerned, its purpose is to uphold legal justice, not moral justice.

Others in Britain may cite HM The Queen as the people's guardian, but Britain has a parliamentary monarchy in which the sovereign reigns only by the consent of Westminster. Given the lack of any Written Constitution, British monarchs are quite powerless to champion individual rights and liberties to any effect. The present heir to the throne has genuinely sought to bypass the restrictions by speaking out from time to time, only to suffer recriminations from the establishment. Like a Victorian child he is supposed to be seen and not heard, while bankers, industrialists and lawyers control the fate of the nation.

So often one hears politicians quoting the British Constitution as if it actually exists by way of a documentary privilege—but it does not. It is simply an accumulation of old customs and precedents concerning parliamentary sanctions, together with a number of specific laws defining certain aspects. Since Scotland's 1320 *Declaration of Arbroath* was nullified by England's *Treaty of Union* in 1707, the oldest Written Constitution now in force is that of the United States of America. It was adopted in 1787, ratified in 1788, and effected in 1789. In that same year began the French Revolution, which abolished feudalism and absolute monarchy in France, thereby influencing politics in much of Europe. Within the two centuries since the Revolution, France and other European States (with Britain as a noticeable exception) have adopted Written Constitutions to protect the rights and liberties of individuals—but who champions these Constitutions on behalf of the people?

A popular alternative to absolute monarchy or dictatorship has been found in Republicanism. The Republic of the United States was created primarily to free the emergent nation from the despotism of Britain's House of Hanover. Yet its citizens still tend to be fascinated by the concept of monarchy. No matter how Republican the spirit, the need for a central symbol remains. Neither a flag nor a president can fulfil this unifying role, for by virtue of the party system presidents are always politically motivated. Republicanism was devised on the principle of fraternal status, yet an ideally classless society can never exist in an environment that promotes displays of eminence and superiority by degrees of wealth and possession.

For the most part, those responsible for the morally inspired Constitution of the United States were Rosicrucians and Freemasons—notable characters such as George Washington, Benjamin Franklin, Thomas Jefferson, John Adams and Charles Thompson. The last, who designed the Great Seal of the United States of America, was a member of Franklin's American Philosophical Society—a counterpart of Britain's *Invisible College*. The imagery of the Seal is directly related to alchemical tradition, inherited from the allegory of the ancient Egyptian Therapeutate. The eagle, the olive branch, the arrows, and the pentagrams are all occult symbols of opposites: good and evil, male and female, war and peace, darkness and light, etc. On the reverse (as repeated on the dollar bill) is the truncated pyramid, indicating the loss of the Old Wisdom, severed and forced underground by the Church establishment. But above this are the rays of ever-hopeful light, incorporating the all-seeing eye, used as a symbol during the French Revolution.

In establishing their Republic, the Americans could still not escape the ideal of a parallel monarchy—a central focus of non-political, patriotic attachment. George Washington was actually offered kingship, but declined because he had no immediately qualifying heritage. Instead he turned to the Royal House of Stuart. In November 1782 four Americans arrived at the Palazzo San Clemente in Florence, the residence of Charles III Stuart in exile. They were Mr. Galloway of Maryland, two brothers named Sylvester from Pennsylvania, and Mr. Fish, a lawyer from New York. They were taken to Charles Edward by his secretary John Stewart. Also present was the Hon. Charles Hervey-Townshend (later Britain's ambassador to The Hague) and the Prince's future wife Marguerite, Comtesse de Massillan. The interview—which revolved around the contemporary transatlantic dilemma—is documented in the US Senate archives and in the *Manorwater Papers*. Writers such as Sir Compton Mackenzie and Sir Charles Petrie have also described the occasion when Charles Edward Stuart was invited to become King of the Americans.

Some years earlier, Charles had been similarly approached by the men of Boston, but once the War of Independence was over George Washington sent his own envoys. It would have been a great irony for the House of Hanover to lose the hitherto North American colonies to the Stuarts — but Charles declined the offer for a number of reasons, not the least of which was his lack of a legitimate male heir at the time. He knew that without a due successor, the United States could so easily fall to Hanover again at his death, thereby defeating the whole Independence effort.

Precept of the Sangréal

Since those days, many other radical events have taken place: the French Revolution, the Russian Revolution, two major World Wars, and a host of changes as countries have swapped one style of government for another. Meanwhile, civil and international disputes continue just as they did in the Middle Ages. They are motivated by trade, politics, religion and whatever other banners are flown to justify the constant struggle for territorial and economic control. The Holy Roman Empire has disappeared, the German Reichs have failed and the British Empire has collapsed. The Russian Empire fell to Communism, which has itself been disgraced and crumbled to ruin, while Capitalism teeters on the very brink of acceptability. With the Cold War now ended, America faces a new threat to her superpower status from the Pacific countries. In the meantime, the nations of Europe band together in what was once a seemingly well conceived economic community, but which is already suffering from the same pressures of individual custom and national sovereignty that beset the Holy Roman Empire.

Whether nations are governed by military-style regimes or elected parliaments, by autocrats or democrats, and whether formally described as monarchist, socialist or republican, the net product is always the same: the few control the fate of the many. In situations of dictatorship this is a natural experience, but it should not be the case in a democratic institution based on the principle of majority vote. True democracy is government *by* the people *for* the people, in either direct or representative form, ignoring class distinctions and tolerating minority views. The American Constitution sets out an ideal for this form of democracy, but in line with other nations there is always a large sector of the community that is not represented by the party in power.

Because presidents and prime ministers are politically tied, and because political parties take their respective turns at individual helms, the inevitable result is a lack of continuity for the nations concerned. This is not necessarily a bad thing, but there is no reliable ongoing institution to champion the civil rights and liberties of people

in such conditions of ever-changing leadership. Britain does, at le
retain a monarchy, but it is a politically constrained monarchy, an
such is ineffectual in performing its role as Guardian of the Rea
The United States, unlike Britain, has a Written Constitution, but has
no one with the power to uphold its principles against successive
Governments who determinedly pursue their own politically vested
interests.

Is there an answer to the anomaly — an answer that could bring not
just a ray of hope but a shining light for the future? There certainly is,
but its energy relies on those in governmental service appreciating
their roles as representatives of society rather than presuming to stand
at the head of society. Alongside the political administration, an
appointed Constitutional champion could be empowered to keep
check on any potential disparities and infringements of the
Constitution that might occur. This can be achieved in the manner first
envisaged by George Washington and the American Fathers. Their
original plan was for a democratic Parliament combined with a
working Constitutional Monarchy bound not to Parliament or the
Church, but to the people and their Written Constitution. In such an
environment, sovereignty would ultimately rest with the people,
while the monarch (as an operative Guardian of the Realm) would
pledge an Oath of Fealty to the Nation — not the reverse as in Britain's
case, whereby the Nation pays homage to the sovereignty of
Parliament and the Monarchy.

The unfulfilled ambition of the American Fathers was that
Government ministers should be elected by the majority vote of the
people, but that their actions be directed within the boundaries of the
Constitution. Because that Constitution belongs to the people, its
champion — as George Washington perceived — should be a monarch
whose obligation is not to politics or religion but to the sovereign
nation. Through the natural system of heredity (being born and bred
to the task), such a Constitutional Guardian would provide an
ongoing continuity of public representation through successive
governments. In this regard both monarchs and ministers would be
servants of the Constitution on behalf of the Community of the Realm.
Such a concept of moral government lies at the very heart of the Grail
Code, and it remains within the bounds of possibility for every
civilized Nation State.

A British prime minister recently claimed that it was not his job to
be popular! Not so — a popular minister is a trusted minister, and
holding a deserved electoral trust facilitates the democratic process.
No minister can honestly expound an ideal of equality in society

when that minister is deemed to possess some form of prior lordship over society. Class structure is always decided from above, never from below. It is therefore for those on self-made pedestals to be seen to kick them aside in the interests of harmony and unity. Jesus was not in the least humbled when he washed his Apostles' feet at the Last Supper; he was raised to the realm of a true Grail King—the realm of equality and princely service. This is the eternal Precept of the *Sangréal*, and it is expressed in Grail lore with the utmost clarity: Only by asking, Whom does the Grail serve? will the wound of the Fisher King be healed and the Wasteland returned to fertility.

NOTES AND REFERENCES

1: ORIGINS OF THE BLOODLINE

1. As also mentioned in Hugh Schonfield, *The Passover Plot*, Element Books, Shaftesbury, 1985, ch. 5, p. 245.

2. Eusebius of Caesarea, *Ecclesiastical History* (trans. C. F. Crusé), George Bell, London, 1874, III, 11.

3. Malachi Martin, *The Decline and Fall of the Roman Church*, Secker and Warburg, London, 1982, p. 43.

4. Massue, Melville Henry, 9th Marquis of Ruvigny and Raineval, *The Jacobite Peerage, Baronetage, Knightage and Grants of Honour*, 1904, Introduction.

5. The date of 4004 was calculated by Archbishop James Ussher of Armagh in his *Annales Veteris Testamenti* of 1650. Adam's creation has been separately dated at 5503 BC by means of Alexandrian texts and at 5411 BC based on the Greek *Septuagint* (produced by 72 translators of Old Testament texts in around 270 BC). The standard Jewish reckoning for the Creation (on which the Judaic calendar relies for its emergent year) is 3760 BC.
   Ussher's date provides a satisfactory mean and is often used in today's chronologies. The *Universal History's* error was in confusing Adam's date (*see* note 7) with the Earth's creation.

6. Darwin was not the first in the field of evolutionary research. The French naturalist Comte George de Buffon, Keeper of the Jardin du Roi, published the *Epochs of Nature* in 1778; the Scottish physician James Hutton (sometimes known as the 'founder of geology') published his *Theory of the Earth* in 1785; the French anatomist Baron Georges Cuvier (the 'father of palaeontology') published his *Tableau elementaire de l'histoire naturelle des animaux* in 1798, followed by his great work *Le regne animal*; the French naturalist le Chevalier Jean Baptiste de Monet Lamark, Professor of Zoology at the University of Paris, published his *Philosophie zoologique* in 1809, and followed it with the *Histoire naturelle des animaux sans vertebres*; and the Scotsman Sir Charles Lyell published his *Principles of Geology* in the early 1830s.

7. For Adam to have appeared somewhere around Ussher's mean year of 4004 BC (*see* note 5) would put him notionally in the tribal Bronze Age of his locality. From around 6000 BC there were villages and organized farming communities. By 5000 BC there was municipal structure, complete with civic councils run by the Halafans of Tel Halaf. In Jordan, Jericho was an established urban residential centre from about 6000 BC and, in China, the Yangtze Basin (the basin of the Chang Jiang) was developed in the same era. By 4000 BC (the said time of Adam), the plough, wheel and sailing ship were all in widespread use.

8. Prior to *The Descent of Man*, Darwin's *On the Origin of the Species by Means of Natural Selection* was published in 1859.

9. The Hebrew language at the time the books of the Pentateuch (the first five books of the Old Testament) were written did not distinguish between past tenses as we do in English. There was only one past tense and it referred to events that 'happened', 'have happened' and 'had happened' with equal relevance. Linguistically, there was no difference between what took place a thousand years ago and what occurred yesterday. Moreover, the Hebrew words for 'day' and 'year' were used with total flexibility, which made translation into languages with more concrete ideas of time very difficult. See Mary Ellen Chase, *Life and Language in the Old Testament*, Collins, London, 1956, ch. 3, pp. 32-39.

10. A derivation of the name Israel is from *ysra* ('ruler'), plus the element *El* (Lofty one or, later, God) — found in various forenames such as Elizabeth and Michael - thus 'El is ruler' or 'El rules'. See Ahmed Osman, *The House of the Messiah*, Harper Collins, London, 1992, ch. 17, p. 96. (Also see note 11 below.)

11. Jacob was renamed Israel (Genesis 32:28, 35:10) after his wrestling with God. Some say, therefore, that Israel means 'God wrestles', but there is no apparent foundation for this. The descendants of Jacob-Israel were called Israelites.

12. *Oxford Concordance to the Bible*, ref. Ramesses (2).

13. Ahmed Osman, *The House of the Messiah*, p. 11.

14. *Ibid.*, ch. 12, p. 67.

15. The Tabernacle of the Congregation (also translated as the Tent of the Meeting) was a wooden-framed rectangular tent or booth covered with cloth and skins. It was used as a portable place of worship during the wanderings in the Wilderness. (*See* the *Oxford Concordance to the Bible*).

2: IN THE BEGINNING

1. The subject is fully covered by Dr. Raphael Patai, a noted authority on historical Judaic culture, in *The Hebrew Goddess*, Wayne State University Press, Detroit, 1967.

2. Some of the Old Testament, however, derived directly from the Book of the Law that was discovered in the Temple of Jerusalem (2-Kings 22:8-13) some 35 years before the Babylonian Exile during the reign of King Josiah of Judah (640-609 BC). The existing Hebrew text of the Old Testament corresponds to that produced by the Massoretic scholars in around AD 900, although it is based on earlier manuscripts, some from the 1st century BC.

3. Eridu (modern Abu Shahrein) was the most sacred city of ancient Mesopotamia — a jewel within a green and fertile land that, to the inhabitants of Canaan, would have seemed a veritable paradise. In acknowledgement of its lush surroundings the city was dedicated to the water god Enki (or Ea), and has been identified with the Garden of Eden.

4. According to Sir Charles Leonard Woolley (one-time Director of the British Museum and of the University of Pennsylvania's archaeological expedition to

Mesopotamia) in *Ur of the Chaldees* (1, 21-32), the Flood, as narrated in Genesis, took place in around 4000 BC.

5. The Tower of Babel, a huge ziggurat, was constructed on the Babylonian Plain of Shinar. Such richly decorated, multi-levelled ziggurats (Babylonian for 'high place' or 'tower') were features of Sumerian cities. They were surmounted by small temples to the primary deities of the regions. The Great Ziggurat was sited at the city of Uruk (from which modern Iraq derives its name) and its temple was consecrated to the goddess Ishtar.

6. To the Jews, the Underworld was known as *Sheol*. It was an equivalent to the Graeco-Roman kingdom of Hades, the infernal region in which souls dwelt in mournful darkness, separated from their earthly bodies.

7. The first five Books of Moses correspond to the first five books of the Old Testament (also called the Pentateuch): Genesis, Exodus, Leviticus, Numbers and Deuteronomy.

8. The Books of the Prophets are technically those written by or about the Jewish prophets, as opposed to books that are narrative histories—although the general definition does include some historical books such as Judges, Samuel and Kings. The balance of the Old Testament is called the Hagiographa (Holy writings).

9. Other Jewish holy writings are the Mishnah and the Talmud. The Mishnah (Repetition) is an early codification of Jewish law, based upon ancient compilations and edited in Palestine by the Ethnarch (Governor) Judah I in the early 3rd century AD. It consists of traditional law (Halakah) on a wide range of subjects, derived partly from old custom and partly from Biblical law (Tannaim) as interpreted by the rabbis (teachers).

The Talmud is basically a commentary on the Mishnah, compiled originally in Hebrew and Aramaic. It derives from two independently important streams of Jewish tradition: the Babylonian and the Palestinian.

10. Rev. John Fleetwood, *The Life of Our Lord and Saviour Jesus Christ*, William MacKenzie, Glasgow, *c.*1900, ch. 1, p. 3: the entry by Dr. G. Redford.

11. The Hasmonaeans were a distinguished and priestly family, prominent in Jerusalem in the 2nd century BC. At the time of Antiochus IV, the head of the household was the high priest Mattathias, who initiated the Jewish Revolt. Before he died, he nominated his third son Judas (nicknamed Maccabaeus or Maccabee: 'the appointed [one]') to be the movement's military commander. Judas was in turn succeeded by his brothers Jonathan and Simeon who, along with all their followers, were thereafter known as Maccabees.

12. *See* Baigent, Leigh and Lincoln, *The Holy Blood and the Holy Grail*, Jonathan Cape, London 1982, ch. 12, p. 285.

13. *See* Baigent, Leigh and Lincoln, *The Dead Sea Scrolls Deception*, ch. 9, p. 141.

14. Twelve other works dating from and related to the last part of the Old Testament era constitute the Apocrypha (Hidden things). Although included in the Greek *Septuagint*, they were not, however, contained in the Hebrew canon. They originated in the Hellenist Judaism of Alexandria, but are not accepted by orthodox Jews. The

books are, nevertheless, included in St. Jerome's Latin *Vulgate* (c.AD 385) as an extension to the Old Testament, and are recognized by the Roman Catholic Church. But, they are omitted by almost all Protestant Bibles, having been sidelined by the prime reformer Martin Luther (1483-1546) and largely ignored by translators. The twelve books are: Esdras, Tobit, Judith, the Rest of Esther, the Wisdom of Solomon, Ecclesiasticus [of Jeremiah], Baruch with the Epistle of Jeremy, the Song of the Three Holy Children, the History of Susanna, Bel and the Dragon, the Prayer of Manasses, and Maccabees.

15. J. T. Milik, *Ten Years of Discovery in the Wilderness of Judaea* (trans. J. Strugnell), SCM Press, London, 1959, ch. 1, pp. 11-19.

16. In the New Testament, 2-Corinthians 4:3-7 similarly states: 'If our Gospel be hid, it is hid to them that are lost .... But we have this treasure in earthen vessels'.

17. James Robinson and the Coptic Gnostic Project, *The Nag Hammadi Library*, E. J. Brill, Leiden, 1977.

18. *Bedouin* is used in English as a singular adjective, whereas it is technically a plural noun. In Arabic, *bedu* is 'desert' and the *bedu'een* are the 'people of the desert'.

19. Josephus, *Antiquities of the Jews* (trans. W. Whiston), Thomas Nelson, London, 1862, XV, ch. 5, p. 2.

20. J. T. Milik, *Ten Years of Discovery in the Wilderness of Judaea*, ch. 3, pp. 51-53.

21. John Allegro, *The Dead Sea Scrolls*, Penguin, Harmondsworth, 1964, ch. 5, p. 94.

22. *Ibid.*, ch. 5, p. 93.

23. Barbara Thiering, *Jesus the Man*, Doubleday/Transworld, London, 1992, ch. 4, pp. 20-21.

24. Eschatology: the study (or branch of theology) that has to do with the end of the world—the Last Things (death or judgement).

25. John Allegro, *The Dead Sea Scrolls*, ch. 6, p. 104.

26. *Pesharim*: 'Interpretations', thus 'Commentary' or 'Exegesis'. The singular is *pesher*.

27. Barbara Thiering, *Jesus the Man, passim*.

28. *Ibid.*, Appendix III, p. 339.

29. Josephus, *The Jewish Wars*, II, ch. 8, p. 6.

30. Barbara Thiering, *Jesus the Man*, ch. 12, p. 65; Appendix III, p. 344.

31. During the earlier era of polytheistic religions, Zoroaster (or Zarathustra) modified the concept and devised the world's first genuinely dualist creed. He became the archpriest and prophet of Ahura Mazda (Ormuzd), god of life and light,

who was opposed by Ahriman (Angra Mainyu), the evil lord of death and darkness. These ancient deities were destined to wage a continual war, Light against Darkness, until Light won in the Final Judgement. At that time, Ahura Mazda would resurrect the dead to create a Paradise on Earth.

Over the centuries thereafter, and as the tradition altered with the differing cultural influences, much of the legend remained fixed. At the time of the Essenes of Qumrân (as the years BC drew to a close), the story of the dualist war was still current, although generally as an allegory related to the hoped-for overthrow of Roman imperialism. Later, Roman Christianity retained the basic idea, with the result that many Christians still believe there is still a Final Judgement to come.

3: JESUS, SON OF MAN

1. Rev. John Fleetwood, *The Life of Our Lord and Saviour Jesus Christ,* ch. 1, pp. 21-22. Various interpretations of the prophecy may be found in *Dr. Smith's Bible Dictionary.*

2. A. N. Wilson, *Jesus,* Sinclair Stevenson, London, 1992, ch. 4, p. 79.

3. Nancy Qualls-Corbett, *The Sacred Prostitute,* Inner City Books, Toronto, 1988, ch. 2, p. 58.

4. The concept that Mary was 'ever-virgin' was established at the Council of Trullo in AD 692.

5. A. N. Wilson, *Jesus,* ch. 4, p. 83.

6. An old monastic complex stood on the outskirts of Qumrân. Among its buildings was the house where Essene children conceived out of wedlock were born. The community referred to this house as 'Bethlehem of Judaea' (as opposed to the quite separate Bethlehem settlement, south of Jerusalem). Matthew 2:5 states that Jesus was born 'in Bethlehem of Judaea'. (*See* Barbara Thiering, *Jesus the Man,* ch. 9, pp. 50-52.)

The Gospel narratives were geared to comply with the prophecy of Micah 5:2, which dates from about 710 BC: 'But thou, Bethlehem Ephratah, though thou be little ... yet out of thee shall he come forth unto me that is to be ruler in Israel'.

7. *Dr. Smith's Bible Dictionary* states that the Hebrew word translated as 'inn' in English more literally signifies a 'lodging-place'. Inns, in the modern sense, were unknown in the ancient Near East, where it was common to invite travellers into one's home, and was regarded as a pious duty to do so.

8. A. N. Wilson, *Jesus,* ch. 4, p. 80.

9. Ahmed Osman, *The House of the Messiah,* ch. 5, p. 31. *Robinson's Bible Researches,* on the other hand, gives the Arabic name as *en Nusara.* (*See* Rev. John Fleetwood, *The Life of Our Lord and Saviour Jesus Christ,* ch. 1, p. 10.)

10. The Old Testament does not refer to Nazareth. Neither does the Hebrew Talmud, and nor does Josephus mention the town in his 1st-century *The Antiquities of the Jews* or in *The Jewish Wars.* Nazareth first appeared around AD 70 and became a place of pilgrimage only from the 6th century (Ahmed Osman, *The House of the Messiah,* ch. 5, pp. 30-32).

11. Rev. John Fleetwood, *The Life of Our Lord and Saviour Jesus Christ,* 1, 4, confirms the information in *Dr. Smith's Bible Dictionary* that the name Gabriel in this context represents a title corresponding to angelic office.

12. Josephus, *The Jew Jewish Wars,* II, ch. 8, p. 7.

13. Barbara Thiering, *Jesus the Man,* Appendix III, pp. 335-8. The name Gabriel means 'Man of God'. Appendix III, p. 340. The name Michael means 'Who [is] like God'.

14. Luke 1:5 — Elizabeth was a daughter of the priestly house of Aaron.

15. Luke 2:25.

16. Rev. John Fleetwood, *The Life of Our Lord and Saviour Jesus Christ,* ch. 1, pp. 10-11; an extract by Dr. Paxton outlines the customary rules of Jewish matrimony as distinct from the more restrictive dynastic regulations.

17. Barbara Thiering, *Jesus the Man,* p. 8; Appendix I, p. 177.

18. Josephus, *The Jewish Wars,* 11, ch. 8, p. 13.

19. Barbara Thiering, *Jesus the Man,* ch. 7, p. 42: Appendix I, p. 209.
   It was not until AD 314 that Emperor Constantine the Great arbitrarily changed the date of Jesus's birthday to 25 December so as to coincide with the pagan sun festival.
   It will be noticed that the dates of some New Testament events as given in this book do not conform to the traditional dates. The year of Jesus's birth, for example, is often considered to have been 5 BC, but herein is 7 BC. The date of the Crucifixion is similarly often shown as AD 30 whereas it is given here as AD 33. The first published sequence of Biblical dates appeared in AD 526, being calculations of the monk Dionysius Exiguus. By his reckoning Jesus was born in the Roman year 754 AUC *(Anno Urbis Conditae:* 'Years after the founding of the City [of Rome]') — equivalent to AD 1. But Herod the Great died four years before this, in 750 AUC (= 4 BC). Because it was known that Herod was still alive at the time of Jesus's birth, the monk's chart was, therefore, adjusted to set the Nativity a year before Herod's death — in the year 749 AUC (= 5 BC). This became the accepted date, and the rest of the Gospel time-frame was recalculated accordingly.

20. In relating Jesus's lineage, Matthew and Luke do not agree on the genealogy from King David. Matthew gives the kingly line from Solomon, whereas Luke details a descent from another of David's sons, Nathan. This segment of the list in Matthew contains 22 ancestors, against 20 in Luke. However, both lists eventually coincide at Zerubbabel, whom they agree was the direct and immediate heir of Shealtiel. But even this is subject to debate for, whereas the Old Testament books of Ezra (3:2) and Haggai (1:1) confirm that Zerubbabel was born into Shealtiel's family, there could have been a generation between the two — a possible son of Shealtiel named Pedaiah, who would then have been Zerubbabel's father. The account in 1-Chronicles 3:19 is confusing in this regard.
   The main difference between Matthew and Luke concerns the ancestors from the time of David to the era of the Israelites's return from Babylonian captivity. For this term, the equivalent list in 1-Chronicles is in general accord with Matthew's genealogy. Then, having converged on Zerubbabel, the lists in Matthew and Luke diverge again. Matthew traces Jesus's descent through a son named Abiud, while Luke takes a course through a son called Rhesa (a titular name meaning 'chieftain').

Jesus's paternal grandfather is called Jacob according to Matthew 1:16 but, in Luke 3:23, he is said to be Heli. Both versions are correct, however, for Joseph's father, Heli, held the distinction of 'Jacob' in his patriarchal capacity. *(See* Barbara Thiering, *Jesus the Man*, ch. 5, p. 29.)

The genealogical list in Matthew, from David to Jacob-Heli (spanning about 1000 years) contains 25 generations at 40 years each. Luke, on the other hand, gives 40 generations at 25 years each. Hence, Luke places Jesus in the 20th generation from Zerubbabel, whereas Matthew places him in the 11th. Through this latter period of around 530 years, the Matthew list supports a 53-year generation standard, while Luke is more comprehensible with its 28-year standard.

21. The original Zadok was the High Priest who anointed David's son King Solomon in around 1015 BC (1-Kings 1:38-40), as celebrated by Handel in the anthem sung at British coronations since the 18th century.

4: THE EARLY MISSION

1. Barbara Thiering, *Jesus the Man*, Appendix II, p. 299.

2. *Ibid.*, Appendix I, pp. 325-30.

3. Rev. John Fleetwood, *The Life of Our Lord and Saviour Jesus Christ*, ch. 1, pp. 11-12; extract from *Dr. Smith's Bible Dictionary*.

4. The Samaritans believed that Simon (Zelotes) Magus represented the 'Power of God' (Acts 8:9-10).

5. Steve Richards, *Levitation*, Thorsons, Wellingborough, 1980, ch. 5, pp. 66-7.

6. Barbara Thiering, *Jesus the Man*, ch. 15, p. 80.

7. Judas the Galilean died in AD 6.

8. The Syrian Semitic verb *skariot* was an equivalent of the contemporary Hebrew *sikkarti*: 'to deliver up'. It has been suggested that Judas Iscariot was therefore 'Judas the Deliverer', referring to his betrayal of Jesus. (*See* Ahmed Osman, *The House of the Messiah*, ch. 15, p. 81.)

9. *Jacob* is synonymous with *Jacobus*, of which there was a Latin variant *Jacomus*, from which (via the Norman French) English now has the variant nominal form of *James*. The connection between the forms has never been forgotten and is the reason why, from the 17th century, adherents of the Stuart King James VII of Scotland (James II of England) were known as Jacobites (i.e. Jacob-ites).

10. Matthew was regarded with considerable hostility by the Pharisees. Their strict, orthodox Jewish outlook caused them to be petty in the extreme about the observance of laws that predated the Books of Moses (the Pentateuch or Torah), to the extent that they believed Israel could not be redeemed until all Jews were purified. To them, such essential purification was incompatible with monetary affairs or political intrigues, and someone who was involved in both—like a publican, and especially one who collected taxes—could only be regarded as a sinner.

11. The Proselytes were Gentile converts to the Jewish faith.

12. Shem was a son of Noah and an ancestor of Abraham; he represents the ancient lineage of the S[h]emitic peoples.

13. The name Bartholomew derives from *Bar-Ptolemy* (Aramaic: 'servant of Ptolemy') and thus has its own Egyptian connotations.

14. Thomas was born Philip, the son of Herod the Great and Mariamne II. In due course he became the first husband of Herod's granddaughter Herodias, with whom he had a daughter, Salome (who requested the head of John the Baptist from Herod-Antipas of Galilee). Well known for her 'dance of the seven veils', Salome is not mentioned by name in the New Testament, but features in Flavius Josephus, *The Antiquities of the Jews,* XVIII, ch. 5, sect 4.

15. Genesis 16:7-12.

16. Numbers 22:21-35.

17. Judges 13:3-19.

18. Judges 6:11-22.

19. The twelve clay tablets recounting the *Epic of Gilgamesh,* ruler of Uruk, derive from the 7th century BC. They were discovered among the effects of King Ashurbanipal of Assyria (669-626 BC) at Nineveh. Among the various events described in the *Epic* is the story of Enkidu who, like Ezekiel and the prophet Elijah, was confronted by a roaring from the heavens. He was seized and transported upwards in the brazen talons of an eagle, with a vertical speed that made his body feel as heavy as an enormous boulder.
Reference of this kind to an eagle also occurs in the *Moses Apocalypse,* in which Eve sees a chariot of light drawn by shining eagles.
Flaming seraphims also appear with regularity in the ancient documents. That they are fiery is consistent with the etymology of the word *seraph,* which is related to an old Hebrew stem meaning 'flame'. But they sometimes have awesome destructive properties, as in Numbers 21:16, when a large proportion of Israel died after the Lord sent fiery serpents (seraphims) among them.
Such stories are not confined to the countries of North Africa and the Near East. from that same period similar accounts come from Tibet, India, Scandinavia and elsewhere. The writings all tell of heavenly chariots that spout fire and quicksilver, and of thunderbirds with brazen wings.

20. The subject is well covered in Erich von Däniken, *Chariots of the Gods,* Souvenir, 1969.

21. 1-Enoch 4:9 and the Qumrân *War Scroll* 9:15-17. *See* also A. Dupont-Sommer, *The Essene Writings From Qumrân* (trans. G. Vermes), Basil Blackwell, Oxford, 1961, V, p. 183 (re. the angelic shields).

22. Josephus, *The Jewish Wars,* II, ch. 7, p. 7.

23. Tabulated details of the angelic and priestly structures are given in Barbara Thiering, *Jesus the Man,* Appendix III.

24. The spiritual energy of springs and streams was numerically represented in the Solar Force as 1080. (*See* John Michell, *Dimensions of Paradise*, Thames and Hudson, London, 1988, ch. 1, p. 18.)

5: THE MESSIAH

1. The Qumrân *Manual of Discipline* (the *Scroll of the Rule*), ch. 6, pp. 4-5; annex 18-20.

2. Barbara Thiering, *Jesus the Man*, ch. 18, p. 91.

3. *Ibid.*, Appendix III, p. 357. There were not actually 5,000 people at this symbolic feeding. The 'Five Thousand' was a name applied to a body of non-Jews native to Palestine and who were described as the 'Sons of Ham' — regarded as the founder of the Hamitic tribes of the region. The Community's liaison officer with the Five Thousand was Jesus's Apostle John Boanerges.

4. Again there were not 4,000 recipients involved. This 'Four Thousand' (the Men of Shem) was another particularized group of Gentiles. Together with the Proselytes (converts to Judaism) called the 'Three Thousand', the Five Thousand and the Four Thousand were held to comprise part of the especially cosmopolitan tribe of Asher.

5. Barbara Thiering, *Jesus the Man*, ch. 18, p. 92; Appendix II, pp. 325-31.

6. There was a good deal of speculation over whether John the Baptist or Jesus was the awaited Messiah. John was, after all, the prevailing Zadok and anointed as such, thereby holding Messianic status (*Messiah:* 'Anointed One'). But when asked directly about the Saviour Messiah, John 'confessed, and denied not; but confessed, I am not the Christ' (John 1:20). The Qumrân Scrolls indicate that the community lived in expectation of two important Messiahs. One was to be of the priestly caste, whom they called the Teacher of Righteousness; the other would be a Prince of the line of David — a warrior who would restore the kingdom of his people.

John the Baptist made it quite clear that he was not the Kingly Messiah (John 3:28): 'I said, I am not the Christ, but that I am sent before him '. For the Qumrân notion of the two Messiahs, *see* also John Allegro, The Dead Sea Scrolls, *ch.* 13, pp. 167-72.

7. The Hebrew calendar was lunar in origin, and its 12-month year totals 354 days although, to make up for the deficiency of 11 days in relation to the solar calendar year, it adds a complete calendar month in 7 years of a 19-year cycle. The Hellenists in Palestine adopted the Romans' Julian (365-day) calendar in 44 BC — a system that suited the Samaritan Magi, who made astronomical calculations according to the solar calendar, which added 10 days per year to the lunar calendar. The difference in calendars over a number of centuries might account for a displacement of seven years in a forecast relating to a time sufficiently far ahead.

8. A 'fuller' was one who beat and scoured the textiles of the washed cloths (using a special grease-absorbent clay and certain herbs) so that the material fluffed up, with an effect much like that provided by today's fabric conditioners. On white garments the result was an extra lustrous sheen. (Some modern Bibles tend to translate the original Greek word as 'bleacher.)

9. Josephus, *The Antiquities of the Jews*, XVIII, ch. 3, p. 2.

10. Barbara Thiering, *Jesus the Man*, ch. 20, pp. 97-100.

11. Spikenard was a fragrant, sweet-smelling ointment compounded from the nard plant, which grew only in the Himalayan mountains at heights of around 15,000 feet (*c*.4570 metres) and was very expensive.

12. In the Gospels of Matthew and Mark, Jesus's entry into Jerusalem occurs before the anointing at Bethany. A political motivation lies behind this textual switch of events in their accounts. In John, the anointing is correctly related in conjunction with the raising of Lazarus and, for Jesus to be accredited as the Messiah, it was imperative that he be anointed.

13. Spikenard was also used as an unguent in funerary rites. It was customary for a grieving widow to place a broken vial of the ointment in her late husband's tomb. *See* Margaret Starbird, *The Woman With the Alabaster Jar*, Bear, Santa Fe, New Mexico, 1993, ch. 2, pp. 40-41.

14. *Ibid.*, ch. 11, pp. 35-36.

15. Of the academic works on the subject of sacred marriage, Samuel Kramer's *The Sacred Marriage Rite* (especially ch. 3, p. 63) is worthy of particular study. From the female standpoint, however, nowhere is the story of the Lost Bride more compassionately conveyed than in the writings of Margaret Starbird.

16. Ahmed Osman, *The House of the Messiah*, ch. 28, p. 152.

17. Barbara Thiering, *Jesus the Man*, Appendix III, pp. 366-71.

18. The Sanhedrin was the Jewish assembly that held supreme authority in all religious and civil matters. It consisted of priests, scribes and elders, who formed the Supreme Court of Judicature (*Oxford Concordance to the Bible*).

19. Salome's baptismal name was Helena. As the spiritual adviser to Salome, daughter of Herodias, she too was called Salome in accordance with custom. Helena-Salome was the spiritual mother of the Apostles, James and John Boanerges.

20. Barbara Thiering, *Jesus the Man*, Appendix III, pp. 366-71.

21. Morton Smith, *The Secret Gospel*.

22. *Ibid.*, ch. 7, p. 51.

23. In the 4th century AD, when the New Testament was first collated, the Gospel manuscripts of Mark ended at the present Chapter 16 verse 8, before the narration of the Resurrection events. These shorter manuscripts are part of the *Codex Vaticanus* and the *Codex Sinaiticus*. *See* Baigent, Leigh and Lincoln, *The Holy Blood and the Holy Grail*, ch. 12, pp. 282-3; notes, p. 432.

24. *Ibid.*, ch. 12, p. 296.

6: BETRAYAL

1. John the Baptist had initially supported a prediction known as the Prophecy of Enoch. This gave a date for the restoration of the Zadokite and Davidic hereditary lines as being 'the end of the eighth World Week' — that is 3920 years after the supposed Creation. This had been calculated to occur in the year now defined as 21 BC, but nothing had happened. Calendar revision allowed for an extension to AD 29, but judicious recalculation further extended the deadline date to AD 31. (*See* Barbara Thiering, *Jesus the Man*, ch. 13, pp. 67-68). John's whole reputation, with all its wild mystique, hung on this prediction. Following John's execution, the prophecy was recalculated yet again to fall on the vernal equinox of AD 33.

2. Josephus, *The Antiquities of the Jews*, XVIII, ch. 1, sect. 3.

3. John Allegro, *The Dead Sea Scrolls*, ch. 7, p. 131; ch. 12, p. 164; ch. 13, p. 168.

4. *Scroll of The Rule*, Annex II, 17-22.

5. Barbara Thiering, *Jesus the Man*, ch. 21, p. 102.

6. Baigent, Leigh and Lincoln, *The Holy Blood and the Holy Grail*, ch. 12, p. 309.

7. Barbara Thiering, *Jesus the Man*, ch. 22, p. 105.

8. Baigent, Leigh and Lincoln, *The Holy Blood and the Holy Grail*, ch. 12, p. 309; notes, p. 433.

9. *The Apostolic Constitutions*, VI, sect. 9. *See* Clement (Cults and Religions) in Bibliography.

10. Gnostic tradition has it that Simon the Cyrene was crucified 'in the place of Jesus'. This does not mean instead of Jesus, but in what should have been Jesus's location. Understanding Jesus to represent the kingly Davidic heritage, with Simon to represent the priestly line (and therefore Judas to represent the line of the prophets), the positioning of the three crosses should have been made to observe the formal hierarchical ranks. According to this scheme, the position of the King should have been to the west (on the left); the position of the Priest should have been in the centre; and the position of the Prophet should have been to the east (on the right). But the Gospels state that Jesus's cross was in the middle. If, though, the Cyrene was crucified in this place instead of Simon (as the Priest), Jesus (as the King) would have been correctly positioned to the west.

7: CRUCIFIXION

1. Barbara Thiering, *Jesus the Man*, ch. 24, p. 113.

2. *Ibid.*, Appendix II, p. 312.

3. *Ibid.,* Appendix III, p. 353.

4. *Ibid.,* ch. 26, p. 122.

5. The translation to 'pound' in this case represents the Greek *litra* (a variant of the Roman *libra),* a measure of weight equal to one ninetieth of a *talantaios (*talent). In modern terms this approximates to 330 grams or 12 ounces *avoirdupois.* 100 New Testament 'pounds' is thus roughly equal in modern terms to 33 kilograms or 75 pounds (more than 5 stones) *avoirdupois*—a considerable quantity for Nicodemus to manage alone.

6. Christianity did survive, although for many the Crucifixion was seen as the blow which should have put an end to it. Senator Cornelius Tacitus (born *c.*AD 55), referring to the Crucifixion, wrote ruefully: 'In spite of this temporary setback, the deadly superstition [Christianity] had broken out afresh, not only in Judaea where the mischief had started, but even in Rome' (Tacitus, *The Annals of Imperial Rome,* XIV, ref. AD 64).

7. *See* Chapter 5, *The King and His Donkey.*

8. Baigent, Leigh and Lincoln. *The Messianic Legacy,* ch. 6, p. 68.

9. Gladys Taylor, *Our Neglected Heritage,* Covenant Books, London, 1974, vol. 1, p. 42.

10. The Gnostics were so called because they were accredited with *gnosis* (Greek: 'knowledge'—especially esoteric insight). The Gnostic movement originated in Samaria, where Simon Zelotes (Simon the Magus) was head of the Samaritan Magi (men of wisdom) of West Manasseh. Later, it was further developed in Syria, again with Simon as its principal proponent, before spreading into the pre-Roman Christian environment.

11. Nag Hammadi *Codex* BG 8502, 1.

12. *See* Chapter 4, *Who Were the Apostles?* (under *Thaddaeus, James and Matthew).*

13. Nag Hammadi *Codex* VII, 3.

14. Nag Hammadi *Codex* II, 2.

8: THE BLOODLINE CONTINUES

1. Barbara Thiering, *Jesus the Man,* Appendix I, p. 177 and p. 196.

2. *Ibid.,* Appendix III, p. 177.

3. The fact that Jesus is mentioned in connection with the 'times of restitution' (Acts 3:21) indicates that he had become a parent and was, therefore, obliged to lead a celibate existence for a predetermined time. There is no suggestion that this child was a son, which means that the child was a daughter. Note that Damaris is mentioned in Acts 17:34.

4. Barbara Thiering, *Jesus the Man*, Appendix I, p. 297 and p. 299; Appendix III, pp. 363-64.

5. *Ibid.*, ch. 29, p. 133.

6. A. N. Wilson, *Jesus*, ch. 2, p. 26.

7. Baigent, Leigh and Lincoln, *The Messianic Legacy*, ch. 6, p. 67.

8. Barbara Thiering, *Jesus the Man*, ch. 30, p. 139.

9. The doctrinal theme of the Qumrân Community was called the 'Way', and those who followed the Way were the 'Children of Light', it was in this context that those who were unsympathetic to the doctrine were 'blind to the way' (Acts 9:17). Symbolically, his instruction in Hellenist principles enabled him to 'see the Way' and, as the English metaphor has it, to 'see the Light'.

10. A. N. Wilson, *Jesus*, ch. 2, pp. 18-19.

11. *Ibid.*, ch. 2, pp. 22-23.

12. Simon is honoured as the first missionary priest in Cyprus. The main church in Larnaca is dedicated to him under his other New Testament name, Lazarus. He is said to have been the first Bishop of Larnaca.

13. Barbara Thiering, *Jesus the Man*, ch. 31, pp. 143-44.

14. *Ibid.*, ch. 31, p. 141.

15. *Ibid.*, Appendix I, p. 268.

16. The colour black, as used for ecclesiastical garb, has associations far older than Christianity.
  The tall black statue of Isis at the Church of St. Germain, Paris, was identified as the Virgin of Paris until the 16th century. The original abbey on the site was built for Childebert I on top of a Temple of Isis. It housed Childebert's relics from the Treasures of Solomon and was a burial-place for the Merovingian kings. (*See* Ean C. M. Begg, *The Cult of the Black Virgin*, Arkana, London, 1985, ch. 2, p. 66.) The Benedictine monks of St. Germain-des-Prés wore black cassocks in the Nazarite tradition.
  A statue of St. Genevieve was erected in the Benedictine chapel. She was perceived as a successor to Isis in France, and was a close friend of King Clovis.

17. It was in AD 62 that Ananus the younger, a Sadducee brother of Jonathan Annas, became High Priest. As such, he was predisposed towards furthering the Sanhedrin's opposition to James and his Nazarene ideals.

18. The stoning took place in AD 62, according to Josephus' 1st-century *Antiquities of the Jews*, XX, ch. 9, p. 1.

19. Tacitus, *The Annals of Imperial Rome*, XV, 43: ref. AD 64.

20. 2-Timothy 2:9: 'The word of God is not bound'.

21. Andreas Faber-Kaiser, *Jesus Died in Kashmir*, Abacus/Sphere, London, 1978.

22. The only time that Jewish forces ever again dented Roman military pride was when, in AD 132, they revolted once more under the leadership of Simon Ben Kochba, Prince of Israel. Simon assembled a large army of native volunteers, together with professional mercenary soldiers from abroad. His battle plan included many strategic operations, some of which made use of tunnels and underground chambers beneath Jerusalem. Within one year, Jerusalem was recaptured from the Romans. Jewish administration was established and maintained for two years. But outside the city the struggle continued and the final strategy depended on military assistance from Persia. However, just when the Persian forces were meant to set out for the Holy Land, Persia was invaded. Its troops had to stay and defend their own territory — with the result that Simon and his gallant band were not able to counter the advance of the twelve Roman legions, who had regrouped in Syria at the command of Emperor Hadrian. Simon's men were eventually overwhelmed at Battin, west of Jerusalem, in AD 135.

23. Julius Africanus made his reputation by translating into Latin a series of works written by the 1st-century disciple Abdias, the Nazarene Bishop of Babylon. *The Books of Abdias* amounted to ten volumes of firsthand Apostolic history. However, like so many other important eyewitness accounts of the era, they were rejected outright for inclusion in the eventual New Testament.

24. Malachi Martin, *The Decline and Fall of the Roman Church*, p. 44.

9: MARY MAGDALENE

1. John W Taylor, *The Coming of the Saints*, Covenant Books, London, 1969, ch. 7, p. 138.

2. As Chief of the Scribes, Judas Sicariote also held the post of the Tempter. It was thus with Judas that Jesus debated when he was 'led up of the Spirit into the wilderness to be tempted of the devil' (Matthew 4:1). Judas was at that time seeking to become the Father in the place of John the Baptist. The basis of Judas's negotiation with Jesus was that if he would aid him to priestly eminence, he would assist him, in return, to become king: 'All this power I will give thee, and the glory of them: for that is delivered unto me; and to whomsoever I will give it. If thou therefore wilt worship me, all shall be thine' (Luke 4:6-7). *See* Barbara Thiering, *Jesus the Man*, ch. 17, p. 88; also ch. 15, pp. 80-81.

3. *Ibid.*, Appendix III, p. 367.

4. Gladys Taylor, *Our Neglected Heritage*, vol. 1, p. 17.

5. Ean C. M. Begg, *The Cult of the Black Virgin*, ch. 4, p. 98.

6. Margaret Starbird, *The Woman With the Alabaster Jar*, ch. 3, p. 50.

7. Henry Lincoln, *The Holy Place*, Jonathan Cape, London, 1991, ch. 7, p. 70.

8. Ean C. M. Begg, *The Cult of the Black Virgin*, Gazetteer, p. 234.

9. Barbara Thiering, *Jesus the Man*, Appendix III, p. 367.

10. Ean C. M. Begg, *The Cult of the Black Virgin*, Introduction, p. 20.

11. Margaret Starbird, *The Woman With the Alabaster Jar*, ch. 6, p. 123.

12. *Ibid.*, ch. 6, p. 123.

13. Nag Hammadi *Codex* BG 8502-1.

14. Elaine Pagels, *The Gnostic Gospels*, Weidenfeld and Nicolson, London, 1980, ch. 3, p. 65.

15. Nag Hammadi *Codex* II, 2.

16. *Ibid.*, II, 3.

17. Ean C. M. Begg, *The Cult of the Black Virgin*, ch. 2, p. 68.

18. Beryl Platts, *Origins of Heraldry*, Proctor Press, London, 1980, ch. 1, p. 33. This much misunderstood subject is refreshingly well covered by Beryl Platts, who sets many heraldic myths to rights.

19. John W Taylor, *The Coming of the Saints*, ch. 6, p. 103.

20. Rev. Père Lacordaire, *St. Mary Magdalene*, Thomas Richardson, Derby, 1880, chs. 106-8.

21. *Dictionnaire étymologique des noms de lieux en France*.

22. *Ibid.*

23. The Merovingians were the dynasty of Frankish kings in the 5th to 8th centuries, who founded and established what became the monarchy of France.

24. *See* also Laurence Gardner, *Realm of the Ring Lords*, MediaQuest, Ottery St. Mary, 2000, ch. 2, pp. 29-30.

10: JOSEPH OF ARIMATHEA

1. In *De Demonstratione Evangelii*, Eusebius wrote: 'The Apostles passed over the ocean to the islands known as Britain '. (*See* Rev. Lionel Smithett Lewis, *Joseph of Arimathea at Glastonbury*, A. R. Mobray, London, 1927, p. 54.)

2. Archbishop Isidore of Seville (600-636) wrote: 'Philip of the city of Bethsaida, whence also came Peter, preached Christ to the Gauls, and brought barbarous nations and their neighbours ... into the light of knowledge. ... Afterwards he was stoned and crucified, and died in Hierapolis, a city of Phrygia '. This information was confirmed by Freculphus, 9th-century Bishop of Lisieux.

3. The Tabernacle of the Hebrews is described in Exodus 26 and 36.

4. Rev. Lionel Smithett Lewis, *Joseph of Arimathea at Glastonbury,* pp. 15-16.

5. Writing in about AD 600, St. Augustine described: 'There is on the western confines of Britain a certain royal island called in ancient speech Glastonia .... In it, the earliest Angle neophytes of the Catholic doctrine—God guiding them—found a church not made by any man, they say, but prepared by God Himself for the salvation of mankind, which church the Heavenly Builder Himself declared (by many miracles and mysteries of healing) he had consecrated to Himself and to Holy Mary, Mother of God '. (*See* William of Malmesbury, *The Antiquities of Glastonbury,* Talbot/JMF Books, Llanerch, 1980, p. 1.)

6. The route used by the Jewish tin traders was described by Diodorus Siculus in the days of Emperor Augustus (63 BC - AD 14): 'The tin ore is transported from Britain into Gaul, the merchants carrying it on horseback through the heart of Celtica to Marseilles and the city called Narbo[nne] '. It was then taken by ship across the Mediterranean to any of several destinations. *See* John W Taylor, *The Coming of the Saints,* ch. 8, p. 143.

7. Tin is essential to the production of bronze, and the most important tin mines were in south-western England—an area also rich in copper and lead, for which there was a great market in the expanding Roman Empire. The British Museum contains two splendid examples of lead from the Mendip mines near Glastonbury, dated AD 49 and AD 60 respectively. In Latin, one bears the name of 'Britannicus, son of the Emperor Claudius', and the other is inscribed, 'British lead: property of the Emperor Nero'.

8. It is important to note that stoning was not generally a method of execution. It was more often a way of hounding a denounced victim out of one area of the city, or out of the city altogether.

9. Rev. Lionel Smithett Lewis, *Joseph of Arimathea at Glastonbury,* p. 15. Following the union of Scotland with England and Wales, the king's title was adjusted to the less pious 'His Britannic Majesty'.

10. The Gaelic term *Scotia* (from which Scots and Scotland derive) was inherited from Princess Scota, daughter of Pharaoh Nechonibus (Nekau I) of Egypt (610-555 BC). She gained the name Scota (Scythian: *Sco-ta* = Ruler of people) when she married Galamh of Scythia (also known as Milidh). Thereafter, she moved to Ireland with her sons following Galamh's death in Spain. It was King Nial Noighiallach and the Dal Riàta who gave the name 'Scotia' to Alba during the 4th century AD. *See* Geoffrey Keating, *The History of Ireland* (trans. David Comyn and rev. P. S. Dinneen), Irish Texts Society, London, 1904-14, vol. I, p. 102; II, pp. 44, 46, 58, 78, 372, 374.

11. Professor Roger Sherman Loomis, in *The Grail: From Celtic Myth to Christian Symbolism,* University of Wales Press, Cardiff, 1963, makes the point that proper names in manuscript transmission sometimes lose their initial letter—although mutation of the initial letters of names is a feature of the Celtic languages. By this process, Morgaine is sometimes found as Orguein and, with specific relevance to the present case, Galains (Galaain) became Alain (Alaain).

12. The *Grand Saint Grail (Estoire del Saint Graal)* confirms that on the death of Alain the Lordship of the Grail passed to Josue — although defining him as Alain's brother rather than his cousin.

13. Including, for example, *De Sancto Joseph ab Arimathea* and William of Malmesbury's *De Antiquitate*.

14. Prof. S. Hewins, *The Royal Saints of Britain*, Chiswick Press, London, 1929, p. 18.

15. Sir Thomas Malory, *Morte d'Arthur*, Book XIII, ch. 20.

16. The shroud was known as Veronica's Veil. St. Veronica was said to have wiped the sweat from Jesus's face with it as he walked to his crucifixion. Legend has it that his facial image was left imprinted on the veil. For centuries this story has been bound up with the length of cloth known as the Turin Shroud, which supports the resemblance of a complete body. The name 'Veronica' would seem to be a corruption of the Latin *vera icona* (true image). *See* Nancy Qualls-Corbett, *The Sacred Prostitute*, ch. 5, p. 151.

17. Herod-Antipas, the Tetrarch of Galilee, was banished by Rome to Lyon in Gaul following his beheading of John the Baptist. It was also at Lyon, from 28 June AD 208, that 19,000 Christians were put to death at the personal direction of Emperor Septimius Severus.

18. Verulam or Verulamium was renamed St. Albans after a 4th-century martyr: the Roman soldier Alban, who was beheaded by his military superiors in AD 303 (the Diocletian era) for sheltering a Christian priest. He is often referred to as 'the first Christian martyr in England' which, of course, he was not. Modern St. Albans is a busy market city in Hertfordshire, with a spectacular abbey.

19. *Genealogies of the Welsh Princes,* Harleian MS 3859, confirms that Anna was the daughter of Joseph of Arimathea.

20. Gladys Taylor, *Our Neglected Heritage*, I, p. 33.

21. *Ibid.,* I, pp. 40-45. Peter was never formally appointed Bishop of Rome. Linus — appointed by Paul in AD 58 (during Peter's lifetime: *Apostolic Constitutions*) — was therefore the first Pope.

11: THE NEW CHRISTIANITY

1. A transcript of Eleutherius' reply to King Lucius in AD 177 is given in John W. Taylor, *The Coming of the Saints*, Appendix K.

2. Lucius died on 3 December 201 and was buried at St. Mary le Lode in Gloucester. His remains were later reinterred at St. Peter's, Cornhill, London.

References in Roman martyrology to the burial of Lucius at Chur in Switzerland are inaccurate on two counts. They actually relate to King Lucius of Bavaria (not to Lucius the Luminary of Britain); also the Bavarian Lucius died at Curia in Germany, not at Chur in Switzerland.

3. Geoffrey Ashe, *Avalonian Quest*, Methuen, London, 1987, ch. 7, p. 126.

4. Paul Broadhurst and Hamish Miller, *The Dance of the Dragon*, Pendragon Press, Launceston, 2000.

5. The reference to Jesus in the *Antiquities of the Jews* (XV111, ch. 3, p. 3) is regarded by some as a later Christian interpolation. Origen, writing before AD 245, does not mention the passage, although Eusebius in his *Demonstration of the Gospel* written in around AD 320, does. It may therefore be held to have been interpolated after Origen but before Eusebius. (*See* Ahmed Osman *The House of the Messiah*, ch. 3, pp. 19-20). But the basis of such a claim is tenuous, to say the least. The passage is not really Christian in sentiment: it defines neither Jesus's status as the Messiah, nor his relationship to God. It states only that he was 'the Christ', a 'wise man', a 'worker of marvels' and a 'teacher — in much the way that the Jews of the era would have perceived him. (*See* A. N. Wilson, *Jesus*, ch. 4, p. 89.)

6. George F. Jowett, *The Drama of the Lost Disciples*, Covenant Books, London, 1961, ch. 12, pp. 125-26.

7. Three British bishops attended the Council of Arles in 314: those of London, York, and Lincoln.

12: RELIGION AND THE BLOODLINE

1. In AD 452, Bishop Leo I of Rome and an unarmed body of monks confronted the fearsome Attila the Hun and his army by the River Po in northern Italy. At that time, Attila's empire stretched from the Rhine right across into Central Asia. His well equipped hordes were ready with chariots, ladders, catapults and every martial device to sweep on towards Rome. The conversation lasted no more than a few minutes, but the outcome was that Attila ordered his men to vacate their encampments and retreat northwards. What actually transpired between the men was never revealed, but afterwards Leo the Great was destined to wield supreme power.

Some time earlier, in AD 434, an envoy sent by the Byzantine Emperor Theodosius II had met the dreaded Hun in similar circumstances by the Morava River (south of modern Belgrade). He had given Attila the contemporary equivalent of millions of dollars as a ransom for peace in the East. Bishop Leo's arrangement was probably much the same. (*See* Malachi Martin, *The Decline and Fall of the Roman Church*. Also, for further reading on the subject, *see* Norman J. Bull, *The Rise of the Church*, Heinemann, London, 1967.)

2. The word 'occult' is today often associated with sinister magic — but it actually means no more than 'hidden' or 'obscure'. Initiates of the occult during the Middle Ages revered the planet Venus as representative of Mary Magdalene, who was regarded as a medium of secret revelation. Over its regular 8-year cycle, Venus traces a precise pentangle (a five-pointed star) in the night sky. This same figure is formed by the five mountain peaks around the Magdalene centre at Rennes-le-Château in Languedoc. See David Wood, *Genisis*, Baton Press, Tunbridge Wells, 1985, *passim*, and Henry Lincoln, *The Holy Place*, ch. 7, pp. 65-70.

3. The esoteric tradition of Solomon spanned the centuries to the era of Gnostic Christianity, which preceded the Merovingian age. The Gnostics, whose texts referred

318

to the *Book of Solomon,* were the inheritors of the early Jewish sects of Babylonia. Their form of Christianity was thus closely allied to the metaphysical doctrines of Plato and Pythagoras; their creeds were largely founded on astrology and on cosmic awareness. In addition they claimed a particular insight *(gnosis:* 'knowledge') into Jesus's teaching that was unknown to the Church of Rome.

4. The hexagon is formed by dividing the circumference of a circle by chords equivalent to its radius, so producing a figure of six equal straight sides — as found in the cells of some organic life. For this reason, bees were held to be endowed with special geometrical forethought, employing strength with economy of space as their guiding principles. King Solomon's Seal (which is made up of two equilateral triangles within a circle) incorporates a natural hexagon. The resultant hexagram symbolically denotes the unity (if not the harmony) of opposites: male and female, fire and water, hot and cold, earth and air, and so on. Prominently used in alchemy, the symbol, in outline, remains specific to the Jews as the Star of David.

5. The town of Ferrières was destroyed by Atilla the Hun in AD 461, but was substantially rebuilt by the Merovingians. *See* Ean C. M. Begg, *The Cult of the Black Virgin,* Introduction, pp. 20-21.

6. What traditional history makes of this baptism is that the pagan Clovis became a Christian. What actually transpired was that the already Christian Clovis became a Roman Catholic.

7. The whole subject of the relationship between Clovis and the Vatican is well covered in Baigent, Leigh and Lincoln, *The Holy Blood and the Holy Grail,* ch. 9, p. 209 and elsewhere.

13: THE PENDRAGONS

1. John Allegro, *The Dead Sea Scrolls,* ch. 7, p. 110.

2. Some art historians maintain that the pomegranates in these paintings denote the Resurrection through classical associations with the story of Persephone. She was the ancient Greek goddess (a daughter of Zeus and Demeter) who was carried off to the Underworld by Hades (Pluto). A condition of her eventual rescue was that she could spend only part of each year thereafter on the Earth's surface, and her annual return is marked by the regeneration of natural life that characterizes the spring.

This story is an allegory of the growth and decay cycle of vegetation and has nothing whatever to do with bodily resurrection from the dead. Such a connotation was conferred on Botticelli's paintings by a fearful establishment wishing to conceal the facts. Botticelli was a Grail student, a leading esotericist and a designer of Tarot cards. His pomegranate seeds represent fertility in accordance with the pomegranates of the *Song of Solomon* and the pillar capitals of Solomon's Temple, which was built around a thousand years before Jesus was crucified.

3. From *The High History of the Holy Grail,* compiled in around 1220 from an earlier manuscript by the clerk Josephus.

4. George F. Jowett, *The Drama of the Lost Disciples,* ch. 6, pp. 45-46.

5. The 13th-century French work, *Sone de Nansai*, identifies Joseph's wife as a Nordic princess.

6. Henry VIII's antiquary, John Leland, in 1542 identified the Iron Age hill-fort at South Cadbury in Somerset as Camelot, mainly on the grounds that a couple of villages nearby included the river-name Camel. Excavations at Cadbury during the 1960s unearthed the remains of a Dark Age feasting-hall but, appealing as it was to the tourist industry, there was nothing to associate the camp with Arthur. Indeed, more than 40 constructions of similar age and type have been found in the south-west of England alone, and there are many more elsewhere in the country. *See* Michael Wood, *In Search of the Dark Ages*, BBC Books, London, 1981, ch. 2, p. 50.

7. Lucius was the grandson of Brân's daughter Penardun of Siluria. She is sometimes held to have been the daughter of Beli Mawr, or sometimes his sister. She was, however, the sister of the later Beli, son of Brân. Penardun was a protégée of Queen Boudicca.

8. Gabràn was a grandson of Fergus mac Erc, who was born of Gaelic Scots royalty in descent from the High King Conaire Mór of Ireland. Fergus left Ireland in the latter 5th century in order to colonize the Western Highlands, taking with him his brothers Loarn and Angus. Loarn's family occupied the region of northern Argyll, thereafter known as Loarna (or Lorne), based at Dunollie, Oban.

9. Individual annals cite different names for this conflict and/or its location. Names for the location include Mount Badon, Mons Badonicus, Dun Baedàn and Cath Badwn (in which *mount* and *mons* imply a hill; *dun* implies either a hill or a hill-fort, and *cath* represents a stronghold). Names for the battle include *Bellum Badonis and Obsessio Badonica* (the first suggesting a war and the second a siege).

10. The battle is cited in the Bodleian Manuscripts, the *Book of Leinster*, the *Book of Ballymote* and the *Chronicles of the Scots* – and all give the date as 516. The Scots commander is generally named as Aedàn mac Gabràn of Dalriada, but Aedàn had not yet been born. The leader was actually his father, Gabràn, who became King of Dalriada in 537. Aedàn and his eldest son, Arthur, fought at the second battle of Dun Baedàn, which took place in 575. Despite the definitive date of 516 quoted in the chronicles, there has been a great deal of speculation about this (first) battle, much of which has arisen because researchers have been directed to the wrong historian Gildas. All too often it is Gildas II who is mistakenly identified as the author of *De Excidio*. But he lived 425-512, and was thus already dead when Gildas III was born in 516 – the very year of the battle, as he made a point of saying.

Other selected works on the subject of Britain in the Dark Ages are Myles Dillon and Nora K. Chadwick, *The Celtic Realms*; Hector Munro Chadwick *et al.*, *Studies in Early British History*; Hector Munro Chadwick, *Early Scotland*; W. F. Skene, *Celtic Scotland*; R. Cunliffe Shaw, *Post-Roman Carlisle and the Kingdoms of the North-West*; Eoin MacNeill, *Celtic Ireland*, and Peter Hunter Blair, *The Origins of Northumbria*.

14: KING ARTHUR

1. In the time of Arthur, the south-west peninsula of the British mainland was called Dumnonia (from which the name Devon derives). The name *Cornwall* did not emerge until the 9th century.

2. *Tract on the Tributes Paid to Baedàn, King of Ulster* in the *Chronicles of the Picts and Scots.*

3. This was at a time before the unified nation of England. It was not until 927 that Alfred the Great's grandson, Aethelstan, was recognized as overall king by the majority of Anglo-Saxon territorial groupings.

4. The distinction of *le Benoic* derives from Latin *ille benedictum:* 'the Blessed'.

5. Urien is most famous for effecting a coalition of Strathclyde rulers against the Northumbrian Angles of Bernicia.

6. Geoffrey Ashe, *Avalonian Quest*, ch. 3, sect. 2, p. 48.

7. The tradition that Arthur had two wives is yet another manifestation of the confusion caused by the convergence in mythology of the two princely Arthurs (Arthur of Dalriada and Arthur of Dyfed) described as if they were one in the *Annales Cambriae.*

8. Thomas F. O'Rahilly, *Early Irish History and Mythology*, Dublin Institute for Advanced Studies, 1946, ch. 6, p. 145.

9. William J. Watson, *The History of the Celtic Place Names of Scotland*, William Blackwood, Edinburgh, 1926, ch. 3, p. 97.

15: INTRIGUE AGAINST THE BLOODLINE

1. Some useful information on Priscillian is to be found in Baigent, Leigh and Lincoln, *The Messianic Legacy*, ch. 8, pp. 99-101.

2. It was Pope Gregory who, in 600, determined that Latin was, and should remain, the sole official language of the Roman Catholic Church—an edict that was not repealed until the 1960s.

3. For further information about the Celtic Church, *See* Nora K. Chadwick, *The Age of Saints in the Celtic Church*, Oxford University Press, 1961; Dom Louis Gougaud, *Christianity in Celtic Lands*, and E. G. Bowen, *The Settlements of the Celtic Saints in Wales*, University of Wales Press, Cardiff, 1956.

4. Notwithstanding the practicalities of the break between Rome and Constantinople, the fact that it resulted in two separate and independent Churches was not formalized by the denominations concerned until 1945.

5. Anna Jameson, *Legends of the Madonna*, Houghton Mifflin , Boston, 1895.

6. Literature on the subject of this latter period of Merovingian history is fairly limited in the English language. Gregory of Tours' 6th-century *History of the Franks* does not extend to this era. It is covered, up to a point, in J. M. Wallace Hadrill, *The Long-Haired Kings*, but the best overview of the story of Dagobert II is recounted in various chapters of Baigent, Leigh and Lincoln, *The Holy Blood and the Holy Grail*. There is also a useful summary of the late Merovingian situation in Margaret Deanesley, *A Medieval History of Europe 476 to 911*, Methuen, London, 1956, ch. 15.

7. The transference of power from the Merovingians to the Carolingians is well narrated in R. H. C. Davis, *A History of Medieval Europe*, Longmans Green, London, 1957, ch. 6, pp. 120-53. Unlike the Dagobert intrigue, which is outside the scope of conventional history books, the rise of the Carolingians is widely documented as a historical subject in its own right.

8. The most comprehensive account to date of the Septimanian kingdom is in Arthur J. Zuckerman, *A Jewish Princedom in Feudal France*, Columbia University Press, New York, 1972.

9. The Jewish faith being represented here by the collective term (i.e. Torah) for the first five scriptural books of the Hebrew Bible.

16: TEMPLE OF THE GRAIL

1. *See* Chapter 12, *The Sorcerer Kings*.

2. Corbenic = *Cors benicon*, from *Corpus benedictum* = 'Body blessed' — thus the Blessed Body. Accordingly, Château du Corbenic = Castle of the Blessed (or Consecrated) Body.

3. Miles Dillon and Nora K. Chadwick, *The Celtic Realms*, Weidenfeld & Nicolson, London 1967, ch. 1, p. 7.

4. Henry Hubert, *The Greatness and Decline of the Celts*, Kegan Paul, London, 1934, III, ch. 2, p. 229.

5. Dom Louis Gougaud, *Christianity in Celtic Lands*, (trans. Maud Joynt), Four Courts Press, Dublin, 1932, VI, ch. 2, p. 204.

6. Myles Dillon and Nora K. Chadwick, *The Celtic Realms*, ch. 1, p. 15.

7. As late as 1632, the Italian scientist Galileo Galilei was summoned to Rome to give his public confirmation of Copernicus's heliocentric principle of cosmology. His explanation was not accepted and he was duly condemned by the Catholic Inquisition.

8. Neoplatonism emerged in about 250 AD.

9. Margaret Starbird, *The Woman With the Alabaster Jar*, ch. 5, p. 102.

10. Louis Charpentier, *The Mysteries of Chartres Cathedral*, Research Into Lost Knowledge Organization / Thorsons, Wellingborough, 1992, ch. 14, p. 113.

11. Nigel Pennick, *Sacred Geometry*, Turnstone, Wellingborough, 1980, Introduction, p. 8.

17: THE GRAIL HALLOWS

1. John Matthews, *The Grail – Quest for the Eternal*, Thames & Hudson, London, 1981, p. 8.

2. *Ibid.*, p. 9.

3. Riane Eisler, *The Chalice and the Blade*, Harper & Row, New York, 1987, p. 72.

4. Harold Bayley, *The Lost Language of Symbolism*, Williams & Norgate, London, 1912, which contains comprehensive details of medieval watermarks in Provence.

5. Lionel Smithett Lewis, *Joseph of Arimathea at Glastonbury*, p. 35.

6. George F. Jowett, *The Drama of the Lost Disciples*, ch. 18, p. 212.

7. Gladys Taylor, *Our Neglected Heritage*, II, pp. 47-8.

8. Geoffrey Ashe, *Avalonian Quest*, ch. 5, sect. 4, pp. 93-97.
    Other selected reading material on the subject of the Holy Grail includes Sebastian Evans, *In Quest of the Holy Grail*; Roger Sherman Loomis, *The Grail - From Celtic Myth to Christian Symbolism*; John Matthews, *The Grail - Quest for the Eternal*; David Nutt, *Studies on the Legend of the Holy Grail*; D. D. R. Owen, *The Evolution of the Grail Legend*; and Arthur E. Waite, *The Hidden Church of the Holy Grail*.

9. John Matthews, The Grail - Quest for the Eternal, p. 6.

10. Margaret Starbird, *The Woman With the Alabaster Jar*, ch. 5, pp. 104-16: an excellent synopsis of the Major Arcana.

11. *Ibid.*, ch. 6, pp. 128-29.

18: GUARDIANS OF THE SACRED RELIC

1. The original Order of Sion was established so that eligible Muslims, Jews and others could be allied to the Christian Order that became the Knights Templars.

2. Cistercian ideals were far removed from the concerns of the curia at the Vatican; they pertained to education, agriculture and the sacred arts.

3. The first Columban mission on Iona was destroyed by Norse pirates in 807. St. Bernard's new monastery on the site was Cistercian rather than Columban.

4. Ean C. M. Begg, *The Cult of the Black Virgin*, ch. 4, p. 103.

5. Louis Charpentier, *The Mysteries of Chartres Cathedral*, ch. 7, p. 55.

6. *Ibid.*, ch. 7, p. 56.

7. *Ibid.*, ch. 8, p. 69.
   Other selected works on the subject of the Templars and the Crusades are John C. Andressohn, *The Ancestry and Life of Godfrey de Bouillon*; Baigent and Leigh, *The Temple and the Lodge*; Desmond Seward, *The Monks of War*, and Steven Runciman, *A History of the Crusades*.

8. Louis Charpentier, *The Mysteries of Chartres Cathedral*, ch. 9, p. 70.

9. The *Notre Dame* ground-plan made use of ley lines and Mother Earth locations in which the terrestrial forces were heightened by deep underground caverns or wells.

10. Louis Charpentier, *The Mysteries of Chartres Cathedral*, ch. 2, p. 29.

11. A dolmen usually comprises two upright stones with a horizontal capstone across the top, as at Stonehenge. From prehistoric times, dolmens were used as gigantic resonators (much like sound-boxes used to amplify acoustic musical instruments) to boost the properties of the Earth's telluric current.

12. Laurence Gardner, *Genesis of the Grail Kings*, Bantam Press, London, 1999, ch. 14, p. 146.

13. Numerical values have often been used to disguise the use of sacred geometry, as in the Old Testament descriptions of King Solomon's Temple (1-Kings 6 and 2-Chronicles 3, 4).

14. Louis Charpentier, *The Mysteries of Chartres Cathedral*, ch. 18, pp. 144-51.

15. Michael Howard, *The Occult Conspiracy*, Rider / Century Hutchinson, London, 1989, ch. 1, pp. 9-10.

16. The system of measurement that is much to be preferred is that which counts in feet and inches, rather than in metres. Indeed, adepts in sacred geometry and metrology regard the metre as nothing more than a 'fashionable folly' because of its determined adherence to tens and hundreds. The decimal base of 10 leads to inevitable inaccuracies and such nonsenses as recurring decimals. Universal measurement is much more accurately founded on a base of 12, which is divisible by five of the first six numbers and provides a more flexible foundation for any numerical calculation than does 10. Similarly, geometry that is founded upon a decagon in inherently unstable. The cardinal factors in sacred mathematics are 3, 4 and 12. *See* John Michell, *The Dimensions of Paradise*.

17. The subject is well covered in Baigent, Leigh and Lincoln, *The Holy Blood and the Holy Grail*, ch. 2, pp. 19-34. Similarly, *The Temple and the Lodge* by Baigent and Leigh (ch 3, pp. 51-62 and ch. 4, pp. 63-76) is informative on the Inquisition of the Templars and the Templar Fleet.

18. A good overview of Provence as a 'cradle of awakening' is given in Margaret Starbird, *The Woman With the Alabaster Jar*, ch. 4, pp. 67-78.

19. Eleanor of Aquitaine (1122-1204) is a good example of female equality in the region. Her importance and influence were a constant embarrassment to the Roman Church bishops.
20. Selected works on the subject of the Albigensian Crusade are Zoe Oldenbourg, *Massacre at Montségur*, and J. Sumption, *The Albigensian Crusade*.

19: KINGDOM OF THE SCOTS

1. The excommunication of Scotland as a nation was not repealed until 1323. This followed Robert the Bruce's defeat of Edward II at Bannockburn in 1314 and the drawing up of the Scottish Constitution (the *Declaration of Arbroath*) in 1320. Subsequently, in 1328, the Treaty of Northampton confirmed Scotland's independence under King Robert I.

2. HRH Prince Michael of Albany, *The Forgotten Monarchy of Scotland*, Element Books, Shaftesbury, 1998, ch. 5, pp. 62-64.

3. Although there were enclaves of celibate monks within the Celtic Church, the priests were permitted to marry. Their clerical ordination was strictly hereditary, passing from father to son. Crinan's ancestors had maintained the hereditary priesthood of Dull (Dule, near Aberfeldy, Perthshire) for more than five generations from around 850. By the late 900s Crinan was Seneschal (Steward) of the Isles, Abthane of Dull and Abbot of Dunkeld.

4. At the time of Malcolm III Canmore's installation, the Celtic Church prevailed. But this was destined to change. Malcolm's wife Margaret (the last Saxon heiress and a great-granddaughter of Aethelred the Unready) had been raised at the Roman Catholic Court of her grandfather King Stephen of Hungary. She also spent time at the court of Edward the Confessor in England. When she married Malcolm, Margaret had no knowledge of the Gaelic language used by the Celtic priests, but her son became King David I of Scots and, accordingly, head of the Sacred Kindred of St Columba. Margaret (later St. Margaret) ignored the Celtic heritage and pursued her Catholic endeavour, so that the two cultures became firmly integrated. Some historical content of this section of the chapter derives from the archives of the Royal House of Stewart, and the tenets of the Sacred Kindred of Columba.

5. The monastery at Dol was founded by the Celtic St. Samson, who first sailed to Brittany from Cornwall in the early 500s during the reign of the Merovingian King Childebert. Dol is on the Brittany coast near Dinan, not far from St. Michel. The spear-carrying Samson, with his long hair and druidic frontal tonsure, had been educated by the Welsh abbot Illtyd. He was installed as Bishop of Dol in about 530. The bishopric was elevated to become an archbishopric in 845. Later still, the ancient town of Dol (in which the main street was subsequently named 'la Grande Rue des Stuarts') became prominent in sovereign history. It was from here that the closely related major-domos of the royal house (the Seneschals of Dol and Dinan) emerged through the female line to found the Royal House of Stewart in Scotland.

6. This error originated in *The History of Shropshire*, 1858.

7. This marriage is correctly recorded in Chalmers' *Caledonia*, 1807.

8. This error was an element of the 1895 book *The Isle of Bute in the Olden Time* by J. K. Hewison, in which he quite wrongly averred that 'Walter, the son of Fleadan, son of Banchu, is identical with Walter, son of Alan'.

The historical content of this section of the chapter is extracted from the Jacobite Records of Saint Germain-en-Laye, the *Cartulary of St. Florent*, the *Cartulary of St. George, Hesdin*, and the *Diocesan Archives of Angers*.

20: THE AGE OF CHIVALRY

1. *See* Laurence Gardner, *Realm of the Ring Lords*, ch. 9, pp. 114-15.

2. *See* Chapter 14, *The Historical Warlord*.

3. Brutus (d. *c*.1103 BC) was the grandson of Ascanius Julius, son of Aeneas and Creusa (daughter of King Priam of Troy.) After the fall of Troy in about 1184 BC, the royal house of Dardanos was scattered. The Trojan Cycle, as listed by Proclus in the 2nd century AD, records that Aeneas went to Italy with 88,000 Trojans in a fleet of 332 ships. Brutus led another party to Britain, where, as cited in Nennius' *Historia*, he founded London, calling it Trinovantium. The Brutus Stone, from which royal accessions were traditionally proclaimed, is at Totnes in Devon. *See* Gladys Taylor, *Our Neglected Heritage*, III, ch. 4, pp. 28-29.

4. Guanhumara of Ireland was the wife of Arthur of Dyfed, whereas Gwenhwyfar of Brittany married Arthur of Dalriada.

5. The historical Sword of Avallon was passed to Lancelot by his mother, Viviane del Acqs. He was to hold it in trust for Modred, Archpriest of the Celtic Kindred and son of the dynastic heiress, Morgaine. Instead, however, Lancelot gave the sword to Modred's father, Arthur—and this was reckoned to have caused the downfall of the kingdom. In the event, both Arthur and Lancelot were denounced by the Celtic Church.

6. Laurence Gardner, *Realm of the Ring Lords*, ch. 4, pp. 47-48.

7. Beryl Platts, *Scottish Hazard*, Proctor Press, London, 1985-90, *passim*.

8. *See* Chapter 19, *Persecution of the Templars*.

9. Baigent and Leigh *The Temple and the Lodge*, Jonathan Cape, London, 1989, ch. 8 p. 113.

10. Andrew Sinclair, *The Sword and the Grail*, Crown, New York, 1992, ch. 7, p. 73.

11. Barbara Thiering, *Jesus the Man*, Appendix III, p. 351.

12. *Dundee Courier*, 12 April 1991.

13. Baigent, Leigh and Lincoln, *The Holy Blood and the Holy Grail*, ch. 6, p. 108.

14. Andrew Sinclair, *The Sword and the Grail*, ch. 7, pp. 77-78.

15. *See* Chapter 10, *Lordship of the Grail*.

16. A good account of Columbus' personal family background is given by Ian F. Brown in the Rosslyn Chapel publication *The Sinclair Genealogist*.

17. Details of the Sinclair-Zeno voyage is to be found in Andrew Sinclair, *The Sword and the Grail*, chs. 9-11, pp. 108-50.

21: HERESY AND INQUISITION

1. Michael Howard, *The Occult Conspiracy*, ch. 3, p. 43.

2. Laurence Gardner, *Realm of the Ring Lords*, ch. 13, pp. 171-76

3. *Lorraine* (as a place name) derives from *Lotharingia*, in turn so called after the Carolingian King Lothar (or Lothair) II.

4. There is an informative section concerning the Scots Guard in Baigent and Leigh, *The Temple and the Lodge*, ch. 7, pp. 103-10.

5. The caduceus corresponds to the winged staff of Mercury, borne by him as a messenger of the gods.

6. Michael Howard, *The Occult Conspiracy*, ch. 4, pp. 73-74.
   Other selected works on the subject of the Rosicrucians are Frances A. Yates, *The Rosicrucian Enlightenment*, and Arthur E. Waite, *The Real History of the Rosicrucians*.

22: HOUSE OF THE UNICORNS

1. The quoted verse refers to the marriage of the Sumerian deities Inanna and Dumuzi (Tammuz). *See* Samuel N. Kramer, *The Sacred Marriage Rite*, Indiana University Press, Bloomington, 1969, ch. 4, p. 84.

2. The sobriquet 'Ironsides' was conferred on Cromwell's troopers by the Rosicrucian general Prince Rupert of Heidelberg, the son of Friedrich of Palatine and Elizabeth Stuart.

3. *Boyle's Law*: At a constant temperature, the volume of a perfect gas varies inversely in relation to its pressure.

23: LIBERTY OF CONSCIENCE

1. An account of this sequence of events is given in Marquis de Ruvigny et Raineval, *The Jacobite Peerage, Baronetage, Knightage and Grants of Honour*, Appendix II.

2. The tax imposed on the manufacture of linen goods provides an example. It was of little consequence in the South of Britain, but linen was a major industrial product in Scotland.

24: THE SANGRÉAL TODAY

1. Horace Round, in his *Studies in Peerage and Family History*, Constable, London, 1901, referred to these contrived entries, stating: "For the source ... we have to penetrate behind *Burke*, to the authors of these fabrications — the heralds and antiquaries".

2. Documents at the Archives Nationales include: *Archives d'Aubignie*, Berri, France; Comte Antoine Marie Chaman de Lavalette, *Memoires et souvenirs de Marguerite Marie Thérèse d'Audibert de Lussan, Comtesse de Massillan et d'Albanie*; Robert Antoine, Chevalier de Beauterne, *La vie du Prince Edouard Jacques Stuart d'Albani*, Paris, 1846; Msr. Foissy (Avocat), *Les Comtes d'Albanie depuis 1766*, Paris Notorial Registers Acts, 1830; Léonce Brotonne, *Les Stuarts et leurs alliances*, Paris 1834; Madame Olivier des Armoises, *Un rapport sur la mort étrange du 4tièm Comte d'Albanie le Prince Charles Benoix Stuart à Msr. le Ministre des Affaires Etrangère a Paris*, 1898; *Memoirs of Cardinal Ercole Consalvi*, Paris, 1864.

3. The House of Lords Archive, Westminster, London.

4. Aspects of this chapter are drawn from the Royal House of Stewart Jacobite records of St. Germain; from the records of Melville Henry Massue, Marquis de Ruvigny et Raineval 1868-1921; the Stewart family papers in Edinburgh and with the Brussels Registrars; along with the archives of the Stuart Trustees in Rome. However, since the first edition of *Bloodline of the Holy Grail* was published in 1996, *The Forgotten Monarchy of Scotland*, by HRH Prince Michael of Albany, was released in 1998. This work expands greatly on the substance of the final two chapters of *Bloodline of the Holy Grail* in its past and present forms.

Genealogical Charts

THE HOUSE OF HEROD

Gospel Kings and Governors of Judaea (37 BC - AD 99)

Antipater the Idumaean
d. 48 BC
= Cypros (Arabian)

Herod the Great
King of Judaea from 37 BC
d. 4 BC

< = *Ten wives, including* = >

1
= *Doris*
(Idumaean)

2
= *Mariamne I*
dau. of
Alexander
the Hasmonean
(Jewess)

3
= *Pallas*

4
= *Phaedra*

5
= *Mariamne II*
dau. of
Simon Boethus
High Priest
(Jewess)

6
= *Malthace*
of Samaria
d. 4 BC
(Samaritan)

7
= *Cleopatra*
of Jerusalem
(Jewess)

Antipater
d. 4 BC

Aristobulous
d. 7 BC
= *Berenice*
niece of
Herod the Great

Alexander
d. 7 BC
= *Glaphyra*

Philip
(Thomas)
= *Herodias* ◆

Salome ●

Archelaus
Ethnarch
of Judaea
deposed AD 6
[exile in Gaul]

Herod-Antipas
Tetrarch of
Galilee
deposed AD 39
[exile in Gaul]
= 2 *Herodias* ◆

Herod-Philip
Tetrarch of
Trachonitis
d. AD 34
= *Salome* ●
d.s.p.

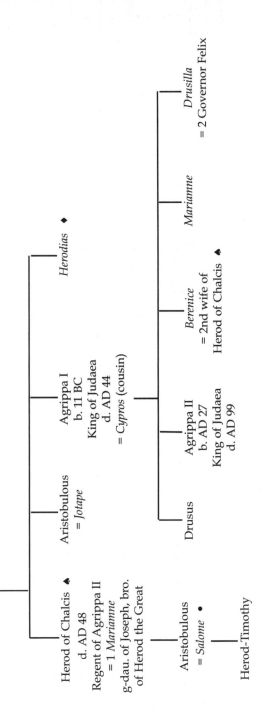

Herod of Chalcis ♠
d. AD 48
Regent of Agrippa II
= 1 *Mariamne*
g-dau. of Joseph, bro.
of Herod the Great

Aristobulous
= *Jotape*

Agrippa I
b. 11 BC
King of Judaea
d. AD 44
= *Cypros* (cousin)

Herodias ◆

Aristobulous
= *Salome* ●

Herod-Timothy

Drusus

Agrippa II
b. AD 27
King of Judaea
d. AD 99

Berenice
= 2nd wife of
Herod of Chalcis ♠

Mariamne

Drusilla
= 2 Governor Felix

EARLY EMPERORS AND BISHOPS OF ROME
To the Time of Constantine the Great (44 BC - AD 337)

Roman Emperors	Year	Bishops	Year
Augustus	44 BC - AD 14		
Tiberius	AD 14-37		
Gaius Caligula	37-41		
Claudius	41-54		
Nero	54-68	Linus	58-78
Galba	68-69	First Bishop of Rome appointed by Paul before death of Peter	
Otho (joint)	69		
+ Vitellius	69		
Vespasian	69-79		
Titus	79-81	Anacletus	78-89
Domitian	81-96	Clement I	89-98
Nerva	96-98		
Trajian	98-117	Evaristus	99-106
		Alexander	107-115
Hadrian	117-138	Sixtus I	116-125
		Telesphorus	125-136
Antoninus Pius	138-161	Hyginus	136-140
		Pius I	140-154
Marcus Aurelius	161-180	Anicetus	155-165
		Soter	165-174
Commodus	180-192	Eleutheriu	174-189
Pertinax (joint)	193	Victor I	189-198
+ Didius Julianus	193		
Lucius Severus	193-211	Zephyrinus	199-217
Caracalla	211-217		
Macrinus	217	Callixtus I	217-222
Heliogabalus	218-222		

Roman Emperors	Year	Bishops	Year
Alexander Severus	222-235	Urban I	222-230
		Pontianus	230-235
Maximinus	235-238	Anterus	235-236
Gordian I (joint)			
+ Gordian II	238	Fabian	236-250
Pupienus (joint)			
+ Balbinus	238		
Gordian III	238-244		
Philip (the Arabian)	244-249		
Decius	249-251		
Gallus	251-253	Cornelius	251-253
Aemilian	253	Lucius	253-254
Valerian (joint)	253-260	Stephen I	254-257
+ Gallienus	253-268	Sixtus II	257-258
Claudius	268-270	Dionysius	259-268
Aurelian	270-275	Felix I	269-274
Tacitus	275	Eutychianus	275-283
Probus	276-282		
Carus	282-283	Gaius	283-296
Carinus (joint)	284		
+ Numerianus	284		
Diocletian (joint)	284-305		
+ Maximianus	286-305	Marcellinus	296-304
Constantius Chlorus	305-306		
Maxentius	306-312	Marcellus I	308-309
Constantine the Great		Eusebius	309
(Britain and Gaul)	306-	Miltiades	310-314
(West)	312-	Silvester I	314-335
(Overall)	324-337	First Imperial Bishop of Rome	

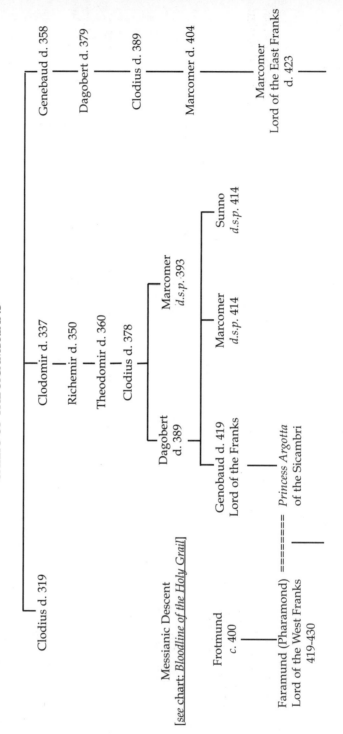

SICAMBRIAN FRANKS AND THE FIRST MEROVINGIANS

Progenitors of the Sorcerer Kings (4th - 6th century)

Descent from King Francio of the Sicambri Tribes d. 11 BC

CHIEFS OF THE SICAMBRIANS

Clodius d. 319

Clodomir d. 337

Richemir d. 350

Theodomir d. 360

Clodius d. 378

Dagobert d. 389

Marcomer *d.s.p.* 393

Genebaud d. 419
Lord of the Franks

Marcomer *d.s.p.* 414

Sunno *d.s.p.* 414

Princess Argotta of the Sicambri

Genebaud d. 358

Dagobert d. 379

Clodius d. 389

Marcomer d. 404

Marcomer
Lord of the East Franks
d. 423

Messianic Descent
[*see chart: Bloodline of the Holy Grail*]

Frotmund
c. 400

Faramund (Pharamond) ========
Lord of the West Franks
419-430

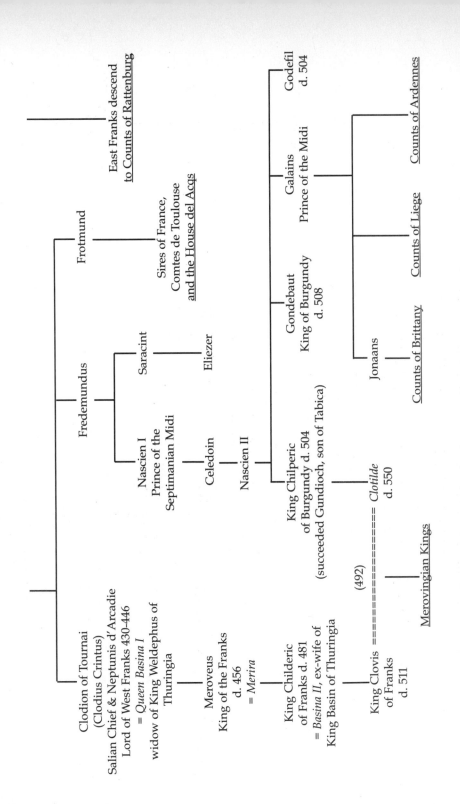

MEROVINGIAN KINGS

The House of Meroveus (5th - 8th century)

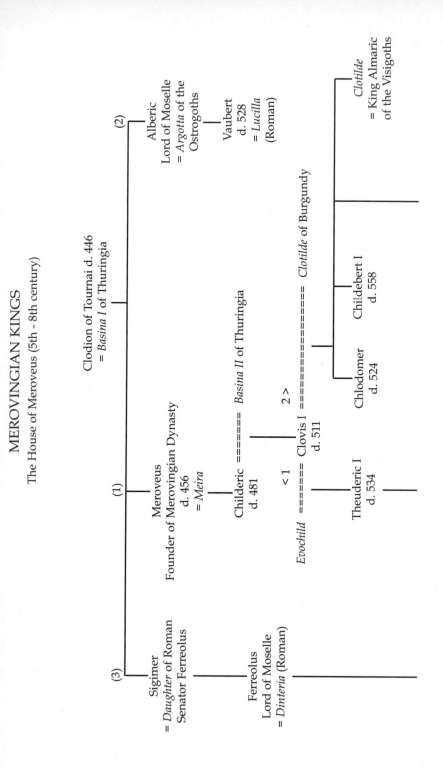

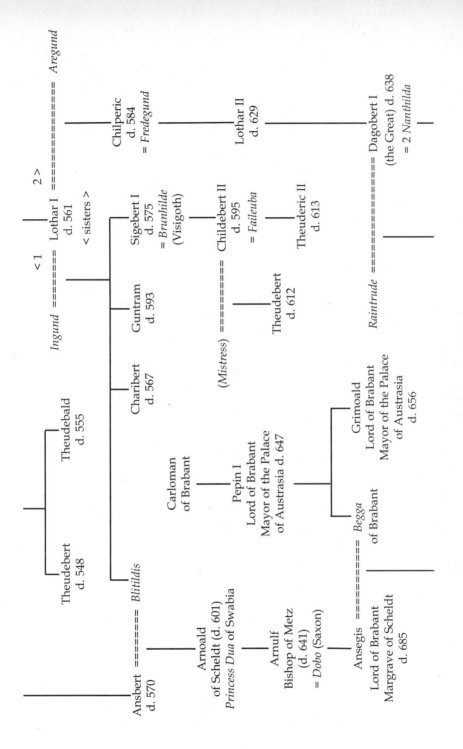

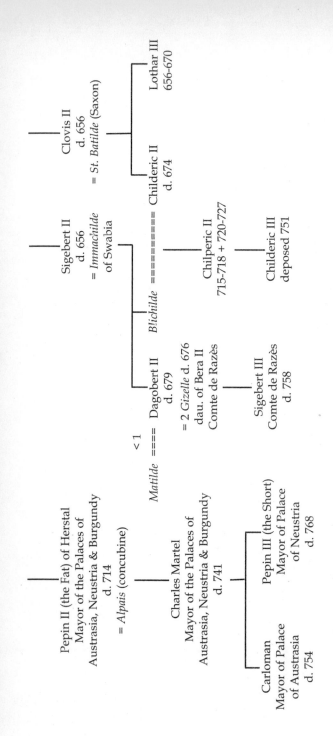

THE CAROLINGIANS

House of Charlemagne (8th - 10th century)

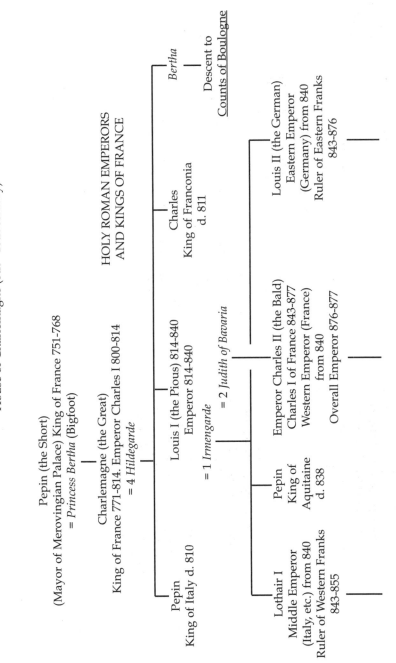

HOLY ROMAN EMPERORS
AND KINGS OF FRANCE

Pepin (the Short)
(Mayor of Merovingian Palace) King of France 751-768
= *Princess Bertha* (Bigfoot)

Charlemagne (the Great)
King of France 771-814. Emperor Charles I 800-814
= *4 Hildegarde*

Pepin
King of Italy d. 810

Louis I (the Pious) 814-840
Emperor 814-840
= *1 Irmengarde*
= *2 Judith of Bavaria*

Charles
King of Franconia
d. 811

Bertha

Descent to
Counts of Boulogne

Pepin
King of
Aquitaine
d. 838

Lothair I
Middle Emperor
(Italy, etc.) from 840
Ruler of Western Franks
843-855

Emperor Charles II (the Bald)
Charles I of France 843-877
Western Emperor (France)
from 840
Overall Emperor 876-877

Louis II (the German)
Eastern Emperor
(Germany) from 840
Ruler of Eastern Franks
843-876

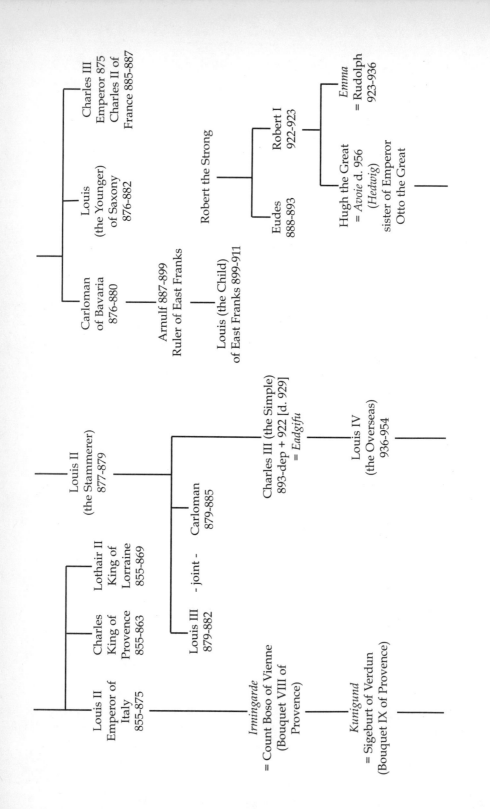

Charles III
Emperor 875
Charles II of
France 885-887

Louis
(the Younger)
of Saxony
876-882

Carloman
of Bavaria
876-880

Arnulf 887-899
Ruler of East Franks

Louis (the Child)
of East Franks 899-911

Robert the Strong

Eudes
888-893

Robert I
922-923

Hugh the Great
= *Avoie* d. 956
(*Hedwig*)
sister of Emperor
Otto the Great

Emma
= Rudolph
923-936

Louis II
(the Stammerer)
877-879

Louis II
Emperor of
Italy
855-875

Charles
King of
Provence
855-863

Lothair II
King of
Lorraine
855-869

Louis III
879-882

- joint -

Carloman
879-885

Charles III (the Simple)
893-dep + 922 [d. 929]
= *Eadgifu*

Louis IV
(the Overseas)
936-954

Irmingarde
= Count Boso of Vienne
(Bouquet VIII of
Provence)

Kunigund
= Sigeburt of Verdun
(Bouquet IX of Provence)

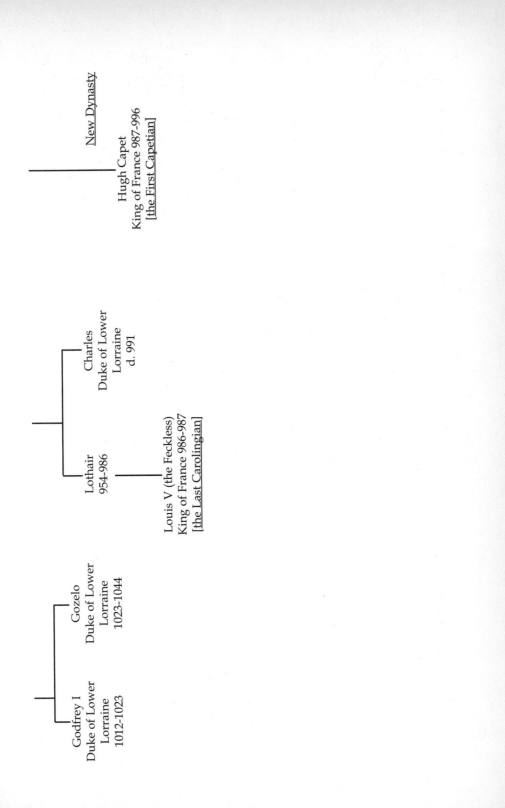

New Dynasty

Hugh Capet
King of France 987-996
[the First Capetian]

Charles
Duke of Lower
Lorraine
d. 991

Lothair
954-986

Louis V (the Feckless)
King of France 986-987
[the Last Carolingian]

Gozelo
Duke of Lower
Lorraine
1023-1044

Godfrey I
Duke of Lower
Lorraine
1012-1023

HOUSES OF WALES AND BRITTANY
Arimatheac Dynasties (1st - 10th century)

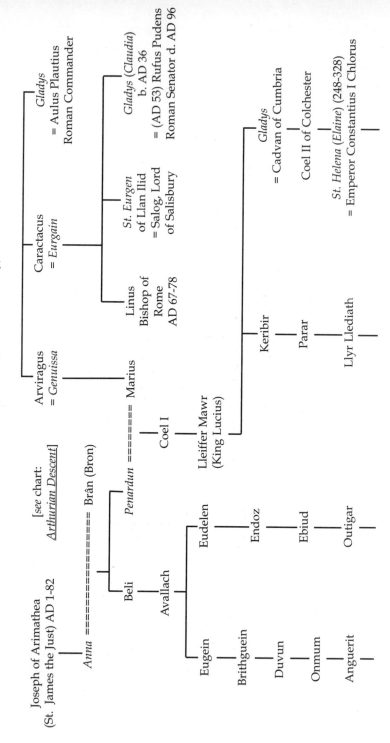

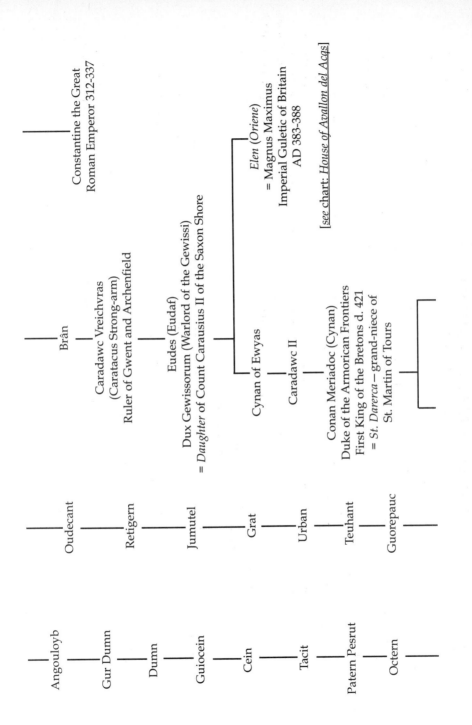

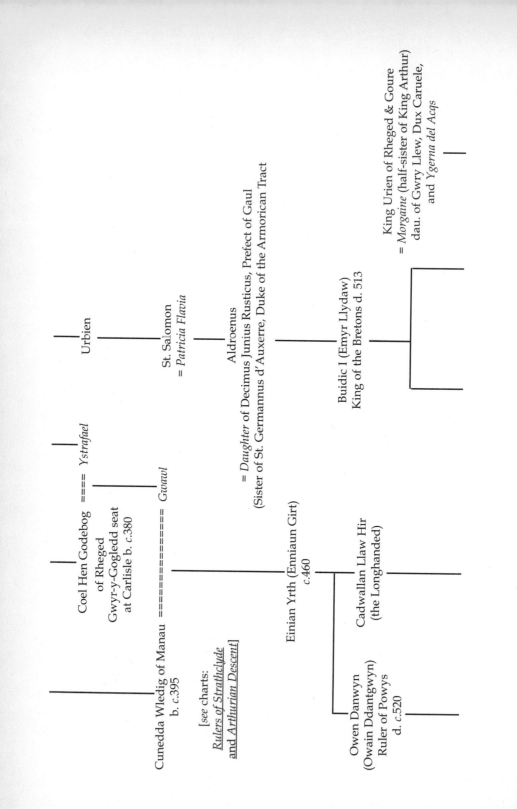

Urbien

Coel Hen Godebog ==== *Ystrafael*
of Rheged
Gwyr-y-Gogledd seat
at Carlisle b. *c.*380

St. Salomon
= *Patricia Flavia*

Cunedda Wledig of Manau ================ *Gwawl*
b. *c.*395

[*see charts:
Rulers of Strathclyde
and Arthurian Descent*]

Aldroenus
= *Daughter of Decimus Junius Rusticus, Prefect of Gaul*
(Sister of St. Germannus d'Auxerre, Duke of the Armorican Tract)

Einian Yrth (Enniaun Girt)
*c.*460

Buidic I (Emyr Llydaw)
King of the Bretons d. 513

King Urien of Rheged & Goure
= *Morgaine* (half-sister of King Arthur)
dau. of Gwry Llew, Dux Caruele,
and *Ygerna del Acqs*

Cadwallan Llaw Hir
(the Longhanded)

Owen Danwyn
(Owain Ddantgwyn)
Ruler of Powys
d. *c.*520

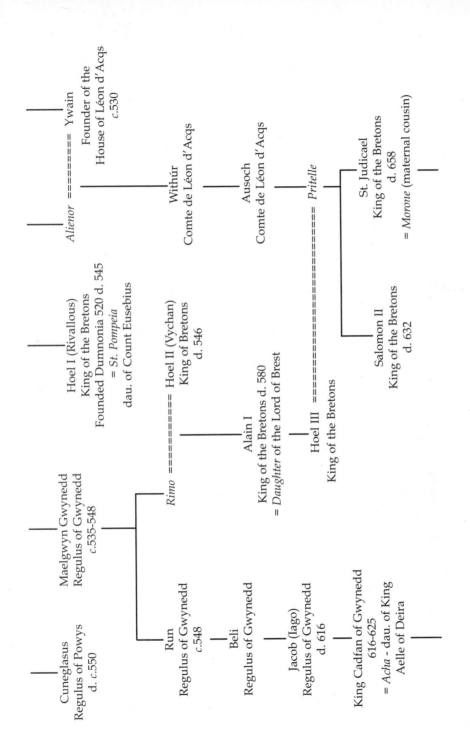

Cuneglasus
Regulus of Powys
d. c.550

Maelgwyn Gwynedd
Regulus of Gwynedd
c.535-548

Hoel I (Rivallous)
King of the Bretons
Founded Dumnonia 520 d. 545
= St. Pompeia
dau. of Count Eusebius

Alienor ======== Ywain
Founder of the
House of Léon d'Acqs
c.530

Run
Regulus of Gwynedd
c.548

Rimo ============ Hoel II (Vychan)
King of Bretons
d. 546

Withúr
Comte de Léon d'Acqs

Beli
Regulus of Gwynedd

Alain I
King of the Bretons d. 580
= Daughter of the Lord of Brest

Ausoch
Comte de Léon d'Acqs

Jacob (Iago)
Regulus of Gwynedd
d. 616

Hoel III =================== Pritelle
King of the Bretons

King Cadfan of Gwynedd
616-625
= Acha - dau. of King
Aelle of Deira

Salomon II
King of the Bretons
d. 632

St. Judicael
King of the Bretons
d. 658
= Morone (maternal cousin)

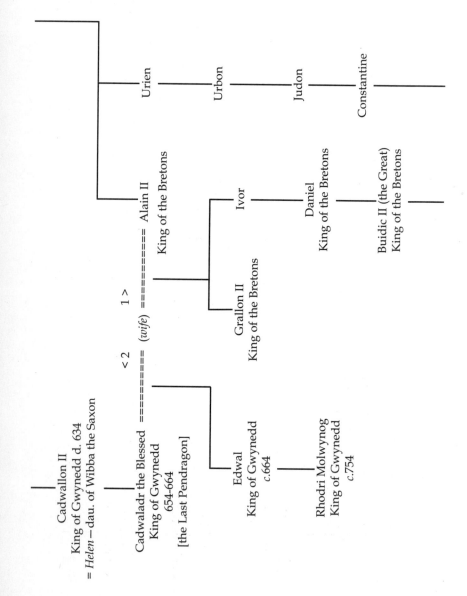

Cadwallon II
King of Gwynedd d. 634
= *Helen* – dau. of Wibba the Saxon

Urien

<2
Cadwaladr the Blessed ==========
King of Gwynedd
654-664
[the Last Pendragon]

1 >
(*wife*) ========== Alain II
King of the Bretons

Urbon

Edwal
King of Gwynedd
*c.*664

Grallon II
King of the Bretons

Ivor

Judon

Rhodri Molwynog
King of Gwynedd
*c.*754

Daniel
King of the Bretons

Buidic II (the Great)
King of the Bretons

Constantine

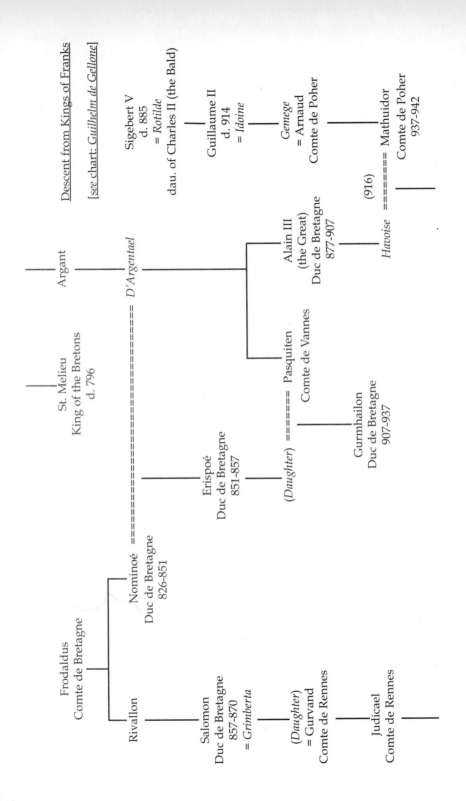

Descent from Kings of Franks

[see chart: *Guilhelm de Gellone*]

Frodaldus
Comte de Bretagne

Rivallon

Nominoé ============ St. Melieu   Argant
Duc de Bretagne   King of the Bretons
826-851   d. 796

                 D'Argentael ================

Salomon   Erispoé
Duc de Bretagne   Duc de Bretagne
857-870   851-857
= *Grimberta*

(*Daughter*)   (*Daughter*) ======== Pasquiten   Alain III
= Gurvand   Comte de Vannes   (the Great)
Comte de Rennes   Duc de Bretagne
                                                                      877-907

Judicael   Gurmhailon   Sigebert V
Comte de Rennes   Duc de Bretagne   d. 885
                                               907-937   = *Rotilde*
                                                                      dau. of Charles II (the Bald)

                                                                      Guillaume II
                                                                      d. 914
                                                                      = *Idoine*

                                                                      Gemege
                                                                      = Arnaud
                                                                      Comte de Poher

                                               (916)
                                               Havoise ======== Mathuidor
                                                                  Comte de Poher
                                                                  937-942

Alain IV
(Strongbeard)
Duc de Bretagne
937-952
= *Gerberge* de Blois

Juhel Berenger
Comte de Rennes
930-937
= *Gerberge*

Conan le Tort
Comte de Rennes
= *Ermengarde*
d'Anjou

Havoise
= Geoffrey
d. 1004

Alain V
Comte de Rennes
Duc de Bretagne
= *Berta* de Blois

THE HOLY FAMILIES OF BRITAIN
Saints and Sovereign Houses (1st - 6th century)

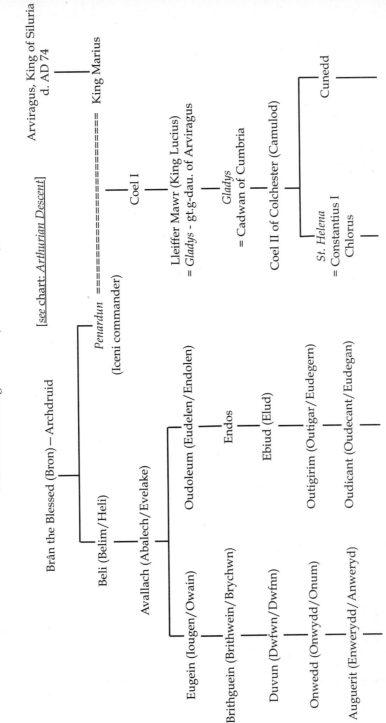

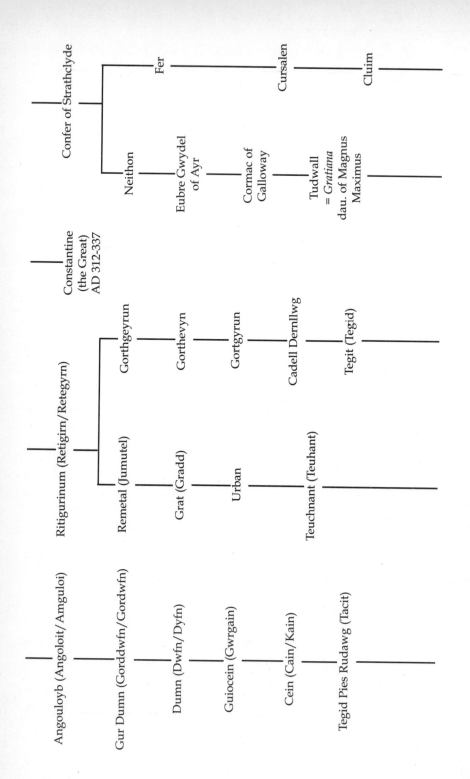

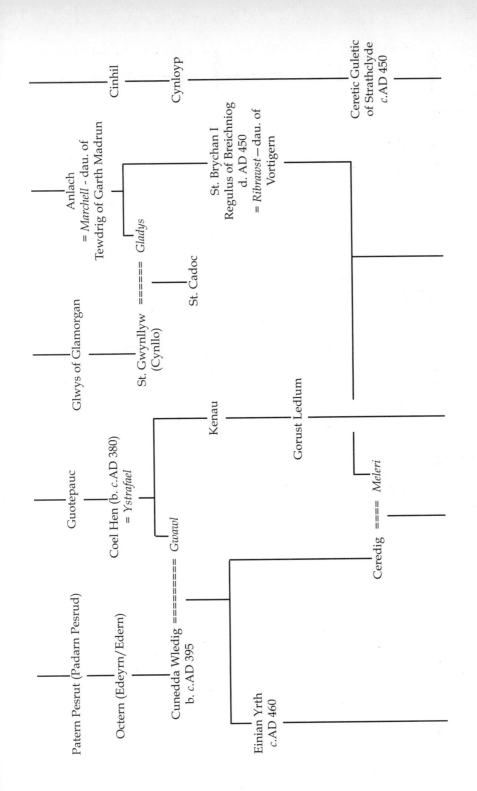

Cinhil

Cynloyp

Ceretic Guletic
of Strathclyde
c.AD 450

Anlach
= *Marchell* - dau. of
Tewdrig of Garth Madrun

St. Brychan I
Regulus of Breichniog
d. AD 450
= *Ribrawst* – dau. of
Vortigern

Gladys

Glwys of Glamorgan

St. Gwynllyw ======
(Cynllo)

St. Cadoc

Kenau

Gorust Ledlum

Guotepauc

Coel Hen (b. c.AD 380)
= *Ystrafael*

Gwawl

Ceredig ==== *Meleri*

Patern Pesrut (Padarn Pesrud)

Octern (Edeyrn/Edern)

Cunedda Wledig ==========
b. c.AD 395

Einian Yrth
c.AD 460

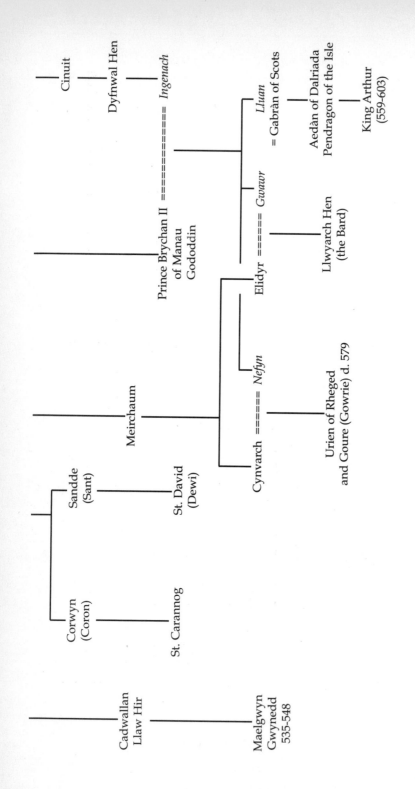

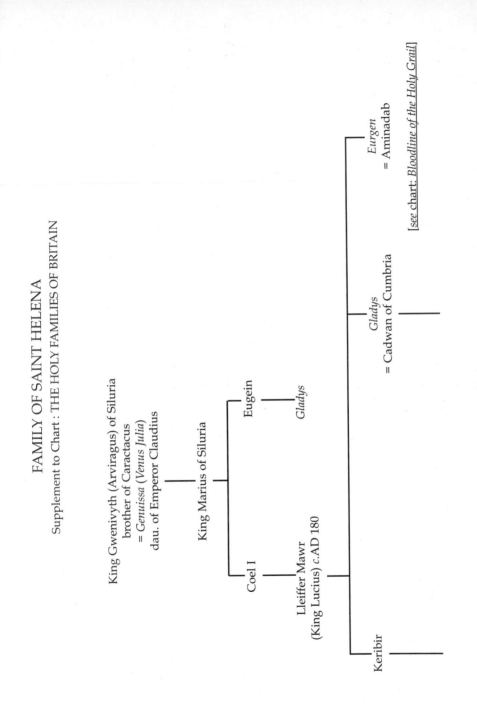

FAMILY OF SAINT HELENA

Supplement to Chart : THE HOLY FAMILIES OF BRITAIN

King Gwenivyth (Arviragus) of Siluria
brother of Caractacus
= *Genuissa (Venus Julia)*
dau. of Emperor Claudius

King Marius of Siluria

Coel I

Eugein

Gladys

Lleiffer Mawr
(King Lucius) c.AD 180

Keribir

Gladys
= Cadwan of Cumbria

Eurgen
= Aminadab

[*see* chart: *Bloodline of the Holy Grail*]

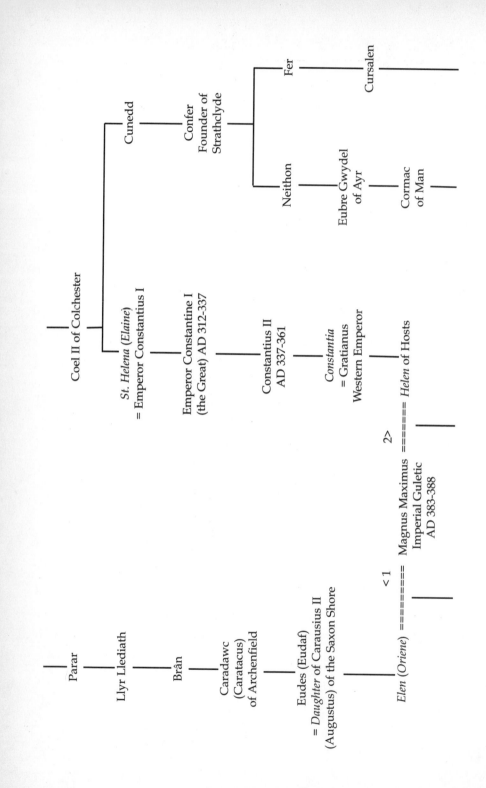

Parar

Llyr Llediath

Brân

Caradawc
(Caratacus)
of Archenfield

Eudes (Eudaf)
= *Daughter* of Carausius II
(Augustus) of the Saxon Shore

Coel II of Colchester

St. Helena (Elaine)
= Emperor Constantius I

Emperor Constantine I
(the Great) AD 312-337

Constantius II
AD 337-361

Constantia
= Gratianus
Western Emperor

Cunedd

Confer
Founder of
Strathclyde

Fer

Cursalen

Neithon

Eubre Gwydel
of Ayr

Cormac
of Man

Elen (Oriene) ========= <1 Magnus Maximus ======= 2> *Helen* of Hosts
                            Imperial Guletic
                            AD 383-388

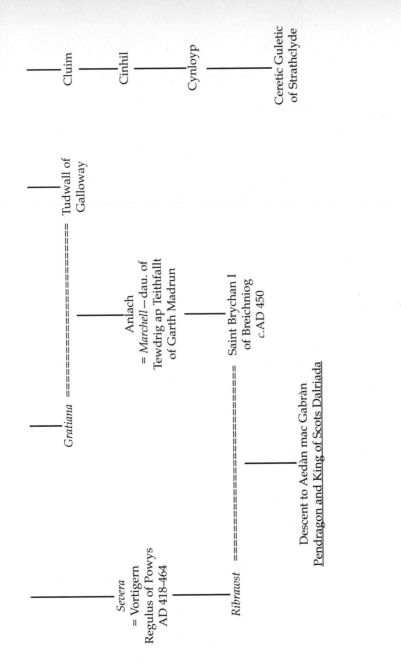

Cluim

Cinhil

Cynloyp

Ceretic Guletic
of Strathclyde

Tudwall of
Galloway

Gratiana ==================================

Anlach
= *Marchell* – dau. of
Tewdrig ap Teithfallt
of Garth Madrun

Saint Brychan I
of Breichniog
*c.*AD 450

Severa
= Vortigern
Regulus of Powys
AD 418-464

Ribrawst ==

Descent to Aedàn mac Gabràn
Pendragon and King of Scots Dalriada

ARTHURIAN DESCENT

Houses of Siluria, Camulod, Dalriada and Gwynedd

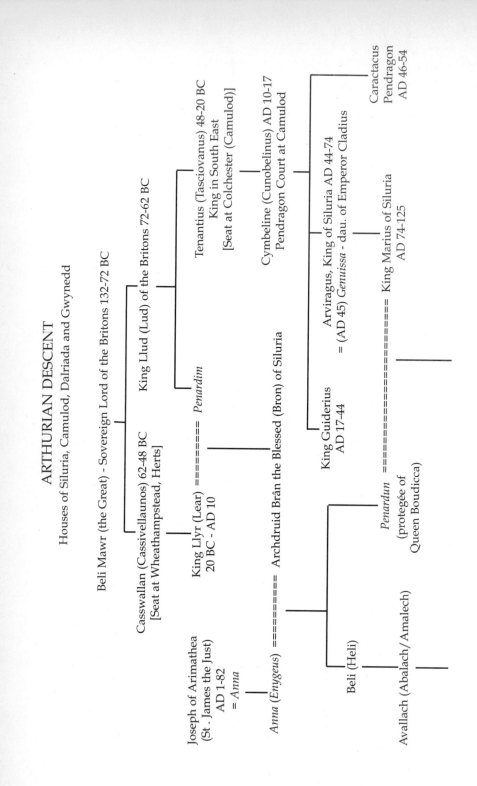

Beli Mawr (the Great) - Sovereign Lord of the Britons 132-72 BC

King Llud (Lud) of the Britons 72-62 BC

Casswallan (Cassivellaunos) 62-48 BC
[Seat at Wheathampstead, Herts]

Tenantius (Tasciovanus) 48-20 BC
King in South East
[Seat at Colchester (Camulod)]

Cymbeline (Cunobelinus) AD 10-17
Pendragon Court at Camulod

King Llyr (Lear) ========= Penardim
20 BC - AD 10

Archdruid Brân the Blessed (Bron) of Siluria

Arviragus, King of Siluria AD 44-74
= (AD 45) Genuissa - dau. of Emperor Cladius

King Guiderius
AD 17-44

Caractacus
Pendragon
AD 46-54

King Marius of Siluria
AD 74-125

Joseph of Arimathea
(St . James the Just)
AD 1-82
= Anna

Anna (Enygeus) ========== Archdruid Brân the Blessed (Bron) of Siluria

Penardun ========================== King Marius of Siluria
(protegée of
Queen Boudicca)

Beli (Heli)

Avallach (Abalach/ Amalech)

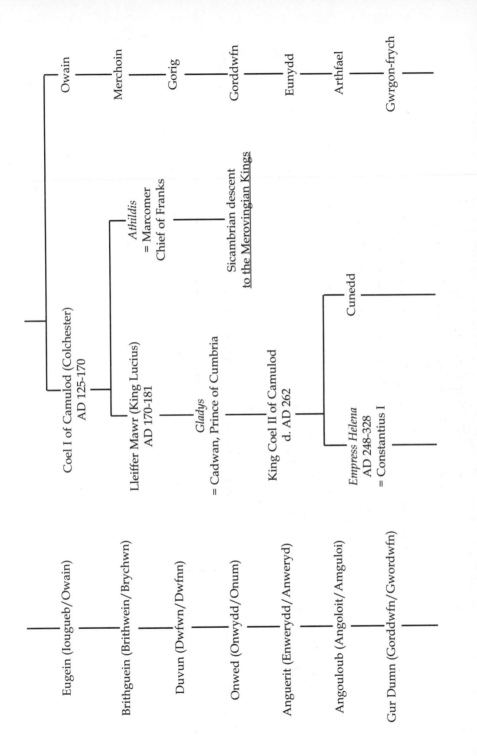

Coel I of Camulod (Colchester)
AD 125-170

Owain

Merchoin

Gorig

Gorddwfn

Eunydd

Arthfael

Gwrgon-frych

Athildis
= Marcomer
Chief of Franks

Sicambrian descent
to the Merovingian Kings

Lleiffer Mawr (King Lucius)
AD 170-181

Gladys
= Cadwan, Prince of Cumbria

King Coel II of Camulod
d. AD 262

Cunedd

Empress Helena
AD 248-328
= Constantius I

Eugein (Iougueb/Owain)

Brithguein (Brithwein/Brychwn)

Duvun (Dwfwn/Dwfnn)

Onwed (Onwydd/Onum)

Anguerit (Enwerydd/Anweryd)

Angouloub (Angoloit/Amguloi)

Gur Dumn (Gorddwfn/Gwordwfn)

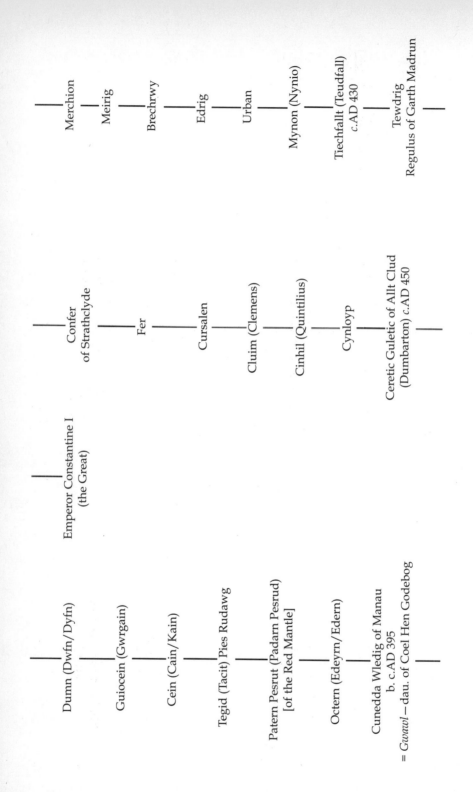

Merchion

Meirig

Brechrwy

Edrig

Urban

Mynon (Nynio)

Tiechfallt (Teudfall)
c.AD 430

Tewdrig
Regulus of Garth Madrun

Comer
of Strathclyde

Fer

Cursalen

Cluim (Clemens)

Cinhil (Quintilius)

Cynloyp

Ceretic Guletic of Allt Clud
(Dumbarton) c.AD 450

Emperor Constantine I
(the Great)

Dumn (Dwfn/Dyfn)

Guiocein (Gwrgain)

Cein (Cain/Kain)

Tegid (Tacit) Pies Rudawg

Patern Pesrut (Padarn Pesrud)
[of the Red Mantle]

Octern (Edeyrn/Edern)

Cunedda Wledig of Manau
b. c.AD 395
= Gwawl—dau. of Coel Hen Godebog

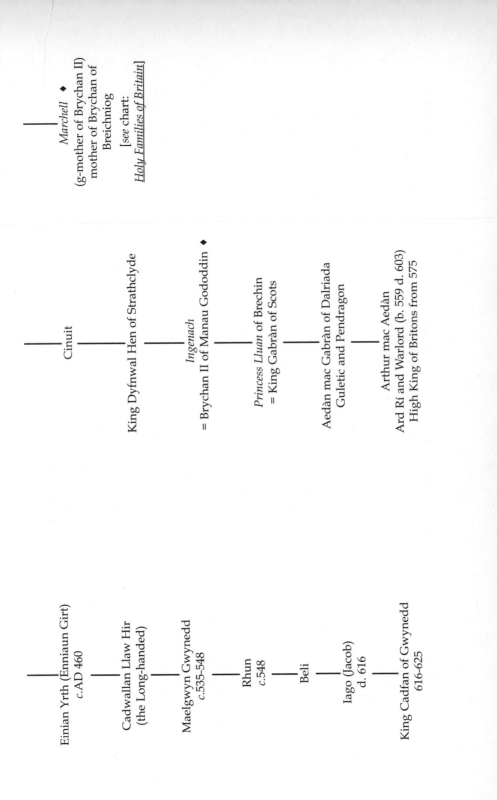

Marchell ◆
(g-mother of Brychan II)
mother of Brychan of
Breichniog
[see chart:
Holy Families of Britain]

Cinuit

King Dyfnwal Hen of Strathclyde

Ingenach ◆
= Brychan II of Manau Gododdin

Princess Lluan of Brechin
= King Gabràn of Scots

Aedàn mac Gabràn of Dalriada
Guletic and Pendragon

Arthur mac Aedàn
Ard Rí and Warlord (b. 559 d. 603)
High King of Britons from 575

Einian Yrth (Enniaun Girt)
c.AD 460

Cadwallan Llaw Hir
(the Long-handed)

Maelgwyn Gwynedd
c.535-548

Rhun
c.548

Beli

Iago (Jacob)
d. 616

King Cadfan of Gwynedd
616-625

ARTHUR AND THE HOUSE OF AVALLON DEL ACQS

Including Merlin, Vortigern and Aurelius (4th - 6th century)

[see chart: *Descent to Wales & Brittany*]

Magnus Maximus (Maxen Wledig)
Imperial Guletic of Britain AD 383-388
= 1 *Elen* – dau. of Eudes (Eudaf) the
Dux Gewissorum

Constantine
Overlord of Britain

Emrys of Wales

Cateyrn

Rulers of Powys

Britu

Severa (Gladys)

Vortigern (Foirtcherrn) ======= *Severa (Gladys)*
King of Powys AD 418
Regulus of Britain AD 425-464

Loigure
of the Boyne

Fedelmid
= *Scotnoe*
Princess of Britons

Anlach
son of Tudwall mac Cormac
of Man and Galloway
= *Marchell* – dau. of
Tewdrig of Garth Madrun

St. Brychan I ============ *Ribrwast*
of Breichniog

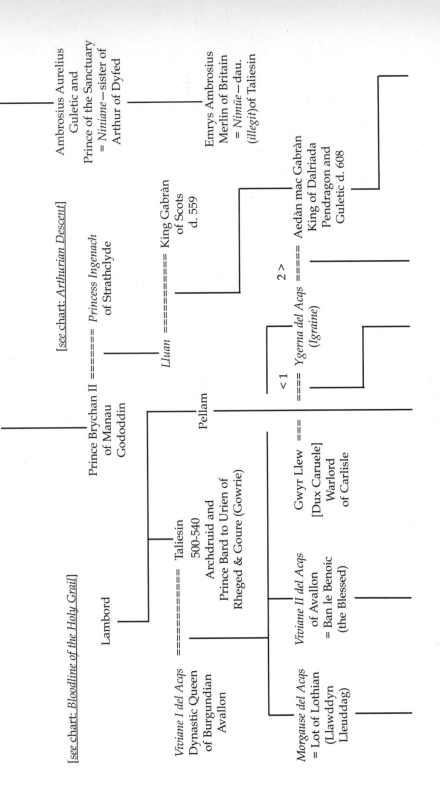

[see chart: Bloodline of the Holy Grail]

[see chart: Arthurian Descent]

Ambrosius Aurelius
Guletic and
Prince of the Sanctuary
= Niniane — sister of
Arthur of Dyfed

Emrys Ambrosius
Merlin of Britain
= Nimue — dau.
(illegit)of Taliesin

Prince Brychan II ======= Princess Ingenach
of Manau   of Strathclyde
Gododdin

Lluan =========== King Gabràn
of Scots
d. 559

Pellam

Aedàn mac Gabràn
King of Dalriada
Pendragon and
Guletic d. 608

2 >

Ygerna del Acqs ====
(Igraine)

< 1

====

Lambord

Taliesin
500-540
Archdruid and
Prince Bard to Urien of
Rheged & Goure (Gowrie)

=============

Viviane I del Acqs
Dynastic Queen
of Burgundian
Avallon

Gwyr Llew ===
[Dux Caruele]
Warlord
of Carlisle

Viviane II del Acqs
of Avallon
= Ban le Benoic
(the Blessed)

Morgause del Acqs
= Lot of Lothian
(Llawddyn
Lleuddag)

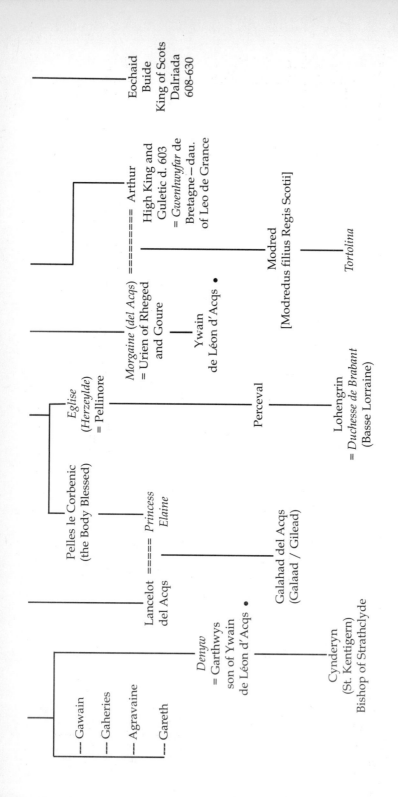

Eochaid
Buide
King of Scots
Dalriada
608-630

Arthur
High King and
Guletic d. 603
= *Gwenhwyfar* de
Bretagne — dau.
of Leo de Grance

Modred
[Modredus filius Regis Scotii]

Tortolina

Morgaine (del Acqs) =======
= Urien of Rheged
and Goure

Ywain
de Léon d'Acqs ●

Perceval

Lohengrin
= *Duchesse de Brabant*
(Basse Lorraine)

Eglise
(Herzeylde)
= Pellinore

Pelles le Corbenic
(the Body Blessed)

Lancelot ===== *Princess*
del Acqs   *Elaine*

Galahad del Acqs
(Galaad / Gilead)

Denyw
= Garthwys
son of Ywain
de Léon d'Acqs ●

Cynderyn
(St. Kentigern)
Bishop of Strathclyde

—— Gawain
—— Gaheries
—— Agravaine
—— Gareth

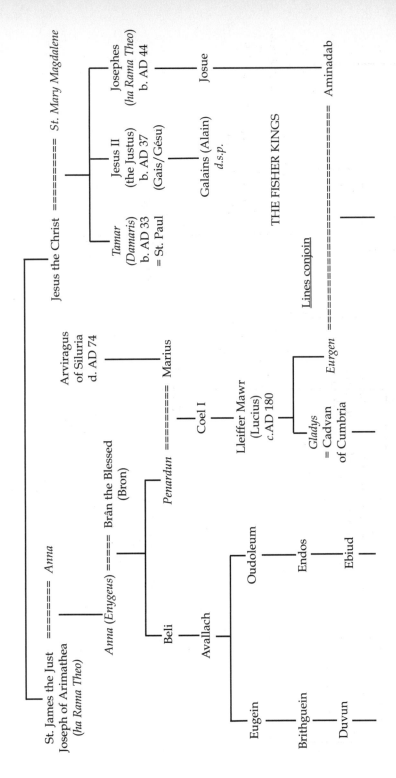

BLOODLINE OF THE HOLY GRAIL
Messianic Descent in Britain and Europe (1st - 7th century)

St. James the Just ======= *Anna*
Joseph of Arimathea
(ha Rama Theo)

Jesus the Christ ========= *St. Mary Magdalene*

Tamar
(Damaris)
b. AD 33
= St. Paul

Jesus II
(the Justus)
b. AD 37
(Gais/Gésu)

Josephes
(ha Rama Theo)
b. AD 44

Galains (Alain)
d.s.p.

Josue

THE FISHER KINGS

Aminadab

Lines conjoin =============

Anna (Enygeus) ===== Brân the Blessed
(Bron)

Arviragus
of Siluria
d. AD 74

Penardun ======= Marius

Coel I

Lleiffer Mawr
(Lucius)
c.AD 180

Gladys
= Cadvan
of Cumbria

Eurgen

Beli

Avallach

Oudoleum

Endos

Ebiud

Eugein

Brithguein

Duvun

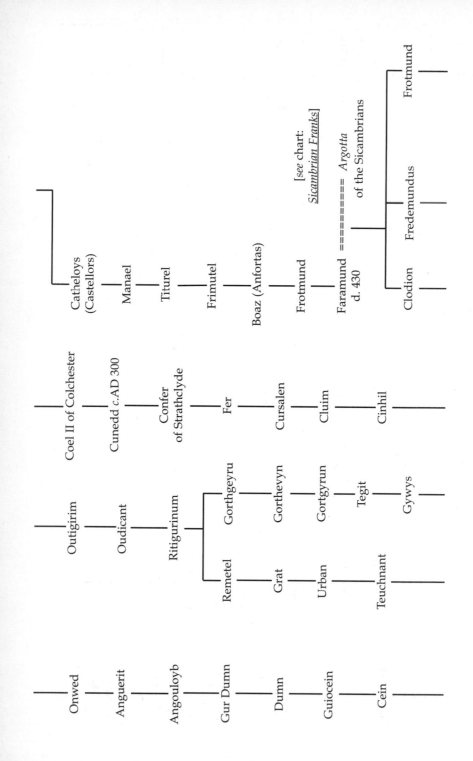

Onwed — Anguerit — Angouloyb — Gur Dumn — Dumn — Guiocein — Cein

Outigirim — Oudicant — Ritigurinum

Gorthgeyru — Gorthevyn — Gortgyrun — Tegit — Gywys

Remetel — Grat — Urban — Teuchnant

Coel II of Colchester — Cunedd *c.*AD 300 — Confer of Strathclyde — Fer — Cursalen — Cluim — Cinhil

Catheloys (Castellors)

Manael — Titurel — Frimutel — Boaz (Anfortas) — Frotmund — Faramund ========= *Argotta* d. 430 ====== of the Sicambrians

[see chart: Sicambrian Franks]

Clodion — Fredemundus — Frotmund

364

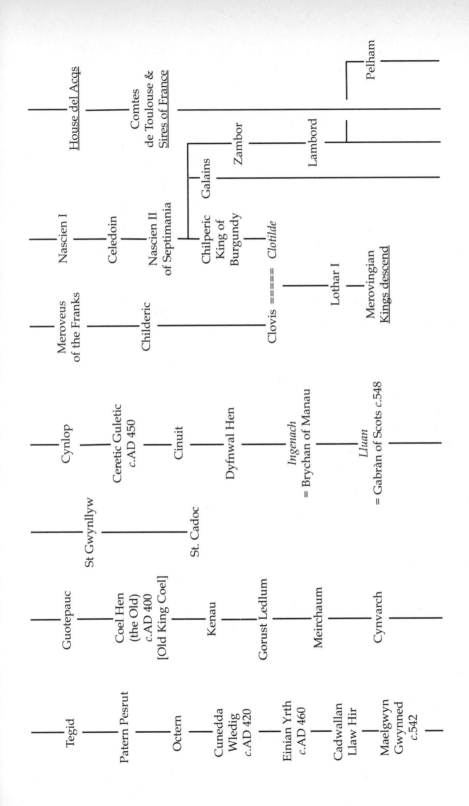

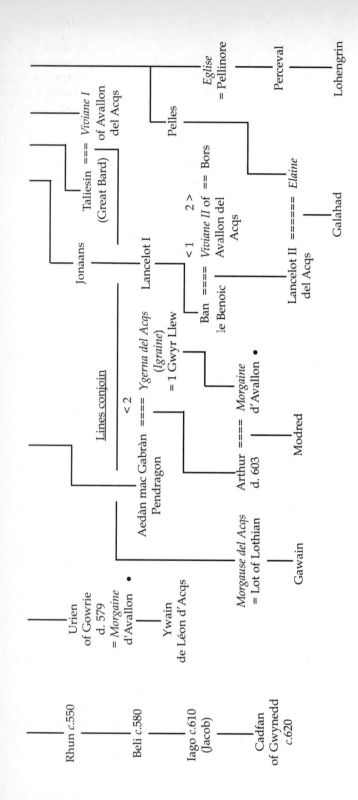

STRATHCLYDE AND THE GWYR-Y-GOGLEDD

Supplement to Chart: ARTHUR AND THE HOUSE OF AVALLON DEL ACQS

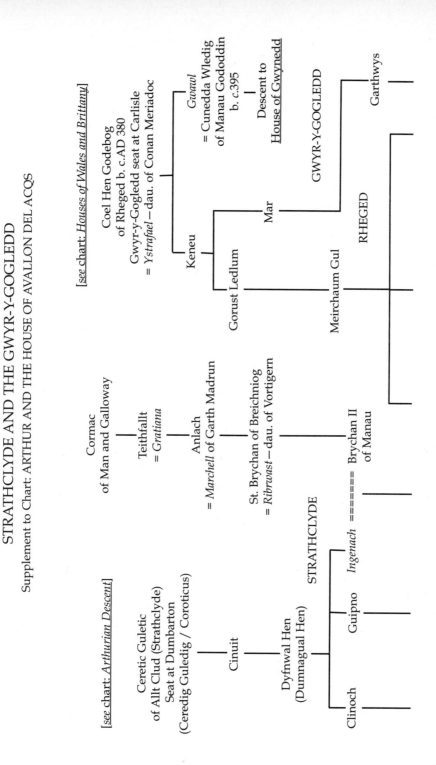

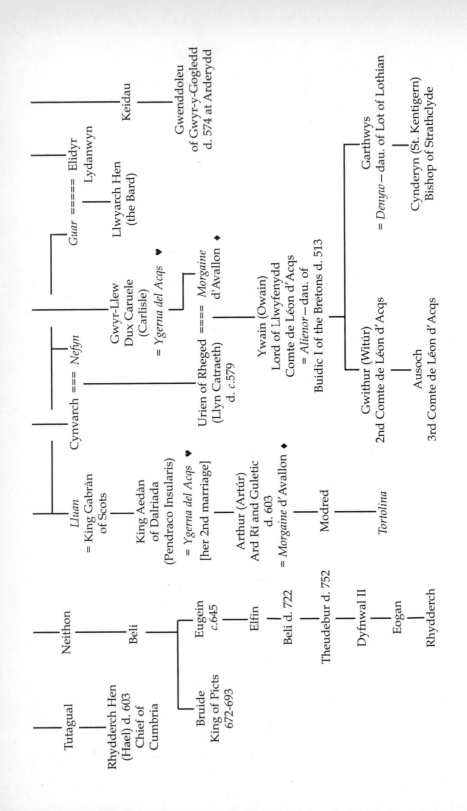

KINGS OF SCOTS DALRIADA

The Western Highlands and Isles (AD 500 - 841)

Erc of Dal n'Araide (Dal Riàta) – Ireland

Fergus Mor
(Kingdom of Alba)
d. 501

Loarn
(Kingdom of Northern Argyll)

Aengus
(Kingdom of Islay)

High Kings of Dalriada

Domangart
501-506

Muiredach

Tribe of Angus

Gabràn
537-559

Comgall
506-537

Eochaid

Aedàn mac Gabràn
574-608

Conall
559-574

Baetàn (Baodan)

Arthur
d. 603

Eochaid Buide
608-630

Connad
d. 630

Colum (Colman)

House of Ulster

Ferchar
643-651

Nechtan

Eoganan
d. 659

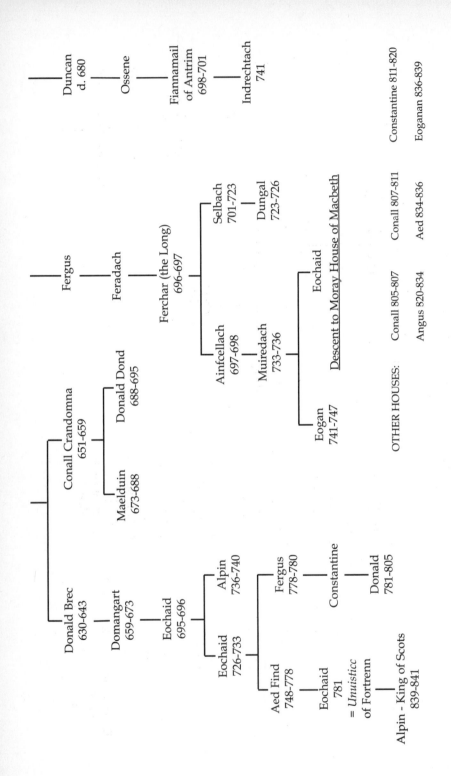

Duncan
d. 680

Ossene

Fiannamail
of Antrim
698-701

Indrechtach
741

Fergus

Feradach

Ferchar (the Long)
696-697

Selbach
701-723

Dungal
723-726

Ainfcellach
697-698

Muiredach
733-736

Eochaid

Descent to Moray House of Macbeth

Eogan
741-747

Conall Crandomna
651-659

Donald Dond
688-695

Maelduin
673-688

Donald Brec
630-643

Domangart
659-673

Eochaid
695-696

Alpin
736-740

Fergus
778-780

Constantine

Donald
781-805

Eochaid
726-733

Aed Find
748-778

Eochaid
781
= Unuisticc
of Fortrenn

Alpin - King of Scots
839-841

OTHER HOUSES:

Constantine 811-820

Eoganan 836-839

Conall 807-811

Aed 834-836

Conall 805-807

Angus 820-834

EARLY KINGS OF SCOTS
Carolingian Contemporaries (8th - 10th century)

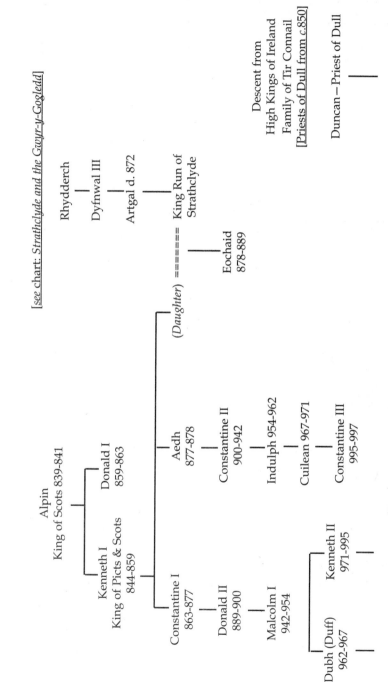

[see chart: *Strathclyde and the Gwyr-y-Gogledd*]

Alpin
King of Scots 839-841

Kenneth I
King of Picts & Scots
844-859

Donald I
859-863

Constantine I
863-877

Aedh
877-878

(*Daughter*) ====== King Run of
Strathclyde

Eochaid
878-889

Donald II
889-900

Constantine II
900-942

Malcolm I
942-954

Indulph 954-962

Dubh (Duff)
962-967

Cuilean 967-971

Kenneth II
971-995

Constantine III
995-997

Rhydderch

Dyfnwal III

Artgal d. 872

Descent from
High Kings of Ireland
Family of Tir Connail
[Priests of Dull from c.850]

Duncan – Priest of Dull

371

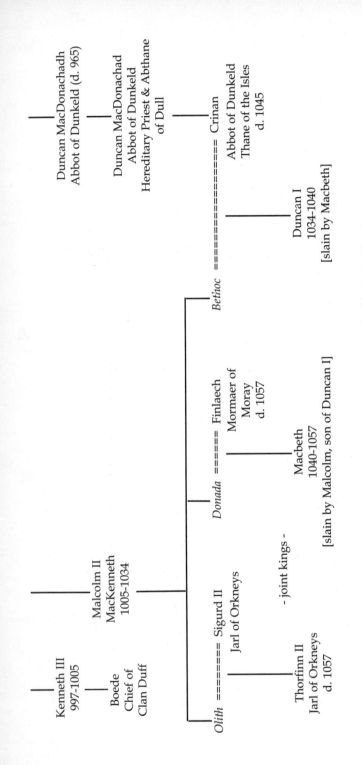

Kenneth III
997-1005

Malcolm II
MacKenneth
1005-1034

Boede
Chief of
Clan Duff

Duncan MacDonachadh
Abbot of Dunkeld (d. 965)

Duncan MacDonachad
Abbot of Dunkeld
Hereditary Priest & Abthane
of Dull

Olith ======== Sigurd II
Jarl of Orkneys

Donada ====== Finlaech
Mormaer of
Moray
d. 1057

Bethoc ===================== Crinan
Abbot of Dunkeld
Thane of the Isles
d. 1045

Thorfinn II
Jarl of Orkneys
d. 1057

- joint kings -

Macbeth
1040-1057
[slain by Malcolm, son of Duncan I]

Duncan I
1034-1040
[slain by Macbeth]

SCOTS IMPERIAL DESCENT

Supplement to Chart: THE HOLY FAMILIES OF BRITAIN

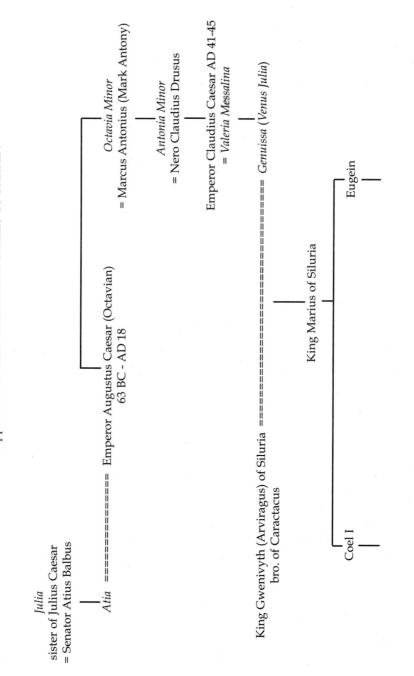

Julia
sister of Julius Caesar
= Senator Atius Balbus

Atia ============ Emperor Augustus Caesar (Octavian)
63 BC - AD 18

Octavia Minor
= Marcus Antonius (Mark Antony)

Antonia Minor
= Nero Claudius Drusus

Emperor Claudius Caesar AD 41-45
= Valeria Messalina

King Gwenivyth (Arviragus) of Siluria ============================ Genuissa (Venus Julia)
bro. of Caractacus

King Marius of Siluria

Coel I

Eugein

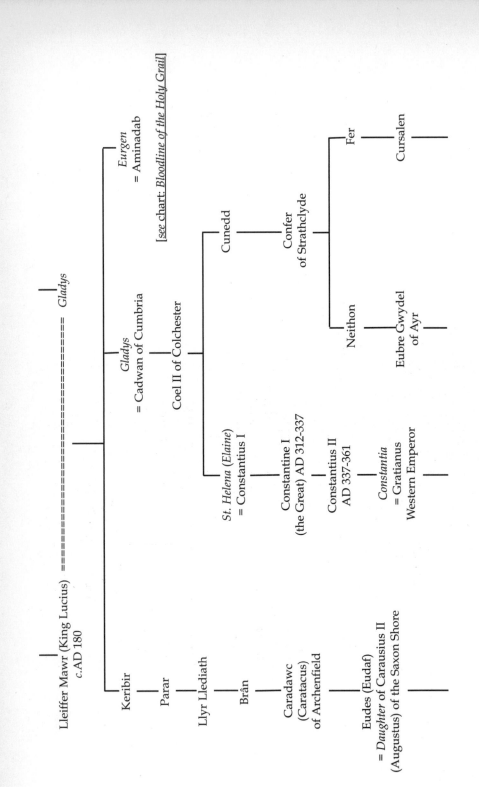

Lleiffer Mawr (King Lucius) =========================== *Gladys*
*c.*AD 180

Keribir

Parar

Llyr Llediath

Brân

Caradawc
(Caratacus)
of Archenfield

Eudes (Eudaf)
= *Daughter* of Carausius II
(Augustus) of the Saxon Shore

Gladys
= Cadwan of Cumbria

Coel II of Colchester

St. Helena (Elaine)
= Constantius I

Constantine I
(the Great) AD 312-337

Constantius II
AD 337-361

Constantia
= Gratianus
Western Emperor

Eurgen
= Aminadab

[*see chart: Bloodline of the Holy Grail*]

Cunedd

Confer
of Strathclyde

Neithon

Fer

Eubre Gwydel
of Ayr

Cursalen

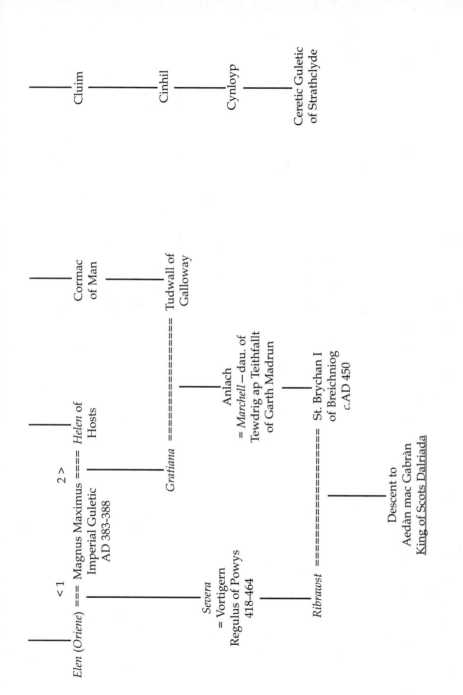

Cluim — Cinhil — Cynloyp — Ceretic Guletic of Strathclyde

Cormac of Man — Tudwall of Galloway

<1   2>

Elen (Oriene) === Magnus Maximus ==== *Helen of Hosts*
Imperial Guletic
AD 383-388

Severa
= Vortigern
Regulus of Powys
418-464

Gratiana ================ Anlach
= *Marchell* – dau. of
Tewdrig ap Teithfallt
of Garth Madrun

Ribrawst ================ St. Brychan I
of Breichniog
c.AD 450

Descent to
Aedán mac Gabrán
King of Scots Dalriada

BISHOP OF ROME AND POPES
From Constantine to the Norman Conquest (AD 336 - 1066)

Bishop/Pope	Year	Pope	Year	Pope	Year
Mark	336	Eugene I	654-657	Benedict IV	900-903
Julius I	337-352	Vitalian	657-672	Leo V	903
Liberius	352-366	Adeodatus	672-676	Sergius III	904-911
Damasus I	366-384	Donus	676-678	Anastasius	911-913
Siricius	384-399	Agatho	678-681	Lando	913-914
Anastasius	399-401	Leo II	682-683	John X	914-929
Innocent I	401-417	Benedict II	684-685	Leo VI	929
Zozimus	417-418	John V	685-686	Stephen VIII	929-931
Boniface I	418-422	Conon	686-687	John XI	931-936
Celestine	422-432	Sergius I	687-701	Leo VII	936-939
Sixtus III	432-440	John VI	701-705	Stephen IX	939-942
Leo I	440-461	John VII	705-707	Marinus II	942-946
Hilarus	461-468	Sisinnius	708	Agapitus II	946-955
Simplicius	468-483	Constantine I	708-715	John XII	955-963
Felix III	483-492	Gregory II	715-731	Leo VIII	963-964
Gelasius I	492-496	Gregory III	731-741	Benedict V	964
Anastasius II	496-498	Zachary	741-752	John XIII	965-972
Symmachus	498-514	Stephen II	752	Benedict VI	973-974
Hormisdas	514-523	Stephen III	752-757	Benedict VII	974-983
John I	523-526	Paul I	757-767	John XIV	983-984
Felix IV	526-530	Stephen IV	768-772	John XV	985-996
Boniface II	530-532	Adrian I	772-795	Gregory V	996-999
John II	533-535	Leo III	795-816	Silvester II	999-1003
Agapitus	535-536	Stephen V	816-817	John XVII	1003
Silverius	536-537	Paschal I	817-824	John XVIII	1003-1009
Vigilius	537-555	Eugene II	824-827	Sergius IV	1009-1012
Pelagius I	556-560	Valentine	827	Benedict VIII	1012-1024
John III	561-578	Gregory IV	827-844	John XIX	1024-1033
Benedict I	575-579	Sergius II	844-847	Benedict IX	1033-1044
Pelagius II	579-590	Leo IV	847-855	Silvester III	1045
Gregory I	590-604	Benedict III	855-858	Benedict	1045
Sabinianus	604-606	Nicholas I	858-867	Gregory VI	1045-1046
Boniface III ◆	607	Adrian II	867-872	Clement II	1046-1047
[◆ first to be styled 'Pope']		John VIII	872-882	Benedict IX	1047-1048
Boniface IV	608-615	Marinus	882-884	Damascus II	1048
Deusdedit	615-618	Adrian III	884-885	Leo IX	1049-1054
Boniface V	619-625	Stephen VI	885-891	Victor II	1055-1057
Honorius I	625-638	Formosus	891-896	Stephen X	1057-1058
Severinus	640	Boniface VI	896	Nicholas II	1059-1061
John IV	640-642	Stephen VII	896-897		
Theodore I	642-649	Romanus	897		
Martin I	649-655	John IX	898-900		

FROM MACBETH TO THE STEWARTS
Kings of Scots (1040 - 1371)

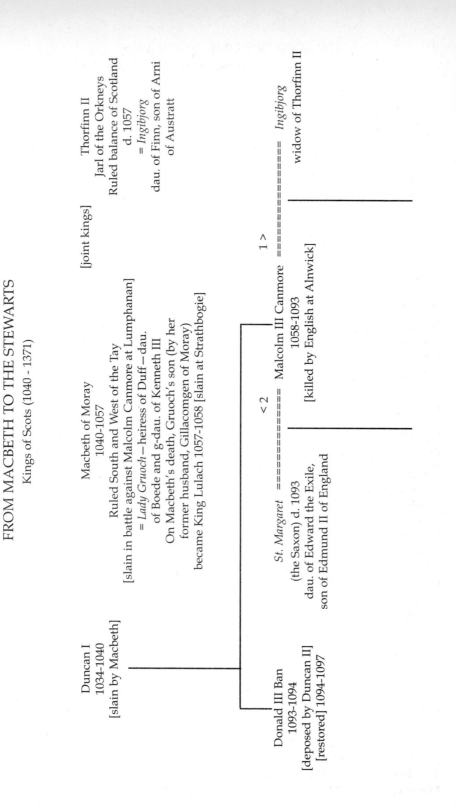

Duncan I
1034-1040
[slain by Macbeth]

Macbeth of Moray
1040-1057
Ruled South and West of the Tay
[slain in battle against Malcolm Canmore at Lumphanan]
= *Lady Gruoch* – heiress of Duff – dau.
of Boede and g-dau. of Kenneth III
On Macbeth's death, Gruoch's son (by her
former husband, Gillacomgen of Moray)
became King Lulach 1057-1058 [slain at Strathbogie]

[joint kings]

Thorfinn II
Jarl of the Orkneys
Ruled balance of Scotland
d. 1057
= *Ingibjorg*
dau. of Finn, son of Arni
of Austratt

St. Margaret ============
(the Saxon) d. 1093
dau. of Edward the Exile,
son of Edmund II of England

< 2   Malcolm III Canmore   1 >
1058-1093
[killed by English at Alnwick]

============ *Ingibjorg*
widow of Thorfinn II

Donald III Ban
1093-1094
[deposed by Duncan II]
[restored] 1094-1097

377

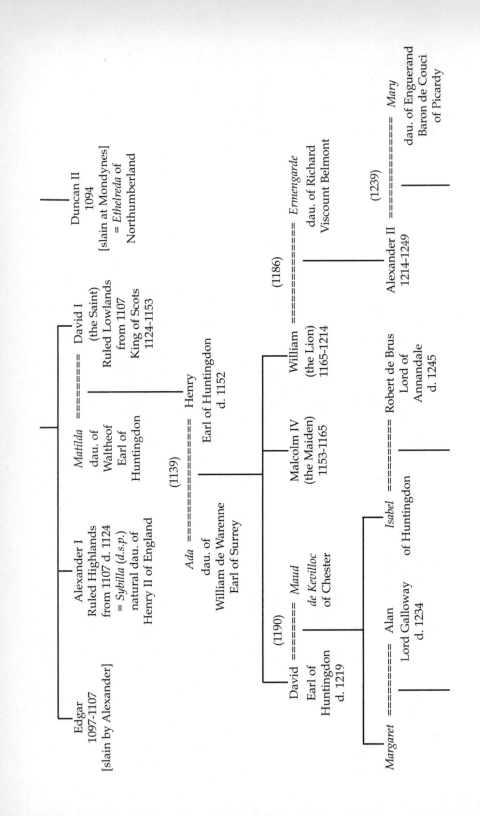

Edgar
1097-1107
[slain by Alexander]

Alexander I
Ruled Highlands
from 1107 d. 1124
= *Sybilla* (*d.s.p.*)
natural dau. of
Henry II of England

David I
(the Saint)
Ruled Lowlands
from 1107
King of Scots
1124-1153
======== *Matilda*
dau. of
Waltheof
Earl of
Huntingdon

Duncan II
1094
[slain at Mondynes]
= *Ethelreda* of
Northumberland

Ada ================ Henry
dau. of   Earl of Huntingdon
William de Warenne   d. 1152
Earl of Surrey
(1139)

David ======= *Maud*
Earl of   *de Kevilloc*
Huntingdon   of Chester
d. 1219
(1190)

Malcolm IV
(the Maiden)
1153-1165

William ============== *Ermengarde*
(the Lion)   dau. of Richard
1165-1214   Viscount Belmont
(1186)

Alexander II ======= *Mary*
1214-1249   dau. of Enguerand
(1239)   Baron de Couci
                     of Picardy

Margaret ========== Alan
            Lord Galloway
            d. 1234

Isabel ========== Robert de Brus
of Huntingdon   Lord of
                    Annandale
                    d. 1245

Genealogical Chart

(1233) Devorguilla d. 1290 ======== John de Balliol d. 1269

(1251) Alexander III 1249-1286 ===== Margaret dau. of Henry III of England

Robert Bruce of Annandale d. 1294 ======== Isabel dau. of Gilbert de Clare, Earl of Gloucester

English Domination

John Balliol 1292-1296 [selected by Edward I of England] = Isobel – dau. of John de Warenne Earl of Surrey [deposed by Edward who ruled 1296-1306]

Margaret = Eric II of Norway

Margaret (Maid of Norway) 1286-1290 [died at sea aged seven]

Crown seized by Edward I of England

Robert Bruce of Annandale Earl of Carrick = Marjorie dau. of Neil Earl of Carrick

Edward Balliol Crowned by English in 1332 but fled Scotland

King Robert I (the Bruce) 1306-1329 Defeated Edward of England at Bannockburn 1314 to reinstate Scottish Independence
= 1 (1295) Isabel dau. of Donald, Earl of Mar
(1302) 2 > Elizabeth du Bourg dau. of Richard Earl of Ulster

Scottish Independence Regained

379

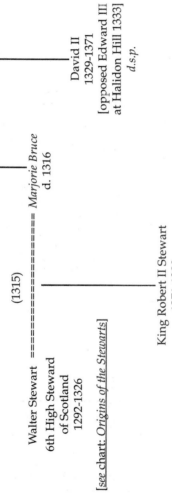

Walter Stewart ============ *Marjorie Bruce*
6th High Steward   *d. 1316*
of Scotland
1292-1326

(1315)

[*see chart: Origins of the Stewarts*]

King Robert II Stewart
1371-1390
Founder of the Royal House of Stewart

David II
1329-1371
[opposed Edward III
at Halidon Hill 1333]
d.s.p.

ORIGINS OF THE STEWARTS

From Steward to Stewart—Scots and Breton Descents

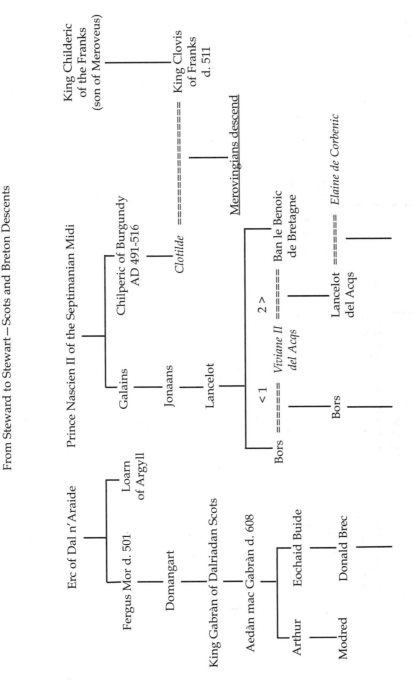

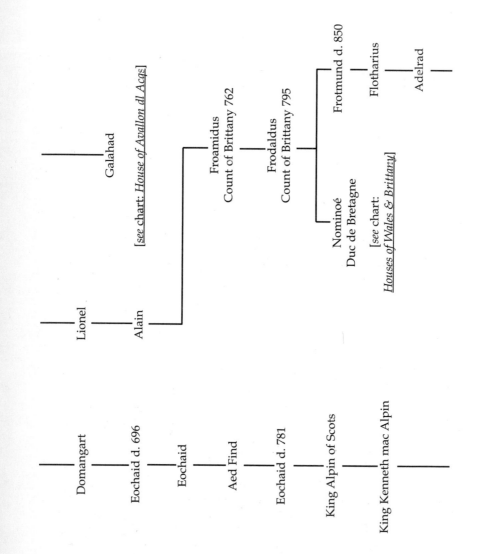

Galahad

[see chart: House of Avallon dl Acqs]

Froamidus
Count of Brittany 762

Frodaldus
Count of Brittany 795

Frotmund d. 850

Flotharius

Adelrad

Nominoé
Duc de Bretagne

[see chart:
Houses of Wales & Brittany]

Lionel

Alain

Domangart

Eochaid d. 696

Eochaid

Aed Find

Eochaid d. 781

King Alpin of Scots

King Kenneth mac Alpin

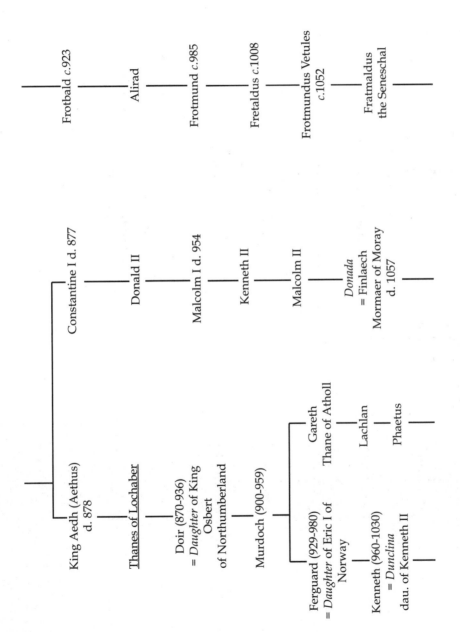

Frotbald *c.*923

Alirad

Frotmund *c.*985

Fretaldus *c.*1008

Frotmundus Vetules
*c.*1052

Fratmaldus
the Seneschal

Constantine I d. 877

Donald II

Malcolm I d. 954

Kenneth II

Malcolm II

Donada
= Finlaech
Mormaer of Moray
d. 1057

King Aedh (Aethus)
d. 878

Thanes of Lochaber

Doir (870-936)
= *Daughter of King
Osbert
of Northumberland*

Murdoch (900-959)

Gareth
Thane of Atholl

Lachlan

Phaetus

Ferguard (929-980)
= *Daughter of Eric I of
Norway*

Kenneth (960-1030)
= *Dunclina*
dau. of Kenneth II

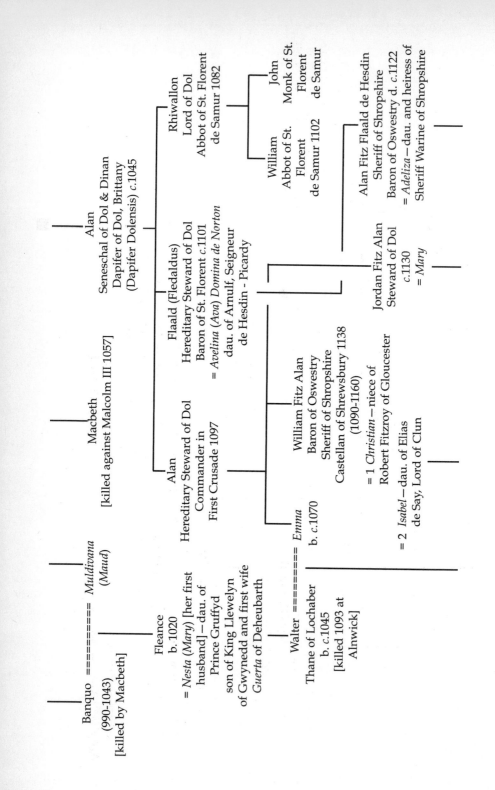

Banquo ============= *Muldivana*
(990-1043)   (*Maud*)
[killed by Macbeth]

Fleance
b. 1020
= *Nesta (Mary)* [her first
husband] – dau. of
Prince Gruffyd
son of King Llewelyn
of Gwynedd and first wife
Guerta of Deheubarth

Walter ========= *Emma*
Thane of Lochaber   b. *c*.1070
b. *c*.1045
[killed 1093 at
Alnwick]

Macbeth
[killed against Malcolm III 1057]

Alan
Seneschal of Dol & Dinan
Dapifer of Dol, Brittany
(Dapifer Dolensis) *c*.1045

Alan
Hereditary Steward of Dol
Commander in
First Crusade 1097

Flaald (Fledaldus)
Hereditary Steward of Dol
Baron of St. Florent *c*.1101
= *Avelina (Ava) Domina de Norton*
dau. of Arnulf, Seigneur
de Hesdin - Picardy

Rhiwallon
Lord of Dol
Abbot of St. Florent
de Samur 1082

William
Abbot of St.
Florent
de Samur 1102

John
Monk of St.
Florent
de Samur

William Fitz Alan
Baron of Oswestry
Sheriff of Shropshire
Castellan of Shrewsbury 1138
(1090-1160)

= 1 *Christian* – niece of
Robert Fitzroy of Gloucester

= 2 *Isabel* – dau. of Elias
de Say, Lord of Clun

Jordan Fitz Alan
Steward of Dol
c.1130
= *Mary*

Alan Fitz Flaald de Hesdin
Sheriff of Shropshire
Baron of Oswestry d. *c*.1122
= *Adeliza* – dau. and heiress of
Sheriff Warine of Shropshire

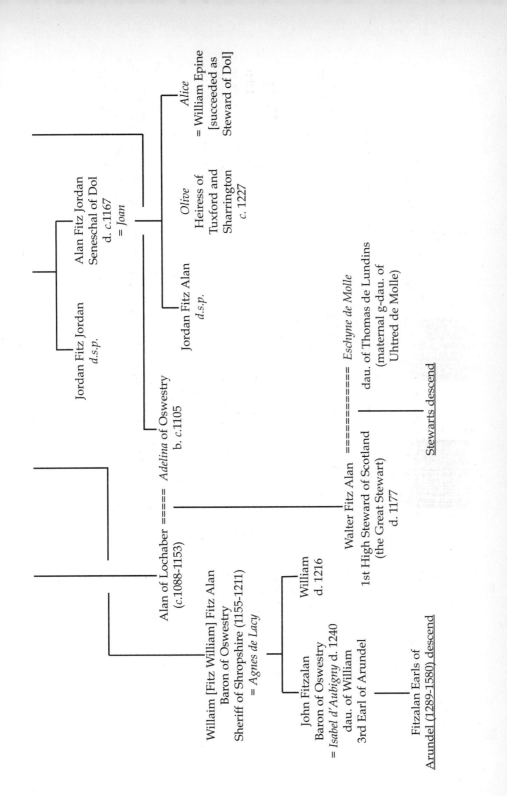

Jordan Fitz Jordan
d.s.p.

Alan Fitz Jordan
Seneschal of Dol
d. *c.*1167
= *Joan*

Alice
= William Epine
[succeeded as
Steward of Dol]

Olive
Heiress of
Tuxford and
Sharrington
c. 1227

Jordan Fitz Alan
d.s.p.

Alan of Lochaber ===== *Adelina* of Oswestry
(c.1088–1153)   b. *c.*1105

Willaim [Fitz William] Fitz Alan
Baron of Oswestry
Sheriff of Shropshire (1155-1211)
= *Agnes de Lacy*

Walter Fitz Alan ============ *Eschyne de Molle*
1st High Steward of Scotland   dau. of Thomas de Lundins
(the Great Stewart)   (maternal g-dau. of
d. 1177   Uhtred de Molle)

William
d. 1216

John Fitzalan
Baron of Oswestry
= *Isabel d'Aubigny* d. 1240
dau. of William
3rd Earl of Arundel

Stewarts descend

Fitzalan Earls of
Arundel (1289-1580) descend

385

THE HIGH STEWARDS OF SCOTLAND
Royal Chancellors (12th - 14th century)

Walter Fitz Alan ================= *Eschyne de Molle*
1st High Steward of Scotland   dau. of Thomas de Lundins
[Dapifer Regis Scotiae]   (sister of Malcolm, 1st Doorward of Scotland,
Benefactor of the Knights Templars   and widow of Robert le Croc, Snr.)
Founder of Paisley Priory 1164
Received Grant of Lands from David I
Ratified by Malcolm IV
d. 1177

Alan Fitz Walter ================= *Eve*
2nd High Steward of Scotland   dau. of Swein of Crawford
Crusader with Richard Coeur de Lion   [ancestor of Ruthvens of Gowrie]
d. 1204

Walter Stewart ================= *Beatrix*
3rd High Steward of Scotland   dau. of Gilchrist
(Walter of Dundonald)   3rd Earl of Angus
Justiciar of Northern Scotland
Raised Paisley Priory to an Abbey
d. 1241

Alexander Stewart ========================= *Jean*
4th High Steward of Scotland   g-dau. of Angus, Lord of Bute
Crusader and co-Regent   and Arran, son of Somerled of the Isles
Lord of Garlies, Galloway
Commander at 1263 Battle of Largs
against King Haakon of Norway
d. 1283

Sir James Stewart ===================== *Jill du Bourg*
5th High Steward of Scotland   dau. of Walter, 1st Earl of Ulster
[supporter of Robert Bruce]
co-Regent & Guardian of the Realm
d. 1309

(1315)
Sir Walter Stewart =============== *Marjorie Bruce*
6th High Steward of Scotland   d. 1316
Commander at Bannockburn 1314   dau. of Robert I Bruce
Regent of Scotland
d. 1326

King Robert II Stewart
1371-1390
(7th High Steward of Scotland)
Founder of Royal House of Stewart

THE STEWART DYNASTY

Noble Families of the Royal House of Scotland

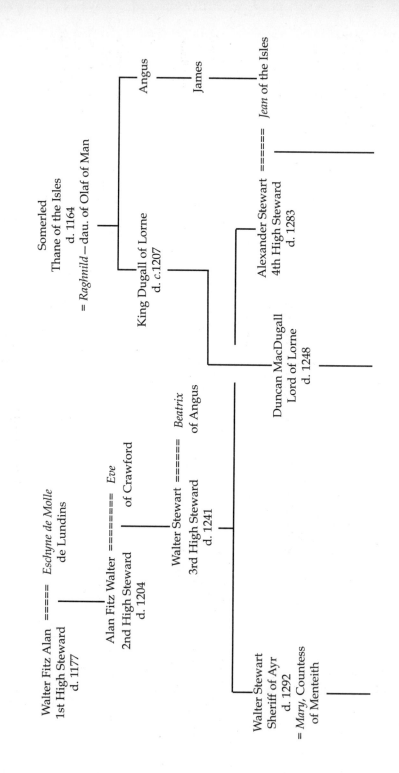

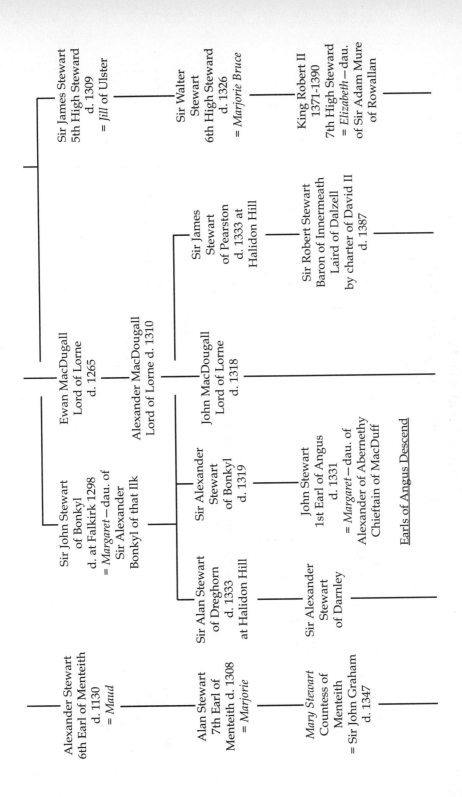

Alexander Stewart
6th Earl of Menteith
d. 1130
= *Maud*

Sir John Stewart
of Bonkyl
d. at Falkirk 1298
= *Margaret* – dau. of
Sir Alexander
Bonkyl of that Ilk

Ewan MacDugall
Lord of Lorne
d. 1265

Sir James Stewart
5th High Steward
d. 1309
= *Jill* of Ulster

Sir Walter
Stewart
6th High Steward
d. 1326
= *Marjorie Bruce*

Alexander MacDougall
Lord of Lorne d. 1310

Sir James
Stewart
of Pearston
d. 1333 at
Halidon Hill

King Robert II
1371-1390
7th High Steward
= *Elizabeth* – dau.
of Sir Adam Mure
of Rowallan

Alan Stewart
7th Earl of
Menteith d. 1308
= *Marjorie*

Sir Alexander
Stewart
of Bonkyl
d. 1319

John MacDougall
Lord of Lorne
d. 1318

Sir Robert Stewart
Baron of Innermeath
Laird of Dalzell
by charter of David II
d. 1387

Mary Stewart
Countess of
Menteith
= Sir John Graham
d. 1347

Sir Alan Stewart
of Dreghorn
d. 1333
at Halidon Hill

Sir Alexander
Stewart
of Darnley

John Stewart
1st Earl of Angus
d. 1331
= *Margaret* – dau. of
Alexander of Abernethy
Chieftain of MacDuff

Earls of Angus Descend

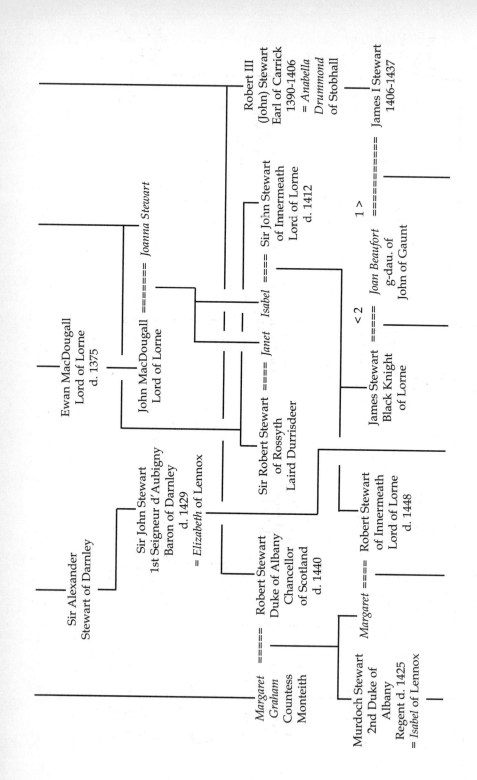

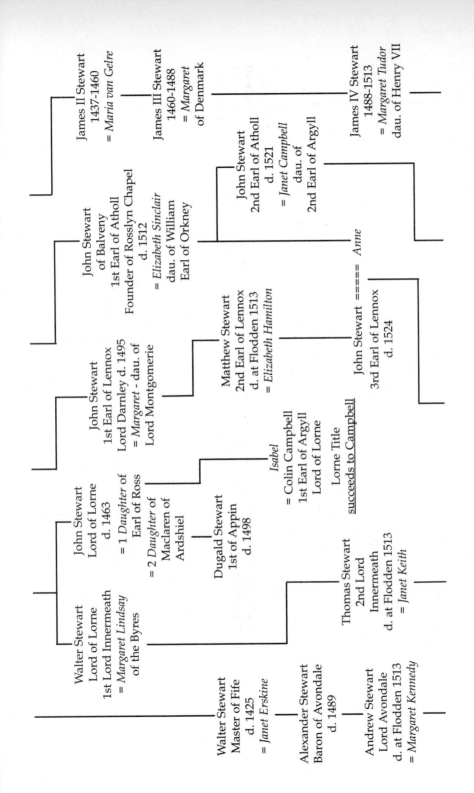

James II Stewart
1437-1460
= *Maria van Gelre*

James III Stewart
1460-1488
= *Margaret*
of Denmark

James IV Stewart
1488-1513
= *Margaret Tudor*
dau. of Henry VII

John Stewart
of Balveny
1st Earl of Atholl
Founder of Rosslyn Chapel
d. 1512
= *Elizabeth Sinclair*
dau. of William
Earl of Orkney

John Stewart
2nd Earl of Atholl
d. 1521
= *Janet Campbell*
dau. of
2nd Earl of Argyll

John Stewart
1st Earl of Lennox
Lord Darnley d. 1495
= *Margaret - dau.* of
Lord Montgomerie

Matthew Stewart
2nd Earl of Lennox
d. at Flodden 1513
= *Elizabeth Hamilton*

John Stewart ===== *Anne*
3rd Earl of Lennox
d. 1524

Walter Stewart
Lord of Lorne
1st Lord Innermeath
= *Margaret Lindsay*
of the Byres

John Stewart
Lord of Lorne
d. 1463
= 1 *Daughter* of
Earl of Ross

= 2 *Daughter* of
Maclaren of
Ardshiel

Dugald Stewart
1st of Appin
d. 1498

Isabel
= Colin Campbell
1st Earl of Argyll
Lord of Lorne

Lorne Title
succeeds to Campbell

Walter Stewart
Master of Fife
d. 1425
= *Janet Erskine*

Alexander Stewart
Baron of Avondale
d. 1489

Andrew Stewart
Lord Avondale
d. at Flodden 1513
= *Margaret Kennedy*

Thomas Stewart
2nd Lord
Innermeath
d. at Flodden 1513
= *Janet Keith*

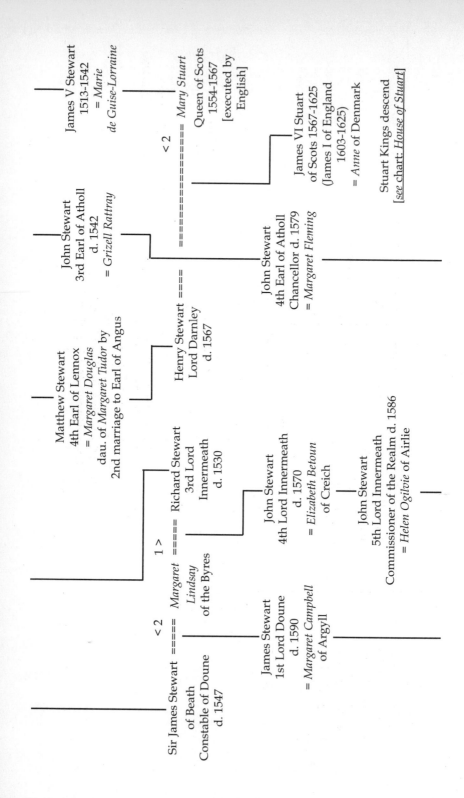

James V Stewart
1513-1542
= Marie
de Guise-Lorraine

John Stewart
3rd Earl of Atholl
d. 1542
= Grizell Rattray

Matthew Stewart
4th Earl of Lennox
= Margaret Douglas
dau. of Margaret Tudor by
2nd marriage to Earl of Angus

< 2   Mary Stuart
Queen of Scots
1554-1567
[executed by
English]

Henry Stewart
Lord Darnley
d. 1567

John Stewart
4th Earl of Atholl
Chancellor d. 1579
= Margaret Fleming

James VI Stuart
of Scots 1567-1625
(James I of England
1603-1625)
= Anne of Denmark

Stuart Kings descend
[see chart: House of Stuart]

Sir James Stewart
of Beath
Constable of Doune
d. 1547

< 2   Margaret   ===== Richard Stewart
Lindsay   3rd Lord
of the Byres   Innermeath
                  d. 1530

1 >

James Stewart
1st Lord Doune
d. 1590
= Margaret Campbell
of Argyll

John Stewart
4th Lord Innermeath
d. 1570
= Elizabeth Betoun
of Creich

John Stewart
5th Lord Innermeath
Commissioner of the Realm d. 1586
= Helen Ogilvie of Airlie

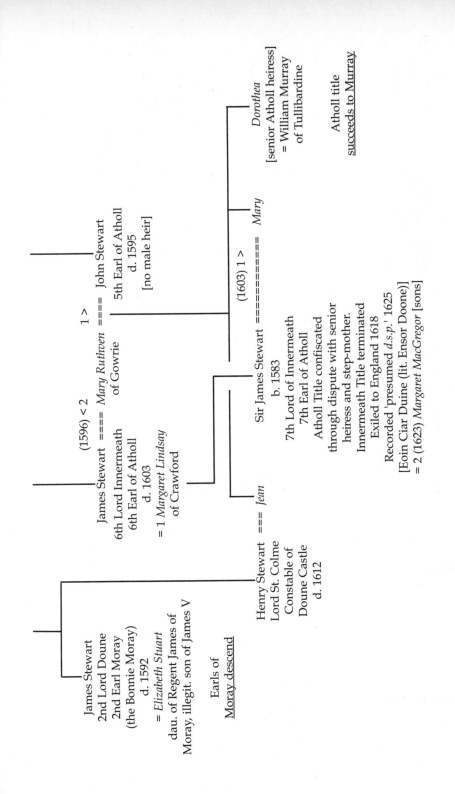

James Stewart
2nd Lord Doune
2nd Earl Moray
(the Bonnie Moray)
d. 1592
= *Elizabeth Stuart*
dau. of Regent James of
Moray, illegit. son of James V

Earls of
Moray descend

Henry Stewart === *Jean*
Lord St. Colme
Constable of
Doune Castle
d. 1612

(1596) < 2   *Mary Ruthven*   1 >
James Stewart ==== of Gowrie ==== John Stewart
6th Lord Innermeath   5th Earl of Atholl
6th Earl of Atholl   d. 1595
d. 1603   [no male heir]
= 1 *Margaret Lindsay*
of Crawford

(1603) 1 >
Sir James Stewart ==============   *Mary*
b. 1583
7th Lord of Innermeath
7th Earl of Atholl
Atholl Title confiscated
through dispute with senior
heiress and step-mother.
Innermeath Title terminated
Exiled to England 1618
Recorded 'presumed *d.s.p.*' 1625
[Eoin Ciar Duine (lit. Ensor Doone)]
= 2 (1623) *Margaret MacGregor* [sons]

Dorothea
[senior Atholl heiress]
= William Murray
of Tullibardine

Atholl title
succeeds to Murray

393

From the Norman Conquest to the Age of Chivalry (11th - 14th century)

ENGLAND	SCOTLAND	FRANCE
Normans	Scots	Capetians
		Robert II 996-1031 son of Hugh Capet = *Constance* of Provence
	Lulach of Moray 1057-1058 stepson of Macbeth	Henri I 1031-1060 son of Robert II = *Anne* of Kiev
William I (the Conqueror) 1066-1087 Duke of Normandy = *Matilda* of Flanders	Malcolm III Canmore 1058-1093 son of Duncan I = 1 *Ingibjorg* of Orkney = 2 *Margaret* the Saxon	
William II (Rufus) 1087-1100 son of William I [unmarried]	Donald Ban 1093-1094 brother of Malcolm III [deposed]	Philip I 1060-1108 son of Henri I = 1 *Bertha* of Holland
	Duncan II 1094 son of Malcolm III and *Ingibjorg*	
	Donald Ban 1094-1097 [restored]	
	Edgar 1097-1107 son of Malcolm III and *Margaret* the Saxon	
Henry I (Beauclerk) 1100-1135 brother of William II = *Maud* – dau. of Malcolm III of Scots	Alexander I 1107-1124 brother of Edgar = *Sybilla* – natural dau. of Henry I of England	Louis VI 1108-1137 (the Fat) son of Philip I = 1 *Lucienne* de Rochefort

ENGLAND	SCOTLAND	FRANCE
Stephen Count of Blois 1135-1154 g-son of William I = *Matilda* of Bologne	David I (the Saint) 1124-1153 brother of Alexander = *Matilda* of Huntingdon	Louis VII 1137-1180 (the Young) son of Louis VI = 2 *Alix* of Champagne

Plantagenets

Henry II (Curtmantel) 1154-1189 g-son of Henry I = *Eleanor* of Aquitaine ex-wife of Louis VII of France	Malcolm IV (the Maiden) 1153-1165 g-son of David I [unmarried]	
Richard I (the Lionheart) 1189-1199 son of Henry II = *Berengaria* of Navarre	William I (the Lion) 1165-1214 bro. of Malcolm IV = *Ermengarde* of Bellomont	Philip II (Augustus) 1180-1223 son of Louis VII = *Isabella* of Hainault
John (Lackland) 1199-1216 brother of Richard I = *Isabel* of Angoulème	Alexander II 1214-1249 son of William I = *Mary* of Picardy	Louis VIII 1223-1226 (the Lionheart) son of Philip II = *Blanche* of Castile
Henry III 1216-1272 son of John = *Eleanor* of Provence	Alexander III 1249-1286 son of Alexander II = *Margaret* — dau. of Henry III of England	Louis IX 1226-1270 (St. Louis) son of Louis VIII = *Margaret* of Provence
Edward I (Longshanks) 1272-1307 son of Henry III = *Eleanor* of Castile		Philip III 1270-1285 (the Bald) son of Louis IX = *Mary* of Brabant
	Margaret 1286-1290 (the Maid of Norway) (g-dau. of Alexander III) dau. of Eric II of Norway [unmarried]	Philip IV 1285-1314 (the Fair) son of Philip III = *Joan* of Navarre
	John Baliol 1292-1296 gt.g-son of Earl of Huntingdon (bro. of William the Lion)	

ENGLAND	SCOTLAND	FRANCE
	Edward I of England 1296-1306 [Scots Crown usurped]	Louis X 1314-1316 (the Headstrong) son of Philip I
Edward II (Caernarvon) 1307-1327 son of Edward I = *Isabella* of France dau. of Philip IV	Robert I (the Bruce) 1306-1329 gt.gt.g-son of Earl of Huntingdon (bro. of William the Lion) = 1 *Isabel* of Mar = 2 *Elizabeth* of Ulster	Philip V 1316-1322 (the Tall) son of Philip IV
Edward III (Windsor) 1327-1377 son of Edward II = *Philippa* of Hainault	David II 1324-1371 *d.s.p.* son of Robert I and *Elizabeth*	Charles IV 1322-1327 son of Philip IV Valois Philip VI 1328-1350 (nephew of Philip IV) son of Count Charles de Valois = 1 *Joan* of Burgundy John 1350-1364 (the Good) son of Philip VI = 2 *Blanche* of Boulogne

GUILHELM DE GELLONE AND GODEFROI DE BOUILLON

Merovingian Descent (7th - 12th century)

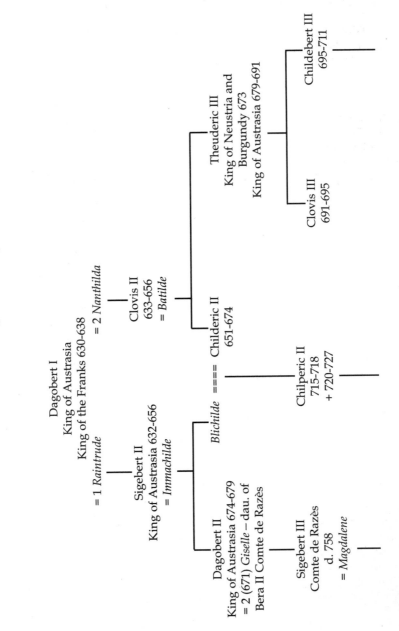

Dagobert I
King of Austrasia
King of the Franks 630-638
= 1 Raintrude
= 2 Nanthilda

Sigebert II
King of Austrasia 632-656
= Immachilde

Clovis II
633-656
= Batilde

Blichilde ==== Childeric II
651-674

Dagobert II
King of Austrasia 674-679
= 2 (671) Giselle – dau. of
Bera II Comte de Razès

Chilperic II
715-718
+ 720-727

Childeric II
651-674

Theuderic III
King of Neustria and
Burgundy 673
King of Austrasia 679-691

Sigebert III
Comte de Razès
d. 758
= Magdalene

Clovis III
691-695

Childebert III
695-711

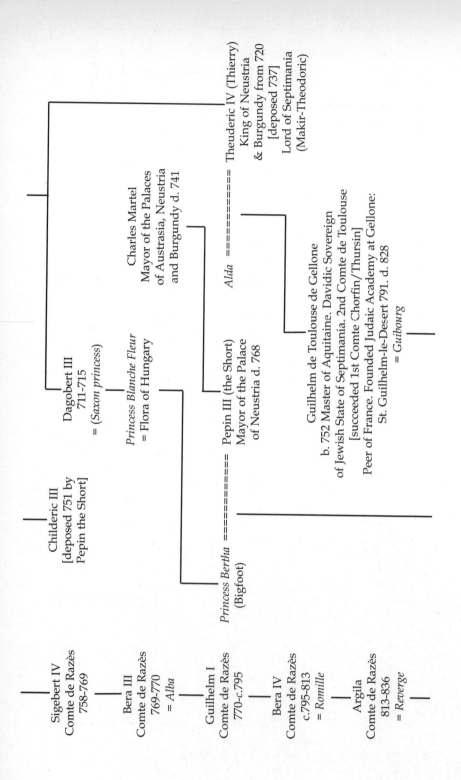

Childeric III
[deposed 751 by
Pepin the Short]

Dagobert III
711-715
= (Saxon princess)

Charles Martel
Mayor of the Palaces
of Austrasia, Neustria
and Burgundy d. 741

Theuderic IV (Thierry)
King of Neustria
& Burgundy from 720
[deposed 737]
Lord of Septimania
(Makir-Theodoric)

Princess Blanche Fleur
= Flora of Hungary

Pepin III (the Short)
Mayor of the Palace
of Neustria d. 768

Alda =============

Princess Bertha ===========
(Bigfoot)

Guilhelm de Toulouse de Gellone
b. 752 Master of Aquitaine. Davidic Sovereign
of Jewish State of Septimania. 2nd Comte de Toulouse
[succeeded 1st Comte Chorfin/Thursin]
Peer of France. Founded Judaic Academy at Gellone:
St. Guilhelm-le-Desert 791. d. 828
= Guibourg

Sigebert IV
Comte de Razès
758-769

Bera III
Comte de Razès
769-770
= Alba

Guilhelm I
Comte de Razès
770-c.795

Bera IV
Comte de Razès
c.795-813
= Romille

Argila
Comte de Razès
813-836
= Reverge

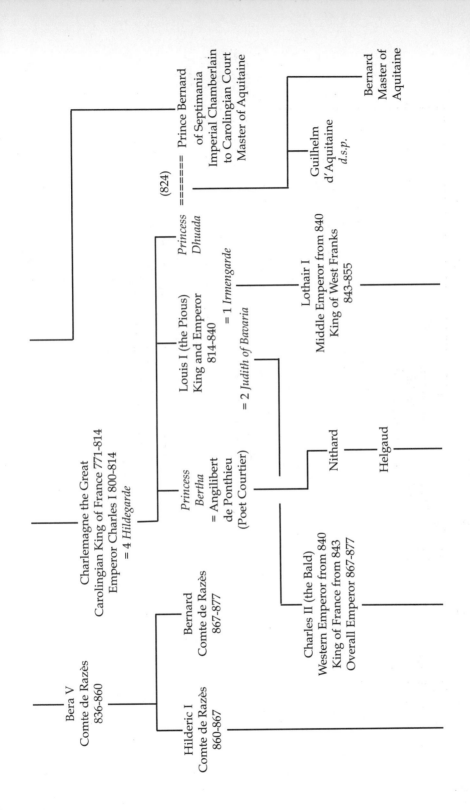

Bera V
Comte de Razès
836-860

Bernard
Comte de Razès
867-877

Hilderic I
Comte de Razès
860-867

Charlemagne the Great
Carolingian King of France 771-814
Emperor Charles I 800-814
= 4 *Hildegarde*

Princess
Bertha
= Angilibert
de Ponthieu
(Poet Courtier)

Louis I (the Pious)
King and Emperor
814-840

= 1 *Irmengarde*

= 2 *Judith of Bavaria*

Princess
Dhuada

(824)

Prince Bernard
of Septimania
Imperial Chamberlain
to Carolingian Court
Master of Aquitaine

Charles II (the Bald)
Western Emperor from 840
King of France from 843
Overall Emperor 867-877

Nithard

Helgaud

Lothair I
Middle Emperor from 840
King of West Franks
843-855

Guilhelm
d'Aquitaine
d.s.p.

Bernard
Master of
Aquitaine

399

Louis II
Emperor of Italy
855-975

Irmengarde
= Count Boso of Vienne
(Bouquet VIII
of Provence)

Louis II (the Stammerer)
King of France 877-879

Charles III (the Simple)
King of France 893-922
[deposed]
= *Eadgifu*

Louis IV (the Overseas)
King of France 936-954
= *Gerberga* – dau. of
Henry I (The Fowler)
of Germany

Herlouin

Roget

William
Comte de Ponthieu *c.*878
[champion of Louis II of France]

Ernicule I
Comte de Ponthieu from 965
Comte de Boulogne by grant of
Lothair, son of Louis II of France
= *Adeline* – heiress of Boulogne

Maud (Mahaut)
= Adolphe, Comte de Guisnes

Rotilde
dau. of
Charles II
(the Bald)

Sigebert V ============
Comte de Razès
877-885

Guilhelm II
d. 914 in England
= *Idoine*

Guilhelm III
d. 936

Arnaud
d. 952

Bera VI
(the Architect)
d. 975

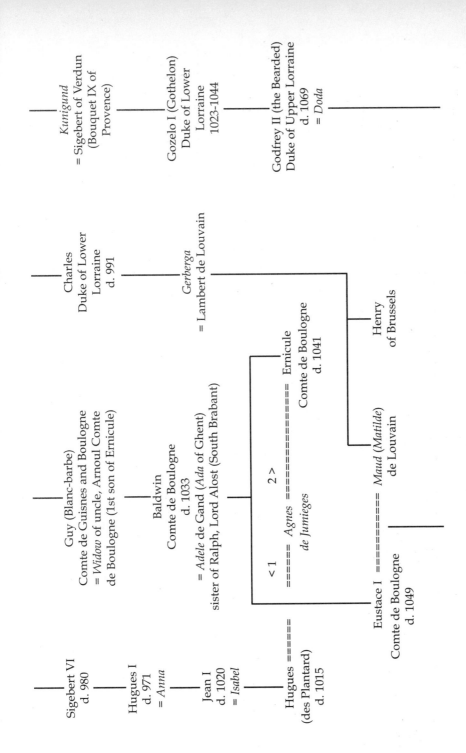

Sigebert VI
d. 980

Hugues I
d. 971
= *Anna*

Jean I
d. 1020
= *Isabel*

Hugues ======
(des Plantard)
d. 1015

Guy (Blanc-barbe)
Comte de Guisnes and Boulogne
= *Widow* of uncle, Arnoul Comte
de Boulogne (1st son of Ernicule)

Baldwin
Comte de Boulogne
d. 1033
= *Adele* de Gand (*Ada* of Ghent)
sister of Ralph, Lord Alost (South Brabant)

Charles
Duke of Lower
Lorraine
d. 991

Gerberga
= Lambert de Louvain

Kunigund
= Sigebert of Verdun
(Bouquet IX of
Provence)

Gozelo I (Gothelon)
Duke of Lower
Lorraine
1023-1044

Godfrey II (the Bearded)
Duke of Upper Lorraine
d. 1069
= *Doda*

Eustace I ========= *Maud* (*Matilde*)
Comte de Boulogne   de Louvain
d. 1049

<1 ===== *Agnes*
         de Jumieges

2 > ============ Ernicule
               Comte de Boulogne
               d. 1041

Henry
of Brussels

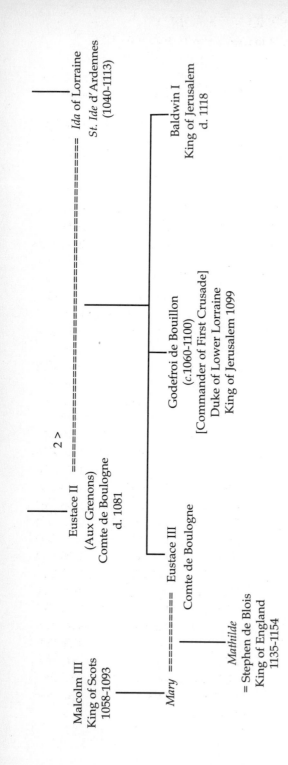

Malcolm III
King of Scots
1058-1093

Eustace II ================================ *Ida* of Lorraine
(Aux Grenons)   *St. Ide* d'Ardennes
Comte de Boulogne   (1040-1113)
d. 1081

2 >

Mary ============ Eustace III
Comte de Boulogne

Godefroi de Bouillon
(c.1060-1100)
[Commander of First Crusade]
Duke of Lower Lorraine
King of Jerusalem 1099

Baldwin I
King of Jerusalem
d. 1118

Mathilde
= Stephen de Blois
King of England
1135-1154

402

POPES (BISHOPS OF ROME)
From the Norman Conquest to the Lateran Treaty (1066 - 1929)

Pope	Year	Pope	Year	Pope	Year
Alexander II	1061-1073	Nicholas IV	1288-1292	Gregory XIII	1572-1585
Gregory VII	1073-1085	Celestine V	1294	Sixtus V	1585-1590
Victor III	1086-1087	Boniface VIII	1294-1303	Urban VII	1590
Urban II	1088-1099	Benedict XI	1303-1304	Gregory XIV	1590-1591
Paschal II	1099-1118	Clement V	1305-1314	Innocent IX	1591
Gelasius II	1118-1119	John XXII	1316-1334	Clement VIII	1592-1605
Callistus II	1119-1124	Benedict XII	1334-1342	Leo XI	1605
Honorius II	1124-1130	Clement VI	1342-1352	Paul V	1605-1621
Innocent II	1130-1143	Innocent VI	1352-1362	Gregory XV	1621-1623
Celestine II	1143-1144	Urban V	1362-1370	Urban VIII	1623-1644
Lucius II	1144-1145	Gregory XI	1370-1378	Innocent X	1644-1655
Eugene III	1145-1153	Urban VI	1378-1389	Alexander VII	1655-1667
Anastasius IV	1153-1154	Boniface IX	1389-1404	Clement IX	1667-1669
Adrian IV	1154-1159	Innocent VII	1404-1406	Clement X	1670-1676
Alexander III	1159-1181	Gregory XII	1406-1415	Innocent XI	1676-1689
Lucius III	1181-1185	Martin V	1417-1431	Alexander VIII	1689-1691
Urban III	1185-1187	Eugene IV	1431-1447	Innocent XII	1691-1700
Gregory VIII	1187	Nicholas V	1447-1455	Clement XI	1700-1721
Clement III	1187-1191	Callistus	1455-1458	Innocent XIII	1721-1724
Celestine III	1191-1198	Pius II	1458-1464	Benedict XIII	1724-1730
Innocent III	1198-1216	Paul II	1464-1471	Clement XII	1730-1740
Honorius II	1216-1227	Sixtus IV	1471-1484	Benedict XIV	1740-1758
Gregory IX	1227-1241	Innocent VIII	1484-1492	Clement XIII	1758-1769
Celestine IV	1241	Alexander VI	1492-1503	Clement XIV	1769-1774
Innocent V	1243-1254	Pius III	1503	Pius VI	1775-1799
Alexander IV	1254-1261	Julius II	1503-1513	Pius VII	1800-1823
Urban IV	1261-1264	Leo X	1513-1521	Leo XII	1823-1829
Clement IV	1265-1268	Adrian VI	1522-1523	Pius VIII	1829-1830
Gregory X	1271-1276	Clement VII	1523-1534	Gregory XVI	1831-1846
Innocent V	1276	Paul III	1534-1549	Pius IX	1846-1878
Adrian V	1276	Julius III	1550-1555	Leo XIII	1878-1903
John XXI	1276-1277	Marcellus II	1555	Pius X	1903-1914
Nicholas III	1277-1280	Paul IV	1555-1559	Benedict XV	1914-1922
Martin IV	1281-1285	Pius IV	1559-1565	Pius XI	1922-1939
Honorius IV	1285-1287	Pius V	1566-1572		

HOLY ROMAN EMPERORS
(1273 - 1806)

Emperor	House	Emperor	House
Rudolph I 1273-1291 of Habsburg (Rudolph I of Austria)	Habsburg	Albert V 1438-1439 gt.gt.g-son of Albert I = *Elizabeth*, Queen of Bohemia-Hungary dau. of Sigismund	Habsburg
Adolph 1291-1298 son of Walram II of Nassau	Nassau		
Albert I 1298-1308 son of Rudolph I	Habsburg	Frederick III 1440-1493 Archduke of Austria cousin of Albert V	Habsburg
Henry VII 1308-1313 of Luxembourg	Luxembourg	Maximillian I 1493-1519 son of Frederick III = *Mary* of Burgundy	Habsburg
Louis III 1314-1346 g-son of Rudolph I (via dau. *Matilda*) son of Louis II Duke of Bavaria	Wittelsbach	Charles V 1519-1558 (g-son of Maximilian) son of Philip of Burgundy and *Joanna* of Castile	Habsburg
Charles IV 1346-1378 King of Bohemia g-son of Henry VII (via son John, and *Elizabeth* of Bohemia)	Luxembourg	Ferdinand I 1558-1564 bro. of Charles V	Habsburg
		Maximillian II 1564-1576 son of Ferdinand I	Habsburg
Wenceslas 1378-1410 King of Bohemia son of Charles IV	Luxembourg	Rudolph II 1576-1612 son of Maximillian II	Habsburg
Sigismund 1410-1437 King of Bohemia bro. of Wenceslas = *Mary* of Hungary	Luxembourg	Matthias 1612-1619 King of Bohemia and Hungary bro. of Rudolph II	Habsburg

Emperor	House	Emperor	House
Ferdinand II 1619-1637 King of Bohemia and Hungary nephew of Matthias	Habsburg	Charles VII 1742-1745 Elector of Bavaria [contested inheritance of *Maria Theresa*]	Wittelsbach
Ferdinand III 1637-1657 son of Ferdinand II	Habsburg	Francis I 1745-1765 Francis of Lorraine = *Empress Maria Theresa*	Habsburg- Lorraine
Leopold I 1657-1705 son of Ferdinand III	Habsburg	Joseph II 1765-1790 son of Francis I [with *mother* to 1780]	Habsburg- Lorraine
Joseph I 1705-1711 son of Leopold I	Habsburg	Leopold II 1790-1792 son of Francis I	Habsburg- Lorraine
Charles VI 1711-1740 bro. of Joseph I	Habsburg	Francis II 1792-1806 Emperor of Austria son of Leopold II [last Holy Roman Emperor]	Habsburg- Lorraine
Empress Maria Theresa 1740-1742 dau. of Charles VI = Francis of Lorraine	Habsburg		

THE HOUSE OF STEWART AND CONTEMPORARY MONARCHS

England, Scotland and France (1371 - 1603)

ENGLAND	SCOTLAND	FRANCE
Plantagenets	Stewarts	Valois
Richard II (Bordeaux) 1377-1399 *d.s.p.* son of the Black Prince, and g-son of Edward III	Robert II 1371-1390 son of Walter, 3rd High Stewart, and *Marjorie Bruce* = *Elizabeth* — dau. of Sir Adam Mure of Rowallan	Charles V (the Wise) 1364-1380 son of John the Good = *Joan de Bourbon*
Henry IV (Bolingbroke) 1399-1413 [House of Lancaster] son of John O'Gaunt (Duke of Lancaster), and g-son of Edward III = *Mary de Bohun*	Robert III 1390-1406 [John, Earl of Carrick] son of Robert II = *Anabella* — dau. of John Drummond of Stobhall	Charles VI (the Mad) 1380-1422 son of Charles V = *Isabeau* of Bavaria [their dau. *Katherine* married Henry V of England]
Henry V (Monmouth) 1413-1422 [House of Lancaster] son of Henry IV = *Katherine de Valois* — dau. of Charles VI of France	James I 1406-1437 son of Robert III = *Joan Beaufort* of Somerset g-dau. of John of Gaunt	
Henry VI (Windsor) 1422-1461 [House of Lancaster] son of Henry V = *Margaret* — dau. of Rayner, Duke of Anjou, titular King of Jerusalem [deposed by Edward Duke of York]	James II 1437-1460 son of James I = *Maria* — dau. of Arnold van Egmond, Hertog van Gelre	Charles VII (the Well Served) 1422-1461 son of Charles VI = *Mary* of Anjou

ENGLAND	SCOTLAND	FRANCE
Edward IV 1461-1483 [House of York] son of Sir Richard Plantagenet, in descent from John of Gaunt's brother, Lionel, Duke of Clarence = *Elizabeth* — dau. of Richard Widville, Earl Rivers	James III 1460-1488 son of James II = *Margaret* — dau. of Christian I of Denmark	Louis XI 1461-1483 son of Charles VII = *Charlotte* of Savoy
Edward V 1483 *d.s.p.* [House of York] son of Edward IV [murdered before coronation, along with brother, Richard]		Charles VIII 1483-1498 son of Louis XI = *Anne* of Brittany
Richard III 1483-1485 [House of York] [killed at Bosworth Field] son of Sir Richard Plantagenet, and brother of Edward IV = *Anne* — dau. of Richard Neville, Earl of Warwick	James IV 1488-1513 son of James III = *Margaret Tudor* — dau. of Henry VII of England	Louis XII 1498-1515 Duke of Orleans grand-nephew of Charles VI = 1 *Joan* de Valois = 2 *Anne* of Brittany — widow of Charles VIII

Tudors

ENGLAND	SCOTLAND	FRANCE
Henry VII 1485-1509 son of Edmund Tudor, Earl of Richmond [in descent from *Katherine de Valois* (widow of Henry V) and her 2nd husband, Owen Tudor] and *Margaret Beaufort*, g-dau. of John O'Gaunt. = *Elizabeth* of York — dau. of Edward IV	James V 1513-1542 son of James IV = 2 *Marie* de Guise — Lorraine, dau. of Claude, Duc de Guise	François I 1515-1547 cousin of Louis XII = 1 *Claude* de France dau. of Louis XII = 2 *Eleanor* of Austria

ENGLAND	SCOTLAND	FRANCE
	Stuarts	

ENGLAND	SCOTLAND	FRANCE
Henry VIII 1509-1547 son of Henry VII = [with offspring] 1 *Catherine* – dau. of Ferdinand V of Aragon and Castille = 2 *Anne* – dau. of Sir Thomas Boleyn, Earl of Ormonde = 3 *Jane* – dau. of Sir John Seymour, and sister of Edward, Duke of Somerset	*Mary*, Queen of Scots 1542-1587 dau. of James V and *Marie* de Guise-Lorraine = 1 François II of France = 2 Henry Stewart, Lord Darnley – son of Matthew Earl of Lennox = 3 James Hepburn, Earl of Bothwell	Henri II 1547-1559 son of Francis I = *Catherine de Medici*
Edward VI 1547-1553 *d.s.p.* son of Henry VII and *Jane Seymour* [unmarried]		François II 1559-1560 *d.s.p.* son of Henri II (as Dauphin and King, he was the first husband of *Mary Stuart*, Queen of Scots)
Jane Grey 1553 dau. of Henry Grey, Duke of Suffolk, and g-dau. of Henry VII (inherited Crown by Will of Edward VI) [executed]		
Mary I (*Bloody Mary*) 1553-1558 *d.s.p.* dau. of Henry VIII and *Catherine* of Aragon = Philip II of Spain		Charles IX 1560-1574 *d.s.p.* son of Henri II and and brother of François II
Elizabeth I 1558-1603 *d.s.p.* dau. of Henry VII and *Anne Boleyn* [unmarried]	James VI of Scots 1567-1625 [James I of England from 1603 Union of Crowns] son of *Mary*, Queen of Scots, and Lord Darnley = *Anne* – dau. of Frederick II of Denmark and Norway	Henri III 1574-1589 *d.s.p.* son of Henri II and brother of François II

THE STUART KINGS AND CONTEMPORARY MONARCHS

Britain and France (1603 - 1688) — From the Union of Crowns to the Whig Revolution

ENGLAND

Elizabeth I Tudor
1558-1603 *d.s.p.*
dau. of Henry VIII and *Anne Boleyn*
[unmarried]

Union of Crowns
James VI of Scots became
James I of England in 1603

Stuart Kings of Britain

James I (VI of Scots)
1603-1625
son of *Mary*, Queen of Scots, and
Henry Stewart, Lord Darnley
= *Anne* — dau. of Frederick II of
Denmark and Norway

Charles I
1625-1649 [executed]
son of James I (VI)
= *Henrietta Maria* — dau. of Henri IV
of France

Commonwealth declared 1649
Oliver Cromwell
Lord Protector 1653-1658
Richard Cromwell
Lord Protector 1658-1659

Stuart Restoration 1660
Charles II
1660-1685 *d.s.p. legit.*
son of Charles I
= *Katherine* of Braganza —
Infanta of John IV of Portugal

James II (VII of Scots)
1685-1688
brother of Charles II
= 1 *Anne* — dau. of Edward Hyde,
Earl of Clarendon
= 2 *Mary D'Este* — dau. of Alphonso
IV of Modena
[deposed by Whig Revolution]

FRANCE

Henry III
1574-1589 *d.s.p.*
son of Henri II and
brother of François II

Bourbon

Henry IV
1589-1610
son of Antoine de Bourbon
and *Jeanne*, Queen of Navarre
= 2 *Marie de Medici*
[their dau. *Henrietta* married
Charles I of Britain]

Louis XIII
1610-1643
son of Henri IV
[policies under Cardinal de
Richelieu 1624-1642]
= *Anne* of Austria

Louis XIV
1643-1715
(The Sun King)
son of Louis XIII
[policies under Cardinal Mazarin
until 1661]
= *Maria Theresa* — Infanta of Philip
IV of Spain

DESCENT TO BONNIE PRINCE CHARLIE

Mary, Queen of Scots, line to Charles Edward Stuart

James V Stewart of Scots
b. 1512 (r. 1513-1542) d. 1542 at Falkland
= 2 (1538) *Marie de Guise-Lorraine*
(d. 1560) dau. of Claude, Duc de Guise

Mary Stuart, Queen of Scots
b. 1542 (r. 1542-1567) – forced abdication
[beheaded 1587 Fotheringay Castle]
= 2 (1565) Henry Stewart, Lord Darnley
Master of Lennox [murdered 1567]

James VI Stuart of Scots
b. 1566 (r. 1567-1625) d. 1625 in Herts
James I of England 1603-1625
= (1589) *Anne* (d. 1619) dau. of
King Frederick II of Denmark & Norway

Charles I Stuart of Britain
b. 1600 (r. 1625-1649) [beheaded 1649 in London]
= (1625) *Henrietta Maria* (d. 1669)
dau. of King Henri IV of France

Charles II Stuart of Britain
b. 1630 [succeeded father in 1649,
but not restored until 1660 after
period of Commonwealth]
(r. 1600-1685) *d.s.p.* legit.
= *Catherine de Braganza*, Infanta of
Portugal — dau. of John IV

James VII Stuart of Scots (James II of England)
b. 1633 (r. 1685-1688) — deposed by Whig Revolution (no abdication)
[succeeded brother, Charles II Stuart] d. at St. Germain 1701
= 2 (1673) *Mary Beatrix D'Este* (d. 1718)
dau. of Duke Alphonso IV of Modena

James Francis Edward Stuart — *de jure* James VIII of Scots (III of England)
(Chevalier St. George) b. 1688 (proclaimed 1701) d. 1766
= (1719) *Mary Clementina Sobieska* (d. 1735) — dau. of Prince
James Lewis Sobieski (son of King Jan III of Poland)

Charles Edward Louis Philip Casimir Stuart
(Bonnie Prince Charlie) *de jure* Charles III of Britain
b. 31 Dec 1720 (figuratively crowned at Holyrood Sept 1745) d. 31 Jan 1788

COUNTS OF ALBANY

De Jure High Stewards of Scotland (1720 to date)

(Nov 1785)

Prince Charles Edward Stuart ============= *Marguerite O'Dea d'Audibert*
1st Count of Albany   *de Lussan, Comtesse de Massillan*
(1720-1788) *de jure* Charles III   *(1749-1820)*
= [declaration 1746 – annulled 1766]
Clementina Walkinshaw of Barrowfield
Comtesse d'Alberstroff

Henry Benedict Stuart
Cardinal - Duke of York
(1725-1807)
de jure Henry I (IX)
d.s.p.

Charlotte de Johnstone Douglas
Duchess of Albany (1753-1789)
= (lover) Ferdinand de Rohan Guémène
Archbishop of Bordeaux

Prince Edward James Stuart (Count Stuarton)
2nd Count of Albany (1786-1845) *de jure* James IX (IV)
= (1809) *Maria Emmanuella Pasquini* (1789-1854)
dau. of Edouardo Guiseppe Pasquini (Italy)
and *Leonora*, Countessa di Vaglio

Prince Henry Edward Benedict Stuart
3rd Count of Albany (1809-1869) *de jure* Henry II (X)
= (1829) *Agnes Beatrix de Pescara* 1810-1878
dau. of Conte Anselmo Bernardo de Pescara
and *Aliena Gabrielle Barberini-Colonna,*
Principessa de Palestrina

Aglae Clementine
(1781-1825)
= (1812) Jehan de
la Tour d'Auvergne
son of Jacques
Prince de Bouillon

Marie Beatrice
(1783-1823)
= Philippe d'Auvergne
g.g-son of Godefroid
Duc de Bouillon

412

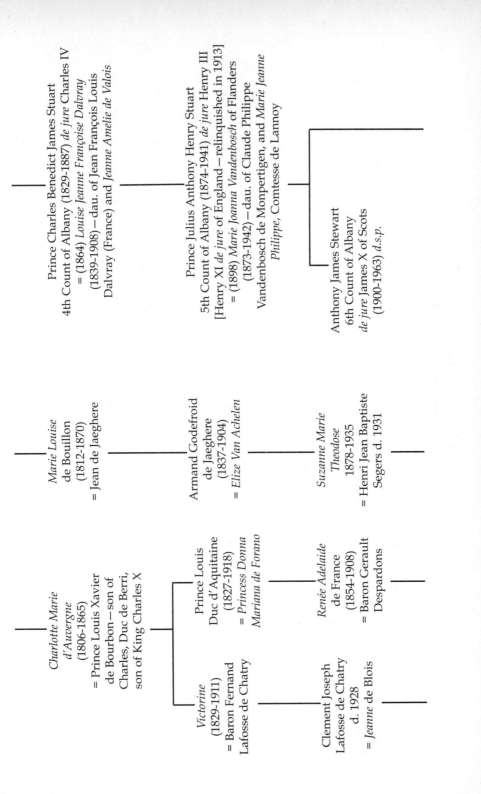

Prince Charles Benedict James Stuart
4th Count of Albany (1829-1887) *de jure* Charles IV
= (1864) *Louise Jeanne Françoise Dalvray*
(1839-1908) – dau. of Jean François Louis
Dalvray (France) and Jeanne Amelie de Valois

Prince Julius Anthony Henry Stuart
5th Count of Albany (1874-1941) *de jure* Henry III
[Henry XI *de jure* of England – relinquished in 1913]
= (1898) *Marie Joanna Vandenbosch of Flanders*
(1873-1942) – dau. of Claude Philippe
Vandenbosch de Monpertigen, and Marie Jeanne
Philippe, Comtesse de Lannoy

Anthony James Stewart
6th Count of Albany
de jure James X of Scots
(1900-1963) *d.s.p.*

Marie Louise
de Bouillon
(1812-1870)
= Jean de Jaeghere

Armand Godefroid
de Jaeghere
(1837-1904)
= *Elize Van Achelen*

Suzanne Marie
Theodose
1878-1935
= Henri Jean Baptiste
Segers d. 1931

Charlotte Marie
d'Auvergne
(1806-1865)
= Prince Louis Xavier
de Bourbon – son of
Charles, Duc de Berri,
son of King Charles X

Prince Louis
Duc d'Aquitaine
(1827-1918)
= *Princess Donna*
Mariana de Forano

Victorine
(1829-1911)
= Baron Fernand
Lafosse de Chatry

Renée Adelaide
de France
(1854-1908)
= Baron Gerault
Despardons

Clement Joseph
Lafosse de Chatry
d. 1928
= *Jeanne de Blois*

Fernand ========= *Josephine*

Maurice Lafosse de Chatry
1907-1978
= *Anne Michielsens*

Baron Gustave Lafosse
de Chatry b. 1935
Comte de Blois

Germaine Elize Segers ===============================
de la Tour d'Auvergne
Princess de Sedan
(1908-1992)

Julius Joseph James Stewart
of Annandale
(1906-1985)

===================================

Renée Julienne Stewart
Princess Royal of Strathearn
Lady Derneley b. 1934

=====================================

Prince Michael James Alexander Stewart
7th Count of Albany b. 1958
de jure High Steward and Alexander IV of Scots from 1963
Dynastic Stewart name inherited from mother and recorded by Registrars at birth
(the same as for Charles Windsor, Prince of Wales, who does not carry his father's name)

MONARCHS FROM THE WHIG REVOLUTION

Britain and France 1688 to the European Union

BRITAIN

Orange & Stuart

William III
1689-1702
Duke of Orange (Dutch)
son of William of Nassau and *Mary
Stuart* – dau. of Charles I
= *Mary Stuart (Queen Mary II)*
d.s.p. 1694 – dau. of James VII (II) and
1st wife *Anne Hyde*

Anne Stuart
1702-1714 *d.s.p.*
dau. of James VII (II)
and *Anne Hyde* of Clarendon

Hanover

George I
1714-1727
[House of Guelph]
Duke of Brunswick-Luneburg
son of Elector of Hanover, Germany
= *Sophia Dorothy* – dau. of George
William, Duke of Zelle

George II
1727-1760
Duke & Elector of Hanover
son of George I
= *Whilhelmina Caroline* – dau. of John
Frederick, Margrave of Brandenburgh-
Anspach

FRANCE

Bourbon

Continuation of Louis XIV
[*see* chart: *Stewart Kings
and Contemporary Monarchs*]
until 1715

Louis XV
1715-1774
(gt.g-son of Louis XIV)
son of Louis, Duke of Burgundy
(d. 1712), son of Louis the
Dauphin (d. 1711)
[policies under Cardinal Fleury
to 1743]
= *Marie Leczinska* of Poland
Mistresses: 1 *Jeanne, Mme de
Pompadour.* 2 *Marie, Mme du Barry*

French Colonies (Canada/India) lost
during Seven Years' War 1756-1763

BRITAIN	FRANCE

BRITAIN

George III
1760-1820
King of Hanover
(g-son of George II)
son of Frederick, Prince of Wales
= *Sophia Charlotte* — dau, of Charles,
Duke of Mecklenburg-Strelitz

FRANCE

Louis XVI
1774-1793
g-son of Louis XV
son of Louis the Dauphin (d. 1765)
= *Marie Antoinette* — dau. of
Emperor Francis I and *Empress
Maria Theresa.*
[Both Louis and *Marie Antoinette*
guillotined (1793) in Revolution]

French Revolution 1789-1799 abolished
absolute monarchy in France. Supreme
Court Parlement of Paris abolished in
1792 when First Republic proclaimed

Louis XVII
1793-1795
Nominal King of France
son of Louis XVI [died in prison]

George IV
1820-1830
King of Hanover
son of George III
= 2 *Caroline Amelia* — dau.
of Charles William Ferdinand,
Duke of Brunswick-Wölfenbuttel

Louis XVIII
1795-1824
Count of Provence. Nominal King of
France (uncle of Louis XVII). Brother of
Louis XVI. Lived in exile until 1814

Coup d'état by Napoleon Bonaparte
brought Revolution to an end in Nov.
1799. He was Consul from 1802 and
Emperor Napoleon I of the French 1804-
1815. Introduced the *Code* (Napoleon)
Civil, which still provides the basis of
French law. d. 1821

Charles X
1824-1830
Count of Artois
brother of Louis XVI and XVIII
English exile in Revolution
Returned to France 1824
Abdicated 1830

BRITAIN

William IV
1830-1837
King of Hanover
brother of George IV
= *Amelia Adelaide* — dau. of George
Frederick, Duke of Saxe Meiningen
[no surviving heir]

Victoria
1837-1901
(Alexandrina Victoria)
Regina et Imperiatrix
Niece of William IV: dau. of his brother,
Edward, Duke of Kent, and *Princess
Victoria Mary* — dau. of Francis
Frederick, Duke of Saxe-Saalfeld-
Coburg
= Francis Albert, Prince of Saxe
Coburg-Gotha, son of Ernest I of Saxe
Coburg and Gotha

Saxe Coburg-Gotha

Edward VII
1901-1910
(Albert Edward)
son of *Queen Victoria*
= *Princess Alexandra* — dau. of Christian
IX of Denmark

Windsor

Family name changed to
Windsor in World War I (1917) to veil
German heritage. Windsor was the
surname of King Edward III (d. 1377)

George V
1910-1936
son of Edward VII
= *Princess Mary* of Teck

Edward VIII
1936 [abdicated]
Duke of Windsor
1st son of George V
= *(Mrs) Wallis Simpson*

FRANCE

Louis Philippe
1830-1848
[The Citizen King]
son of Duke of Orleans in descent from
Philip of Orleans. Originally supported
Revolution against Bourbon monarchy.
Styled King of the French (not of
France). Abdicated — d. (England) 1850

1848 Revolution proclaimed Second
Republic, with forty-four successive
governments between 1918 and 1940

Subsequent to the 1830 abdication of
King Charles X, the House of Bourbon
retained its *de jure* heritage irrespective
of the politically elected Louis Philippe

Charles X's nominated successor was
his grandson, the Duc de Chambord
who was Henri V 1830–1833. He was
succeeded by his nephew, Louis, Duc
d'Aquitaine, as Louis XIX 1833–1918.

Louis died with no son, but nominated
the Spanish Bourbon line to succeed.
Thus, James, Duke of Segovia, 2nd son
of Alfonso XIII, became Jacques I of
France 1918–1975. His son, the Duc
d'Anjou and Cadiz, became Alfonse I
1975– 1989. The present successor is his
son, Louis Alfonso, Duc d'Anjou and
Cadiz, who has been *de jure* King Louis
XX from 1989

BRITAIN	FRANCE
George VI 1936-1952 [Prince Albert] 2nd son of George V = *Elizabeth Bowes-Lyon,* dau. of Claude, Earl of Strathmore	France fell to Germany in World War II Liberated in 1944. General De Gaulle established provisional government. Fourth Republic proclaimed in 1946
Elizabeth II 1952- dau. of George VI = (1947) Philip (Duke of Edinburgh) — son of Prince Andrew, son of King George I of Greece. Gt.g-son of Christian IX of Denmark. Descended in female line via mother, *Princess Alice* of Battenberg, from the German House of Hesse, and from *Queen Victoria*	
When Saxe Coburg-Gotha became Windsor in 1917, the Battenberg name was also changed to Mountbatten. Philip assumed the family name of Mountbatten on gaining British citizenship in 1947	
European Union (European Economic Community) (European Common Market) — an organization of Western States — was created in 1957 by the Treaty of Rome	De Gaulle recalled as President of the Fifth Republic 1958. Resigned 1969

BIBLIOGRAPHY

Aaron, Robert, *Jesus of Nazareth the Hidden Years* (trans. Frances Frenhaye), Hamish Hamilton, London, 1962.

Adam, Frank, Clans, Septs and Regiments of the Scottish Highlands (rev. Sir Thomas Innes of Learney), Johnston & Bacon, Edinburgh, 1965.

Adamnan, Saint, *A Life of Saint Columba* (trans. Wentworth Huyshe), George Routledge, London, 1908.

Adams, Henry, *Mont Saint Michel and Chartres*, Houghton Mifflin, Boston, 1913.

Albany, HRH Prince Michael of, *The Forgotten Monarchy of Scotland*, Element Books, Shaftesbury, 1998.

Allegro, John M., *The Dead Sea Scrolls*, Penguin, Harmondsworth, 1964.

Ames, Delano (trans.), *Greek Mythology* [from *Mythologie Générale Larousse*], Paul Hamlyn, London, 1963.

Anderson, Alan Orr, *Early Sources of Scottish History* (ed. Marjorie Anderson), Paul Watkins, London, 1990.

Anderson, Flavia, The Ancient Secret, Research into Lost Knowledge Organization - Thorsons, Wellingborough, 1953.

Anderson, Hugh, *Jesus and Christian Origins*, Oxford University Press, Oxford, 1964.

Anderson, Joseph, *Scotland in Early Christian Times*, David Douglas, Edinburgh, 1881.

Andressohn, John C., *The Ancestry and Life of Godfrey of Bouillon*, University of Indiana Press, Bloomington, 1947.

Aradi, Zsolt, *Shrines of Our Lady*, Farrar, Strauss & Young, New York, 1954.

Arrien, Angeles, The Tarot Handbook, Aquarian Press, Wellingborough, 1987.

Ashe, Geoffrey, *Camelot and the Vision of Albion*, Heinemann, London, 1971.

   —*Avalonian Quest*, Methuen, London, 1982.

Aveling, S. T., *Heraldry, Ancient and Modern*, Frederick Warne, London, 1873.

Baigent, Michael, with Leigh, Richard and Lincoln, Henry, *The Holy Blood and the Holy Grail*, Jonathan Cape, London, 1982.

   —*The Dead Sea Scrolls Deception*, Jonathan Cape, London, 1991.

   —*The Messianic Legacy*, Jonathan Cape, London, 1986.

Baigent, Michael and Leigh, Richard, *The Temple and the Lodge*, Jonathan Cape, London, 1989.

Bain, J., *Calendar of Documents Relating to Scotland*, H. M. Stationery Office, Edinburgh, 1881-88.

Bain, Robert, *The Clans and Tartans of Scotland*, Fontana - Collins, Glasgow, 1981.

Baldock, John, *Christian Symbolism*, Element Books, Shaftesbury, 1990.

— *The Alternative Gospel*, Element Books, Shaftesbury, 1998.

Bander, P., *The Prophecies of St. Malachy and St. Columbkille*, Colin Smythe, Gerrards Cross, 1979.

Barber, M., *The Trial of the Templars*, Cambridge University Press, Cambridge, 1978.

Barber, Richard, *The Knight and Chivalry*, Longman, London, 1970.

— *Arthur of Albion*, Boydell Press, London, 1971.

— *The Figure of Arthur*, Longman, London, 1972.

— *King Arthur in Legend and History*, Cardinal / Sphere, London, 1973.

- *The Arthurian Legends: An Illustrated Anthology*, Barnes & Noble, New York, 1993.

Barbour, John, *The Bruce*, William Mackenzie, Glasgow, 1909.

Barclay, James, *The Mind of Jesus*, Harper & Row, New York, 1960.

Baring-Gould, S. and Fisher, J., *The Lives of the British Saints*, Cymmrodorion Society, London, 1907-1913.

Barrow, G. W. S., *Robert Bruce and the Community of the Realm of Scotland*, Eyre & Spottiswoode, London, 1965.

— *The Kingdom of the Scots*, Edward Arnold, London, 1973.

Bartrum, Peter C., *Early Welsh Genealogical Tracts*, University of Wales Press, Cardiff, 1966.

Bayley, Harold, *The Lost Language of Symbolism*, Williams & Norgate, London, 1912.

Bede, The Venerable of Jarrow, *The Ecclesiastical History of the English Nation* (trans. J.A. Giles), Dent - Everyman, London, 1970.

Begg, Ean C. M., *The Cult of the Black Virgin*, Arkana, London, 1985.

Bernard de Clairvaux, *On the Song of Songs* (trans. Kilian Walsh), Cistercian Publishers, Michigan, 1976.

Birks, W. and Gilbert, R. A., *The Treasure of Montségur*, Crucible - Thorsons, London, 1987.

Black, Matthew, *The Scrolls and Christian Origins*, Thomas Nelson, London, 1961.

Blair, P. Hunter, *The Origins of Northumbria*, Northumberland Press, Gateshead, 1948.

Bogdanow, Fanni, *The Romance of the Grail*, Manchester University Press, Manchester, 1966.

Bowen, E. G., *The Settlements of the Celtic Saints in Wales*, University of Wales Press, Cardiff, 1956.

Brandon, S. G. F., *The Fall of Jerusalem and the Christian Church*, SPCK, London, 1951.

— *Jesus and the Zealots*, Charles Scribner's Sons, New York, 1967.

Broadhurst, Paul, *Tintagel and the Arthurian Myths*, Pendragon Press, Launceston, 1995.

— (with Miller, Hamish), *The Dance of the Dragon*, Pendragon Press, Launceston, 2000.

Bromwich, Rachel (trans.), *The Welsh Triads*, University of Wales Press, Cardiff, 1961.

Brooke, G., Temple Scroll Studies, Sheffield Academic Press, Sheffield, 1989.

Brook-Little, J. P., *Boutell's Heraldry*, Frederick Warne, London, 1969.

Bryant, Nigel (trans.), *Perlesvaus*, D. S. Brewer, Cambridge, 1978.

Bull, Norman J., *The Rise of the Church*, Heinemann, London, 1967.

Bultmann, Rudolf, *Primitive Christianity in its Contemporary Setting* (trans. R.H. Fuller), Fontana - Collins, Glasgow, 1960.

Burns, Jane E. (ed.), *The Vulgate Cycle*, Ohio State University Press, 1985.

Butler, E.M., *The Myth of the Magus*, Cambridge University Press, Cambridge, 1948.

Butterworth, G. W. (trans.), *Clement of Alexandria*, Heinemann, London, 1968.

Capellanus, Andreas, *The Art of Courtly Love* (trans. J. J. Parry), Columbia University Press, New York, 1941.

Cartwright, E. H., *Masonic Ritual*, Lewis Masonic, Shepperton, 1985.

Castries, Duc de, *The Lives of the Kings and Queens of France* [for Académie Francaise] (trans. Anne Dobell), Weidenfeld & Nicolson, London, 1979.

Catchpole, David R., *The Trial of Jesus*, E. J. Brill, Leiden, 1971.

Cavendish, Richard, *The Tarot*, Michael Joseph, London, 1975.

— *King Arthur and the Grail*, Weidenfeld & Nicolson, London, 1978.

Chadwick, Hector Munro, *Early Scotland, The Picts, Scots and Welsh of Southern Scotland*, Cambridge University Press, Cambridge, 1949.

— *Priscillian of Avila*, Oxford University Press, Oxford, 1976.

— *The Early Church*, Penguin, Harmondsworth, 1978.

Chadwick, Nora K. (ed.), *Studies in Early British History*, Cambridge University Press, Cambridge, 1954.

— *The Age of the Saints in the Early Celtic Church*, Oxford University Press, Oxford, 1961.

— *Celtic Britain*, Praeger, New York, 1963.

— *Celt and Saxon*, Cambridge University Press, Cambridge, 1964.

— *Early Brittany*, University of Wales Press, Cardiff, 1969.

— *The Celts*, Penguin, Harmondsworth, 1970.

Chambers, A.K., *Arthur of Britain*, Sidgwick & Jackson, London, 1966.

Charlsworth, M. P., *The Lost Province*, University of Wales Press, Cardiff, 1949.

Charpentier, Louis, *The Mysteries of Chartres Cathedral*, Research into Lost Knowledge Organization - Thorsons, Wellingborough, 1972.

Chase, Mary Ellen, *Life and Language in the Old Testament*, Collins, London, 1956.

Chrétien de Troyes, *The Story of the Grail* (trans. R. W. Linker), North Carolina Press, Chapel Hill, 1952.

— *Le Conte del Graal* (trans. Ruth Harwood Cline), University of Georgia Press, 1985.

— *Arthurian Romances*, Dent, London, 1987.

Clarke, G. (ed.), *Life of Merlin*, University of Wales Press, Cardiff, 1973.

Clement, Saint of Alexandria, *Clementine Homilies and Apostolical Constitutions* (trans.), Ante-Nicene Library, T. & T. Clark, Edinburgh, 1870.

Comfort, W. W., *Arthurian Romances*, E. P. Dutton, New York, 1914.

Conran, Anthony, *The Penguin Book of Welsh Verse*, Penguin, Harmondsworth, 1967.

Constantinus of Lyons (*c*.AD 480), *The Life of Saint Germanus of Auxerre* [in *The Western Fathers*] (ed. W. Levinson; trans. F.R. Hoare), Sheed & Ward, London, 1954.

Copley, Gordon K., *The Conquest of Wessex in the Sixth Century*, Phoenix House, London, 1954.

Cranfield, C. E. B., *The Gospel According to St. Mark*, Cambridge University Press, Cambridge, 1959.

Crankshaw, Edward, *The Fall of the House of Habsburg*, Longman, London, 1963.

Crossley-Holland, Kevin, *British Folk Tales*, Macmillan, London, 1971.

Cunliffe, Barry, *The Celtic World*, Bodley Head, London, 1979.

Currer-Briggs, N., *The Shroud and the Grail*, Weidenfeld & Nicolson, London, 1987.

Curtin, J., *Hero Tales of Ireland*, Macmillan, London, 1894.

Daniel, Glyn (ed.), *Encyclopedia of Archaeology*, Macmillan, London, 1978.

Danielou, Jean, *The Dead Sea Scrolls and Primitive Christianity* (trans. Salvator Attansio), New American Library, New York, 1962.

Dart, John, *The Laughing Saviour*, Harper & Row, New York, 1976.

Davidson, H. E., *Gods and Myths in Northern Europe*, Penguin, Harmondsworth, 1964.

Davidson, Marshall B., *The Concise History of France*, American Heritage, New York, 1971.

Davis, R. H. C., *A History of Medieval Europe*, Longmans Green, London, 1957.

Deacon, Richard, *A History of the British Secret Service*, Grafton - Collins, London, 1982.

Deanesly, Margaret, *A History of Early Medieval Europe 476-911*, Methuen, London, 1956.

Delaforge, G., *The Templar Tradition in the Age of Aquarius*, Threshold, Vermont, 1897.

Delaney, Frank, *Legends of the Celts*, Hodder & Stoughton, London, 1989.

　　— *The Celts*, Grafton - Collins, London, 1989.

Dill, Sir Samuel, *Roman Society in Gaul in the Merovingian Age*, Macmillan, London, 1926.

Dillon, Myles, *The Cycles of the Kings*, Oxford University Press, Oxford, 1946.

　　— (with Chadwick, Nora), *The Celtic Realms*, Weidenfeld & Nicolson, London, 1967.

Dobbs, B. J. T., *The Foundations of Newton's Alchemy*, Cambridge University Press, Cambridge, 1975.

Dodd, C. H., *Historical Tradition in the Fourth Gospel*, Cambridge University Press, Cambridge, 1963.

Doresse, Jean, *The Secret Books of the Egyptian Gnostics* (trans. Philip Mairet), Hollis & Carter, London, 1960.

Douglas, Alfred, *The Tarot*, Victor Gollancz, London, 1972.

Duncan, Anthony, *Celtic Christianity*, Element Books,Shaftesbury, 1992.

Dupont-Sommer, André, *The Essene Writings from Qumrân* (trans. G. Vermes), Basil Blackwell, Oxford, 1961.

— *The Jewish Sect of Qumrân and the Essenes*, Vallentine Mitchell, London, 1954.

Durman, Edward, *The Templars, Knights of God*, Aquarian Press, Wellingborough, 1988.

Eisenman, R. H., *Maccabees, Zadokites, Christians and Qumrân*, E. J. Brill, Leiden, 1983.

— *James the Just in the Habakkuk Pesher*, E. J. Brill, Leiden, 1986.

Eisler, Riane, *The Chalice and the Blade*, Harper & Row, New York, 1987.

Ellis, P. B., *The Celtic Empire*, Constable, London, 1990.

Eusebius of Caesaria, *History of the Church from Christ to Constantine* (trans. G.A. Williamson), Penguin, Harmondsworth, 1981.

— *Ecclesiastical History*, (trans. C.F. Crusé), George Bell, London, 1874.

Evans, Sebastian, *In Quest of the Holy Grail*, Dent, London, 1898.

— *The High History of the Holy Grail* [*Perlesvaus*] (trans.), Dent - Everyman, London, 1912.

Faber-Kaiser, Andraeus, *Jesus Died in Kashmir*, Abacus - Sphere, London, 1978.

Fairweather, Barbara, *Highland Heritage*, Glencoe and North Lorne Folk Museum, Argyll, 1984.

Farmer, D. H., *The Oxford Dictionary of Saints*, Clarendon Press, Oxford, 1978.

Feiling, Keith, *A History of England*, Book Club Associates, London, 1972.

Fell, Charlotte, *John Dee*, Constable, London, 1909.

Fife, Graham, *Arthur the King*, BBC Books, London, 1990.

Filliette, Edith, *Saint Mary Magdalene, Her Life and Times*, Society of St. Mary Magdalene, Newton Lower Falls, MA, 1983.

Finkel, A., *The Pharisees and the Teacher of Nazareth*, E. J. Brill, Leiden, 1964.

Fleetwood, Rev. John, *The Life of Our Lord and Saviour Jesus Christ*, William Mackenzie, Glasgow, 1900.

Foster, Joseph, *The Dictionary of Heraldry*, Studio Editions, London, 1994.

Fox-Davies, Arthur C., *A Complete Guide to Heraldry*, T. C. & E. C. Jack, Edinburgh, 1929.

Franz, Marie Louise Von, *Alchemy*, Inner City Books, Toronto, 1980.

Frappier, Jean, Chrétien de Troyes and his Work (trans. Raymond Cormier), Ohio State University Press, 1982.

Fuller, Jean Overton, *Sir Francis Bacon*, East-West Publications, London, 1981.

Furnival, Frederick J. (ed.), *The History of the Holy Grail* [from *Roman l'Estoire dou Saint Graal* by Sires Robert de Boron] (trans. Henry Lonelich Skynner), Early English Text Society - N. Turner, London, 1861.

Gantz, Jeffrey (trans.), *The Mabinogion*, Penguin, Harmondsworth, 1976.

Gardner, Laurence, *Genesis of the Grail Kings*, Bantam Press, London, 1999.

— *Realm of the Ring Lords*, MediaQuest, Ottery St. Mary, 2000.

Garmonsway, G. N. (trans.), *The Anglo-Saxon Chronicle*, Dent - Everyman, London, 1967.

Gaster, T. H., *Samaritan Eschatology — Oral Law and Ancient Traditions*, Search, London, 1932.

Geoffrey of Monmouth, *The Life of Merlin* (ed. J. Parry), University of Illinois Press, 1925.

— *The History of the Kings of Britain* (ed. Lewis Thorpe), Penguin, Harmondsworth, 1966.

Gildas, *De Excidio et Conquestu Britanniae* (trans. Michael Winterbottom), Phillimore, Chichester, 1978.

Gilson, Etienne, *The Mystical Theology of Saint Bernard* (trans. A. H. C. Downes), Sheed & Ward, London, 1940

Gimbutas, Marija, *The Gods and Goddesses of Old Europe*, Thames & Hudson, London, 1974.

Giot, P. R., *Brittany*, Thames and Hudson, London, 1960.

Godwin, Joscelyn, *Mystery Religions in the Ancient World*, Thames & Hudson, London, 1981.

Goodrich, Norma, *Merlin*, Franklin Watts, New York, 1989.

— *Arthur*, Franklin Watts, New York, 1989.

Gougaud, Dom Louis, *Christianity in Celtic Lands* (trans. Maud Joynt), Four Courts Press, Dublin, 1932.

Gould, R. F., *Gould's History of Freemasonry*, Caxton, London, 1933.

Grant, M., *The Jews in the Roman World*, Weidenfeld & Nicolson, London, 1973.

— *Herod The Great*, Weidenfeld & Nicolson, London, 1971.

Graves, Robert, *The White Goddess*, Faber & Faber, London, 1961.

— *Mammon and the Black Goddess*, Cassell, London, 1965.

— (with Podro, Joshua), *The Nazarene Gospel Restored*, Cassell, London, 1953.

Gray, Tony, *The Orange Order*, Bodley Head, London, 1972.

Green, Miranda, *The Gods of the Celts*, Alan Sutton, Gloucester, 1986.

Green, V. H. H., *The Hanoverians 1714-1815*, Edward Arnold, London, 1948.

Gregory of Tours, *A History of the Franks* (trans. Lewis Thorpe), Penguin, Harmondsworth, 1964.

Guest, Lady Charlotte (trans.), *The Mabinogion*, John Jones, Cardiff, 1977.

Guilliame de Tyre, *A History of Deeds Done Beyond the Sea* (trans, Emily A. Babcock and A .C. Krey), Columbia University Press, New York, 1943.

Gurney, Robert, *Celtic Heritage*, Chatto & Windus, London, 1969.

Guthrie, W. K. C., *The Greeks and Their Gods*, Methuen, London, 1950.

Hadas, Moses and Smith, Morton, *Heroes and Gods*, Freeport, New York, 1965.

Halsberghe, G. S., *The Cult of Sol Invictus*, E. J. Brill, Leiden, 1972.

Hamill, J., The Craft - *A History of English Freemasonry*, Crucible - Thorsons, London, 1986.

Harrison, Michael, *The Roots of Witchcraft*, Frederick Muller, London, 1973.

Harry, Rev. George Owen, *The Genealogy of the High and Mighty Monarch, James,* Simon Stafford, London, 1604.

Harvey, John, *The Plantagenets*, B. T. Batsford, London, 1959.

Hawking, Stephen, *A Brief History of Time*, Bantam Press, London, 1992.

Herford, R. Travers, *Christianity in Talmud and Midrash*, Williams & Norgate, London, 1903.

Herm, G., *The Celts*, Weidenfeld & Nicolson, London, 1976.

Hewins, Prof. W. A. S., *The Royal Saints of Britain*, Chiswick Press, London, 1929.

Hewison, James King, *The Isle of Bute in the Olden Time*, William Blackwood, Edinburgh, 1895.

Hodgkin, R. H., *A History of the Anglo-Saxons*, Oxford University Press, Oxford, 1952.

Hooke, S. H., *The Siege Perilous*, SCM Press, London, 1956.

Horne, Alexander, *King Solomon's Temple in the Masonic Tradition*, Aquarian Press, Wellingborough, 1972.

Howard, Michael, *The Occult Conspiracy*, Rider - Century Hutchinson, London, 1989.

Howarth, Stephen, *The Knights Templar*, Collins, London, 1982.

Hubert, Henry, The Rise of the Celts, Keegan Paul, London, 1934.

— *The Greatness and Decline of the Celts*, Keegan Paul, London, 1934.

Hulme, Edward F., *Symbolism in Christian Art*, Swann Sonnenschein, London, 1891.

Jacobus de Voragine, *The Golden Legend* (trans. William Caxton; ed. George V. O'Neill), Cambridge University Press, Cambridge, 1972.

James, B. S., *Saint Bernard of Clairvaux*, Harper, New York, 1957.

James, E. O., *The Cult of the Mother Goddess*, Thames & Hudson, London, 1959.

James, Montague R. (ed.), *The Apocryphal New Testament*, Clarendon Press, Oxford, 1924.

Jameson, Anna, *Legends of the Madonna*, Houghton Mifflin, Boston, 1895.

Jarman, A. O. H., *The Legend of Merlin*, University of Wales Press, Cardiff, 1960.

Jeremias, J., *Jerusalem in the Time of Jesus*, SCM Press, London, 1969.

Johnston, Rev. Thomas J., *A History of the Church of Ireland*, APCK, Dublin, 1953.

Joinville, Sire Jean de, *Chronicles of the Crusades* (trans. Margaret Shaw), Penguin, Harmondsworth, 1976.

Jonas, Hans, *The Gnostic Religion*, Routledge, London, 1992.

Jones, B. E., *Freemasons' Guide and Compendium*, Harrap, London 1956.

— *Freemasons' Book of the Royal Arch*, Harrap, London, 1957.

Josephus, Flavius, *The Jewish Wars* (trans. G. A. Williamson), Penguin, Harmondsworth, 1959.

— *Antiquities of the Jews* and *Wars of the Jews* (trans. W. Whiston), Thomas Nelson, London, 1862.

— *The Works of Flavius Josephus*, Milner & Sowerby, London, 1870.

Jowett, George F., *The Drama of the Lost Disciples*, Covenant Books, London, 1961.

Joyce, Donovan, *The Jesus Scroll*, Angus & Robertson, London, 1973.

Jung, Emma and Von Franz Marie Louise, *The Grail Legends* (trans. Andrea Dykes), Hodder & Stoughton, London, 1971.

Keating, Geoffrey, *The History of Ireland, 1640* (trans. David Comyn and Rev. P. S. Dinneen), Irish Texts Society, London, 1902-1914.

Kendrick, T. D., *A History of the Vikings*, Frank Cass, London, 1930.

Kennedy, B., *Knighthood in the Mort d'Arthur*, D. S. Brewer, Cambridge, 1986.

Kenney, James F., *The Sources for the Early History of Ireland*, Four Courts Press, Dublin, 1966.

Kenyon, K. M., Jerusalem: *Excavating 3000 Years of History*, Thames & Hudson, London, 1967.

Kermack, William R., *Scottish Highlands: A Short History c.300-1746*, Johnston & Bacon, Edinburgh, 1957.

Kersten, Holger and Gruber, Elmar R., *The Jesus Conspiracy*, Barnes & Noble, New York, 1995.

Knight, Christopher and Lomas, Robert, *The Hiram Key*, Century, London, 1996.

— *The Second Messiah*, Century, London, 1997.

Knight, G., *The Secret Tradition in Arthurian Legend*, Aquarian Press, Wellingborough, 1983.

Knight, S., *The Brotherhood, The Secret World of the Freemasons*, Granada, St. Albans, 1984.

Knowles, David, *The Monastic Order in England*, Cambridge University Press, Cambridge, 1950.

Knox, Wilfred, *Sources of the Synoptic Gospels*, Cambridge University Press, Cambridge, 1959.

Kramer, Samuel, *History Begins at Sumer*, Thames & Hudson, London, 1958.

— *The Sacred Marriage Rite*, Indiana University Press, Bloomington, 1969.

Lacordaire, Rev. Père, *Saint Mary Magdalene*, Thomas Richardson, Derby, 1880.

Lawrence, J., *Freemasonry, a Religion*, Kingsway, Eastbourne, 1987.

Layamon, *Arthurian Chronicles* (trans. Eugene Mason), Dent, London, 1972.

Lewis, Rev. Lionel Smithett, *Glastonbury, the Mother of Saints*, St. Stephen's Press, Bristol, 1925.

— *St. Joseph of Arimathea at Glastonbury*, A. R. Mobray, London, 1927.

Lincoln, Henry, *The Holy Place*, Jonathan Cape, London, 1991.

Lindsay, Jack, *The Normans and Their World*, Purnell, London, 1974.

Lloyd, Lewis C., *The Origins of Some Anglo-Norman Families* (ed. Charles Clay and David Douglas), Harleian Society, Leeds, 1951.

Lomax, Frank (trans.), *The Antiquities of Glastonbury*, Talbot - JMF Books, Llanerch, 1980.

Loomis, Roger Sherman, *The Grail - From Celtic Myth to Christian Symbolism*, University of Wales Press, Cardiff, 1963.

— *Celtic Myth and the Arthurian Romance*, Columbia University Press, New York, 1977.

— *Arthurian Literature in the Middle Ages*, Clarendon Press, Oxford, 1979.

Lucie-Smith, Edward, *Symbolist Art*, Thames & Hudson, London, 1972.

MacIain, R. R., *The Clans of the Scottish Highlands*, Webb & Bower, Exeter, 1983.

Mackenzie, Sir George, *A Defence of the Antiquity of the Royal Line of Scotland*, H. M. Printers, Andrew Anderson, Edinburgh, 1685.

Mackie, J. D. A, *A History of Scotland*, Pelican, Harmondsworth, 1964.

Maclean, G. R. D., *Praying With the Highland Christians*, Triangle - SPCK, London, 1988.

MacNeill, E., *Celtic Ireland*, Martin Lester, Dublin 1921, Academy Press, Dublin, 1981.

Malory, Sir Thomas, *Mort D'Arthur*, New York University Books, New York, 1961

— *Tales of King Arthur* (ed. Michael Senior), Book Club Associates, London, 1980.

Malvern, Marjorie, *Venus in Sackcloth*, Southern Illinois University Press, 1975.

Margoliouth, D. S., *Mohammed and the Rise of Islam*, Putnam, London, 1931.

Markale, Jean, *King Arthur, King of Kings* (trans. Christine Hauch), Gordon & Cremonesi, London, 1977.

— *Women of the Celts* (trans. A. Mygind, C. Hauch and P. Henry), Inner Traditions, Vermont, 1986.

Marsden, J., The Illustrated Colmcille, Macmillan, London, 1991.

Martin, Malachi, *The Decline and Fall of the Roman Church*, Secker & Warburg, London, 1982.

Matarasso, P. M. (trans.), *The Quest of the Holy Grail* [from the *Queste del Saint Graal*], Penguin, Harmondsworth, 1976.

Mathers, S. L. M., *Astral Projection, Ritual Magic and Alchemy*, Aquarian Press, Wellingborough, 1987.

Matthews, Caitlin, *The Celtic Tradition*, Element Books, Shaftesbury, 1989.

— *Arthur and the Sovereignty of Britain*, Arkana, London, 1989.

Matthews, John, *The Grail - Quest for the Eternal*, Thames & Hudson, London, 1981.

— *The Arthurian Tradition*, Element Books, Shaftesbury, 1989.

— *The Grail Tradition*, Element Books, Shaftesbury, 1990.

— *Household of the Grail*, Aquarian Press, Wellingborough, 1990.

McKendrick, Malvena, *A Concise History of Spain*, Cassell, London, 1972.

McMahon, Norbert, *The Story of the Hospitallers of Saint John of God*, M. H. Gill, Dublin, 1958.

Mead, G. R. S., *The Gnostic John the Baptiser*, John M. Watkins, London, 1924.

Meade, Marion, *Eleanor of Aquitaine*, Frederick Muller, London, 1978.

Michell, John, *Ancient Metrology*, Pentacle Books, Bristol, 1981.

— *The Dimensions of Paradise*, Thames & Hudson, London, 1988.

Milik, J. T., *Ten Years of Discovery in the Wilderness of Judaea* (trans. J. Strugnell), SCM Press, London, 1959.

Moncrieffe, Sir Iain of that Ilk, *The Highland Clans*, Barrie & Jenkins, London, 1982.

Morris, John, *The Age of Arthur*, Weidenfeld & Nicolson, London, 1973.

— *Annales Cambriae: The Annals of Wales*, Phillimore, Chichester, 1980.

Munch, P. A and Goss Rev. Dr., *The Chronicle of Man*, The Manx Society, Isle of Man, 1974.

Murray, John, *7th Duke of Atholl*, Chronicles of Atholl and Tullibardine Families, Ballantyne, London, 1908.

Nash-Williams, V. E., *The Early Christian Monuments of Wales*, University of Wales Press, Cardiff, 1950.

Nennius, *Historia Brittonium* (trans. John Morris), Phillimore, Chichester, 1980.

Newstead, Helaine., *Brân the Blessed in Arthurian Romance*, Columbia Univ. Press, New York, 1939.

Oldenbourg, Zoé, *Massacre at Montségur* (trans. Peter Green), Pantheon, New York, 1961.

Oman, Sir Charles, *England Before the Norman Conquest*, Methuen, London, 1938.

O'Rahilly, Cecile, *Ireland and Wales*, Longmans Green, London, 1924.

O'Rahilly, Thomas, *Early Irish History and Mythology*, Dublin Institute for Advanced Studies, Dublin, 1946.

Osman, Ahmed, *The House of The Messiah*, Harper Collins, London, 1992.

— *Moses Pharaoh of Egypt*, Grafton / Collins, London, 1990.

Owen, D. D. R., *The Evolution of the Grail Legend*, Oliver & Boyd, London, 1968.

Pagels, Elaine, *The Gnostic Gospels*, Weidenfeld & Nicolson, London, 1980.

Paine, Lauren, *Britain's Intelligence Service*, Robert Hale, London, 1979.

Painter, Sidney, *A History of the Middle Ages*, Macmillan, London, 1973.

Patai, Raphael, *The Hebrew Goddess*, Wayne State University Press, Detroit, 1967.

Pennick, Nigel, *Sacred Geometry*, Turnstone, Wellingborough, 1980.

Perowne, S., *The Life and Times of Herod the Great*, Hodder & Stoughton, London, 1956.

— *The Later Herods*, Hodder & Stoughton, London, 1958.

Petrie, Sir Charles, *The Stuarts*, Eyre & Spottiswoode, London, 1937.

Phillips, Graham and Keatman, Martin, *King Arthur, the True Story*, Century, London, 1992.

— *The Shakespeare Conspiracy*, Century, London, 1994.

Piggot, Stuart, *The Druids*, Penguin, Harmondsworth ,1974.

Pincus-Witten, R., *Occult Symbolism in France*, Garland, London, 1976.

Platt, Rutherford H. (ed.), *The Lost Books of the Bible*, World Publishing, New York, 1963.

Platts, Beryl, *Origins of Heraldry*, Proctor Press, London, 1980.

— *Scottish Hazard*, Proctor Press, London, 1985-1990.

Pollard, Alfred, *The Romance of King Arthur*, Macmillan, London, 1979.

Pope, Marvin H., *Song of Songs*, Garden City - Doubleday, New York, 1977.

Price, Glanville (trans.), *William, Count of Orange* [French trad.], Dent, London, 1975.

Pryde, G. S., *The Treaty of Union Between Scotland and England 1707*, Thomas Nelson, London, 1950.

Qualls-Corbett, Nancy, *The Sacred Prostitute*, Inner City Books, Toronto, 1988.

Rees, Alwyn and Brinley, *Celtic Heritage*, Thames & Hudson, London, 1961.

Rees, Rev. W. J. Rice, *An Essay on the Welsh Saints*, Longman, London, 1836.

— *Lives of the Cambro-British Saints*, Welsh MSS Society - Longman, London, 1853.

Rhys, John, *Celtic Folklore*, Clarendon Press, Oxford, 1901.

— (with Brynmore-Jones D.), *The Welsh People*, T. Fisher Unwin, London, 1900.

Richards, Steve, *Levitation*, Thorsons, Wellingborough 1980.

Richey, Margaret Fitzgerald, *Studies of Wolfram Von Eschenbach*, Oliver & Boyd, London, 1957.

Ringgren, Helmer, *The Faith of Qumrân* (trans. Emile T. Sander), Fondress Press, Philadelphia, 1973.

Roberts, J. M., *The Mythology of the Secret Societies*, Granada, St. Albans, 1974.

Robinson, James M., *The Nag Hammadi Library*, Coptic Gnostic Library: Institute for Antiquity and Christianity, E. J. Brill, Leiden, 1977.

Roget, F. F., *French History, Literature and Philology*, Williams & Norgate, London, 1904.

Rohl, David, *A Test of Time*, Century, London, 1995.

Ross, Anne, *Pagan Celtic Britain*, Cardinal - Sphere Books, London, 1974.

Rougemont, Denis de, *Love in the Western World* (trans. Montgomery Belgion), Princeton University Press, New Jersey, 1983.

Round, J. Horace, *Calendar of Documents Preserved in France 918-1206*, Eyre & Spottiswoode, London, 1899.

— *Studies in Peerage and Family History*, Constable, London, 1901.

Roux, George, Ancient Iraq, Penguin, Harmondsworth, 1988.

Runciman, Steven, *A History of the Crusades*, Cambridge University Press, Cambridge, 1951.

Rutherford, Ward, *The Druids and Their Heritage*, Gordon & Cremonesi, London, 1978.

Sackville-West, V., *Saint Joan of Arc*, Michael Joseph, London, 1936.

Schonfield, Hugh J., *The Authentic New Testament*, Denis Dobson, London, 1956.

— *The Essene Odyssey*, Element Books,Shaftesbury, 1984.

— *The Passover Plot*, Element Books,Shaftesbury, 1985.

Scott, John, *The Early History of Glastonbury*, Boydell Press, London, 1981.

Seton, Walter, *Relations of Henry, Cardinal York, With the British Government*, The Royal Historical Society, London, 1919.

Seward, Desmond, *The Monks of War*, Paladin - Granada, St. Albans, 1974.

Shaw, R. Cunliffe, *Post Roman Carlisle and the Kingdoms of the North-West*, Guardian Press, Preston, 1964.

Silberer, Herbert, *Hidden Symbolism of Alchemy and the Occult Arts*, Dover Publications, New York, 1971.

Simms, Katharine, *From Kings to Warlords*, Boydell Press, London, 1987.

Sinclair, Andrew, *The Sword and the Grail*, Crown, New York, 1992.

Skeels, Dell, The Romance of Perceval, University of Washington Press, 1966.

Skeet, Francis J. A, *The Life and Letters of HRH Charlotte, Duchess of Albany*, Eyre & Spottiswoode, London, 1922.

Skene, William Forbes, *Chronicles of the Picts and Scots*, H. M. General Register, Edinburgh, 1867.

— *The Four Ancient Books of Wales*, David Douglas, Edinburgh, 1868.

— *Celtic Scotland*, David Douglas, Edinburgh, 1886-1890.

Smallwood. E. M., *The Jews Under Roman Rule*, E. J. Brill, Leiden, 1976.

Smith, George A., *The Historical Geography of the Holy Land*, Fontana - Collins, Glasgow, 1966.

Smith, Jonathan Riley, *The Knights of Saint John of Jerusalem and Cyprus*, Macmillan, London, 1987.

Smith, Morton, *The Secret Gospel*, Victor Gollancz, London, 1974.

Spence, Keith, *Brittany and the Bretons*, Victor Gollancz, London, 1978.

Stanley, John Edgcumbe, *King René d'Anjou and his Seven Queens*, John Long, London, 1912.

Starbird, Margaret, *The Woman With the Alabaster Jar*, Bear, Santa Fe, 1993.

Steiner, R., *An Outline of Occult Science*, Anthroposophic Press, New York, 1972.

Stenton, F. M., *Anglo-Saxon England*, Oxford University Press, Oxford, 1950.

Stewart, Maj. John of Ardvorlich, *The Stewarts*, Johnston & Bacon, Edinburgh, 1954.

Stewart, R. J., *The Mystic Life of Merlin*, Arkana, London, 1986.

Stone, Merlin, *When God Was a Woman*, Dial Press, New York, 1976.

Tacitus, *The Annals of Imperial Rome* (trans Michael Grant), Cassell, London, 1963.

Tatlock, J. S. P., *The Legendary History of Britain*, University of California, 1950.

Taylor, Gladys, *Our Neglected Heritage*, Covenant Books, London, 1969-74.

Taylor, J. W., *The Coming of the Saints*, Covenant Books, London, 1969.

Thackery, H. St. John, *Josephus the Man and Historian*, KTAV, Hoboken, NJ, 1967.

Thiering, Barbara, *Jesus the Man*, Doubleday Transworld, London, 1992.

Thomas, Charles, *Britain and Ireland in Early Christian Times*, Thames & Hudson, London, 1971.

—*Celtic Britain*, Thames & Hudson, London, 1986.

Thomson, E. A., *A History of Atilla and the Huns*, Clarendon Press, Oxford, 1948.

Thompson, J. M., *The French Revolution*, Basil Blackwell, Oxford, 1964.

Thorpe, Lewis (trans.), *The Life of Charlemagne*, Penguin, Harmondsworth, 1979.
Times, The, *Atlas of the Bible*, Times Books, London, 1987.

Tolstoy, Count Nikolai, *The Quest for Merlin*, Hamish Hamilton, London, 1985.

Topsfield, L. T., *A Study of the Arthurian Romances of Chrétien de Troyes*, Cambridge University Press, Cambridge, 1981.

Ullman, W., *A History of Political Thought in the Middle Ages*, Penguin, Harmondsworth, 1970.

Vermes, Geza, *The Dead Sea Scrolls in English*, Pelican, Harmondsworth, 1987.

Von Däniken, Erich, *Chariots of the Gods*, Souvenir Press, London, 1969.

Von Eschenbach, Wolfram, *Parzival* (ed. Hugh D. Sacker), Cambridge University Press, Cambridge, 1963.

Wace, Robert, *Arthurian Chronicles* (trans. Eugene Mason), Dent, London, 1972.

Wade-Evans, Arthur W., *Welsh Christian Origins*, Alden Press, Oxford, 1934.

Waite, Arthur E., *The Hidden Church of the Holy Grail*, Rebman, London, 1909.

—*The New Encyclopedia of Freemasonry*, Weathervane, New York, 1970.

Walker, Benjamin, *Gnosticism*, Aquarian Press, Wellingborough, 1983.

Wallace-Hadrill, J. M., *The Long Haired Kings*, Methuen, London, 1962.

Wallace-Murphy, Tim and Hopkins, Marilyn, *Rosslyn*, Element Books, Shaftesbury, 1999.

Ward, J. S. M., *Who Was Hiram Abiff?*, Baskerville, London 1925.

—*Freemasonry and the Ancient Gods*, Baskerville, London, 1926.

Warren, F. E., *The Liturgy of the Celtic Church*, Oxford University Press, Oxford, 1881.

Watson, W. J., *The History of the Celtic Place Names of Scotland*, William Blackwood, Edinburgh, 1926.

Webster, K. G. T. (trans.), *Lanzelet*, Columbia University Press, New York, 1951.

Wells, H. G., *The Outline of History*, Cassell, London, 1920.

Westwood, Jennifer, *A Guide to Legendary Britain*, Paladin, London, 1987.

Whitelock, Dorothy, *English Historical Documents AD 500-1042*, Eyre & Spottiswoode, London, 1955

William of Malmesbury, *Chronicles of the Kings of England*, Bell and Daldy, London, 1866.

Williams, A. H., *An Introduction to the History of Wales*, University of Wales Press, Cardiff, 1962.

Williamson, G. A, *The World of Josephus*, Secker & Warburg, London, 1964.

Williamson, John, *The Oak King, the Holly King and the Unicorn*, Harper & Row, New York, 1986.

Wilson, A. N., *Jesus*, Sinclair Stevenson, London, 1992.

Wilson, E., *The Dead Sea Scrolls*, Collins, London, 1971.

Wood, David, *Genisis*, Baton Press, Tunbridge Wells, 1985.

    (with Campbell, Ian), *Geneset*, Bellevue Books, Sunbury On Thames, 1994

Wood, Michael, *In Search of the Dark Ages*, BBC Books, London, 1981.

Woolley, C. Leonard, *Ur of the Chaldees*, Ernest Benn, London, 1930.

Yadin, Yigael, *The Temple Scroll: Hidden Law*, Weidenfeld & Nicolson, London, 1985.

    —*Masada — Herod's Last Fortress*, Weidenfeld & Nicolson, London, 1966.

Yates, Frances A., *The Rosicrucian Enlightenment*, Routledge & Kegan Paul, London, 1972.

Zuckerman, Arthur J., *A Jewish Princedom in Feudal France*, Columbia University Press, New York, 1972.

Peerages and Registers

Anderson, James, *Royal Genealogies*, 1732-1736.

Burke's *Peerage and Baronetage*, 1840.

Burke's *Landed Gentry*, 1848.

Burke's *Extinct and Dormant Peerages*, 1952.

Douglas, Sir Robert of Glenbervie, *The Peerage of Scotland*, 1764.

    — *Baronage of Scotland*, 1798.

The Great Seal Register of Scotland.

Massue, Melville Henry, 9th Marquis of Ruvigny & Raineval, *The Royal Blood of Britain*, 1903.

    — *The Jacobite Peerage, Baronage, Knightage and Grants of Honour*, 1904.

    — *The Titled Nobility of Europe*, 1914.

Paul, Sir James Balfour, Lord Lyon, *Ordinary of Scottish Arms*, 1903.

    — *The Scots Peerage*, 1904-1914

The Privy Seal Register of Scotland

Nag Hammadi Codices and Gnostic Tractates

Prayer of the Apostle Paul, Apocryphon of James, Gospel of Truth, Treatise on Resurrection, Tripartite Tractate, Apocryphon of John, Gospel of Thomas, Gospel of Philip, Hypostatis of the Archons, On the Origin of the World, Exegesis on the Soul, Book of Thomas the Contender, Gospel of the Egyptians, Eugnostos the Blessed, Sophia of Jesus Christ, Dialogue of the Saviour, Apocalypse of Paul, Apocalypse of James, Apocalypse of Adam, Acts of Peter and the Twelve Apostles, Thunder — Perfect Mind, Authoritative Teaching, Concept of Our Great Power, Plato Republic, Discourse on the Eighth and Ninth, Prayer of Thanksgiving, Asclepius, Paraphrase of Shem, Second Treatise of the Great Seth, Apocalypse of Peter, Teachings of Sylvanus, Three Steles of Seth, Zostrianos, Peter's Letter to Philip, Melchizedek, Thought of Norea, Testimony of Truth, Marsanes, interpretation of Knowledge, Valentinian Exposition, On the Anointing, On Baptism, On the Eucharist, Allogenes, Hypsiphrone, Sentences of Sextus, Trimorphic Protennoia, Act of Peter, Gospel of Mary.

Apocryphal Gospels, Acts, Epistles and Discourses
(Including Testimonies and Fragments)

Gospel According to the Hebrews, Gospel of the Ebionites, Gospel According to the Egyptians, Gospel of Matthias, Gospel of Peter, The Preaching of Peter, The Pistis Sophia, The Fayoum Gospel, Acts of Paul, Book of James, Book of Thomas, Gospel of Nicodemus, Gospel of Bartholomew, Book of John the Evangelist, Assumption of the Virgin, Acts of John, Acts of Andrew, Acts of Thomas, Acts of Philip, Letters of Christ and Abgarus, Letter of Lentulus, Epistle to the Laodiceans, Correspondence of Paul and Seneca, Unknown Gospel, Birth of Mary, Gospel of Eve, Lesser Questions of Mary, Prophecies of Parchor, Ascents of James, Book of Elxai, Memoria of the Apostles, Gelasian Degree, Stichometry of Nicephorus, Synopsis of Pseudo-Athanasius, Secrets of Enoch.

Annals, Chronicles and Manuscripts

Anglo-Saxon Chronicles:
Compiled from the 9th century (monastic various), ed. B. Thorpe, 1861

Annales Cambriae:
Compiled 10th century — MS to 924 Edited by Egerton Phillimore — *Y Cymmrodor 9* — Cymmrodorion Society 1888.

Annals of Clonmacnoise:
Trans. 1627 (from early MS) by Conell Mageoghagan. Including *Synchronisms of Fland Mainistrech* — Compiled 11th century in Bute. Continuations: *The Book of Lecain*, 1418, ed. Denis Murphy, Royal Society of Antiquities of Ireland, 1896.

Annals of Innisfallen:
Compiled 1215, Co. Kerry — Bodleian MS. Dr. C. O'Connor edition — *Rerum Hibernicarum Scriptores,* 1825.

Annals of the Kingdom of Ireland of the Four Masters:
Compiled 1632-1636 — *Annals of Donegal*, Michael O'Clery + 3 O'Clerys and Forfeasa O'Mulconry, ed. John O'Donovan, Dublin, 1851.

Annals of Tigernach:
Compiled 1017-1088 — Tigernach Ua-Broein of Clonmacnoise, ed. Whitley Stokes, *Revue Celtique*, 1896.

Annals of Ulster:
Compiled pre-1498 — Cathal MacManus, Fermanagh + Continuation, ed. W. M. Hennessey and R. MacCarthy — Dublin, 1887-1901.

Archaelogica Britannica:
Edward Lloyd — published 1707. Ref. *Hengwrt MSS*, catalogued by William Maurice, 1658 (*Wynnstay MS 10*, Nat.Lib. Wales), *Hengwrt MS 33* edit from *Wynnstay MS 10* by Prof. A. O. H. Jarman in *Ymddiddan Myrddin a Thaliesin*. *Hengwrt MS 33* (Hanesyn Hen), copies in *Cardiff* and *Penairth* MSS. Including *Achu Brenhinoedd a Thywysogion*, *Bonedd yr Arwyr, Hen Lwythau Gwynedd a'r Mars & Plant Brychan*.

Bonedd Gwyr-y-Gogledd:
Lineage of the Men of the North — *Penairth* (Nat.Lib.Wales) *MS 45* (13th cty); *Penairth MS 75* (16th cty); *Penairth MS 127* (*c*.1510); *Penairth MS 128* (*c*. 1560); *Penairth MS 129* (early 16th cty); *Penairth MS 253* (16th cty.).

Bonedd-y-Saint:
Lineage of the Saints — 12th cty. Various as given in MSS: *Harleian* (Brit.Mus.); *Cae Cyriog MS 3* (Nat.Lib.Wales); *Llangibby MSS* (Nat.Lib. Wales); *Llanstephan MS 28* (Nat.Lib. Wales); *Penairth MSS* (Nat.Lib. Wales); *Rawlinson B MSS* (Bodleian); *Achau'r Saint* tract — Pedigress of the Saints in MSS *Cardiff* and *Penairth*.

Book of Ballymote:
Compiled 15th century. Photo-fac., ed. Robert Atkinson, Royal Irish Academy, Dublin, 1887.

Book of Kells:
Compiled (MS copied) 12th century—ed. J. O'Donovan, Irish Archaeological Society. 1846.

Book of Leinster:
Compiled 1160/1170—*Book of Glendalough*. Including *Tract on the Picts*—*Leabhar Gabhala*, R. Atkinson edition, Dublin, 1880. Transcript by Joseph O'Longan— Facsimile, Royal Irish Academy, Dublin, 1880.

Book of Lismore:
Compiled 15th century—*Saints from B of L* edition, W. Stokes, 1890.

Book of Llandaff:
Compiled *c.* 1132—ed. W. J, Rees, Llandovery, 1840.

Book of Ui Maine:
Orig. *c.*1394—Irish Manuscripts Commission; facsimile, Dublin, 1942.

Breviary of Aberdeen:
Compiled 1509/10—Coll. Bishop William of Aberdeen. Editions: Spalding Club, Maitland Club, Bannantyne Club—all 1854.

Chronicle of Holyrood:
Compiled *c.*12th century Holyrood Abbey—trans. Joseph Stevenson in *Church Historians of England*, 1856.

Chronicle of Man:
Compiled 13th century—trans. Joseph Stevenson in *Church Historians of England*, 1856.

Chronicle of Melrose:
Compiled from 12th century—trans. Joseph Stevenson in *Church Historians of England*, 1856.

*Chronicles of the King*s:
Including *Chronicle of the Picts*; *Chronicle of the Scots of Dalriata*; *Chronicle of Scotland*. Compiled from 14th century: *Chronicles of the Picts and Scots* , William Forbes Skene, 1867.

Cognatio Brychan:
Cotton MS (Brit.Mus.) *Domitian i*—Sir John Price of Brecon, 1502-55. Egerton Phillimore text in *Y Cymmroder 9*, 1888. Wade-Evans text in *Y Cymmroder 19*, 1906 and *Vita Sanctorum Britanniae et Genealogiae* , Cardiff, 1944.

De Situ Brecheniauc:
Cotton MS (Brit.Mus.) *Vespasian A xiv*—*c.*1200. Egerton Phillimore text in *Y Cymmroder 9*, 1888. Wade-Evans text in *Y Cymmroder 19*, 1906 and *Vita Sanctorum Britanniae et Genealogiae*, Cardiff, 1944.

De Excidio et Conquestu Britanniae:
Compiled 6th century, Gildas III—trans. J. A. Giles, 1841-48 and Hugh Williams, Cymmrodorion Society, 1899.

Domesday Book:
Compiled 1086 — trans. *Victoria County Histories*.

Duan Albanach:
Compiled 11th century. Irish MS. Dudley M'Firbis, 1650. 19th century edit. William Forbes Skene.

Hanes Gruffudd ap Cynan:
Cotton MS (Brit.Mus.) *Vitellius C ix — c.*1600; *Penairth MS 17* (Nat.Lib. Wales); *Penairth MS 267*, John Jones, 1641. Text edits Arthur Jones in *The History of Gruffydd ap Cynan*, Manchester, 1910.

Historia Britonum:
Nennius edition 858 — *Harleian MS — Vatican MS — Paris MS*. Saxon and Welsh additions/Irish and Pictish additions, trans. J. A. Giles, 1848. *Chartres MS 98 Z — c.* 900. *Vatican MS Reginae*, 1964 M, 11th cty. *Harleian MS* (Brit.Mus.) *3859 H — c.*1100. Egerton Phillimore text in *Y Cymmrodor 7*, 1886. Wade-Evans edit. in *Y Cymmrodor 19*, 1906. *Cotton MS* (Brit.Mus.) *Vespasian D xxi* – 12th cty. *Cotton MS* (Brit.Mus.). *Caligula A viii* – 12th cty.

Historia Ecclesiastica Gentis Angolorum:
Compiled 731, Bede of Jarrow. Ed. C. Plummer, Oxford, 1896. (2) Edit. Bertram Colgrave and R. A. B. Mynors, Oxford, 1969.

Historia Regum Britannie:
Compiled *c.*1147, Geoffrey of Monmouth. Trans. J. A. Giles. Caxton Society, 1844.

History of Ireland:
Compiled *c.*1640, Geoffrey Keating. Trans. David Comyn and Rev. Patrick S. Dinneen, Irish Texts Society, 1902-1914.

History of Scotland:
Compiled 14th century — John of Fordun, Chaplain of Church of Aberdeen. Edit. William Forbes Skene, 1891-92. Recension: *Scotichronicon*, Walter Bower, Abbot of Inchcolm — Compiled 1441, including *Book of Paisley, Book of Scone, Book of Cupar, Chronicle of Icolmkill* — ed.Thomas Hearne, Oxford, 1722 and Walter Goodall, Edinburgh, 1759.

Jesus College MSS:
Oxford MS 20 (Bodleian) — Pedigrees: *Ach Cunedda, Ach Gryg, Ach Llewelyn ap Iorwerth, Ach Morgan ab Owain, Ach Rhodri Mawr, Gwehelyth Brycheiniog, Gwehelyth Buellt, Gwehelyth Ceredigion, Gwehelyth Dogfeiling, Gwehelyth Dunoding, Gwehelyth Meirionydd, Gwehelyth Rhos, Gwyr-y-Gogledd, Plant Brychan, Plant Ceredig, Plant Cunedda*, 14th cty. *J.C. MS 20* — copies: *Penairth MS 120* (Nat.Lib. Wales) — Edward Lluyd, *c.*1700; *Panton MS 15* (Nat.Lib. Wales), 18th cty., Evan Evans; *Harleian MS 4181* (Brit.Mus.) — Hugh Thomas, *c.*1700.

Mostyn MSS:
Mostyn 117 (Nat.Lib. Wales) — 13th cty. Edits. J. G. Evans in **Report on Manuscripts in the Welsh Language**, Historical MSS Commission, London, 1898-1910.

Vitae Sanctii:

Lives of Saints: *Vita Beatissimi Cadoci* – *Cotton MS* (Brit.Mus.), *Vespasian A xiv* – c.1200 – orig.Lifris of Llancarfan, c.1100. A. W. Wade-Evans edits – *Vita Sanctorum Britanniae et Genealogiae,* Cardiff, 1944. *Vita Sancti Carantoci* – *Cotton MS* (Brit.Mus.), *Vespasian A xiz* – orig. 12th cty. A. W. Wade-Evans edit in *Vita Sanctorum Britanniae et Genealogiae. Vita Beati David* – *Cotton MS* (Brit.Mus.), *Vespasian A xiv* – orig. Ricemarchus, c.1090. A. W. Wade-Evans edit in *Vita Sanctorum Britanniae et Genealogiae. Vita Sancti Kentegerni* – *Cotton MS* (Brit.Mus.), *Titus A xix* – orig. Anon c.1150. *Vita Sancti Samsonis* – *Bibliotheque Municipale, Metz, MS 195* (11th cty.); *Bibliotheque Mazarine, Paris, MS 1708* (c.1000); *Bibliotheque Nationale, Paris, MS 11758* (13th cty.).

INDEX

246, 247
Nefertiti, Queen 10
Nennius 160, 164
Nero, Emperor 42, 94-95, 131
Nesta of Gwynedd 228, 230
Nestorian Creed 174
Nestorius, Patriarch of
Constantinople 141-142, 174
Neustria 149, 170, 184, 185
New Testament scribal codes 38
Newton, Sir Isaac 263, 273-275
Nicene Creed, 139
Nicodemus, Gospel of 204
Notre Dame 102, 104, 108, 217-219,
220, 262

Octavius, Gaius (Octavian) 17, 18
Olith, Princess 227, 228
Order of the Rosy Cross 260-263
Origen of Alexandria 107
Osman, Ahmed 10

Paris, Matthew 100, 115
Parzival (Grail romance), 192, 193,
194, 198, 201, 212, 239
Passover 53, 61, 63, 65, 66, 67, 146,
156, 177, 191
Patrick, St. 114, 172, 175, 177
Paul (Saul), St. 88, 89-91, 92, 94-95,
108, 113, 123-124, 131, 132, 138, 139,
141, 178
Paul III, Pope 206, 258
Paul VI, Pope 179
Pauline Christians 81, 95, 131, 132,
139, 175
Pelles 151, 189, 192, 195
Pendragons 150-157
Pepin the Fat 183, 184
Pepin the Short 184, 195
Pepys, Samuel 263, 273
Perceval 125, 189, 190, 192, 193, 194,
199, 207, 238, 239, 253
Perlesvaus (Grail romance) 192, 193,
212, 239
Peter (Simon), Apostle, St. 33, 37, 39,
42, 46, 50, 64, 65, 75, 80, 81, 82, 88,
90, 91, 92, 93, 95, 102, 103, 105, 107,
113, 116, 131, 135, 178
Peter the Hermit 210
Philip Augustus of France 210

Philip (Apostle) 37, 41, 50, 57, 99,
105, 107, 113, 115
Philip II of Spain 258, 264
Philippe II of France 222
Philippe IV of France 224, 226, 249
Philippe d'Alsace 212, 238
Picts 153, 155, 158, 164, 167, 169, 226,
247
Pilate, Pontius 34, 40, 52, 56, 62, 65-
68, 71, 72, 74, 89, 130, 131, 174, 191
Pierlot, Hubert 294
Pistis Sophia 105
Pius IX, Pope 179
Pius XII, Pope 179
Plato 79, 198, 200, 261
Platts, Beryl 242
Pompey the Great 17
Poussin, Nicolas 180
Powys 123, 153, 155, 158, 162, 163
Prieuré Notre Dame de Sion 151,
201, 248, 260, 274
Priscillian of Avila 175, 178
Propaganda, The (Council of
Cardinals) 136
Protestant Reformation 257, 258, 263,
264, 268
Provost, Jan 88
Puritans 263, 265, 270-271, 275
Pythagoras 50, 79, 197, 198, 261, 275

Qabala 213

Ramesses II, Pharaoh 9, 11
Raphael Sanzio 182, 258
Realm of the Ring Lords (Gardner)
184, 237, 256
Remy, Bishop of Reims 148
religious art 180-183
Renaissance 184, 257, 266
René d'Anjou 248-250, 253, 262, 293
Rennes-le-Château 101, 185
Resurrection 8, 52, 59, 75, 77, 78, 79,
80, 81, 83, 219
Rheged 155, 167
Rhydderch of Strathclyde 158, 164
Richard I (Lionheart) Plantagenet
171, 210, 231
Richard III of England 240
Robert I of Scots, the Bruce 224, 226,
236, 245, 247, 263, 267, 294

The contents of this book are also available in other formats:

E-book in Acrobat PDF

The audio edition set read by Laurence Gardner
Unabridged cassette edition
Abridged edition on cassette and double CD

Realm of the Holy Grail — Volume III CD Rom
(MP3 audio read by Laurence Gardner)

Other releases in 2001 (In hardback):
Genesis of the Grail Kings (Author's US special edition)

Information is available on all Laurence Gardner's books and formats from the MediaQuest Site at:

http://www.mediaquest.co.uk/lgardner.html

Also, for more on Laurence Gardner's work, lectures and updates visit:
laurencegardner.com

MEDIAQUEST